The Battle of Pinkie, 1547

The last battle between the independent kingdoms of Scotland and England

by
David Caldwell, Vicky Oleksy and Bess Rhodes

OXBOW | books
Oxford & Philadelphia

Published in the United Kingdom in 2023 by
OXBOW BOOKS
The Old Music Hall, 106–108 Cowley Road, Oxford, OX4 1JE

and in the United States by
OXBOW BOOKS
1950 Lawrence Road, Havertown, PA 19083

Hardback Edition: ISBN 978-1-78925-973-5
Digital Edition: ISBN 978-1-78925-974-2

A CIP record for this book is available from the British Library

Library of Congress Control Number: 2023936681

Printed in the United Kingdom by Short Run Press

For a complete list of Oxbow titles, please contact:

UNITED KINGDOM
Oxbow Books
Telephone (0)1226 734350
Email: oxbow@oxbowbooks.com
www.oxbowbooks.com

UNITED STATES OF AMERICA
Oxbow Books
Telephone (610) 853-9131, Fax (610) 853-9146
Email: queries@casemateacademic.com
www.casemateacademic.com/oxbow

Oxbow Books is part of the Casemate Group

Front and back cover: The Battle of Pinkie Roll, sheet 4. The Scottish army is beginning to break up and English horsemen are pursuing the fleeing Scots
(Bodleian Library, MS. Eng. Misc. C 13 (R))

Contents

List of figures ... v
List of tables ... x
Acknowledgements ... xi
Abbreviations ... xii

1. Introduction ... 1
    Slaughter near Musselburgh ... 1
    Modern understandings of Pinkie ... 6
    Purpose of this book ... 13

2. Causes of conflict in 1547 ... 16
    Warning of war ... 16
    Dynastic ambitions ... 17
    Religious conflict ... 21
    Attack on Langholm ... 28
    Objectives in September 1547 ... 31

3. The English forces ... 39
    The commanders ... 39
    Cavalry ... 42
    Infantry ... 44
    Artillery ... 48
    Naval forces ... 50
    Logistics and supply ... 52

4. Scotland's military capability ... 58
    The host ... 58
    Wappenshaws ... 59
    The mobilisation ... 60
    The Scottish commanders ... 69
    The structure of the army ... 74
    Scottish battlefield successes ... 89

5. Early sources for the battle: a review ... 96
    Scottish and English governmental and legal records ... 96
    Newsletters and diplomatic reports ... 98

Accounts by eye-witnesses and close relatives of combatants ... 102
Visual sources ... 112
English chronicles, ballads and other histories ... 121
Scottish chronicles ... 124
Overview ... 131

6. Pinkie Battlefield: topography and archaeology ... 137
What's in a name? ... 137
Topographical overview ... 140
Lordships and lands ... 143
Settlements ... 145
Communications ... 148
Land use ... 150
On manoeuvres, September 1547 ... 154
The archaeology of the Battle of Pinkie ... 169

7. A new interpretation of the Battle of Pinkie ... 188
The English advance into Scotland ... 188
Scottish preparations ... 194
Thursday 8 and Friday 9 September ... 196
Saturday 10 September ... 203

8. Pinkie: first and last ... 221
After Pinkie: the English policy ... 221
After Pinkie: the Scottish response ... 230
Pinkie and military change in early modern Britain ... 239
Pinkie: future directions ... 246

Bibliography ... 257
Index ... 269

List of figures

Figure 1.1: Copperplate engraving of the English victory at Musselburgh (Pinkie), about 1547–49 ... 2
Figure 1.2: Pinkie location map showing the route taken by the English army from Berwick, the Scottish muster site at Fala and the way from there to their camp on the west bank of the River Esk ... 3
Figure 1.3: Edward Seymour, Duke of Somerset (?) A portrait miniature dated 1550 ... 3
Figure 1.4: The Scottish Governor, the Earl of Arran, playing political chess, as imagined by a contemporary artist, John Halliday ... 3
Figure 1.5: King Edward VI of England, about 1547 ... 4
Figure 1.6: Billon penny of Mary Queen of Scots minted in 1547 ... 4
Figure 1.7: The Pinkie battlefield monument at Salters Road, erected in 1998 ... 6
Figure 1.8: Monument commemorating the Battle of Pinkie by Gardner Molloy, unveiled at Almond Park, Wallyford, in 2021 ... 7
Figure 1.9: Sir Charles Oman. Photograph by Bassano Ltd, 1926 ... 7
Figure 1.10: Pinkie, 10 September. The battle as interpreted by Charles Oman in 1937 ... 8
Figure 1.11: 'Pinkie, c. 10.00 hours, 10 September'. Interpretative plan published by David Caldwell in 1991 ... 9
Figure 1.12: Pinkie, 10 September. Phases in the development of the battle as envisaged by David Caldwell in 1991 ... 10
Figure 1.13: Aerial view of the battlefield with the boundary of the Inventory area marked ... 11
Figure 2.1: A map of the British Isles by Giovanni Scorcioni, gifted to Henry VIII in 1537 ... 18
Figure 2.2: The royal castle of Roxburgh, the site of an English fort started in September 1547 ... 20
Figure 2.3: St Andrews, plan, c. 1580, by John Geddy ... 22
Figure 2.4: John Dudley, successively Viscount Lisle and Earl of Warwick, line engraving published in 1786 ... 24
Figure 2.5: Lord Clinton (later Earl of Lincoln), c. 1560–65 ... 25
Figure 2.6: Broughty Castle in 1807 ... 26
Figure 2.7: Langholm Castle, a tower house in a strategic location in the Scottish West March ... 29
Figure 2.8: Berwick, Lord's Mount, a state-of-the-art fortification built in 1541–42 at the northeast angle of the town walls ... 31

Figure 3.1: Battle formation calculations for the English army 40
Figure 3.2: Recent military experience of the English Army Commanders at Pinkie 40
Figure 3.3: Lord Grey of Wilton (?) Portrait by Gerlach Flicke, 1547 41
Figure 3.4: Sir James Wilford, dated 1547. A fanciful depiction of the siege of Haddington is shown in the background 41
Figure 3.5: Shaffron, early sixteenth century 43
Figure 3.6: English demilances at Pinkie, as illustrated in the 1577 edition of Holinshed's *Chronicles* 43
Figure 3.7: 'Spanish' morion, a type of helmet extensively used by English foot soldiers in the early sixteenth century 45
Figure 3.8: Typical English bill of the sixteenth century 45
Figure 3.9: Matchlock long gun (hackbut), Italian, mid-sixteenth century 47
Figure 3.10: The Pease, a deep and wide ravine on the route from Berwick to Edinburgh 49
Figure 3.11: The *Galley Subtle*, a Mediterranean-style galley as depicted on the 2nd Anthony Roll, 1546 51
Figure 3.12: The *Pauncy*, a carrack, from the 1st Anthony Roll, 1545 52
Figure 4.1: The Scottish mobilisation in August 1547; the delivery of letters of proclamation 61
Figure 4.2: Location of bale fires for warning of an English invasion 62
Figure 4.3: Fala Moor from Soutra Aisle, with the Pentlands in the distance 62
Figure 4.4: Possible invasion routes into Scotland 63
Figure 4.5: Edinburgh Castle, as represented on the Battle of Pinkie Roll 63
Figure 4.6: The artillery blockhouse in Dunbar Castle, constructed about 1517–23 64
Figure 4.7: Hume Castle 65
Figure 4.8: Leith, as represented on the Battle of Pinkie Roll 65
Figure 4.9: The royal castle of Blackness 66
Figure 4.10: Tantallon Castle 67
Figure 4.11: Annan in the aftermath of the English siege; detail from Thomas Petit's plat of Castlemilk 68
Figure 4.12: Bird's eye view of Edinburgh by Richard Lee at the time of the English invasion in 1544 71
Figure 4.13: Archibald Douglas, 6th Earl of Angus 72
Figure 4.14: The Scottish army in line of battle and on the march 75
Figure 4.15: Diagram of one of the Scottish battles of footmen showing how its size has been calculated 78
Figure 4.16: Jack padded with iron plates, a type of protective garment worn by many on both sides at Pinkie 80
Figure 4.17: Grave slab of the early or mid-sixteenth century at Keills in Knapdale with a sword and buckler, flanked to the left by a battle-axe and a bow to the right 81

Figure 4.18: How to marshall a unit of footmen composed of pikemen and halberdiers. From Digges, *Stratioticos* ... 81
Figure 4.19: Woodcut by Hans Burgkmair the Elder (1473–1531) of a fight between pikemen and billmen, actually the Scots and English at Flodden in 1513 ... 82
Figure 4.20: Diagram showing how the size of the formations of light horsemen have been calculated ... 83
Figure 4.21: Grave slab of the mid-sixteenth century at Finlaggan, Islay, showing Donald MacGillespie, a gentleman of Clan Donald, wearing an aketon ... 86
Figure 4.22: Two panels, now built into the outer gatehouse of Edinburgh Castle, with pieces of artillery and their equipment ... 87
Figure 4.23: Cast bronze gun with the arms and initials of King James V of Scotland, probably made in Edinburgh Castle in 1526 ... 88
Figure 5.1: William Patten's first table ... 105
Figure 5.2: William Patten's second table ... 105
Figure 5.3: William Patten's third table ... 106
Figure 5.4: Patten's key to the symbols and letters on his three tables of the battle on 10 September ... 106
Figure 5.5: Title page of *Stratioticos*, a mathematical treatise for use by the military, published in London in 1579. Its author, Leonard Digges, fought at Pinkie ... 109
Figure 5.6: The Battle of Pinkie Roll, sheet 1, showing the cavalry engagement on 9 September ... 113
Figure 5.7: The Battle of Pinkie Roll, sheet 2. The English army is shown in marching order. The Scottish army, approaching from the right, is manoeuvring into battle order ... 115
Figure 5.8: The Battle of Pinkie Roll, sheet 3. The English army is shown in line of battle. Some of its artillery and the baggage train are adjacent to Falside Castle while a large force of horse attacks the Scottish foot ... 117
Figure 5.9: The Battle of Pinkie Roll, sheet 4. The Scottish army is beginning to break up and English horsemen are pursuing the fleeing Scots ... 118
Figure 5.10: The Battle of Pinkie Roll, sheet 5. The Scots are in full flight, chased by English horsemen and footmen ... 119
Figure 5.11: The Battle of Pinkie Roll, sheet 6. A view of Edinburgh, partially obscured by Calton Hill. The English camp is near the port of Leith ... 120
Figure 5.12: Raphael Holinshed, *Chronicles*, 1577 edition, title page of the second volume ... 123
Figure 5.13: The Battle of Pinkie, as illustrated in the 1577 edition of Holinshed's *Chronicles* ... 124

Figure 5.14: John Knox, wood engraving, 1580, after Adrian Vanson 125
Figure 5.15: John Leslie, bishop of Ross, painted after 1580 127
Figure 5.16: George Buchanan, a portrait attributed to Arnold Bronckorst, 1581 130
Figure 6.1: Topographical analysis of the Pinkie battlefield and surrounding area 138
Figure 6.2: Map of battlefield with places and features mentioned in the text 139
Figure 6.3: Pinkie Cleugh, now the location of Edenhall Hospital, surrounded by trees 139
Figure 6.4: Map of area of battlefield in 1547, based on interpretation of archival and cartographic sources 142
Figure 6.5: Dunfermline town and abbey, Fife, from John Slezer's *Theatrum Scotiae*, 1693. 143
Figure 6.6: Musselburgh tolbooth. Only the tower pre-dates 1547 146
Figure 6.7: Cousland Castle, probably incorporating the remains of a tower house destroyed by the English in 1547 147
Figure 6.8: Falside Castle 148
Figure 6.9: The old ('Roman') bridge over the River Esk 149
Figure 6.10: Howe Mire, looking south-eastwards, now well drained arable land 153
Figure 6.11: View from the River Esk westwards up the slope of Haugh Park to Monktonhall Terrace, the forward edge of the Scottish camp 156
Figure 6.12: The medieval church of St Michael at Inveresk, from a painting reproduced in 1857 158
Figure 6.13: LiDAR analysis of the Pinkie battlefield 165
Figure 6.14: Aerial view of Colton Dean from the southeast 166
Figure 6.15: Monument in Lewisvale Park claiming to mark the site of Somerset's camp on 9 September 169
Figure 6.16: Plan of trial trenches excavated at Gula Flats (Area 3) with significant small finds marked 170
Figure 6.17: Map showing the extent of archaeological surveys within the Inventory area of the battlefield 171
Figure 6.18: Photograph showing the extent of ground disturbance in 1985 associated with building the A1 dual carriageway 172
Figure 6.19: Distribution map of round shot recovered from the Inventory area of the battlefield 176
Figure 6.20: Part of the rim and handle mount of a medieval bronze laver, found at Crookston 179
Figure 6.21: Copper alloy mount in the form of an imperial crown, found at Crookston 179

Figure 6.22: Broken silver badge in the form of a rose, with traces of red enamel, found at Crookston 180
Figure 6.23: Broken copper alloy badge in the form of a crowned flower, found at Crookston 180
Figure 7.1: A plat of Castlemilk made in late 1547 by the English surveyor, Thomas Petit 189
Figure 7.2: A fanciful representation of the taking of Thornton Castle on 6 September from the 1577 edition of Holinshed's *Chronicles* 192
Figure 7.3: Innerwick Castle in 1790 192
Figure 7.4: The bridge across the River Tyne at East Linton 193
Figure 7.5: Hailes Castle, the residence of the Earl of Bothwell 194
Figure 7.6: Plan of the Pinkie battlefield showing the approximate locations of the camps of the opposing sides and the areas where fighting took place on 9 and 10 September 198
Figure 7.7: Supplies and equipment being unloaded from the English ships to the English camp before the battle. Detail from the Copperplate Engraving of the English victory at Musselburgh 199
Figure 7.8: The English galley shown positioned near the mouth of the River Esk and firing at the Scots. Detail from the Copperplate Engraving of the English victory at Musselburgh 199
Figure 7.9: Battle Phasing, 10 September – 1: The Scots form a line of battle overlooking Pinkie Cleugh while the English march from their camp towards Inveresk Church 206
Figure 7.10: Battle Phasing, 10 September – 2: Both armies head inland towards Falside Hill 206
Figure 7.11: Battle Phasing, 10 September – 3: A cavalry attack is launched by the English on the Scottish vanguard while the English army is drawn up in line of battle. The Scots horse manoeuvres away, aiming to launch an attack along Falside Hill 210
Figure 7.12: Battle Phasing, 10 September – 4: The English cavalry make a disorderly retreat after failing to break the Scottish vanguard. The Scots attempt to form a battle line but are under increasing fire from English artillery and hackbutters 213
Figure 8.1: Map showing the route home taken by the English army and the garrisons left behind 221
Figure 8.2: Inchcolm Abbey, on an island in the Firth of Forth 226
Figure 8.3: Aerial view of the fort at Eyemouth 227
Figure 8.4: Mary of Guise 231
Figure 8.5: Inchmahome Priory, on an island in the Lake of Menteith 232
Figure 8.6: Stirling Castle 233
Figure 8.7: Dumbarton Castle, from John Slezer's *Theatrum Scotiae*, 1693 237

List of tables

Table 3.1: Composition of the English Army at Pinkie ... 42
Table 5.1: Data on army sizes, numbers of casualties and prisoners, derived from early sources ... 99
Table 5.2: Pinkie casualties recorded in two or more early histories ... 128
Table 6.1: Summary of finds possibly associated with the Battle of Pinkie ... 174

Acknowledgements

The authors are grateful to several friends and colleagues who have provided advice and insights, answered questions and reviewed earlier drafts of their manuscripts. They include Amy Blakeway, Colin Martin and Roger Mason of the University of St Andrews; Simon Egan of Trinity College in Dublin; Jon Cooper of the Siege of Haddington Research Group; Andrew Coulson of the Pinkie Cleugh Battlefield Group; William Hepburn of Aberdeen University; Neil Murphy of Northumbria University; Tim Neighbour of CFA Archaeology Ltd; Alison Morrison-Low, Calum Robertson and Ella Paul of the National Museum of Scotland; Elizabeth Roads (previously of Lyon Court of Arms); Tico Seifert of the National Galleries of Scotland; Thomas Tolley of Edinburgh University; Eleanor Wilkinson-Keys of the Royal Armouries; Louise Rhodes and Ashley Stevens.

Staff of Historic Environment Scotland, especially Kevin Munro and Philip Robertson, and Andy Robertson, Heritage and Archaeology Officer for East Lothian Council have been of considerable assistance in providing information and their considerable expertise on Pinkie Battlefield and more generally on sites, monuments and pertinent legislation.

Colleagues at AOC Archaeology Group have been particularly supportive, especially Rob Engl who managed much of the fieldwork undertaken by AOC across the battlefield, Dawn McLaren who worked on the finds recovered, Rafa Soler Rocha who processed the LiDAR data and Tom Lovekin who photographed the battle monument at Almond Park. A considerable debt of gratitude is owed to Bob Salter and Rob Miller of Geddes Consulting Ltd for devising and producing diagrams and plans, to Howard Wallace for providing access to a drone survey of the battlefield, and to Ronnie Weir for photographs taken during the construction of the A1. Two metal detectorists, David Harvey and Robert Dale, provided much useful information on Crookston and their finds. We are very grateful to Gerry Kane at Chatelherault Country Park for facilitating access to John Halliday's picture of the Earl of Arran.

Generous financial support for the book's publication has been provided by the Dorothy Dunnett Society, the Society of Antiquaries of Scotland and AOC Archaeology Group.

Abbreviations

ADC:	*Acts of the Lords of Council in Public Affairs, 1501–54*
APC:	*Acts of the Privy Council of England*
Berteville:	Le Sieur de Berteville, *Recit De L'Expedition En Ecosse L'An MDXLVII Et De La Battayle de Muscleburgh*
BL:	British Library
Canmore:	National Record of the Historic Environment (HES)
CSP Dom Add:	*Calendar of State Papers Domestic for the Reign of Elizabeth, 1601–1603 And Addenda, 1547–65*
CSP Edward VI:	*Calendar of State Papers Domestic of the Reigns of Edward VI, Mary, Elizabeth 1547–1580*
CSP For:	*Calendar of State Papers, Foreign Series, of the Reign of Edward VI, 1547–1553*
CSP Mary:	*Calendar of State Papers Domestic of the Reign of Mary I 1553–1558*
CSP Scot:	*Calendar of the State Papers relating to Scotland and Mary, Queen of Scots*
CSP Spain:	*Calendar of Letters, Despatches and State Papers relating to the Negotiations between England and Spain*
Dalrymple:	Leslie, John, *The Historie of Scotland, translated in Scottish by Father James Dalrymple*
DES:	*Discovery and Excavation in Scotland*
Diurnal:	*Diurnal of Remarkable Occurrents in Scotland A.D. M.D.XIII – A.D. M.D.LXXV*
DSL:	*Dictionaries of the Scots Language Online*
Dunfermline Reg:	*Registrum de Dunfermelyn*
ELHER:	East Lothian Council Historic Environment Record
ER:	*Exchequer Rolls of Scotland*
Fourquevaux *Instr:*	Fourquevaux, Raymond de Rouer, baron de, *Instructions sur le faict de la Guerre*
Fourquevaux *Miss:*	*Mission de Beccarie de Pavie, Baron de Fourquevaux, en Ecosse, 1549.*
Hertford Exp:	*Late Expedicion in Scotlande Made By the Kynges Hyhnys Armye, Under the Conduit of the Ryght Honorable the Erle of Hertforde, The Yere of Oure Lorde God 1544*
HES:	Historic Environment Scotland
Holyrood Lib:	*Liber Cartarum Sancte Crucis*

HP:	*Hamilton Papers: Letters and Papers Illustrating the Political Relations of England and Scotland in the XVIth Century*, 2 vols
L&P:	*Letters and Papers, Foreign and Domestic, of the Reign of Henry VIII*
MLSC:	Mary of Lorraine, *Scottish Correspondence*
Navy of Edward VI:	Knighton, C. S. and David Loades (eds), *The Navy of Edward VI and Mary I*
Newbattle R:	*Registrum S. Marie de Neubotle*
NLS:	National Library of Scotland
NRHE:	National Record of the Historic Environment
NRS:	National Records of Scotland
NSA:	*New Statistical Account*
ODNB:	*Oxford Dictionary of National Biography (Online)*
OED:	*Oxford English Dictionary*
OSA:	*Old Statistical Account*
Patten:	William Patten, *The Expedicion Into Scotlande of the most worthy fortunate Prince Edward, Duke of Soomerset*
Pitscottie:	Robert Lindesay of Pitscottie, *The Historie and Cronicles of Scotland*
PSAS:	*Proceedings of the Society of Antiquaries of Scotland*
Retours:	*Inquisitionum Ad Capellam Domini Regis Retornatarum*
RMS:	*Registrum Magni Sigilli Regum Scotorum, Register of the Great Seal of Scotland*
RPC:	*Register of the Privy Council of Scotland*
RPS:	Records of the Parliaments of Scotland to 1707
RSS:	*Registrum Secreti Sigilli Regnum Scotorum, Register of the Privy Seal of Scotland*
Selve:	*Correspondance Politique de Odet de Selve, Ambassadeur de France en Angleterre, 1546–1549*
SHR:	*Scottish Historical Review*
SHS:	Scottish Historical Society
SP:	*Scots Peerage*
SRS:	Scottish Record Society
STS:	Scottish Text Society
TA:	*Accounts of the Treasurer of Scotland*
Teulet:	*Papiers d'état, pièces et documents inedits ou peu connus relatifs à l'histoire de l'Écosse au XVIeme siècle*, ed. A. Teulet
TNA:	The National Archives (Kew)
Yester Writs:	*Calendar of Writs preserved at Yester House, 1166–1625*

1

Introduction

Slaughter near Musselburgh

On Friday 9 and Saturday 10 September 1547 bloody fighting took place beside the Scottish coastal town of Musselburgh, near a ravine known as Pinkie Cleugh. This confrontation is now commonly called the Battle of Pinkie (Figures 1.1 and 1.2). Pinkie was the last pitched battle between the independent kingdoms of Scotland and England, and, unusually, was also a clash between two regents. An English invading army led by Edward Seymour, Duke of Somerset, then head of government for the boy king Edward VI, was resisted by James Hamilton, Earl of Arran, governor for the young Mary Queen of Scots (Figures 1.3 and 1.4). The causes of the fighting at Pinkie were complex, but partly arose from Somerset's wish to force a marriage between the child monarchs of Scotland and England, enabling 'the perpetual uniting of both realms' – a project that was opposed by many (though by no means all) Scots (Figures 1.5 and 1.6).[1] Intersecting with this dynastic ambition was a divisive religious conflict, in which increasingly Protestant English forces sought to 'deliver' Scotland from the 'dreadful danger' of Catholicism.[2]

The forces that faced each other outside Musselburgh in September 1547 were national armies of a large size for the period. The English had a fighting force of about 16,800 men on land, as well as 1,400 pioneers, an extensive baggage train, and significant naval support.[3] The Scots had in the region of 23,000 fighting men, the vast majority of whom were infantry.[4] Despite this imbalance in numbers, the English won what they described as 'a most valiant victory', and inflicted heavy casualties on the Scots.[5] The Edinburgh-based author of the mid-sixteenth-century *Diurnal of Remarkable Occurrents* claimed that 600 English soldiers were killed, whilst 7,000 Scots were 'taken' or 'slain' on 10 September – a tragedy that led to the day becoming known as 'Black Saturday'.[6] Others thought that the losses were even greater. The young Edward VI wrote in his personal chronicle that 'there were slain' 10,000 Scottish soldiers.[7] The schoolboy monarch also incorrectly asserted that English deaths were restricted to '51 horsemen, which were almost all gentlemen, and but one footman'.[8] Meanwhile, Francis van der Delft, the Holy Roman Empire's ambassador in London, reported that there were 'some 15,000 [Scots] either killed or taken prisoner'.[9] Van der Delft further claimed that the English were acknowledging losses of 'not more than two hundred men, although

Figure 1.1: Copperplate engraving of the English victory at Musselburgh (Pinkie), about 1547–49 (© The British Library Board, Maps.C.C.5.a.409)

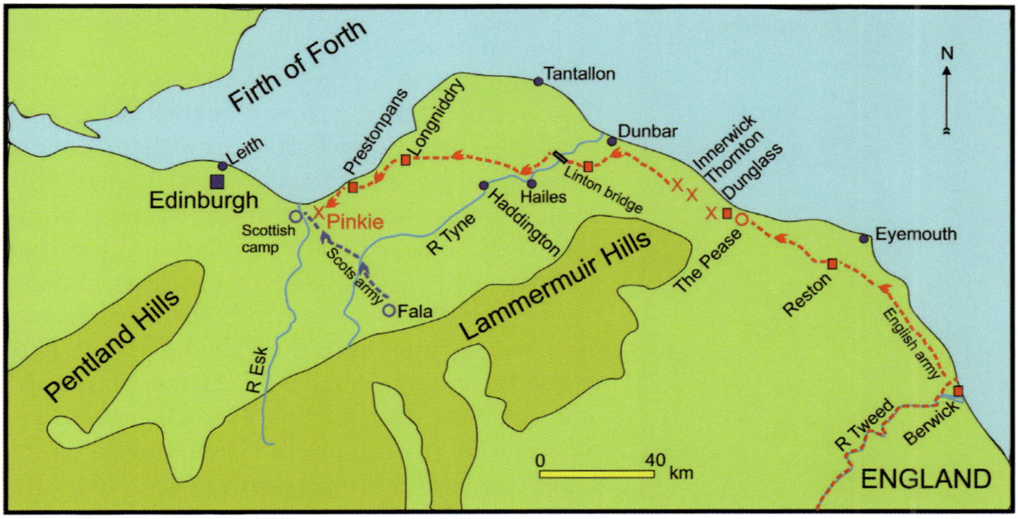

Figure 1.2: Pinkie location map showing the route taken by the English army from Berwick, the Scottish muster site at Fala and the way from there to their camp on the west bank of the River Esk (David Caldwell)

Figure 1.3: Edward Seymour, Duke of Somerset (?) A portrait miniature dated 1550 in the manner of Nicholas Hilliard (© Victoria and Albert Museum, London, P.25–1942)

Figure 1.4: The Scottish Governor, the Earl of Arran, playing political chess, as imagined by a contemporary artist, John Halliday. Halliday has successfully adapted his image of Arran from a portrait of him dating to 1578 to suggest how he would have looked in 1547. The painting is at Chatelherault, Lanarkshire (Bess Rhodes, copyright South Lanarkshire Council)

Figure 1.5: King Edward VI of England, born 1537, succeeded his father Henry VIII as king in January 1547. The painting was produced in the workshop of 'Master John' about 1547 (© National Portrait Gallery, London)

Figure 1.6: Billon penny of Mary Queen of Scots minted in 1547. Mary was six days old when she became queen on the death of her father James V in December 1542 (private collection, used with permission)

private letters are to hand which speak of five or six hundred'.

Whatever the exact number who died at Pinkie, the fighting was clearly brutal. The Englishman William Patten described how at the site of the main English cavalry charge on 10 September 'there found we our horses slain, all gored and hewn, and our men so ruefully gashed and mangled in the head specially, as not one by the face could be known'.[10] The Scots had an even worse time. Patten recalled how the path of the retreating Scottish forces was marked by 'corpses lying dispersed abroad, some their legs off, some but [hamstrung] and left lying half dead, some thrust quite through the body, others the arms cut off, diverse their necks half asunder, many their heads cloven, of sundry the brains pashed out'.[11]

News of the slaughter rapidly spread across Europe, with many observers expecting it to shift the balance of power in Scotland. For a brief moment, it seemed as though Britain's political and religious future might have been redefined by Somerset's army. An anonymous letter from London dated 18 September 1547 and preserved in the archives at Simancas in Spain notes with relish 'the great destruction of the Scots' and declares that 'it may be hoped' the English would soon 'have the whole country subject . . . either by force or agreement'.[12] Van der Delft similarly reported the assumption in London that because of Pinkie the English 'hold the whole of Scotland in the hollow of their hand'.[13] Meanwhile, Mary of Hungary (then governing the Netherlands on behalf of her brother, Emperor Charles V) expressed her pleasure at Somerset's victory and thought it would 'provide a favourable opportunity' to renegotiate the relationship between the Habsburgs and the Scots.[14] In Paris the news of Pinkie was received less positively. King Henry II of France was apparently extremely anxious about the invasion of a traditional ally and feared that Scotland would be 'utterly lost and nearly ruined', a concern that eventually led the French to offer the Scots military aid.[15] Of course in the long run, Pinkie was less conclusive than many contemporaries anticipated – contrary to the hopes of the English churchman John Hooper the quarrel between Scotland and England was not settled on the fields of Musselburgh.[16] What the battle did do was usher in several years of bitter Anglo-Scottish warfare, thereby devastating many Scottish communities, undermining English royal finances, and leading to the political ruin of Protector Somerset.

Despite its muddled legacy, for many survivors of Pinkie, the battle appears to have been a defining moment in their lives. The English cavalry commander Lord Grey of Wilton, who was wounded in the mouth by a blow from a pike at Pinkie, would tell his family about his exploits 'at the day of the battle' – recollections which his son and heir dutifully wrote down.[17] William Cecil, later Lord Burghley, recorded his own presence at Pinkie in his family chronicle, alongside significant events such as births, deaths, and the accession of Queen Elizabeth I.[18] Cecil, who served Somerset in a judicial and administrative capacity, also kept a series of 'notes' regarding 'occurrences' during the 1547 invasion. He generously shared these with his colleague and fellow Pinkie veteran William Patten, who wrote one of the first books about the battle, namely *The Expedition into Scotland of the Most Worthily Fortunate Prince Edward, Duke of Somerset,* which was printed in London in 1548.[19] Patten's memoir is one of several descriptions of Pinkie published during the sixteenth century. Further Scottish and English accounts of the battle were preserved in manuscript form.[20] Indeed, Pinkie is perhaps the best recorded battle to have been fought in Britain prior to the civil wars of the seventeenth century. Pinkie even inspired a number of illustrations, including a contemporary copperplate engraving (Figure 1.1) and a remarkable panoramic depiction of the battle now preserved in the Bodleian Library.[21]

In the years immediately after Pinkie, both Scots and English seem to have regarded the battle as a key moment in their national stories. However, over time Pinkie slipped from prominence. The reasons for this lower profile are unclear, but the fact that Arran and Somerset were in their different ways quite problematic rulers, and not obvious heroes, may have contributed to limited popular interest. The battle also fitted uncomfortably in emerging patriotic narratives of Scotland, England, and ultimately Great Britain. Whilst Somerset's vision of joining the Tudor and Stewart realms was eventually accomplished, it was by dynastic accident and negotiation, not military might. For later generations of 'Britons' the Battle of Pinkie was mostly an irrelevance and on occasions a source of awkwardness. Indeed, when the novelist and travel writer Daniel Defoe visited Pinkie in the early eighteenth century, he chose not to give a long description of the battle on the grounds that it 'would not be using the Scots fairly' and he did not wish to 'throw the English [triumph] in their faces'.[22] In at least some people's eyes the dead bodies beside Musselburgh were best forgotten.

Modern understandings of Pinkie

Today, many (perhaps most) residents of the British Isles have never heard of the Battle of Pinkie. Whilst confrontations such as Bannockburn (fought in 1314 near Stirling) and Culloden (fought in 1746 near Inverness) have captured the imagination of modern Scots, Pinkie is often overlooked. This relative neglect is echoed in the physical memorialisation of the battle. Unlike the large heritage centres that welcome tourists to better known Scottish battlefields, the chief monuments to the Battle of Pinkie are a simple carved stone near the Wallyford junction on the A1 (the main road from north-eastern England to Edinburgh), and a pink and yellow sculpture of two soldiers commissioned by the building firm Taylor Wimpey for their housing development at Almond Park (Figures 1.7 and 1.8). Neither memorial is on the site of the actual fighting.

Over the past century, the Battle of Pinkie has received a degree of attention from historians and, in recent years, archaeologists. However, the current scholarly understanding of what happened in September 1547 is patchy and increasingly contested. There are a number of unresolved issues, not least about the site of the actual battlefield. Some basic points can be stated with (relative) confidence about the fighting on Saturday 10 September. That morning both the English and Scots left their camps (the exact locations of which are debatable although the Scots were clearly to the west of the River Esk whilst the English were to the east). After some marching, which has often been interpreted as an attempt by both sides to gain control of the high ground at Falside Hill about three miles southeast of Musselburgh, the Duke of Somerset launched a cavalry attack on the Scots, which they resisted with some success. In ensuing manoeuvres, the Scottish army fell into disarray, before breaking and fleeing. A rout then followed in which the Scots suffered heavy losses as they were ridden down by the English horsemen. Yet much that relates to these basic points is less clear. There are major questions about the locations of these events, what happened on preceding days, the motivations of both Somerset and Arran for committing to a pitched battle, the exact movements of the troops, the reasons for the English cavalry charge, the cause of the Scottish collapse, and the choices made by the English high command in the aftermath of the fighting. This book is an effort to tackle some of these questions, utilising the extensive written and visual sources for the battle, and drawing on analysis of the local landscape and archaeological record. It will argue that many frequently repeated assumptions about the Battle of Pinkie require

Figure 1.7: The Pinkie battlefield monument at Salters Road, erected in 1998 (David Caldwell)

Figure 1.8: Monument commemorating the Battle of Pinkie by Gardner Molloy, unveiled at Almond Park, Wallyford, in 2021. It takes the form of two soldiers in combat with each other (Tom Lovekin)

further consideration – often being rooted in theories developed nearly a century ago on the basis of limited evidence.

Much of the modern scholarship on Pinkie is heavily influenced by the writings of Sir Charles Oman, who in 1933 published a paper on an illustrated roll in the Bodleian Library depicting the fighting at Pinkie and the eventual Scottish flight (Figure 1.9).[23] Oman was the person who correctly identified this series of scenes as showing the Battle of Pinkie. However, his attempt to make sense of how the forces moved in the landscape was significantly flawed. Oman discussed Pinkie further in his 1937 survey of sixteenth-century European warfare – again drawing problematic conclusions regarding the locations and timings of events.[24] Among other basic errors, Oman regarded the geographic feature of Pinkie Cleugh as an enclosure, despite the fact that the word 'cleugh' was long established in Scots as a term for a steep valley or a ravine.[25] Still more remarkably,

Figure 1.9: Sir Charles Oman, Chichele Professor of Modern History at Oxford University. He had a considerable reputation as a military historian. Photograph by Bassano Ltd, 1926 (© National Portrait Gallery, London)

he misdated a key cavalry engagement between the English and the Scots that took place a little before the main battle – Oman assigned this to 8 May when most contemporary sources clearly state that it took place on Friday 9 September.[26] Oman also relied on a relatively restricted range of sources, focusing heavily on William Patten's memoir and the Battle of Pinkie Roll in the Bodleian Library, to the exclusion of other records of the battle.

Nevertheless, Charles Oman's writings have cast a long shadow and his core assertions are therefore worthwhile outlining. According to Oman, the battle was preceded by a cavalry engagement in which the Scots were roundly defeated, meaning the Scottish horsemen played little or no part in the main pitched battle, which unfolded as follows. On the morning of Saturday 10 September the Scots were in a well defended camp on the west bank of the River Esk, whilst the English were positioned on higher ground to the southeast, with their left wing by Falside Castle at the top of Falside Hill, and their right wing beside the sea – an interpretation which implies that Protector Somerset's forces were stretched across a front significantly in excess of 2 km (Figure 1.10). Somerset supposedly assumed that the Scots would not leave their camp, and so resolved to bombard their position with artillery mounted on a hillock by Inveresk Church and with the guns of the English ships lying off the coast. Arran

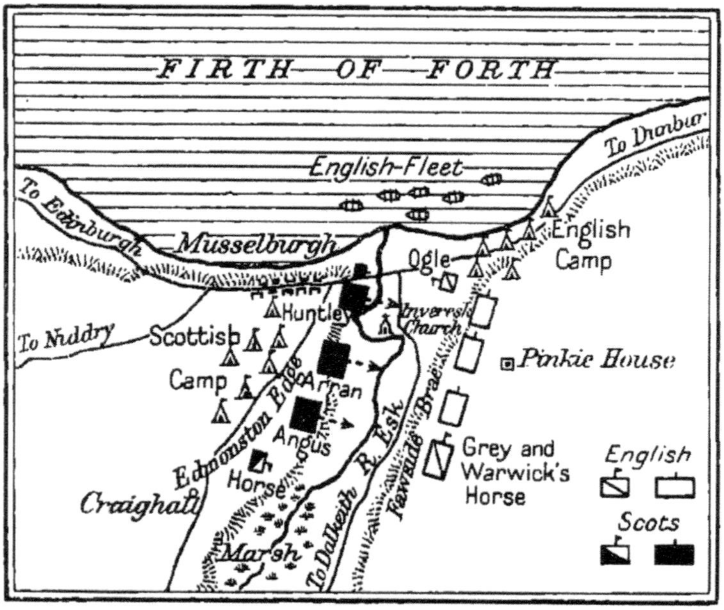

Battle of Pinkie, September 10, 1547.

Figure 1.10: Pinkie, 10 September. The battle as interpreted by Charles Oman in 1937. This plan neither represents the geography of the battlefield accurately nor relates the disposition of the opposing forces to information provided by early sources

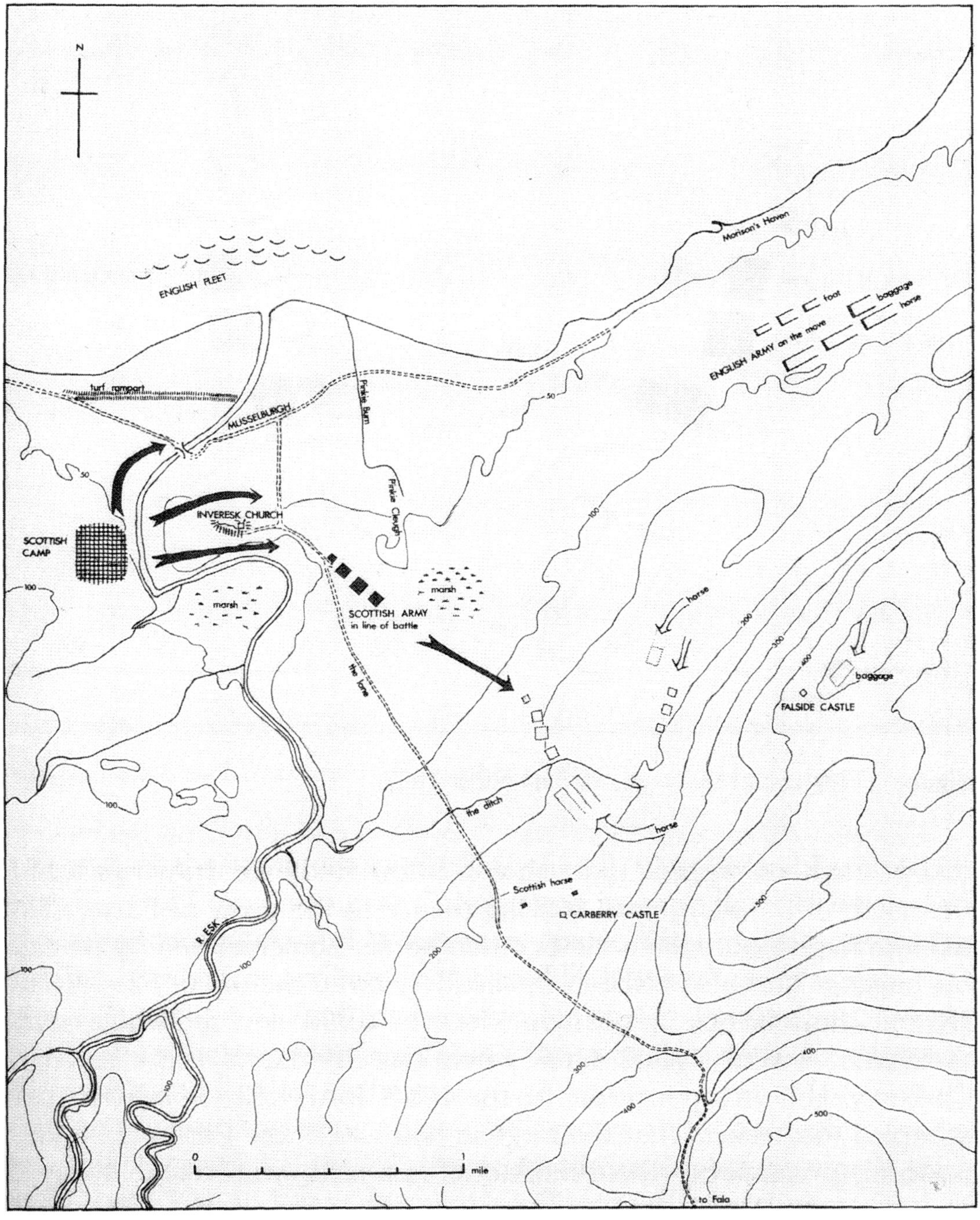

Figure 1.11: 'Pinkie, c. 10.00 hours, 10 September'. Interpretative plan published by David Caldwell in 1991. It attempted to provide accurate geographical detail and show the armies to scale

misinterpreted the preparations for this bombardment as a withdrawal and ordered his forces across the River Esk to attack the English flank. In order to gain time to organise the English forces into line of battle, Somerset launched two cavalry attacks which the Scots repulsed. As this was going on, the three main Scottish foot units had coalesced into one formation, whilst a contingent of Highland archers had fled because of bombardment from the sea. Somerset then brought his artillery, archers, and hackbutters to bear on the Scottish army, which broke and fled – ultimately leading to a bloody rout.

This version of events was for many years the dominant interpretation of the Battle of Pinkie and has been adhered to in a number of general overviews of the period.[27] Part of the reason for Oman's lasting influence, is the fact that many historians have been more interested in the broader implications of Pinkie than in the actual events of the battle.[28] There is of course nothing wrong with focusing on the wider consequences of Pinkie, rather than the bloody details of what happened on the ground. However, the tendency of many historians to look at the bigger picture means that a number

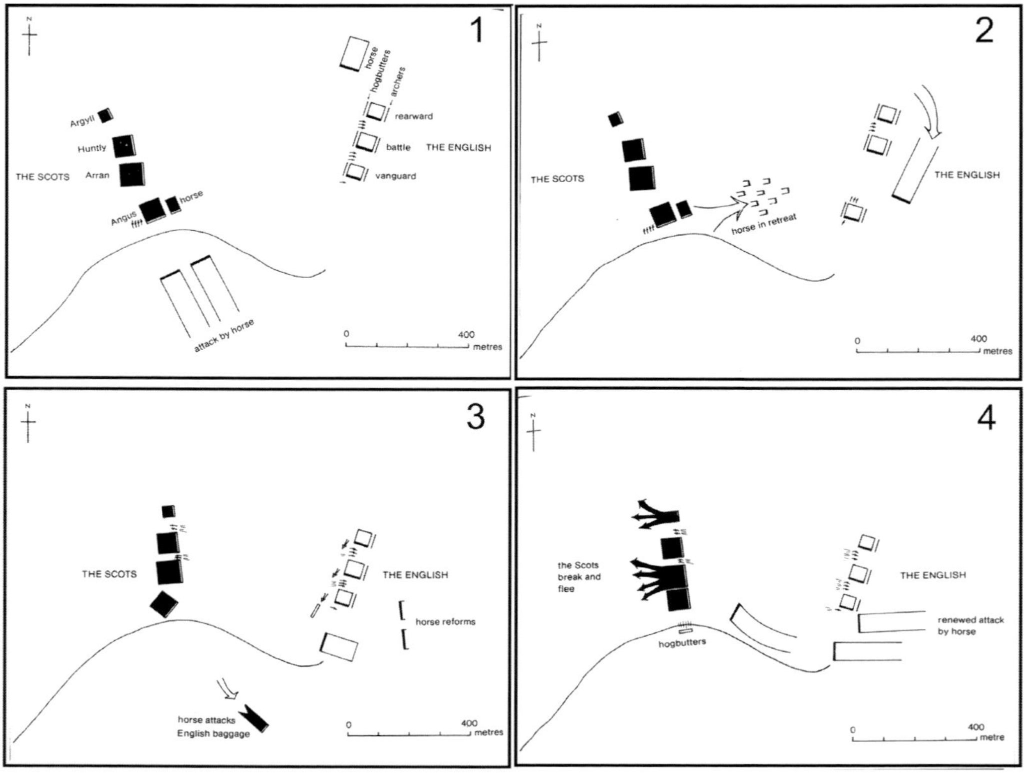

Figure 1.12: Pinkie, 10 September. Phases in the development of the battle as envisaged by David Caldwell in 1991

of problematic assumptions about the movements and actions of both the Scots and English stand unquestioned in major historical works.

Another scholar whose analysis of Pinkie has left a complicated legacy is Sir James Fergusson. In the 1960s, Fergusson sought to understand the landscape of Pinkie, looking beyond the houses, fields and industrial activity of his own day to create a picture of the geography in 1547. In envisioning this, Fergusson mentioned morasses, particularly the Howe Mire, which 'lay, rather awkwardly, before the English right wing and north-east from the camp on the shore'.[29] This appears to be the first time that the Howe Mire features in a serious description of the battle. It is not mentioned in any early accounts, but has come to bedevil recent studies of the battlefield and will be discussed further below.

It was in the 1990s that major questions about Oman's work were raised. In 1991, David Caldwell (one of the authors of this book) published a paper on Pinkie, which linked the evidence from a range of contemporary sources to the realities of the landscape around Musselburgh, Wallyford and Inveresk (Figure 1.11).[30] He argued that on the morning of 10 September, the Scottish army was already crossing the River Esk as the English were leaving their camp, probably located at Preston near to the shore. The Earl of Arran proceeded to draw up his army in line of battle to the east of Inveresk Church whilst the English army was still in marching order. Arran then decided to wheel his army inland to gain advantage of the higher ground

Figure 1.13: Aerial view of the battlefield with the boundary of the Inventory area marked (AOC Archaeology Group)

at Falside Hill and Somerset followed suit. Realising that the Scots would win the race for the high ground, Somerset launched a cavalry charge to slow them down. Although the English horse were repulsed, their attack had the desired effect of delaying the Scots and enabling the rest of Somerset's forces to draw up a line of battle. Caldwell's account also located the fighting on 10 September more precisely than previous analyses, placing it to the south of (the present) A1 dual carriageway (Figure 1.12) – a conclusion he reached by identifying the Crookston Burn as relating to the 'slough', which William Patten describes the English cavalry crossing on their way to attack the Scots during the race for the high ground.

This revised interpretation of Pinkie was partially adopted by Gervase Phillips in his book on *The Anglo-Scots Wars*, which was published in 1999 and sought to place the battle in wider debates about an early modern military revolution (a lively area of discussion in the 1990s).[31] Phillips' work highlighted the way in which military practices in sixteenth-century Britain showed an awareness of trends in Continental Europe, and challenged perceptions of the perceived backwardness of English and Scottish forces. In this context, Pinkie became an invaluable case study, with its relatively large armies, increased use of guns, and the presence of a number of military specialists. The extent to which concepts of 'modernity' and 'military revolution' are helpful lenses for understanding Pinkie will be examined in later sections of this book.

Since the beginning of the twenty-first century, much of the in-depth discussion about Pinkie has been driven by archaeologists and heritage organisations. There has also been a resurgence of interest in the battle among local residents, leading to the creation of the Pinkie Cleugh Battlefield Group, the erection of several interpretation panels and signs, and annual commemorations near the memorial stone by the A1.

The recent concentration on the physical site of Pinkie is linked to efforts by national heritage bodies to foster an appreciation of battlefields and give them a degree of protection in the planning process. In 2011 Historic Scotland (now renamed Historic Environment Scotland) established an Inventory of Historic Battlefields. Sites on the Inventory must meet a number of criteria. In particular, it must be possible to 'identify the location of the site and to map boundaries of the overall area of interest'.[32] Pinkie was among the first battles to be placed on the Inventory, and as part of the process of designation Historic Scotland defined on a map what they perceived to be the 'area of interest' (Figure 1.13). The prioritising of this area was based upon earlier research undertaken by the Battlefields Trust.

The Battlefields Trust's analysis was heavily influenced by their identification of the Howe Mire, now arable farmland (see Figure 6.10), bounded on the west by the old Crookston Road and on the east by Barbachlaw and Wallyford, with 'the slough' described by William Patten in 1548 as a key feature in the battlefield landscape. They therefore located the main engagement to the north of the (present) A1 dual carriageway.[33] The authors of this book disagree with that interpretation.

From about 2000 onwards a number of commercially funded landscape and archaeological investigations have challenged the interpretation of Pinkie set out by the Battlefields Trust and Historic Environment Scotland. As of June 2019, East Lothian Council Historic Environment Record noted 134 archaeological investigations within the boundary of the Battlefield Inventory.[34] Many of these interventions were small scale, often in urban areas (particularly Musselburgh and Wallyford), and not primarily concerned with the Battle of Pinkie. However, others placed the battlefield at the heart of their research questions. In recent years, projects focused on the battlefield have been undertaken, amongst others by AOC Archaeology Group and by CFA Archaeology Ltd.[35] None of these activities has successfully identified the site of the battlefield. However, the findings have raised significant questions regarding previous assumptions about where the English and Scots moved through the landscape on 9 and 10 September 1547, which this book will consider.

Purpose of this book

Pinkie is an exceptionally well-documented battle. Yet current understandings of what happened and where key events took place are rather confused. This is unfortunate. Pinkie was a military engagement that involved a great many people, a significant proportion of whom lost their lives. It was perhaps the largest battle ever fought in mainland Scotland.[36] That alone makes it a topic worthy of consideration.

There are, though, additional reasons to regard Pinkie as an incident of interest. The fighting at Musselburgh in September 1547 took place during a transitional period in the military history of Scotland and England. In some respects the battle has features that are reminiscent of the Middle Ages. For example, there were a significant number of archers in the English and Scottish armies. Yet there were signs of the changes that gunpowder weapons were bringing. For instance, both sides at Pinkie had artillery trains, and experience of using guns effectively. Pinkie provides a valuable insight into how the leaders of Scotland and England sought to navigate a shifting military landscape, and the murky boundaries between 'medieval' and 'modern' warfare.

In many respects Pinkie hints at a new era of larger armies, joint operations, and increasing reliance on military specialists. These were changes with which the English, and later British, state would ultimately engage – if at times in a somewhat belated and parsimonious fashion. Yet the fighting in September 1547 was also the end of a pathway in Scotland's military evolution. After the Earl of Arran's defeat at Pinkie, no monarch or regent of Scotland ever again used a mostly Scottish army in a pitched battle against a foreign power. In a sense, Pinkie is the final chapter in a story that stretches back to Bannockburn and beyond. The catastrophe outside Musselburgh cast a long shadow, and arguably profoundly shaped the Scottish state's subsequent military choices. What went wrong in the autumn of 1547 is therefore of considerable importance for making sense of Scotland's complex military past.

Yet Pinkie has a significance beyond military history. The battle was part of a long-running struggle to determine how the people of Scotland would align religiously and politically. Would the Scots embrace a new relationship with an increasingly Protestant

England, or would they stick with an older alliance with Catholic France? The Battle of Pinkie was a key moment in this protracted dilemma and took place at a time when a number of Scots were uncertain where the best future for their country lay. The actions of both sides during and immediately after the battle profoundly shaped the experience of Scotland in the 1540s and 1550s. Pinkie did not lead to the total redefining of Britain's political map, but it was a moment of disruption and crisis. The choices made by the Duke of Somerset and the Earl of Arran in September 1547 had major implications for how the next few years of Anglo-Scottish relations played out, with attendant human and economic costs. The casualties of Pinkie were not just the soldiers who died at Musselburgh, but also the men, women and children who suffered in the succeeding years of conflict.

The Battle of Pinkie deserves to be more widely known and better understood. Recent years have seen several innovative perspectives regarding this significant moment in British history. These new concepts have come from a variety of disciplines and have often been published in forms that are not particularly accessible to the general reader. At the same time, some rather flawed traditional assumptions are still repeated relatively unquestioningly in overviews of the period, and on occasions by influential national organisations. It therefore seems that there is a need for a work which brings together the new thinking on Pinkie, and which examines carefully the historical, archaeological and geographic evidence regarding the battle. This volume seeks to provide a detailed and approachable study of the battle, exploring why Pinkie happened, the nature of the forces that took part, how events unfolded in September 1547, the location of the fighting, and its legacy and significance. The authors believe these are questions of considerable importance for our understanding of the landscape around Musselburgh, but which also have a relevance for wider understandings of Britain's past. Broader historical works, covering big themes in national life or major developments in warfare, are an aggregate of the thinking on specific events and individuals. It is important that the building blocks from which these wider syntheses are constructed are reliable and evidence-based. This book seeks to compare and integrate the wealth of evidence available on Pinkie, and so provide a firmer foundation for future discussions about the battle. The authors do not expect this to be in any sense the last word on Pinkie. Instead, in the words of William Patten, it is a starting point for others to see 'what else they can utter, either further or better'.[37]

Notes

1 TNA, SP 50/1, f. 111r.
2 Patten, f. 30r.
3 Patten, ff. 35r–v.
4 See chapter 4 for discussion of the size of the Scottish army.
5 Patten, f. 4v.
6 *Diurnal*, 44–45.

7 W. K. Jordan (ed.), *The Chronicle and Political Papers of Edward VI* (London, 1966), 8.
8 Jordan, ed. *Chronicle of Edward VI*, 8.
9 *CSP Spain* 9, 152.
10 Patten, ff. 111v–112r.
11 Patten, f. 104r.
12 *CSP Spain* 9, 150.
13 *CSP Spain* 9, 152.
14 *CSP Spain* 9, 165.
15 *CSP Spain* 9, 176. For an in-depth analysis of the French reaction to Pinkie see E. Bonner, 'The French Reactions to the Rough Wooings of Mary Queen of Scots', *Journal of the Sydney Society for Scottish History* 6 (1998), 78–161.
16 *Original Letters relating to the English Reformation*, vol. 1, ed. Rev. Hastings Robinson (Cambridge, 1846), 44.
17 A. Grey, *A Commentary of the services and charge of William Lord Grey of Wilton* (Camden Society, 1847), 15.
18 Hatfield House, CP 140/13.
19 Patten, ff. 150v–151r.
20 See Chapter 5 for further discussion of the primary sources for the Battle of Pinkie.
21 C. Anderson and C. Fleet, *Scotland: Defending the Nation: Mapping the Military Landscape* (Edinburgh, 2018), 33–34.
22 D. Defoe, A *Tour Thro' The Whole Island of Great Britain* (1724–1727), https://www.visionofbritain.org.uk/travellers/Defoe/36 (accessed 9 December 2022).
23 C. W. C. Oman, 'The Battle of Pinkie, Sept. 10, 1547', *Archaeological Journal* 90 (1933), 1–25.
24 Sir C. Oman, *History of the Art of War in the Sixteenth Century* (London, 1937), 358–67.
25 See *DSL*, https://dsl.ac.uk/entry/dost/cleuch (accessed 9 December 2022).
26 For instance, Patten clearly indicates that the cavalry engagement took place on 9 September. Patten ff. 64v–79r.
27 W. K. Jordan, *Edward VI: The Young King: The Protectorship of the Duke of Somerset* (Cambridge, MA, 1968), 257–60; M. Scard, *Tudor King in All but Name: The Life of Edward Seymour* (Cheltenham, 2020), 180–84.
28 M. L. Bush, *The Government Policy of Protector Somerset* (London, 1975), 1, 12–13; M. Merriman, *The Rough Wooings: Mary Queen of Scots 1542–1551* (East Linton, 2000), 236–37.
29 Sir J. Fergusson, *The White Hind* (London, 1963), 18.
30 D. H. Caldwell, 'The Battle of Pinkie', in N. Macdougall (ed.), *Scotland and War AD 79–1918* (Edinburgh, 1991), 61–94.
31 G. Phillips, *The Anglo-Scots Wars 1513–1550* (London, 1999), 191–200. Phillips covered the same ground in a more recent paper focusing on the Scottish contribution, 'Scotland in the Age of the Military Revolution, 1488–1560', in E. M. Spiers, J. A. Crang and M. J. Strickland (eds), *A Military History of Scotland* (Edinburgh, 2014), 182–208.
32 HES, *Designation Policy & Selection Guide* (2019), Annex 4 para 12. This document can be accessed at https://www.historicenvironment.scot/archives-and-research/publications/publication/ (accessed 9 December 2022).
33 Battlefields Trust report on the Battle of Pinkie, http://www.battlefieldstrust.com/resource-centre/medieval/battleview.asp?BattleFieldid=68 (accessed 24 April 2020).
34 ELHER, https://www.eastlothian.gov.uk/info/210596/archaeology/12108/historic_environment-record (accessed 24 April 2020).
35 See Chapter 6 for discussion of these investigations.
36 Assertion made in Battlefields Trust report on Pinkie, section 2.6.
37 Consult the Musselburgh Museum website for updates and new research on the battle, https://www.musselburghmuseum.org.uk/events/battle-of-pinkie-cleugh/ (accessed 16 February 2023).

2

Causes of conflict in 1547

Warning of war

During the spring of 1547 the Scottish ambassador to England was a worried man. Adam Otterburn was a skilled lawyer and diplomat, with considerable experience negotiating between the Stewart and Tudor courts. He was regarded by contemporaries as one of the wisest men in Edinburgh and in the 1530s had been praised as 'a solicitor of peace and concord' between Scots and English.[1] Yet by the late spring of 1547 Otterburn was feeling isolated and increasingly ineffectual. In a letter from London, dated 17 May, he informed Mary of Guise, the Queen Dowager, that he was 'so evil treated [in] many ways that it is both shame and pain to rehearse'.[2] The Scottish ambassador confessed that he was out of the diplomatic loop and had 'no credence' in London because notable Englishmen 'dare not' treat him with courtesy. Most alarming of all, Otterburn judged that the English were preparing 'for war against us [Scots]' and were daily checking weapons, insisting that even priests 'find harness for one man'.[3]

When the English invaded Scotland at the beginning of September 1547, there had for several months been signs of impending conflict, with both sides checking defences and readying their forces (Figure 2.1). As early as 19 March, the Scottish Privy Council was advised that their 'old enemies of England' intended to invade 'both by sea and land'.[4] In response, the Scottish Government ordered proclamations to be made at market crosses for men to be in readiness for resisting an invasion and to be prepared to gather 'at such day and place as shall be assigned . . . with such provision and furnishing as they shall be advertised . . . to bring with them'. At the same time, the Privy Council ordered communities across the kingdom to organise wappenshaws (reviews of weapons and equipment).[5]

Scotland's martial preparations appear to have alarmed the English Government, whose plans for invasion at the beginning of March may have been more nebulous than the Scots believed. When the English Privy Council learned how 'proclamation was made in Edinburgh to charge all men to be in readiness upon [24] hours warning', they immediately told Berwick-upon-Tweed and the coastal ports to prepare so that if the Scots or 'others minding to do annoyance' attacked, they could be swiftly repulsed.[6] On 16 April, letters were sent to the English shires ordering checks on weapons and defences, and instructing the nobility to be ready to provide cavalry at one hour's notice any time after 20 May.[7] These orders seem to have been obeyed, although at the end of May the Bishop of Durham complained that despite having told all the chief gentlemen of the Northeast to be in readiness when required, there was still a 'great lack of bows and arrows', a deficiency blamed on a Danish merchant who was monopolising the import trade for bow staves.[8]

Large-scale fighting broke out in the late summer, but an aggressive intent was there several months before. Why did the leaders of Scotland and England commit to warfare in 1547? What drove the Tudor state to undertake the vast cost, risk, and effort of invading a neighbouring country? Last, but by no means least, why did the confrontation at Pinkie take place when it did?

Dynastic ambitions

The beginning of 1547 was an unstable time in English politics. In January, King Henry VIII died, leaving the throne to his nine-year-old son Edward. The final illness and death of the domineering Henry created a struggle for power at the Tudor court, from which Edward Seymour, brother of Henry's third wife Jane, and uncle of the new king Edward VI, emerged triumphant.[9] On 1 February, Edward Seymour was recognised as Lord Protector, a public acknowledgement of his control of the child monarch and the English government.[10] By the end of the month, Seymour had also become Duke of Somerset. It was a remarkable ascent for a man who started life as the son of a Wiltshire knight.

Upon gaining power, Somerset rapidly turned his attention to Scotland where the political situation was even more precarious than in London. The Scots also had a child monarch, the young Mary Queen of Scots, who in the Autumn of 1547 was not quite five years old. Mary had come to the throne as a baby, when her father James V unexpectedly died a few days after her birth. As a result, since January 1543 the Scottish government had been led by James Hamilton, Earl of Arran, who would command his country's forces at the Battle of Pinkie. Arran was a distant cousin of the child queen and during the late 1540s was also heir to the Scottish throne. He appears to have tried to rule effectively and to protect his monarch's interests.[11] However, Arran was far from universally liked, and his regency was later remembered as a time of 'great dissension' in the 'administration and governing of the realm'.[12] By no means the least of these divisions related to plans for the young queen's eventual marriage.

As a female monarch, Mary was an exceptionally desirable marriage prospect. There was a high likelihood that whoever married her would gain control of Scotland. From the perspective of the English government, a match between the young Edward VI and the even younger Mary Queen of Scots provided a unique opportunity to expand the Tudor sphere of influence northwards. The fact that the line of succession in Scotland and England had produced a boy and girl of similar ages, who would each rule over their respective nations, was described by Somerset and his advisors as 'a marvel' that had not chanced for 800 years.[13] It was an opportunity that the English, and their sympathisers, were determined to exploit. As the propagandist James Henrisoun (by birth a Scot, but whose Protestant convictions made him a supporter

Figure 2.1: A map of the British Isles by Giovanni Scorcioni, gifted to Henry VIII in 1537. This provides an insight to the extent of knowledge in governing circles in England of the geography of Scotland in the years immediately prior to the invasion of 1547. Scotland appears much bigger in relation to England than it is in reality (© The British Library Board, Cotton Augustus I.1.9)

of Somerset) declared, there was the possibility of the Tudors acquiring 'the whole monarchy of Britain'.[14] However, other Scots were less enthusiastic, fearing that if both realms were united it would be the King of England who would benefit most and Scotland would be 'utterly beggared'.[15]

A match between Edward and Mary was suggested as early as 1543 when it briefly seemed as though the Tudor and Stewart dynasties might be united by peaceful means. That summer, the Earl of Arran and Scottish diplomatic representatives, including Adam Otterburn, agreed to a betrothal between Mary and Edward (then still Prince of Wales). Yet, in December 1543 the Scottish Parliament, probably acting in line with popular opinion in Edinburgh, rejected the proposed English marriage and renounced the treaties that the diplomats had recently negotiated and Arran had signed. Instead, the Parliament asserted its support for 'the old, ancient leagues, contracts and considerations of amity and kindness passed . . . before between the kings of Scotland and France'.[16]

The Scottish legislators' rejection of the English marriage and their affirmation of friendship with France enraged Henry VIII, who in the spring of 1544 despatched a punitive expedition led by the Duke of Somerset (then Earl of Hertford) to revenge and punish what he saw as 'the notable falsehood and disloyalty of the Scots'.[17] Having failed with diplomacy, the English now sought by more brutal means to secure the Scottish marriage. There followed two years of intermittent Anglo-Scottish warfare. Yet for Henry VIII, Scottish matters usually took second place to Continental affairs. When Somerset was sent north in April 1544, he was told to subdue Edinburgh quickly and then bring his forces south to join Henry VIII's invasion of France in June, with strict instructions that too much time should not be 'consumed' in Scotland.[18] Indeed, the future Duke of Somerset was specifically informed by the English Privy Council that the principal cause for sending an army into Scotland was to create disruption so the Scots did not have sufficient resources to annoy England whilst the king 'in his most royal person' attacked France.[19]

The timetable for the 1544 campaign in Scotland was unreasonably tight and restricted any lasting gains. After capturing Leith in early May, Somerset's forces failed to take Edinburgh Castle. They instead burned part of the capital and sacked Holyrood Abbey, before returning south, leaving a trail of destruction through the Lothians and Borders. The expedition was hailed as a success at the Tudor court but brought little strategic benefit. During the Scottish campaign, Somerset expressed his frustration with the limits posed by Henry VIII's strict schedule. On 6 May 1544, shortly after entering Leith, he and his fellow commanders, John Dudley and Ralph Sadler (who would both hold key roles at Pinkie) wrote to Henry VIII stating that 'if your Majesty's former determination had continued to fortify this town, we think it could not but have served to great purpose'.[20] The same letter noted that the English *Galley Subtle* had razed a blockhouse on the island of Inchgarvie (in the Forth, now overshadowed by the Forth Rail Bridge) 'which if your Highness' first determination to fortify here had continued, had been worth the keeping'.

The future Protector Somerset led another army into Scotland in 1545, again producing short-term disruption, but securing little of long-term value. Once more, Somerset advocated long-term occupation and fortification, informing Henry VIII in September 1545 that the old castle at Roxburgh was 'one of the strongest sites' for a fortification that he had seen, and stressing the potential benefits if the king should decide to take it (Figure 2.2).[21] Yet, as before, such recommendations were not implemented.

The insubstantial achievements of the Scottish expeditions of 1544 and 1545 seem to have haunted Somerset, and almost certainly influenced his decision to invade again in 1547. Interestingly, immediately before he entered Scotland *en route* to Pinkie, Somerset told his officers of a recent nightmare where he returned victorious to court but realised 'he had done nothing at all'.[22] Filled with guilt at the great costs of the war and the efforts of his soldiers, the 'shamefast abashment of the thing did wake him' from sleep. The invasion of 1547 was a deeply personal project for Somerset, which he pursued with much greater fervour than Henry VIII usually applied to Scottish affairs.

By the time of Henry VIII's death in January 1547, England had signed a peace treaty with France and diplomatic relations had been reopened with Scotland – circumstances that may have led to expectations of more cordial Anglo-Scottish relations during Edward VI's minority. If so, such hopes were soon disappointed. On 3 February 1547, a mere two days after his appointment as Protector, the soon-to-be Duke of Somerset met with Adam Otterburn. The new Lord Protector informed the Scottish ambassador of his desire for 'a treaty of peace with some treaty of the marriage but not with so straight and rigorous conditions as was in the first contract'.[23] Yet even at this initial meeting, Somerset may have hinted that if peaceful means did not achieve the match he was willing to contemplate force. In a letter to Mary of Guise dated 4 February, Adam Otterburn advised the Scottish government

Figure 2.2: The royal castle of Roxburgh on the bank of the River Tweed had long been abandoned but was deemed by Somerset an appropriate place to build a fort. He was finally able to have work started on it in September 1547 (Brown, The Royal Palaces of Scotland, 1830)

to improve the defences of Edinburgh and 'the Queen's houses of Lothian' to avert the 'danger of conquest'.[24] By 8 March, Somerset seems to have been showing open hostility towards the Scottish ambassador, with Otterburn complaining that in London the French diplomats were treated as friends whilst the Scots were regarded as enemies.[25]

Right from the start of his protectorate, the Duke of Somerset looked at Scotland with acquisitive eyes. In a notable contrast to Henry VIII's foreign policy, Somerset saw Britain, rather than France, as the key place to expand English influence. He was even willing to consider an immediate hand over to the French of Henry VIII's prized stronghold at Boulogne in order to free up resources for campaigning within the British Isles.[26] Unlike many of his contemporaries, Somerset seems to have recognised the geopolitical possibilities of an Anglo-Scottish alliance and wished to secure that end either by diplomacy or force. According to the English Lord Protector, if Britain was united, with 'the sea for wall', it need not be afraid of 'any worldly or foreign power'.[27]

Throughout the summer and autumn of 1547, Somerset and his propagandists emphasised the benefits of a united Britain. In July 1547 congregations in English churches were urged to pray 'for this small Isle of Britain' and that its people 'might forever live hereafter in one love... knit into one nation by the most happy and Godly marriage of the King's Majesty and the young Scottish Queen'.[28] A similar theme was emphasised in the proclamation issued by Somerset the week before Pinkie, which declared that the English sought only to bring together:

> [The] good men of both the Realms, to unite them . . . in one name, by the name of Britons, and in one such a friendly kind of living . . . as they shall well find . . . the honour of both the Realms preserved, and the subjects of the same well satisfied and contented.[29]

The point was repeated by Somerset in the aftermath of the battle, when the Norroy herald was sent to inform the Scottish leaders of the advantages if the peoples of Britain lived 'together as one nation of one tongue and one land'.[30] Somerset felt he had a divine calling to unify Britain and bring to an end the 'unnatural and unchristian' conflict between two countries alike in 'manner, form, language, and all conditions'.[31]

Religious conflict

Somerset's belief that he had a God-given mission to bring together Scotland and England was given particular potency by the complex religious situation of the time. The English invasion of 1547 was not simply a push for dynastic union, but also a confessional conflict. According to Somerset's own proclamations, an Anglo-Scottish union would advance 'the glory of God' and help abolish 'the bishop of Rome's usurped jurisdiction'.[32] Since Henry VIII's break with the Papacy in the early 1530s, Protestant ideas had been gaining ground in England. The Reformist party was given a major boost by the accession of Edward VI and Somerset's seizure of power. At the coronation of the child king on 20 February 1547, Archbishop Cranmer urged the new regime to see 'God truly worshipped, and idolatry destroyed'.[33] The Archbishop of Canterbury's remarks were an early indication of the radical religious policies that would characterise Edward VI's reign.

Although there has been some historical debate about the degree of Somerset's personal interest in religious affairs, he repeatedly declared that his regency served a divine purpose.[34] Upon becoming protector, Somerset gave thanks to God for His 'providence' in allowing him to rule, and prayed to follow the Lord's 'calling'.[35] Somerset was surrounded by keen advocates for religious reform (including his second wife Anne Stanhope), and his political and military appointees were overwhelmingly sympathetic to Protestant ideas.

While preparations for the invasion of Scotland were gathering pace, the English Church was experiencing revolutionary change. The summer of 1547 saw Somerset's government advocating the destruction of religious images (including stained glass windows), banning votive candles and forbidding religious processions.[36] That autumn, as the armies of the Duke of Somerset and the Earl of Arran faced off near Musselburgh, royal visitations were descending on English churches and zealous Londoners were smashing the images in St Paul's Cathedral.[37] An increasingly assertive Protestant identity was developing within England, which some evangelicals wanted to spread across the British Isles. As William Patten declared, the English having 'received with most humble thanks' God's word in their 'own tongue' now desired for the Scots likewise to enjoy 'such goodly benefits'.[38]

At the time of the Battle of Pinkie, Scotland was still an officially Catholic country. Yet it was far from religiously united. There had been a Protestant presence in Scotland since at least the late 1520s. During the political and military upheavals of the early and mid-1540s Scottish support for religious reform had expanded and become more radical.[39] Scotland's internal religious divisions were brutally highlighted in May 1546 when the Archbishop of St Andrews, Cardinal David Beaton, was murdered by a group of Reformist activists. The Cardinal's assassins then proceeded to occupy the archbishop's residence of St Andrews Castle in Fife for over a year and hold hostage Arran's eldest son and heir (who at the time of the murder was being educated in

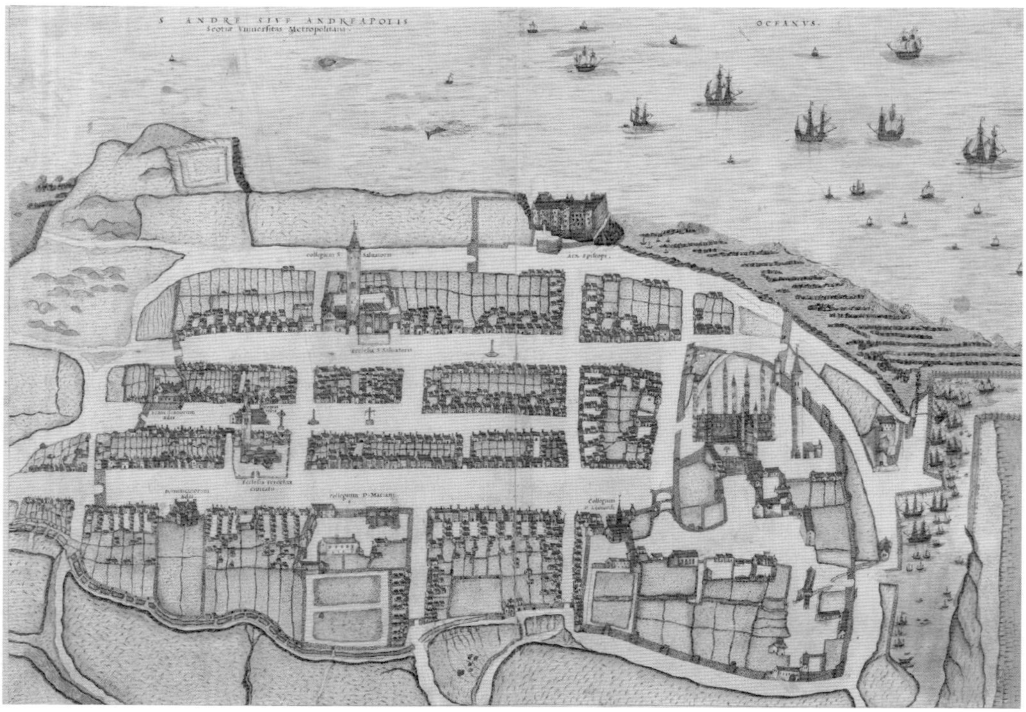

Figure 2.3: St Andrews, plan, c. 1580, by John Geddy. The archepiscopal castle on the coast, largely ruined in the French bombardment in 1547, has by now been restored (The Trustees of the National Library of Scotland)

Beaton's household). The Protestant occupation of St Andrews Castle deeply unnerved Scottish Catholics, created a major problem for Arran's government, and arguably contributed to the English decision to attack Scotland in 1547 (Figure 2.3).

During the final months of Henry VIII's reign there was intermittent contact between the so-called Castilians in St Andrews Castle and the English Government. By the end of 1546 the situation at St Andrews had become problematic for both the occupiers and the besiegers of the castle. The Castilians had issues with supplies. Meanwhile members of the Scottish nobility were getting restive at the resources Arran was expending on the siege. In a meeting of the Scottish Privy Council held in St Andrews on 19 December 1546 there were criticisms of the long time spent by Arran at the siege of the castle and how this had been 'very costly to him and the whole realm'.[40] After extensive consultation, Arran agreed that (ultimately fruitless) negotiations should be opened with 'the persons being in the Castle' – a decision that was hastened by the privy councillors' fears that the Castilians might be victualed by the English and even perhaps Arran's young son delivered to them.[41]

In reality, the aid given by the English during Henry VIII's last days was limited. This changed following Somerset's seizure of power. On 4 February 1547 Adam Otterburn regretfully noted 'that ambassadors of St Andrews' were given a good hearing at the English court. Two days later, with Henry VIII still unburied, and in the midst of processing the considerable business necessitated by a new monarch, the English Privy Council agreed to send £1180 for the wages of soldiers in St Andrews Castle and the pensions of several nobles 'and others' defending the castle.[42] The privy councillors depicted the aid as 'accomplishment of the promise' made by Henry VIII.

On 27 February (a week after the coronation of Edward VI), Somerset and the Privy Council gave instructions to Andrew Dudley, newly appointed Admiral of the King's Fleet, to sail northwards with seven ships 'for annoyance of the Scots bruited to prepare to pass towards France, and for the interruption of such munition as is looked to be brought for Scotland out of France'.[43] The English naval forces were also instructed to assist the Protestants in St Andrews Castle. Dudley was told to sail 'before St Andrews to the terror of our enemies of Scotland and the comfort of our friends' and to make contact with the castle's defenders.[44] Around the same time William Elmes, who that spring became Vice-Admiral of the English fleet in the North Sea, was sent north with three vessels (*Minion*, *Dragon*, and a smaller craft known as 'the great pinnace') to guard a convoy of ships transporting victuals and munitions for the relief of St Andrews.[45] This naval intervention in early March 1547 led to the first outright violence of Edward VI's regime against the Scots, when Andrew Dudley's forces boarded and captured the Scottish ship the *Lion*, and reportedly sank a further two vessels.[46]

The English continued to send aid to St Andrews Castle throughout the spring and early summer of 1547, apparently sending the Castilians 'the best gunner in England' in May and delivering victuals and gunpowder in late June.[47] By the middle of the summer the English seem to have decided to give more far-reaching support. Indeed,

Figure 2.4: John Dudley, successively Viscount Lisle and Earl of Warwick, line engraving, after unknown artist, published in 1786 by Richard Godfrey (© National Portrait Gallery, London)

the campaign that led to Pinkie may have been partly envisaged as a liberation effort for St Andrews, or at least was meant to capitalise on the presence of this Protestant-held castle on the Fife coast. The role that the situation in St Andrews played in plans for the English invasion is often downplayed by modern scholars. Yet contemporaries regarded it as a factor in how military activities developed in the summer of 1547. In the aftermath of the surrender of the castle on 30 or 31 July, the English ambassador to France informed the Imperial ambassador at the same court that before news of this capitulation reached London, Somerset and William Paget (Comptroller of the Royal Household) had made up their minds to help the castle hold out.[48] Furthermore, the ambassador confided that the Earl of Warwick (who commanded the vanguard at Pinkie) was 'already on the Scottish frontier waiting for his army, which was to be large, and which he intended to march through Scotland' (Figure 2.4).[49]

It is worthwhile remembering that although the English army that fought at Pinkie only entered Scotland at the start of September 1547, the process of planning for the campaign began significantly sooner, when the defenders of St Andrews Castle seemed likely to hold out for some time. Preparations for invasion were already taking place in June, when Adam Otterburn wrote from London that 'there is no appearance of motion in this country except against us'.[50] That same month, the French ambassador in London, Odet de Selve, complained to Somerset about rumours that the English had resolved to attack Scotland in August both by sea near St Andrews and by land.[51] In a letter dated 22 June, de Selve also informed King Henry II of France that many in London were saying there were plans for nine or ten thousand footmen, as well as numerous horsemen, to be sent secretly to the Scottish border for an invasion.[52]

The surrender of St Andrews Castle to the Italian mercenary Leone Strozzi and his fleet of French galleys at the end of July 1547 came as a shock to the English, not least because up until that point the newly ascended Henry II had largely avoided military intervention in Britain.[53] Although Strozzi's galleys were seen passing Dover and heading north, the English were uncertain of their destination. On 23 July, Somerset informed the Imperial ambassador Francis van der Delft that he had 24 'well-armed ships' ready for dealing with the French galleys and that they would 'sail very shortly to take up their position either at the mouth of the Forth leading to Edinburgh or else at St Andrews' and thus 'prevent the French galleys from getting out so easily as they got in'.[54] In the same meeting, Somerset also noted that he had already gathered all the 'needful stores' for a wider invasion of Scotland, which with God's blessing would secure England 'for the future against both Scots and French'.[55] At this time, the English had little idea that Strozzi would bombard the Protestants in St Andrews Castle into submission over a few days during the final week of July 1547. The English government's failure to recognise the potential frailty of St Andrews becomes a little more explicable if one considers that the Scottish Privy Council had itself concluded that the castle was only winnable by starving the Protestant defenders.[56]

On 1 August, a day or so after the Castilians had surrendered but before news of their capitulation had reached London, Lord Clinton (soon to be commander of the English fleet at Pinkie), was sent north with 12 ships and six row barges for the assistance of St Andrews Castle (Figure 2.5). Clinton was ordered to ascertain the situation and, if it seemed the Protestants could hold out, to send to the castle 100 men and 'such victuals or munition as shall be necessary'.[57] In reality of course it was already too late. Clinton's orders were written a day or so after the Castilians had surrendered. Strong 'contrary' winds meant that Clinton was delayed, only making it as far as Holy Island at Lindisfarne by 16 August.[58] News of the winning of St Andrews had already reached Lindisfarne and London and Clinton ended up focusing on revictualling activities around Berwick and preparing for the wider English invasion.

Figure 2.5: Lord Clinton (later Earl of Lincoln), c. 1560–65, artist unknown (© National Portrait Gallery, London)

When the Duke of Somerset crossed into Scotland at the start of September 1547, Scotland's Catholic authorities were firmly in control of St Andrews. Nevertheless, the siege there seems to have shaped how the English invasion was originally conceived. St Andrews stands on the east coast of Fife, a county which is bounded to the north by the

River Tay and to the south by the River Forth. This section of coastline was integral to Somerset's initial planning. In the early summer of 1547, the English twice sent an Italian military engineer to St Andrews to 'devise' where best to build fortifications on the Fife coast.[59] The area had several attractions for the English as a foothold for attacking the rest of Scotland. First, control of the Tay and the Forth brought with it influence over three of Scotland's richest burghs (Edinburgh, Dundee and Perth) and much of the country's most fertile farmland. Second, fortifications on these estuaries and the adjacent coastline could be accessed from the sea, reducing, though not eliminating, problems with supply. Third, the region had a significant number of Protestant sympathisers, a proportion of whom saw England as a possible ally in the struggle against Catholicism. It was a state of affairs that alarmed supporters of the Scottish Government.[60]

Messages between the English Government and Scottish collaborators provide helpful insights into plans during the spring and early summer of 1547. The English appear to have wanted to occupy burghs and fortifications on the east coast and use these as hubs to spark a wider religious revolt. In March 1547, in an agreement witnessed at St Andrews Castle, the Scottish nobleman Lord Gray pledged to deliver Broughty Castle at the mouth of the River Tay to the English (which he actually did in the aftermath of Pinkie), and to assist them with taking the burgh

Figure 2.6: Broughty Castle in 1807, by Robert Scott, after Patrick Nasmyth. This tower house was the property of a prominent protestant, Patrick, Lord Gray who delivered it to be occupied by the English on 21 September 1547 (National Galleries of Scotland. Purchased 2004)

of Perth (Figure 2.6).[61] Around the start of July, the Scottish exile James Henrisoun updated Somerset on recent communication with his countrymen regarding their shared aims of ensuring that proposed English 'sea fortresses' may be supplied, the Scottish Government kept 'otherwise occupied', the Catholic clergy and 'resisters to Godliness suppressed', and St Andrews fortified.[62] To this end, Henrisoun's informants stated that with little cost the English might gain key fortifications in 'the most rich country of Fife', namely Inchgow (now known as Lochore), Lochleven, Ravensheugh (now known as Ravenscraig), and Rosyth.

Discussions regarding more ambitious plans to spark religious war across the kingdom seem to have taken place with the fiercely Protestant Earl of Glencairn who had extensive lands in Western Scotland. Following a meeting with the Duke of Somerset in June 1547, Glencairn provided the English with a summary of the aid he could offer and advice on how to take Scotland.[63] This briefing was created at Somerset's request and the original has survived with additional comments in the margin, possibly reflecting the views of the English Protector himself.[64] The document has traditionally been dated to July 1547, following Glencairn's return to Scotland.[65] Yet its opening sentence implies that it was drafted while the Earl was still in southern England (so is from mid-June at the latest), as Glencairn remarks that in his conversation with Somerset he 'declared at length the occasion of my coming here, which is to serve at your Grace's pleasure with my body, kin, and friends, in setting forward the King's Majesty's Godly purpose'.[66]

Among other commitments, Glencairn pledged to provide aid if Somerset and his army were ready to invade Scotland – an offer which received the cryptic annotation that the English did not intend any such thing 'without cause of [the Scots] part given'.[67] Glencairn appears to have been aware of Somerset's interest in establishing English garrisons, declaring that he supposed the Protector would 'fortify St Andrews or Leith for the East seas' and advising that for 'the West seas' it might be advisable to build at Ardmore on the Clyde.[68] This idea was deemed 'very good' by the English annotator of the document. However, arguably the most striking of Glencairn's proposals was his willingness to raise 1,000 of his own men and 1,000 other 'favourers of the word of God' and together 'break the country and make division unto the time your grace invades'.[69] This strategy likewise met with English approval, assuming an invasion took place.

Protestant hopes of triggering a religious rising in Scotland were not completely far-fetched. The spring of 1547 saw Catholic churchmen petitioning the Scottish Privy Council regarding the alarming spread of the 'pestilential heresies of Luther' not only in the distant parts of the realm but also among people close to the government.[70] According to the churchmen, if action was not taken soon these 'damnable heresies' would increase 'daily more and more'. The clerics' concerns were not completely unfounded. A significant number of Scots in the 1540s had Reformist sympathies, and a proportion considered collaboration with England to further their religious agenda. During the siege of St Andrews Castle supposedly as many as 200 lords, lairds and gentlemen made promises to England.[71] Their names were recorded in a register, which was rather incompetently left in the castle when it surrendered. Despite (or perhaps because of) this misfortune, several Protestant nobles and lairds remained in contact with the English throughout the late summer of 1547, with some such as James Cockburn, the laird of Langton, specifically entreating Somerset to invade.[72] Following Pinkie, further Protestant Scots offered assistance to the English. Indeed, in December 1547 Andrew Dudley, then commanding the English at Broughty on the Tay, claimed that 'the whole country was ready to come in, both great and small', and that he was being offered control of towns and many 'handsome piles', if only he had men to put in them.[73]

A significant proportion of both Scots and English appear to have seen the campaign of 1547 through the lens of religious conflict. When, in the aftermath of Pinkie, the provost and bailies of Dundee agreed to assist the English at Broughty they first and foremost promised to be 'favourers of God's word' and 'setters forth of the same' and accepted Somerset's intervention in Scotland as fulfilling a Godly purpose.[74] Francis van der Delft noted that when news of Pinkie reached London, the courtiers did not boast about the English success, regarding 'this great victory' as something that was won by 'the grace of God alone'.[75] The young Edward VI put the English perspective even more pithily when, in September 1547, he wrote to Somerset that 'we fight for the cause of God, they for that of the pope'.[76] Catholic Scots were likewise keen to frame the fighting as a confessional conflict. In the autumn of 1547, David Paniter, the Scottish ambassador at the French court, spoke bitterly of the need for the injustice of Pinkie to be revenged with God's help.[77] He 'prayed that all good princes and Christians and friends of the Catholic faith would assist his country'. What was being fought over at Pinkie was not merely a dynastic struggle; it was a battle for the souls of the people of Scotland.

Attack on Langholm

Despite Somerset's preparations for war, it was the Scots who actually initiated land warfare against the English with the capture of Langholm Castle in July 1547 (Figure 2.7). The tower house of Lord Maxwell at Langholm had been occupied by an English garrison since 1544. Although not an exceptionally strong fortification, it was regarded by English leaders in the Borders as a convenient place from which to 'annoy' Scotland.[78] Somerset appears to have been less convinced of Langholm's value, informing Francis van der Delft that the 'fort' was of very little importance.[79] Nevertheless, it would acquire a disproportionate significance in the months prior to Pinkie.

The Scottish Government had developed plans to retake Langholm as early as January 1547.[80] At the start of April, Arran gathered an army and was only discouraged from attacking Langholm by a combination of 'evil weather' and the Earl of Huntly saying that he could not bring his men into 'those far places' at that time of the year.[81] In June, preparations were again put in place for an attempt

Figure 2.7: Langholm Castle, a tower house in a strategic location in the Scottish West March, held by an English garrison but recaptured by Arran in the summer of 1547. In order to strengthen it the English commander, Lord Wharton, had proposed taking down its top storey to make a fighting platform and filling in its stair, chimney and windows (David Caldwell)

on Langholm, and pieces of artillery were moved from Edinburgh to Peebles in advance of the attack.[82] Arran, with a large army (perhaps as many as 25,000 men), then advanced on Langholm around 10 July.[83] A spy report sent to the English described Arran's army as 'the starkest host' and 'with the best order that was since Flodden'.[84] Faced with such an overwhelming force, the small English garrison, a few hundred men at most, surrendered on 17 July, supposedly after withstanding several cannon shots.[85]

Arran's reasons for bringing such a substantial army to capture a relatively small fortification are far from clear. On the surface it was perhaps an effort to exert control over a troubled area of the Borders, where a proportion of local residents had been collaborating with the English. Supposedly, Arran made commitments to the inhabitants of the west borders of Scotland, specifically the residents of Annandale, Ewesdale, Eskdale and Liddesdale, that he would cast down Langholm and bring them under his protection, if they would be 'true Scottish men' and loyal 'to the realm of Scotland'.[86] However, the scale of the forces Arran committed to Langholm suggest that additional factors may have been shaping the Scottish governor's decisions.

By attacking Langholm, the Scots reopened hostilities with England. In some respects this was a reckless move. Yet Arran probably believed that an English invasion was already inevitable. The Scots had been preparing for Somerset to attack since at least March, and the decision to besiege Langholm took place against a wider background of organising for war. Orders gathering Scottish forces and weaponry in the Langholm area were sent out at the beginning of June.[87] Only a few weeks earlier, on 20 May, the Scottish Privy Council noted that they had received information that the 'old enemies of England' were in readiness 'to come and invade' with a navy and ordered beacons to be established to warn of their approach.[88] Faced with this impending crisis Arran sought to depict himself as a strongman and a protector of Scotland, declaring that he would 'defend this realm and liberty thereof and [expend] his life thereupon, with the help of God, the noblemen and subjects of the same'.[89] In this context, Arran may have seen advantages in striking the first blow against the English. He perhaps also hoped that a quick victory, and the retaking of a Scottish stronghold would help unite a divided nation and inspire his countrymen to resist determinedly subsequent English attacks. If so, it was not an entirely successful scheme, as later in August when Arran sought to gather his forces for Pinkie, several lairds complained that they had so recently been out in arms that 'their men would not rise again'.[90]

From the perspective of the English the loss of Langholm was embarrassing, but it also gave them grounds to seem like the wronged party. On 23 July, in a meeting with the Imperial ambassador, Somerset complained that the Scots were not fulfilling treaties and, as they had now attacked again, the English had 'decided to go against them both by land and sea'.[91] By 7 August, Anglo-Scottish relations had deteriorated so much that Otterburn sought to end his embassy to the court of Edward VI and return to Scotland. Straight after an official audience with the boy king at Hampton Court, Otterburn had a deeply hostile conversation with Somerset. During the argument Somerset apparently declared that 'the King's majesty was dishonoured by the taking of the Langholm, which was conquest in time of war and his just dominion'.[92] Otterburn left Hampton Court convinced that an English invasion was imminent. Indeed, during the audience with the king, Otterburn complained how he had seen with his own eyes 'very great preparation for war' against Scotland. A day after the meetings at Hampton Court an urgent message was brought asking Otterburn to return. Upon arriving at the palace, Somerset told the Scottish ambassador that on reflection there were 'better ways' than 'the effusion of blood and the destruction of the poor people'.[93] Somerset therefore proposed continuing negotiations, suggesting that he met with Scottish representatives at Newcastle on 27 August.

In reality, this proposal was disingenuous, as Otterburn himself suspected. Orders had already been sent out in mid-July ordering English forces to gather at Newcastle on 24 August.[94] Planning for an invasion of Scotland was taking place prior to the fall of both Langholm and St Andrews. Indeed, as the Scottish forces were advancing on Langholm, Somerset informed van der Delft that although he hoped the Scots would not be able to take it, the outcome was relatively unimportant as once the Scottish forces 'had done their utmost he would take from them more than they could get back'.[95] Furthermore, Somerset told him that the English had already 'made full preparations to this effect'. The Scottish reoccupation of Langholm was presented by the English as a grievous hurt and became a pretext for war.[96]

Objectives in September 1547

By the end of August 1547, both Scotland and England were on a war footing. As harvest came to an end, Somerset's long-awaited invasion began. On Saturday 27 August he met with English cavalry forces at Newcastle, prior to joining the rest of the army at Berwick-upon-Tweed, the base from which the attack on Scotland would be launched (Figure 2.8). According to Patten, Somerset wanted 'speedily to further that [which] he had deliberately taken in hand', and to that end rode rapidly 'all the way' from London to Newcastle, notwithstanding the 'weariness of the way'. [97] Somerset's need for speed was partly dictated by the tight timetable he had set for the invasion. The day before he left the English capital *en route* to Scotland, Somerset informed van der Delft that he hoped to be back in London again within six weeks.[98]

Figure 2.8: Berwick, Lord's Mount, a state-of-the-art fortification built in 1541–42 at the northeast angle of the town walls which were then largely dilapidated. It has large casemates for pieces of artillery. Somerset would almost certainly have viewed this before setting out on his expedition into enemy territory (David Caldwell)

A number of factors probably encouraged Somerset to plan for a short campaign. First and foremost, there were major challenges attendant on keeping sixteenth-century armies in the field for any length of time. These were heightened in a region such as the Scottish Borders where there were significant problems with supply.[99] The time of year also added pressure as by the middle of autumn conditions for campaigning would be worsening. August had already been characterised by bad weather, with storms impacting the movement of English ships in the Channel and North Sea.[100] Somerset may have also been concerned about the prospect of renewed fighting in mainland Europe. Supposedly, part of the reason why he joined his forces so late was because he was detained by rumours that the French had 'collected a great force' to threaten English holdings on the Continent.[101] Last, but by no means least, a combination of court politicking, religious divisions and economic upheaval made it unwise for the English head of government to absent himself from London for a long period. Somerset's desire to return quickly from Scotland is therefore understandable. Yet what did he actually hope to achieve during his six weeks in the north of Britain?

At his most optimistic, Protector Somerset may have believed that a decisive military victory would shock the Scottish government into agreeing to the betrothal of their queen to the young Edward VI. In the immediate aftermath of Pinkie, Somerset demanded that the Scots consent to 'the Godly' marriage of Britain's two child monarchs, and that Mary Stewart be handed over to the English 'to be nourished and brought up. . . in the company of the King's Majesty'.[102] With hindsight this seems rather unrealistic. Yet it should be remembered that Arran had in 1543 assented to this match, and a significant number of Protestant-sympathising Scots were still expressing their support for the marriage during the summer of 1547.[103] Indeed, it was reported in June 1547 that every day there arrived at the Tudor court 'Scots who favour the English side' and they had 'frequent secret conferences with the Protector'.[104] It is likely that Somerset underestimated the extent of opposition to the marriage amongst Scottish elites and thought that a convincing show of force would bring about a change in policy.

Yet the invasion of 1547 was not just about bullying Scottish politicians into delivering up their queen. Somerset was determined to establish an English military presence in the southeast of Scotland. To this end, he sought to capture strategic locations, particularly around the Tay and Forth, which could be fortified and so provide a foothold for wider expansion. On 6 September 1547 van der Delft wrote to Mary of Hungary (then Governor of the Netherlands) noting that even if Somerset's enterprise against the Scots 'did not succeed entirely' he was given to understand that the English would nevertheless construct two fortresses on Scottish territory, located in 'such a position as would enable them to make themselves masters of the rest of the country with ease'.[105] Furthermore, the Protector himself had apparently 'made much of this plan'. Somerset subsequently discussed the merits of planting garrisons in Scotland with the French ambassador Odet de Selve in December 1547, supposedly claiming that in previous centuries English attempts at conquering

Scotland 'depended on the chance of one battle' rather than building 'fortifications to keep what they had conquered'.[106]

We should also not overlook the extent to which the campaign of 1547 was intended as a war of religious liberation and a gesture of support to Scottish Protestants. The fall of St Andrews Castle had seriously alarmed elite supporters of religious reform. Several were fearful for their futures and saw English intervention as potentially saving their own skins and their countrymen's souls. On 18 August, the Protestant laird James Cockburn wrote to Somerset emphasising the need for an army from England and claiming that if there was no invasion many Scottish supporters of reform were likely 'to be in danger'.[107] In late August Glencairn informed the English that he was 'at a hard point', although he did still agree to distribute the proclamation that Somerset sent north immediately in advance of the Pinkie campaign.[108] The fate of Scottish Protestants was a matter of concern to the English during the late summer of 1547. Interestingly, one of the points that Somerset raised during his acrimonious meeting with Otterburn at Hampton Court on 7 August was the persecution of the 'king's friends'.[109] Of course, quite apart from any confessional solidarity Somerset perhaps felt, the increasing religious divisions in Scotland potentially provided the English with a fifth column. As an intelligence report sent to the English government in August 1547 maintained, those 'that profess the word of God' were inclined 'to follow the favourers and forthputters of the same'.[110]

The openness of many reformist sympathisers to interaction with the English profoundly shaped how the invasion of 1547 was approached. In comparison to earlier interventions in Scotland, Somerset placed an unusual degree of emphasis on winning hearts and minds and sought to present himself as a friendly ally. Whilst in 1544 Henry VIII had told the army attacking Scotland to put 'man, woman and child to fire and sword', the 1547 campaign was framed rather differently.[111] The proclamation Somerset issued before Pinkie declared that the English came into Scotland as 'friend and a conservator' for the 'Godly fulfilling of God's pleasure'.[112] Furthermore, Somerset stated that his forces intended 'to pass amicably' without doing to the 'well willers of both the Realms', hurt or damage, saving 'somewhat in forage, which cannot be avoided where an army marcheth'.[113] This message of (relative) restraint appears to have been circulated within the English army. William Patten subsequently claimed that 'according to the promise of the Proclamation, neither force nor fire was used wittingly' during the English army's time in Scotland.[114] Similarly, on 8 October 1547, Andrew Dudley, then commanding the English forces at Broughty, noted that 'according to your grace's commandment for ordering myself to the country I use them with all gentleness'.[115]

Such statements did not mean that the English completely avoided violence and the threat of force. Towards the end of October 1547 the supposedly 'gentle' Andrew Dudley threatened to bombard Dundee, and actually ordered the *Bark Auger* and the *Mary Hambrough* to fire some shots to get the town to agree to his demands.[116] However, in the weeks around Pinkie, deliberate devastation was not a core English policy. Significantly, the letter in which Dudley threatened the Dundonians, also noted that: 'they are much desirous here in the country of Angus and Fife to have a good preacher and bibles and testaments and other good English books of Tyndale and Frithe's translation which I have promised them'.[117] Dudley further advocated for a 'book binder' to be sent north, which he believed would do 'very much good'. In the autumn of 1547 a proportion of the English commanders perceived their role as protecting and extending Protestantism – they arrived bearing guns in one hand and bibles in the other.

If English aims at the time of Pinkie can be broadly summarised as faith, forts and royal marriage, what were the objectives of the Scottish leaders in September 1547? Unsurprisingly, Arran's priority was repelling an invading army and maintaining his country's independence. This was reflected in the Scottish government's official pronouncements, for example on 8 September decreeing special concessions for the heirs of anyone killed in the army gathered for 'defence' of the realm.[118] Yet Arran's responsibility to defend Scotland did not necessarily mean fighting a pitched battle. There were other ways to resist an invasion – including various forms of guerrilla warfare. Arran chose not to take these alternative pathways but determined on a large-scale confrontation with Somerset from at least the start of September. Intelligence sent to the English Government from John Cockburn (the Protestant sympathising Laird of Ormiston) on 2 September 1547, noted that Arran was intending to 'haste his army' down to the Peaths (the ravine now known as the Pease, near Cockburnspath) and there abide the coming of the English.[119] Ultimately Arran chose to fight further west, but the intention to pick a strongpoint and make a stand was clearly there some days in advance of Pinkie.

Why did Arran commit his forces to an all or nothing confrontation with the English, rather than adopting a less high-risk strategy? It is likely that divisions among the Scots drove Arran to gamble on the possibility of a rapid and definitive victory, rather than a longer campaign in which the English were gradually worn down and picked off. According to John Cockburn's report of 2 September, Arran feared an English delay in attacking as he believed he could not hold his army together for any length of time once it was convened.[120] That same week, the Earl of Glencairn informed the English that the governor 'fears his own folks in one part as mickle as your army'.[121] Similarly, Lord Wharton and the Earl of Lennox reported that there was great division amongst the noblemen of Scotland at this time.[122] The problems were real. A number of Scots were actively colluding with the English and praying that God would assist Somerset's 'army to work His glory'. [123] Even more were rather cynical and dispirited.[124] In late August the Laird of Barr expressed considerable displeasure at being expected to turn out his men once again, and declared that the English were welcome to 'take the bishops and priests' – a point on which many of his fellows agreed.[125]

Against this unhappy background, Arran appears to have decided to use resisting the English as a litmus test of loyalty to his regime. Intelligence reports from late August and early September repeatedly refer to how Scots were 'most dreadly commanded' to join Arran's forces, and that those who stayed at home would be regarded as traitors.[126] Furthermore, Arran may have anticipated that if he won a pitched battle alongside the chief figures in the Scottish kingdom it would silence his opponents and bolster his position, rather as Robert the Bruce had managed at Bannockburn in 1314. Arran probably hoped an overwhelming victory would unite the Scots and quickly tackle the problem of an English presence within Scotland – something that, in the words of the Scottish Privy Council later that autumn, would 'engender a great inconvenience' if it was not hastily remedied.[127] It was an understandable conclusion to draw. Arran almost certainly knew that he could call on more men than the invading English had brought with them. Furthermore, Arran and his fellow commanders were defending familiar territory and may have assumed that this would bring them an advantage. Unfortunately for thousands of Scots, these strengths were not enough to outweigh the capabilities of the English army they faced in the fields beside Musselburgh.

Notes

1 J. Finlay, 'Otterburn, Sir Adam (d. 1548)', *ODNB*.
2 *MLSC*, 185.
3 *MLSC*, 184.
4 *RPC* 1, 62.
5 *RPC* 1, 62.
6 *APC* 2, 470–71.
7 *CSP Edward VI*, 3; TNA, SP 10/1.
8 *HP* 2, 596.
9 For discussion of the machinations surrounding Henry VIII's final days see C. Skidmore, *Edward VI: The Lost King of England* (London, 2007), 40–54.
10 B. L. Beer, 'Seymour, Edward, duke of Somerset [known as Protector Somerset] (c.1500–1552), *ODNB*.
11 Arran's effectiveness as a regent has recently been re-evaluated by A. Blakeway, *Regency in Sixteenth-Century Scotland* (Woodbridge, 2015).
12 Dalrymple 1, 263.
13 Duke of Somerset, *An Epistle or Exhortacion, to Unitie and Peace, sent from the Lorde Protector, and Others the Kynges moste Honorable Counsaill of England: to the Nobilitie, Gentlemen, and Commons, and al Others the Inhabitauntes of the Realme of Scotlande* (London, 1548), f. 7r.
14 J. Harrison, *An Exhortation to the Scotts to Conforme Themselves to the Honourable Expedient and Godly Union Betwene the Two Ralmes of Englande and Scotland* (London, 1547), 12.
15 These are the sentiments of a Scottish messenger, Archibald Douglas, passing though England in January 1543 and questioned by Viscount Lisle (later to be made Earl of Warwick) and the Bishop of Durham. *HP* 1, 358.
16 RPS, 1543/12/32.
17 *HP* 2, 343.
18 *HP* 2, 342–43.
19 *HP* 2, 325.
20 *HP* 2, 365.
21 TNA, SP 49/8, f. 177r.

22 Patten, f. 40r–v.
23 *MLSC*, 174.
24 *MLSC*, 174–75.
25 *MLSC*, 176.
26 Somerset considered an immediate hand-over of Boulogne as early as 1548. Bush, *The Government Policy*, 2, 4, 10.
27 Somerset, *Epistle*, f. 17r.
28 TNA, SP 10/2, f. 11r.
29 Somerset, E., Duke of, 'Proclamation' (London, 1547).
30 TNA, SP 50/1, f. 112v.
31 Somerset, *Epistle*.
32 Somerset, Proclamation. Compare Patten, f. 24r.
33 Cranmer address at coronation, quote in D. McCulloch, *Tudor Church Militant. Edward VI and the Protestant Reformation* (London, 2001), 62.
34 See for instance J. Loach, *Edward VI* (New Haven and London, 1999), 47.
35 Quoted in Skidmore, *Edward VI*, 66.
36 E. Duffy, *The Stripping of the Altars: Traditional Religion in England, 1400-1580* (New Haven, 1997), 450–52.
37 Duffy, *Stripping of the Altars*, 453.
38 Patten, f. 29r.
39 A. Ryrie, *The Origins of the Scottish Reformation* (Manchester, 2006), 64–78.
40 *RPC* 1, 58.
41 *RPC* 1, 58.
42 *APC* 2, 12–13.
43 *APC* 2, 44; *Navy of Edward VI*, 14–16.
44 TNA, SP 10/1, 87v–88r; *Navy of Edward VI*, 15.
45 TNA, SP 50/1, f. 23r–24r; *Navy of Edward VI*, 17.
46 *APC* 2, 452. *CSP Spain* 9, 499. *MLSC*, 176. Compare the report of its shipwreck in *CSP Scot* 1, 3–4. It does, however, appear clear that the ship was boarded by the English. See *CSP Scot* 1, 7; *Navy of Edward VI*, 19.
47 *MLSC*, 184. *CSP Scot* 1, 8.
48 *CSP Spain* 9, 515.
49 *CSP Spain* 9, 515.
50 *MLSC*, 187.
51 Selve, 153.
52 Selve, 154.
53 Surrender details in J. Knox, *History of the Reformation in Scotland*, ed. W. C. Dickinson, 2 vols (Edinburgh, 1949), vol. 1, 96.
54 *CSP Spain* 9, 127.
55 *CSP Spain* 9, 127.
56 *RPC* 1, 58; *CSP Spain* 9, 140. For an account of the siege operation by Strozzi see E. Bonner, 'The recovery of St. Andrews Castle in 1547: French Naval Policy and Diplomacy in the British Isles', *English Historical Review* 111(1996), 578–98.
57 *Navy of Edward VI*, 25.
58 *Navy of Edward VI*, 26.
59 *MLSC*, 188.
60 *MLSC*, 188.
61 *CSP Scot* 1, 2.
62 TNA, SP 50/1, f. 55r; *CSP Scot* 1, 11.

63 Glencairn visited England during the summer of 1547, travelling back through Carlisle and seemingly reaching Scotland at the very end of June. TNA, SP 50/1, f. 48r. TNA, SP 15/1, f.34r–v.
64 TNA, SP 50/1, ff. 57r–58v.
65 This is how it is dated in *CSP Scot* 1, 10.
66 TNA, SP 50/1, f. 57r.
67 TNA, SP 50/1, f. 57r.
68 TNA, SP 50/1, f. 57v.
69 TNA, SP 50/1, f. 57v.
70 RPC 1, 63.
71 TNA, SP 50/1 f. 76r–v; CSP Scot 1, 14.
72 TNA, SP 50/1 f. 76r–v; CSP Scot 1, 14.
73 TNA, SP 50/2, f. 159v; *CSP Scot* 1, 53.
74 TNA SP 50/2, f. 69r. Also *CSP Scot* 1, 33.
75 *CSP Spain* 9, 152.
76 Letter from Edward VI to Protector Somerset quoted in Skidmore, *Edward VI*, 78.
77 *CSP Spain* 9, 214.
78 TNA SP 15/1, f.1r; *CSP Dom Add*, 320.
79 *CSP Spain* 9, 122.
80 Pitscottie 2, 87. Rumours regarding an attack on Langholm were already circulating in January 1547, TNA SP 50/1, f. 1r.
81 *Diurnal*, 44; TNA, SP 15/1, f. 22r; *CSP Dom Add*, 323.
82 *TA* 9, 79.
83 *CSP Spain* 9, 126; *TA* 9, 80, 85–94; *CSP Dom Add*, 325–26.
84 *CSP Scot* 1, 8.
85 Merriman, *Rough Wooings*, 224. *CSP Spain* 9, 126.
86 TNA, SP 15/1, f. 37r; *CSP Dom Add*, 325.
87 *TA* 9, 78–80.
88 *RPC* 1, 73.
89 *RPC* 1, 74.
90 TNA SP/1 f. 78r
91 *CSP Spain* 9, 127
92 *MLSC*, 193.
93 *MLSC*, 193.
94 *CSP Edward VI*, 4.
95 *CSP Spain* 9, 125.
96 *MLSC*, 193.
97 Patten, f. 36r.
98 *CSP Spain* 9, 143.
99 Jordan, *Edward VI*, 250.
100 *CSP Spain* 9, 143.
101 *CSP Spain* 9, 135.
102 TNA, SP 50/1, ff. 112r–113r.
103 TNA, SP 50/1, f. 57r.
104 *CSP Spain* 9, 103.
105 *CSP Spain* 9, 147.
106 Selve 248. Compare the interpretation of this conversation by Merriman, *Rough Wooings*, 246.
107 TNA, SP50/1, f.76r–v; *CSP Scot* 1, 14–15.
108 *CSP Scot* 1, 17.
109 *MLSC*, 192.

110 TNA, SP 50/1, f. 90r.
111 Merriman, *Rough Wooings*, 144.
112 Somerset, Proclamation.
113 Somerset, Proclamation.
114 Patten, f. 33v.
115 TNA, SP 50/2, f.10.
116 *CSP Scot* 1, 35.
117 TNA, CSP 50/2, f. 78r.
118 RPS, A1547/9/1
119 TNA, SP50/1, f. 95r (*CSP Scot* 1, 18).
120 TNA, SP50/1, f. 95r (*CSP Scot* 1, 18).
121 TNA, SP50/1, f. 99r (*CSP Scot* 1, 18).
122 TNA, SP50/1, f. 97r (*CSP Scot* 1, 18).
123 TNA, SP50/1, f. 95r (*CSP Scot* 1, 18).
124 TNA, SP50/1, f. 95r (*CSP Scot* 1, 18).
125 *CSP Scot* 1, 15.
126 *CSP Scot* 1, 16–17.
127 *RPC* 1, 80.

3

The English forces

The commanders

The English forces at Pinkie were led by Protector Somerset as 'general of the army'.[1] By personally taking command, Somerset was departing from typical Tudor practice. The last time that an English head of government had been present on an invasion of Scotland was more than a hundred years earlier, during the reign of Henry IV.[2] Protector Somerset's decision to lead the invasion of 1547 himself reflects both the significance he attached to the campaign and his confidence in his own military abilities. Somerset was regarded as a highly competent commander and had played a significant role in Henry VIII's campaigning around Boulogne in 1544 and 1545. Indeed, early in 1545 the future Duke of Somerset had defeated a French force of 14,000 with less than 5,000 English troops.[3] He appears to have been popular with his soldiers, and at least some of the men at Pinkie idolised him. William Patten claimed that Somerset's presence made his forces 'certain' of victory and that many men said 'they had rather in field be a mean soldier under his grace, than under any other [be] a great Captain'.[4]

At Pinkie, Somerset had direct control of the main battle – a typical role for a Renaissance general (Figures 1.3 and 3.1).[5] The other land forces on the 1547 campaign were largely led by men Somerset had previously served alongside. The vast majority were, like the Lord Protector himself, able, upwardly mobile, and supportive of religious reform (Figure 3.2). The English vanguard was commanded by John Dudley, the newly created Earl of Warwick, who had worked closely with Somerset on the Scottish campaign of 1544 as well as enjoying considerable success in naval warfare against the French (see Figure 2.4).[6] Somerset and Warwick had a history of rivalry, but at the time of Pinkie appear to have been cooperating effectively. According to Francis van der Delft, during the summer of 1547, Warwick was 'contenting himself' with the responsibilities Somerset had given him.[7]

Another veteran of the 1544 attack on Scotland, Sir Ralph Sadler, was made treasurer to the English forces – a tribute to the administrative abilities of a man who had risen to prominence in the household of Henry VIII's fixer and advisor Thomas Cromwell.[8] Somerset also gave responsibilities to officers he had worked with during his time in France. The cavalry in particular were dominated by veterans from the French campaigns, including Lord Grey of Wilton (high marshal of the army and

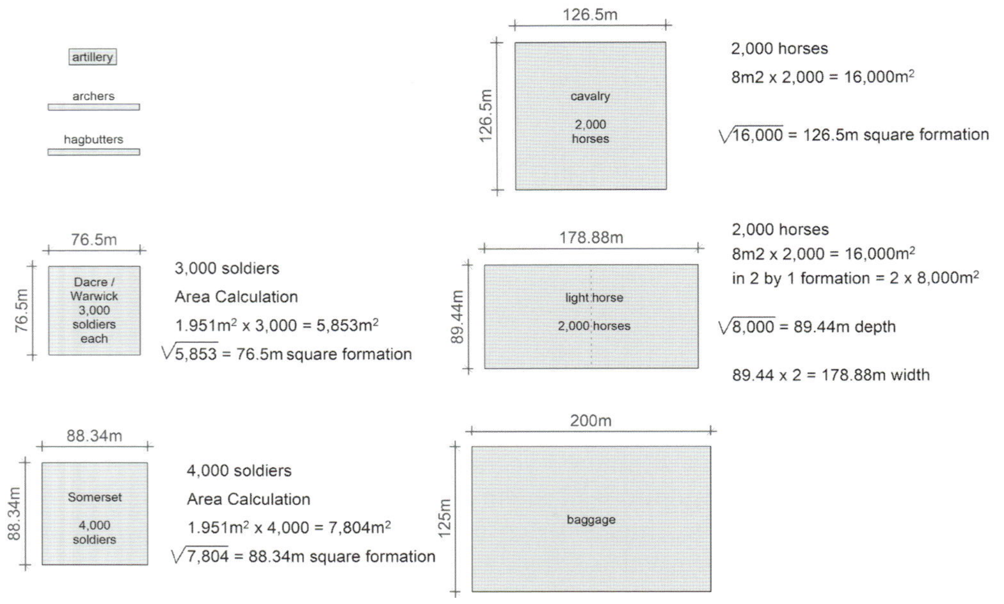

Figure 3.1: Battle formation calculations for the English army. Compare Figures 4.15 and 4.20 for units in the Scottish army. The information on the spacing for individual men is derived from sixteenth-century military manuals (Geddes Consulting Ltd)

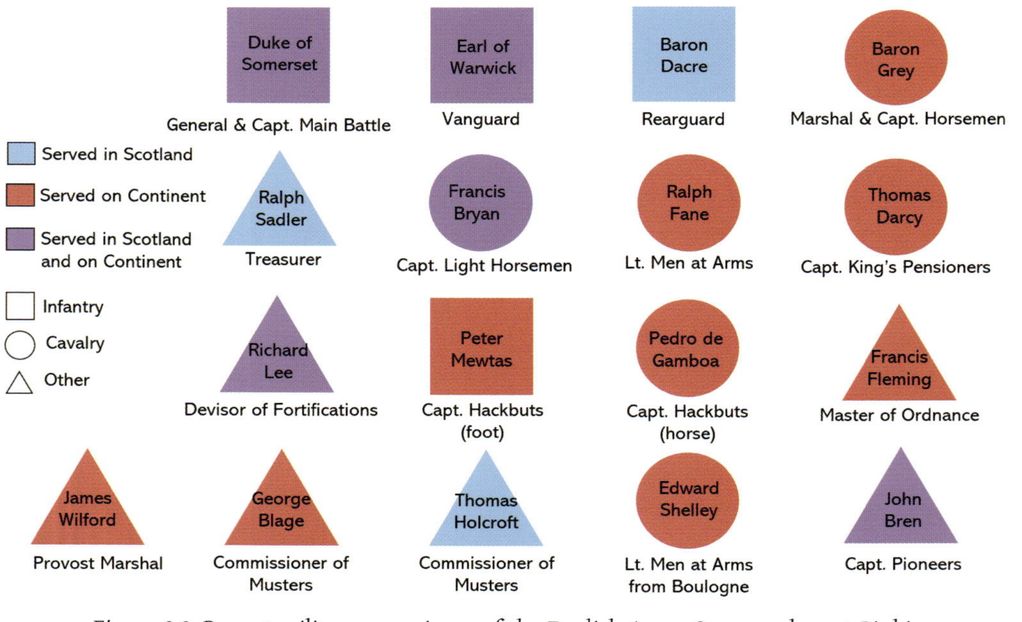

Figure 3.2: Recent military experience of the English Army Commanders at Pinkie

captain general of all the horsemen) (Figure 3.3), Sir Francis Bryan (captain of the light horsemen), Sir Ralph Fane (lieutenant of the men-at-arms and demilances), Sir Thomas Darcy (captain of the king's pensioners and men-at-arms) and Edward Shelley (lieutenant of the men-at-arms brought across from Boulogne).[9] The provost marshal of the army, Sir James Wilford (Figure 3.4), was similarly a colleague from Somerset's stint in Boulogne. Meanwhile, the commander of the naval forces in 1547, Lord Clinton (see Figure 2.5), had served on both the expedition to Scotland in 1544 and the subsequent campaign in France. These were experienced commanders who were familiar with recent conflict.

By the mid-sixteenth century, warfare was becoming increasingly professionalised, and the 1547 campaign had several military specialists, such as the Spanish mercenary Sir Pedro de Gamboa, who commanded the horsemen armed with hackbuts (a type of long gun), and Sir Francis Fleming, who was master of the ordnance. Both men had served in France, while Gamboa also had extensive experience on the Anglo-Scottish border.[10] Further military experts who were veterans of both the French and Scottish campaigns included Sir Peter Mewtas (who led 600 footmen with hackbuts), John Brende (captain of the pioneers), and the military engineer Sir Richard Lee (who had

Figure 3.3: Lord Grey of Wilton (?) Portrait by Gerlach Flicke, 1547. If the identification is correct, it may have been painted in London in the early part of 1548 (National Galleries of Scotland. Bequest of the 11th Marquess of Lothian, 1941)

Figure 3.4: Sir James Wilford, artist unknown, dated 1547. A fanciful depiction of the siege of Haddington, of which Wilford was commander in 1548–49, is shown in the background (National Galleries of Scotland. Given by the Marquess of Tweeddale, 1892)

recently returned from overseeing the English fortifications at Calais and Boulogne). To an overwhelming degree, Somerset's officers were men of proven competence. The English leaders at Pinkie were a capable and close-knit group, many of whom had personal ties to the protector, and who mostly shared his reformist religious ideology. Somerset seems to have chosen men he could work with, and to have left behind less reliable characters such as his brother Thomas Seymour.

Lord Dacre, who at Pinkie commanded the rear-guard, was an exception. While other officers were self-made men (for example, Sir Ralph Fane was illegitimate and started his career as a servant to Thomas Cromwell), Dacre was a scion of a traditional border family. A religious conservative, he clearly fell outside Somerset's inner circle of Protestant modernisers. Furthermore, questions were raised about the competence of his border troops, with fellow English soldiers complaining that while the rest of the camp observed silence the 'Northern prickers' caused 'troublous and dangerous noises all the night long'.[11] However, Dacre brought with him decades of knowledge of the Anglo-Scottish border. Indeed, his connections with the Scottish aristocracy were so close that in 1534 he was tried for treasonous communication with the Scots – an accusation he managed to refute, making him the only English noble to be acquitted of a treason charge during the reign of Henry VIII.[12] Despite ideological differences, Dacre clearly served a practical purpose in Somerset's army.

Cavalry

What, though, was the nature of the forces these men commanded (Table 3.1)? At the Battle of Pinkie, Somerset probably had over 4,000 men-at-arms and demilances, along with 2,000 light horse.[13] Many had seen recent service in France and arrived for the Scottish campaign in good order. Indeed, the contemporary writer William Patten praised the cheerful spirit and high-quality equipment of the cavalry at Pinkie, noting the great number of 'likely men and ready horses' each with 'sure armour, weapon, and apparel'.[14]

Table 3.1: Composition of the English Army at Pinkie

Type	*Number in English Army at Pinkie*
Main Battle	4,000 footmen
Vanguard	3,000 footmen
Rearguard	3,000 footmen
Men-at-Arms and Demi-Lances	4,000 horsemen
Light Horsemen	2,000 horsemen
Mounted Hackbutters	200 horsemen
Foot Hackbutters	600 footmen
Pioneers	1,400 footmen
Artillery	15 great guns drawn 'by horse'
Carriages	900 carts and 'many waggons'

The most high-status heavy cavalry were the men-at-arms, who, when the army was in camp, would lodge about the general.[15] Men-at-arms typically fought with lances, and both they and their horses wore extensive plate armour (Figure 3.5). The armour brought considerable protection but was a substantial burden even for specially bred 'great horses'. Indeed, Thomas Audley, author of a military treatise presented to the young Edward VI, warned that men-at-arms should never ride fast in the chase, but should 'follow softly in a troop together keeping their horses in breath'.[16]

Figure 3.5: Shaffron, of steel, for the protection of a horse's head; North European, early sixteenth century, as used by men-at-arms for their mounts (Royal Armouries, VI.40)

Because of the limitations of horses in heavy armour, most Tudor armies also had a substantial number of demilances and light horsemen. Like the men-at-arms the demilances wore plate, but their legs were less heavily protected, and their horses were largely unarmoured, giving them greater freedom of movement.[17] The demilances were therefore slightly more suitable for skirmishing and pursuing the enemy than the true men-at-arms (Figure 3.6).

At Pinkie, the light horsemen were under the command of Sir Francis Bryan, an experienced soldier and courtier,

Figure 3.6: English demilances at Pinkie, as illustrated in the 1577 edition of Holinshed's Chronicles. *The riders are in armour, but not their horses, and they carry lances. Scottish light horsemen flee to the right*

whose anti-clericalism and scandalous private life had earned him the nickname 'the Vicar of Hell'.[18] His men rode slightly smaller horses, wore much less armour, and carried a range of weapons including spears, swords and bows.[19] Whereas the heavy cavalry were used for their impact in battle, the light horsemen were for scouting, skirmishing and pursuing the enemy, roles which would all prove significant in the Pinkie campaign.[20] The light horsemen were much less highly valued, and in 1546 English forces in France experimented with having no light horse and just relying on men-at-arms – something they soon came to regret, concluding that 'they be necessary as well both for the skirmish and to be van-couriers' (i.e. the advance-guard).[21]

Alongside these traditional types of horsemen, Somerset also had a force of 200 mounted mercenaries armed with hackbuts and led by Sir Pedro de Gamboa.[22] They were largely of Spanish origin, possibly because of the more limited use of fire-arms by mounted units in the British Isles.[23] It is likely that the mounted hackbutters at Pinkie mostly used their horses to move around the battlefield and then dismounted to fire their guns – rather in the manner of later dragoons. Perhaps significantly, Gamboa's hackbutters spent part of the Battle of Pinkie fighting alongside Sir Peter Mewtas' infantry hackbutters and the English archers, with 'the hot continuance of their shot' preventing the Scots from gaining ground.[24] Somerset clearly valued his Spanish mercenaries. When in 1545 Henry VIII discharged several mercenary companies, Somerset (then still Earl of Hertford) successfully lobbied for Gamboa's men to be retained and to be deployed on the Scottish border.[25] Towards the end of the Pinkie campaign, on 28 September 1547, Somerset knighted three of the Spanish mercenaries, including Sir Pedro Negro – perhaps the earliest example of an English leader knighting a black man.[26]

Both light and heavy cavalry played important roles during the Scottish campaign. The heavy cavalry gave the English an advantage over the Scots who lacked men-at-arms. It took considerable nerve and training for light horsemen and infantry to resist the impact of a heavy cavalry charge. Yet such charges were not without risk for the attackers. At Pinkie, the English are said to have lost 51 horsemen, which were 'almost all gentlemen'.[27] Among the dead was the lieutenant of the men-at-arms from Boulogne, Edward Shelley, who was praised by contemporaries as a 'valiant captain'.[28] When Shelley's corpse was found it was so 'pitifully disfigured and mangled' he was only recognisable by his beard.[29] Even the highest-ranking cavalry officers could be exposed to harm, with the high marshal of the army at Pinkie, Lord Grey of Wilton, receiving a 'great wound' from a pike 'three fingers deep into the roof of the mouth'.[30]

Infantry

As was usual in early modern armies, the majority of the English forces at Pinkie were foot soldiers. The largest contingent was the main battle of 4,000 men, directly commanded by Somerset. At least 3,000 footmen were assigned to the vanguard, and a similar number to the rear-guard. There were also 600 foot soldiers armed with hackbuts. In total, in excess of 10,000 English footmen seem to have been present at Pinkie.[31] The bulk of them were probably drawn from the county militias – the armed men each shire provided to the Crown for war at home or abroad. They were ordinary labourers and craftsmen who found their lives interrupted by the martial demands of the government. As Raphael Holinshed's *Chronicles of England, Scotland and Ireland* commented in the 1570s, there was 'almost no village so poor in England ... that hath not sufficient furniture in a readiness to set forth three or four soldiers, or one archer, one gunner, one pike and a bill man at the least' (Figure 3.7).[32]

Figure 3.7: 'Spanish' morion, a type of open-faced helmet extensively used by English foot soldiers in the early sixteenth century (Royal Armouries, IV.490)

The most common weapon carried by early Tudor footmen was the bill, which had a curved blade (Figure 3.8) attached to a long shaft ranging in length from about five to as much as nine feet (about 1.52 m to 2.74 m).[33] Bills are the most frequently listed weapon in English muster rolls from the 1540s, and many of the infantry at Pinkie will have been armed in this manner.[34] For example, the muster records for February 1548 for the county militia in the area around Portsmouth reveal that out of 298 men, 97 were archers, 197 were billmen, and four were armed with hackbuts.[35] A muster that same spring for the area around Northwich in Cheshire recorded 14 archers and 389 billmen.[36] Meanwhile, contemporary muster records from York list 249 archers, 788 billmen, eight hackbutters, and a small number of horsemen.[37]

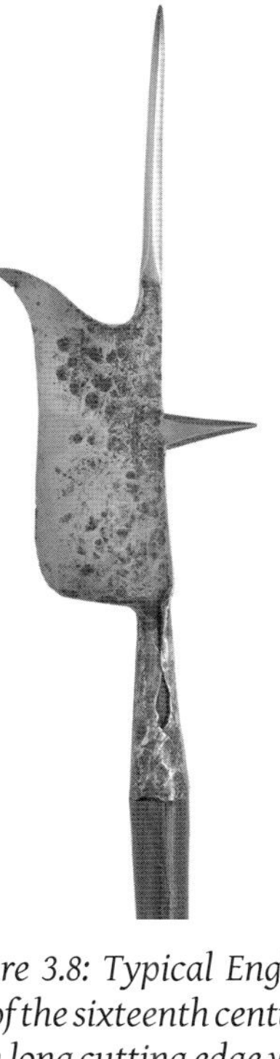

Figure 3.8: Typical English bill of the sixteenth century, with long cutting edge with curved hook, vertical spike and horizontal fluke at the back (Royal Armouries, VII.940)

By the end of the sixteenth century the English had largely abandoned bills in favour of pikes – a rather longer pole weapon which typically took more drilling to use effectively. At the time of Pinkie, the English army had access to pikes and bills, with the shorter weapon still being more widespread. When Somerset (then Earl of Hertford) invaded Scotland in 1544 he planned for his original landing party near Leith to consist of 1,500 archers, 1,500 billmen, 1,000 pikemen, and 250 hackbutters.[38] Unfortunately, we do not have as precise a breakdown for Pinkie. However, the English clearly had both types of pole weapon in 1547. For example, an inventory of the English garrison at Inchcolm that winter records 50 pikes and 40 bills.[39] Pikes appear to have been particularly used by garrisons, on ships, and for semi-professional troops outfitted by aristocratic commanders. Interestingly, in his account of Pinkie William Patten thought it necessary to describe how the Scots used pikes standing 'shoulder to shoulder' with the 'fore ranks well nigh to kneeling' in front of 'their fellows behind' so they were like an 'angry hedgehog'.[40] Patten clearly did not assume that the normal arrangement of a pike unit would be familiar to his readers. Indeed, in the 1540s English officials typically referred to the standard pikes of about 16 ft (4.88 m) as 'morris' or Moorish pikes – a name which reflects the weapon's perceived foreign origins.[41]

In comparison to the cavalry, foot soldiers were much more lightly armoured. Their usual body protection appears to have been the padded tunic known as a jack (see Figure 4.16), although there are frequent mentions of 'steel coats' and some references to 'white harness' (the contemporary term for plate armour).[42] However, even military theorists thought only a small proportion of footmen required plate armour. Thomas Audley advised Edward VI that for every 100 footmen only 20 needed the plate body-armour known as 'corslets'.[43] These were given to the men in the front of the battle as having them in white harness would supposedly fill the enemy with 'terror' from a distance. [44] Audley further suggested that as corslets were 'not easy for poor men to come by' the king should provide 'a sufficient number' – an early hint of the state taking responsibility for individual soldiers' equipment.[45] The pattern of better armed foot soldiers being placed in the front line appears to have been followed at Pinkie. Patten noted how in 'the foremost' of the vanguard were 300 men led by Sir John Luttrell 'all with harness and weapon, and in all points else so well trimmed for war' that it was obvious that great cost had been spent on their 'perfect appointment and furniture'.[46]

Archers remained a component in English armies throughout the Tudor Period and were regarded as a symbol of national pride. In 1557 the Venetian ambassador described bows and arrows as the 'proper and natural weapons' of the English.[47] Even as late as the 1570s the poet and soldier Thomas Churchyard boasted that: 'The bow is feared as far as flies our fame, / And bows I ween won Englishmen the name'.[48] The bow in question was the famous English longbow. The average length of the longbows retrieved from the wreck of the *Mary Rose*, which sank in July 1545, is 6.5 ft (198 cm).[49] Using these weapons took considerable strength. According to modern estimates the draw weight of the *Mary Rose* bows could be as great as 180 lbs (81 kg).[50] In comparison, the bows of present-day Olympic archers have a draw weight of about 50 lbs (22 kg). To ensure enough trained men, Henry VIII passed legislation stating that from the age of seven all boys should be trained in archery, and that all men under 40 who were not exempt by reason of infirmity or rank should regularly 'exercise shooting in longbows'.[51] As Bishop Latimer pointed out in 1549 'men shall never shoot well, except they be brought up in it'.[52]

Like most other early modern soldiers, archers were responsible for providing their own weapons and armour, at least at the start of a campaign. When Henry VIII launched his invasion of France in 1544 he gave instructions for each archer to bring a bow and a sheaf of at least 28 arrows.[53] The archers also had to take an oath 'that his harness, bow, and arrows be his own, or his master's or captain's'.[54] The extent and type of armour worn by Tudor archers varied. An assessment of the weapons held by the citizens of York in February 1548 reveal that while some bowmen were equipped with a coat of plate and a steel cap, others only wore a jack, and many just had a bow and half a sheaf of arrows.[55]

During the campaign of 1547 the English used archers to protect other infantry soldiers while on the move and in battle. Yet, despite English pride in their bowmen, by the 1540s archers did not have quite the military importance they had held in previous centuries. The advent of gunpowder meant that other forms of projectile weapons were available, and some English commentators were beginning to doubt the effectiveness of bowmen. The military author Humfrey Barwick later claimed that during the English campaigns in France in the 1540s he never saw or heard of archers doing anything 'with their long bows, to any great effect'.[56]

Warfare was changing and that was reflected in the English forces present at Pinkie. The 600 foot-hackbutters led by Sir Peter Mewtas played a significant role in the 1547 campaign and appear to have been relatively trusted by Somerset (Figure 3.9). Patten notes how the infantry armed with hackbuts were deployed 'hard at the faces of the enemies' at a critical point in the fighting around the slough at Pinkie and apparently conducted themselves valiantly.[57] Mewtas, the commander of the hackbutters, had been knighted for his service in France in 1544, where he had led 500 men with hackbuts.[58] It is likely that some of these men were also present at Pinkie.

The English forces at Pinkie were a blend of old and new. Many of the infantry were still armed with bow and bill, as most English soldiers had been for generations. Yet recent experience fighting on the Continent was leading some to question this approach. Professional and semi-professional soldiers armed with firearms were increasingly important and were deployed at pivotal moments by Somerset. Despite the 'affection' that many English men had for the long bow, it was beginning to appear 'inferior unto the fiery weapons'.[59]

Figure 3.9: Matchlock long gun (hackbut) from Gardone or Brescia in Italy, perhaps one of a large order made in 1545 for Henry VIII. Hackbutters had to be able to charge these with gunpowder, ram home a piece of lead shot, then aim and fire them with the aid of a lock mechanism that lowered a lighted match into priming power – all potentially when they themselves were under fire or in danger of being attacked (Royal Armouries, XII.5315)

Artillery

The English at Pinkie had a small but highly significant artillery presence. Because the master of the ordnance and his men were able to get two or three cannons onto high ground the English acquired an advantage in the fighting on Saturday 10 September.[60] Supposedly, the guns on the hillside 'did gall' the Scots 'with hail-shot' and other projectiles, whilst artillery placed on the flank of the English rearguard also fired 'with great puissance and vehemence'.[61]

The exact details of the artillery used in this way at Pinkie are unfortunately unclear. However, Patten records that 'there were in the army of great ordnance drawn forth with us by horse 15 pieces'.[62] These great guns needed to be mounted on carriages for firing. Inventories compiled during the winter of 1547 to 1548 provide further hints regarding the artillery that Somerset brought to Pinkie. In December 1547 the English garrison at Roxburgh had two demi-culverins, three sakers, one falcon, three port-pieces, one fowler, six bases (each with two chambers), and another six 'small bases'.[63] The Roxburgh garrison was established by Somerset at the end of the Pinkie campaign, and may have been provided with guns used in the recent battle.

Our understanding of English guns from the 1540s was greatly increased by examples preserved in the wreck of the *Mary Rose*.[64] The guns employed by the Scots would have been similar. The following list provides some guidance on interpreting pieces named in connection with Pinkie:

- ***Cannons*** – Very large muzzle-loading guns, usually bronze. They fired iron shot of 6 inches (152 mm) or more.
- ***Culverins*** – Relatively long muzzle-loading guns, usually bronze or cast iron. Culverins came in several sizes with labels including 'grose' and 'demy'. 'Battards' (or 'bastards'), 'sakers' and 'moyens' were smaller sizes of culverins. Bores ranged from about 4.67 inches to 2.75 inches (119 mm to 70 mm). Note that the term culverin was also used to describe types of firearms.
- ***Falcons*** – Smaller muzzle-loading guns, usually bronze or cast iron. Varieties are described as 'small' or as 'falconets'. Bores ranged from about 2.34 inches to 1.8 inches (59 mm to 46 mm).
- ***Wrought iron breech-loading guns*** – English guns of this type were named as port pieces, fowlers and bases in descending order of size. The Scots named smaller guns of this type as cutthroat guns and berses. The largest fired stone shot with a calibre of 10 inches. The smaller ones fired stone or composite shot as little as 1 inch (25.5 mm) in diameter.

With just 15 great guns on land the English army at Pinkie may not have been as well provided as the Scots. As by the 1540s England had a thriving industry manufacturing cannons, and the English monarch had a large collection of artillery weapons, this situation presumably arose from a deliberate tactical choice on the part of Somerset. He may have been reluctant to have too many great guns on land because of issues with logistics. Transporting heavy artillery across country was no mean feat. To enable ordnance to be moved the army's route had to be flattened, or made 'plain'. The task of constructing suitable crossings and roadways was undertaken by the pioneers. At Pinkie the English had with them no less than 1,400 pioneers under the command of John Brende, who had previously held a series of responsible military roles on the Continent, including recruiting mercenaries for Henry VIII.[65]

Somerset invaded via the coast road running from Berwick to Edinburgh. This route had two major river crossings, namely the Tyne at East Linton and the Esk at Musselburgh. In 1547 both these rivers had bridges. A greater difficulty for a large body of men with horses, carts, and artillery was the ravine known as the Pease or the Peaths.[66] The name 'pease' is derived from the plural of the Scots word 'peth', meaning a steep path up a hillside.[67] Patten recalled it was so steep on both sides and deep that anyone going straight down was in danger of tumbling, while people striving to climb out of it were 'sure of puffing and pain' (Figure 3.10).[68] Yet the labour of the pioneers meant the English army and their ordnance were able to cross. The sheer effort involved was considerable.[69] Somerset was probably also willing to have relatively few guns on land because of the significant firepower of his naval forces. The great guns drawn by horses were never intended, and did not prove to be, the only artillery at the disposal of the English commander.

Figure 3.10: The Pease (Peaths), a deep and wide ravine on the route from Berwick to Edinburgh that had to be crossed by the English Army (David Caldwell)

Naval forces

The 1540s saw major growth in England's naval capabilities. This was largely driven by Henry VIII's war with France. Between 1542 and 1547 the English Crown spent more than £265,000 on naval forces, of which more than £45,000 went on building and rigging new ships.[70] To put this figure in context, at the end of Henry VIII's reign the Crown's ordinary annual income was around £50,000, although extraordinary taxation and other exceptional sources of revenue meant that closer to £120,000 per annum was typically coming into the hands of the monarch.[71] As a result, when preparing for Pinkie, Somerset had available a significant number of newly built warships. Indeed, it is probable that most of the fighting ships used in 1547 were less than ten years old, with many having been built in 1544 or even more recently. The newness of much of Somerset's fleet was less extraordinary in the sixteenth century than it would be today (wooden vessels of the time typically had a short active life).[72] Nevertheless, the late 1540s were a high point in terms of the modernity of the Tudor navy.

Much of this expansion in the royal navy had been presided over by John Dudley, Earl of Warwick, during his time as lord admiral. The English naval forces in 1547 were led by Lord Clinton, one of Warwick's former subordinates. He had previously served on land and sea in the wars against Scotland and France in 1544 and 1545.[73] Like many of the land commanders, Clinton was an experienced officer with a history of working closely with Somerset. Indeed, he had been knighted by Somerset at Leith in May 1544.[74] His vice-admiral was Sir William Woodhouse, who had served in the same role during the 1544 expedition against Scotland (where he too gained his knighthood).[75] Woodhouse was a self-made man who won advancement through his excellence as a naval officer and administrator.[76]

Patten claims that Clinton and Woodhouse had 'upon the sea 65 vessels', of which 'the galley' and 34 'good ships' were 'perfectly appointed for war'. The rest of the vessels were for the 'carriage of munition and victual'.[77] Unfortunately, it is difficult to align Patten's figures with the English government records for the Pinkie campaign. The galley mentioned by Patten was almost certainly the *Galley Subtle*, the only full rowing galley constructed on the orders of Henry VIII.[78] The *Anthony Roll* (an illustrated inventory of the English navy compiled in the mid-1540s) lists the *Galley Subtle* as weighing 200 tonnes, and states that it was manned by 242 mariners and eight gunners and armed with one cannon and two sakers (Figure 3.11).[79]

However, the rest of the fleet is slightly more complex to identify. In the summer of 1547, an English administrator put together a list of vessels and crew headed 'the names of the ships appointed for the enterprise'.[80] This document is generally assumed to relate to Somerset's preparations for the invasion of Scotland. Interestingly, it does not mention the *Galley Subtle*. Instead, it lists 55 ships, plus six 'galliasses, shallops, and other rowing pieces' (all of which could be propelled by oars), eight 'boats of Rye' (typically crewed by about 30 men), and 11 boats described as 'western men with oars' (again usually with a crew of about 30). The recorded craft include both royal navy ships and merchant vessels. This is unsurprising as in times of war the Tudor government frequently conscripted merchant shipping for its own needs.

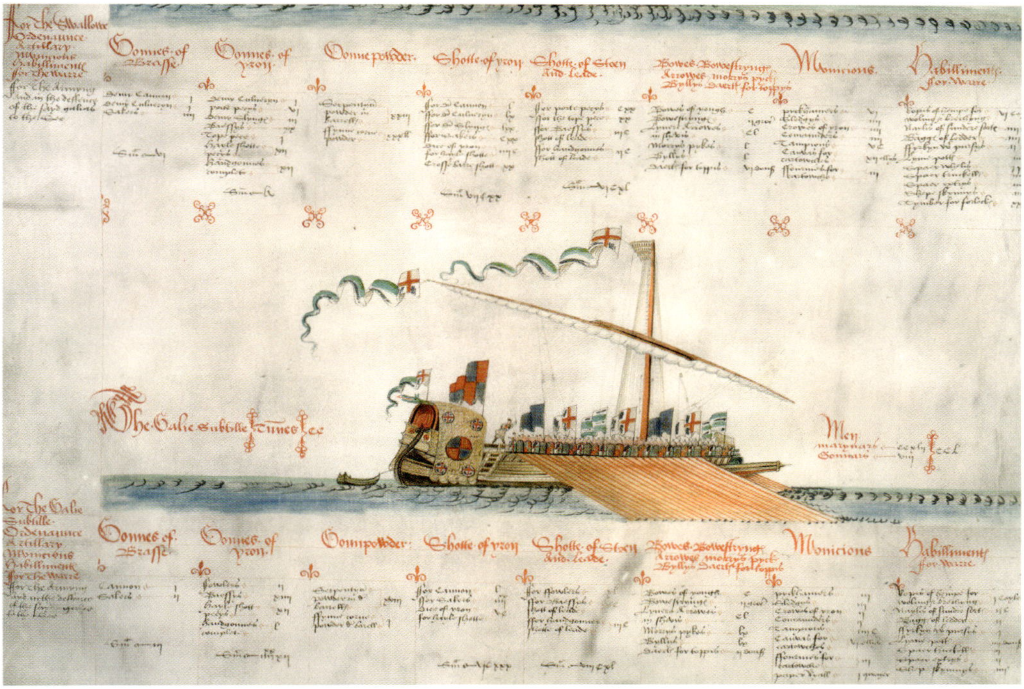

Figure 3.11: The Galley Subtle, *a Mediterranean-style galley as depicted on the 2nd Anthony Roll, 1546. She was the only ship of this type to be built by Henry VIII and played an important part in the 1547 expedition because she could be rowed close to shore for firing her ordnance (© The British Library Board, Add MS 22047, f.5r)*

The largest vessel on the list of 'ships for the enterprise' was the 1,000 tonne *Henry Grace à Dieu* or *Great Harry*, which had 700 men on board. A further seven ships were over 500 tonnes, namely Clinton's flagship *Pauncy* (Figure 3.12), *Aragozia* of Hampton, *Great Venetian*, *Peter Pomegranate*, *Jesus* of Lubeck, *Aragozia* of London, and the *Great Galley* (which confusingly was not a galley but was a sailing ship of about 500 tonnes also sometimes known as the *Great Bark*).[81] All of these larger ships had seen service in the Channel in 1545 during the war with France. No less than 35 ships, plus two rowing vessels (*Anne Gallant* and *Falcon*), of between 100 and 500 tonnes are also on the list – again most had seen service in the Channel. The list from the summer of 1547 gives a fascinating insight into the scale of the English preparations for the invasion, and the figures it provides imply that more than 9,300 men were intended to be on the ships Somerset took to Scotland.

We cannot be certain that this list 'for the enterprise' is the final version of the fleet that actually sailed. Indeed there is evidence that suggests alterations were made to the forces sent north. Instructions for victualling issued in August 1547 in preparation for the attack on Scotland refer to 8,000 men at sea, of which 2,000 were 'mariners' who were required to sail the ships, whilst the rest were intended to be

Figure 3.12: The Pauncy, *a carrack, from the 1st Anthony Roll, 1545. Pepys Library 2991 (by permission of the Pepys Library, Magdalene College, Cambridge)*

set on land.[82] More significantly, when Clinton was given orders on 1 August to set sail in advance of the main expedition and attack the coast of Fife, the list of 12 ships and six rowing barges appended to those orders included several vessels that were not on the longer and probably earlier list (*Jennet*, *Antelope*, *Unicorn*, *Bull* and *New Bark*) as well as several that were (*Morian*, *Swallow*, *Pauncy*, *Anne Gallant*, *Salamander*, *Falcon* and *Saker*).[83] It seems likely that at various points plans changed, and it may prove impossible to identify the exact ships that sailed north in support of Somerset's invasion. What is clear, though, is that a sizeable and relatively up-to-date naval force was prepared and set out for Scotland in the summer of 1547.

Logistics and supply

A central part of the English fleet's role in the invasion of 1547 was supplying the land forces with 'victuals and all kind of munitions'.[84] Sixteenth-century armies got through vast quantities of food for men and animals, as well as requiring regular deliveries of items such as shot, powder, bows, bow strings, arrows, wheels and axle-trees, both for carts and for moving artillery.[85] It was essential that supplies reached the necessary places in a timely fashion. As Thomas Audley remarked, without them an army could be 'overcometh without stroke of the enemy'.[86] Indeed, so important was feeding an army that Audley reckoned 'above all things provision is chiefly to be foreseen'.[87]

It was a challenge for most armies to obtain and transport enough food. However, the logistics of supplying an army attacking Scotland were particularly problematic.[88]

The north of England had limited surplus resources. Supplying a large army as well as the local population placed a considerable, and at times unsustainable, burden on the region's economy. When planning the invasion of Scotland in 1544, the English Privy Council was advised that grain needed to be sent north, not only for the army, but 'also for the relief of the King's poor subjects' who could potentially face such severe food shortages they might 'leave the Borders'.[89] The causes of such shortages become obvious when one considers the scale of an English great army in comparison to the size of regional centres of population. In the early sixteenth century the largest city in the north of England was York, which had about 6,000 residents. The total English land forces at Pinkie were more than three times the population of York.[90] In such a context, it is hardly surprising that contemporary military theorists referred to an army camp as being 'like a city' and requiring equivalent 'victuallers and merchants'.[91]

To provision the expedition to Scotland, Somerset gave orders for stocks of food and munitions to be built up at Berwick-upon-Tweed, Wark Castle and Ipswich, the latter for sending supplies northwards by sea.[92] Victuals and munitions were also stored on Holy Island at Lindisfarne.[93] These locations had all previously been used by Somerset as supply depots during his campaign of May 1544.[94]

The victuals collected at these depots drew from much wider economic networks. Records of supplies sent to Berwick between October 1546 and March 1549 reveal that wheat came from Newcastle, Norfolk and Portsmouth, as well as being purchased in the local area; butter and cheese were sent from Hull, Suffolk and London; whilst salt beef was acquired in Newcastle, Hull, Norfolk, Harwich, London and Dover.[95] By gathering provisions from a wider area the English government presumably intended to avoid problems like those that had arisen in the spring of 1544, when it was feared that Newcastle was likely to have 'famine' unless 'relief of corn' was sent to the city.[96]

Compounding the supply challenges in 1547 was the fact that as well as needing to provision the great army attacking Scotland up the east coast, the English government also had to provision military forces in the west. On 16 September 1547, Lord Wharton wrote from Carlisle to report on English raiding activity and noted how his offensive capabilities were hampered by shortages of food and ordnance.[97] Yet initially the supply networks for the army heading from Berwick towards Musselburgh seem to have held up – arguably a tribute to the experience Somerset and his fellow officers and administrators had gathered on earlier expeditions.

According to Patten, the English at Pinkie had 900 carts for carriage of food and munitions, as well as 'many waggons'.[98] Interestingly, this is significantly more than the number of carts the Duke of Suffolk had calculated would be needed to invade Scotland in 1544, when he advised the English Privy Council that 320 carts could supply an army of 20,000 men for 21 days, with some additional provisions brought by sea.[99] The large number of carts at Pinkie may indicate a wish on Somerset's part to take enough provisions to avoid having to take supplies from the surrounding area – an activity that usually alienated the local population.

Gathering together 900 carts was no easy task. In 1544 there had been issues getting the requisite number of carts for carriage of supplies in Scotland and France.[100] Meanwhile, shortages of carts had seriously impacted English military activity in France in 1523.[101] The fact that Somerset was able to acquire this quantity of carts and waggons was a significant administrative and logistical achievement. It is likely that many of the carts came from Yorkshire, thought to be the source of 'the best wains'.[102] Typically, each cart was drawn by 12 oxen, whilst the artillery had to be drawn by 'strong horses'.[103] These animals themselves provided challenges of supply. It is likely that the English army at Pinkie was accompanied by more than 10,000 oxen as well as a similar (or perhaps greater) number of horses. Fodder and clean water for the animals accompanying armies was an important priority.[104] Thomas Audley advised that when looking for a suitable 'ground for the lodging of an army' the marshal ought to look for the three 'commodities' of water, wood and pasture, with water being particularly essential for both 'man' and 'beast'.[105] Although water was not usually in short supply in Scotland, finding sufficient grass for large numbers of animals could be difficult. Meanwhile, efforts to carry enough animal feed for an army's horses and oxen were not only costly, but also contributed greatly to the need for carts.[106]

Such challenges with land transport were the context to Somerset's decision to supply his forces partly from the sea. There was precedent for using ships to carry a significant proportion of the provisions for an English army invading Scotland. Somerset himself had relied on water transport to move many of his supplies in 1544, as had many English commanders before him, right back to King Edward I in the 1290s. It is likely that about half of the vessels Somerset took to Scotland were primarily intended for supply, whilst several of the war ships also carried additional provisions for land forces. Many of the supply boats were smaller vessels of under 200 tonnes, largely drawn from southern ports, including Bristol, Falmouth, Dartmouth, Plymouth, Hastings and Rye.[107]

Bringing provisions by sea was an integral part of how Somerset approached the invasion of 1547. Patten recalled how the English fleet 'took the seas from Berwick toward Scotland and ... though they might not have always wind at will to keep their course still with us, yet ... with the driving of tides, they might upon any [of] our need of munition or victual not long be from us'.[108] As Patten's comment implies, provisioning from the sea brought with it the challenge of keeping contact between naval and land forces. It effectively determined the routes that Somerset could take and meant that a significant section of the English army had to cling to the coast. In the main it appears to have worked. In the months, weeks and days leading up to the battle of Pinkie, Somerset and his officials seem to have been relatively competent in matters of supply, and to have avoided some of the more spectacular failures of earlier English military ventures. In the short term the approach of gathering food and materials from broader economic networks and bringing them north by land and sea largely worked. However, it was not sustainable in the longer term, particularly when the English government became distracted by other problems in the south.

Ultimately, a failure to create secure provisioning networks would undercut the gains won at Pinkie. As Somerset himself recognised, successfully occupying territory was even harder than winning battles.

Notes

1 Patten, f. 35r.
2 Merriman, *Rough Wooings*, 240. It should perhaps be noted that Henry VIII did accompany English expeditions to France – arguably a reflection of the greater status accorded by the king to conflict in Continental Europe as against fighting in more northerly parts of the British Isles.
3 Beer, 'Seymour, Edward, duke of Somerset'.
4 Patten, f. 11r.
5 Patten, f. 35r.
6 Patten, f. 35r.
7 *CSP Spain* 9, 122.
8 Patten, f. 35r.
9 N. Murphy, *The Tudor Occupation of Boulogne* (Cambridge, 2019), 44, 114.
10 G. J. Millar, 'Henry VIII's Colonels', *Journal of the Society for Army Historical Research* 57/231 (Autumn 1979), 129–36.
11 Patten, f. 118v.
12 S. G. Ellis, 'Dacre, William, third Baron Dacre of Gilsland and seventh Baron Greystoke (1500–1563)', *ODNB*.
13 Patten, f. 35r–v; *CSP Spain* 9, 143.
14 Patten, f. 32r.
15 T. Styward, *The Pathwaie to Martiall Discipline* (London, 1582), 126.
16 T. Audley, 'A Treatise on the Art of War', *Journal of the Society for Army Historical Research* 6/24 (April–June, 1927), 70.
17 A. J. Hodgkins, Rebellion and Warfare in the Tudor State. Military Organisation, Weaponry and Field Tactics in Mid-Sixteenth Century England (Leeds University PhD Thesis, 2013), 70.
18 S. Brigden, 'Bryan, Sir Francis [called the Vicar of Hell] (d. 1550)', *ODNB*.
19 Hodgkins, Rebellion and Warfare, 71.
20 Hodgkins, Rebellion and Warfare, 71.
21 Audley, 'Treatise on the Art of War', 70.
22 Patten, f. 35v.
23 Hodgkins, Rebellion and Warfare, 72. See also M. Kaufmann, 'Sir Pedro Negro: What Colour was his Skin?', *Notes & Queries*, 253/2 (June 2008), 142–46.
24 Patten, f. 99r.
25 Millar, 'Henry VIII's Colonels', 134.
26 Kaufmann, 'Sir Pedro Negro: What Colour was his Skin?'. Patten, f. 144r.
27 Jordan, *Chronicle and Political Papers*, 8.
28 Patten, f. 112r.
29 Patten, f. 112r.
30 J. Lock, 'Grey, William, thirteenth Baron Grey of Wilton (1508/9–1562)', *ODNB*.
31 Patten claims there were 10,000 ordinary footmen, plus the hackbutters. Francis van der Delft states that the English had 12,000 footmen – a figure that probably includes the 10,000 ordinary infantry soldiers, the 600 foot hackbutters, and the 1,400 pioneers. *CSP Spain* 9, 143; Patten, f. 35r.
32 R. Holinshed, *The Firste Volume of the Chronicles of England, Scotlande, and Irelande* (London, 1577) 1, f. 87r.

33 G. Silver, *Paradoxes of Defence* (London, 1599), 29–31.
34 Muster for the City of York, 29 February 1548. TNA, SP 10/3, f. 46r.
35 Muster for the Hundreds of Portsdown and Bosmer, February 1548. TNA, SP 10/3, ff. 140r–145v.
36 Muster for the Hundred of Northwich, 27 February 1548. TNA, SP 10/3, ff. 25r–42v.
37 Muster for the City of York, 29 February 1548. TNA, SP 10/3, ff. 45r–94v.
38 *HP* 2, 356.
39 D. Starkey and P. Ward (eds), *The Inventory of King Henry VIII* (London, 1998), 144.
40 Patten, f. 86v.
41 Morris pikes was the usual term used in the inventory of Henry VIII's navy produced in the 1540s. C. S. Knighton and D. M. Loades (eds), *The Anthony Roll of Henry VIII's Navy: Pepys Library 2991 and British Library Additional MS 22047 with Related Documents* (Ashgate, 2000).
42 See, for instance, Muster for the City of York, 29 February 1548. TNA, SP 10/3, ff. 45r–94v.
43 Audley, 'Treatise on the Art of War', 69.
44 Audley, 'Treatise on the Art of War', 69.
45 Audley, 'Treatise on the Art of War', 69.
46 Patten, f. 96v.
47 J. Davies, 'Painful Pastime Versus Present Pleasure: Tudor Archery and the Law', *Journal of the Society for Army Historical Research*, 85, no. 343 (autumn 2007), 228–29.
48 T. Churchyard, *The Firste parte of Churchyardes Chippes* (London, 1575), f. 6v.
49 D. Whetham, 'The English Longbow: A Revolution in Technology', in L. J. Andrew Villalon and D. J. Kagay (eds), *The Hundred Years War: Pt. 2. Different Vistas* (Leiden, 2008), 222. The original figures are from R. Hardy, *Longbow: A Social and Military History* (Sparkford, 1992), 209–17.
50 Whetham, 'English Longbow', 222.
51 Anonymous, *The Statutes Which the Justices of Peace, Mayors, Sheriffs, Bailiffs, Constables and Other Officers Were of Late Commanded by the King's Majesty to put in Execution* (London, 1538), ff. 4v–8r.
52 T. Esper, 'The Replacement of the Longbow by Firearms in the English Army', *Technology and Culture* 6/3 (summer 1965), 391.
53 Anonymous, *Statutes and Ordinances for the War* (London, 1544), f. 3r.
54 Anonymous, *Statutes and Ordinances for the War*, f. 3r.
55 TNA, SP 10/3, f. 46r.
56 H. Barwick, *A breefe discourse, concerning the force and effect of all manuall weapons of fire and the disability of the long bowe or archery, in respect of others of greater force now in use* (London, 1592), 12.
57 Patten, f. 99r.
58 D. M. Ogier, 'Mewtas [Mewtis], Sir Peter, d. 1562', *ODNB*.
59 Barwick, *Breefe Discourse*, 1, 11.
60 Patten, f. 100v.
61 Patten, f. 100v. Hailshot consisted of quantities of small iron dice (cubes) which at close range would spread out and cause carnage to enemy formations.
62 Patten, f. 35v.
63 Starkey and Ward, eds, *The Inventory of King Henry VIII*, 143.
64 A. Hildred (ed.), *Weapons of Warre. The Armaments of the Mary Rose*, 2 parts (Portsmouth, 2011), especially part 1, 17–306.
65 Patten, f. 35r; *L&P* 21/1, 264, 293, 363.
66 A. Graham, 'Archaeology on a Great Post Road', *PSAS* 96 (1965), 318–47.
67 *DSL*, https://dsl.ac.uk/entry/dost/peth (accessed 22 May 2022).
68 Patten, f. 44v.
69 In 1554 during Wyatt's rebellion a gun coming off its carriage delayed the rebels by 'many hours' so that when they reached London the government forces were already gathered to resist them. Hodgkins, 'Rebellion and Warfare', 278.
70 D. Potter, *Henry VIII and Francis I: The Final Conflict, 1540–47* (Leiden, 2011), 511–12.

71 D. M. Loades, *Tudor Government: Structures of Authority in the Sixteenth Century* (Oxford, 1997), 61.
72 Potter, *Henry VIII and Francis I*, 366.
73 A. Duffin, 'Clinton, Edward Fiennes de, first earl of Lincoln (1512–1585)', *ODNB.*
74 Duffin, 'Clinton, Edward Fiennes de'.
75 Patten, f. 35v; *Navy of Edward VI*, 573.
76 D. Loades, 'Woodhouse, Sir William, (b. in or before 1517, d. 1564), *ODNB*.
77 Patten, f. 35v.
78 J. Bennell, 'The Oared Vessels' in Knighton and Loades (eds), *The Anthony Roll*, p. 34.
79 Knighton and Loades (eds), *The Anthony Roll*, p. 73.
80 TNA, SP50/1, ff. 68r–69v.
81 *Navy of Edward VI*, 483.
82 TNA, SP 50/1 f. 72r.
83 TNA, SP 50/1, 71v.
84 Audley, 'Treatise on the Art of War', 71.
85 Audley, 'Treatise on the Art of War', 71.
86 Audley, 'Treatise on the Art of War', 71.
87 Audley, 'Treatise on the Art of War', 71.
88 C. S. L. Davies, 'Provisions for Armies, 1509-50: A Study in the Effectiveness of Early Tudor Government', *Economic History Review*, new series 17/2 (1964), 236; Potter, *Henry VIII and Francis I*, 237.
89 *HP* 2, 257.
90 This figure assumes English land forces at Pinkie in excess of 18,200.
91 Audley, 'Treatise on the Art of War', 71.
92 TNA, SP 50/1 f. 72r. (*CSP Scot* 1, 14).
93 TNA, SP 50/1 f. 70r. (*CSP Scot* 1, 13).
94 *HP* 2, 287.
95 C. S. L. Davies, Supply Services of English Armed Forces (Oxford University Thesis, 1963), 322–24.
96 *HP* 2, 292. In this context, the fact that Somerset's invasion in 1547 took place at the end of summer (when much of the harvest had just been brought in), rather than in the spring (when grain stocks were lower) may have also helped reduce wider grain shortages in northern England.
97 TNA, SP 50/1 f. 109r, 16 Sep. 1547 (*CSP Scot* 1, 20).
98 Patten, f. 35v.
99 *HP* 2, 258.
100 Davies, 'Provisions for Armies', 239.
101 Davies, 'Provisions for Armies', 239.
102 *HP* 2, 258.
103 *HP* 2, 258.
104 See, for instance, Styward, *The Pathwaie to Martiall Discipline*, 33; Audley, 'Treatise on the Art of War', 74.
105 Audley, 'Treatise on the Art of War', 74.
106 *HP* 2, 257.
107 TNA, SP50/1, ff. 68r–69v.
108 Patten, f. 39r–v.

4

Scotland's military capability

The host

In the sixteenth century, Scotland's military capability depended on the premise that it was the duty of the male population to equip itself to defend the realm. This long-established tradition had the backing of many elite Scots. Supposedly, when in 1556 Scottish nobles objected to a tax for hiring mercenaries to resist the English, they maintained that it was both the custom and the law that the nobility should defend the monarch's rights. According to these noble advocates for low taxes, hired soldiers were not as zealous in fighting for liberty as those defending their wives, children, goods and dwellings. Moreover, Scotland was not rich enough 'to sustain idle men' in the numbers needed to defend the Borders against the English.[1]

The Scottish army, or host, was traditionally made up of men between the ages of 16 and 60. They could be called out to serve for a maximum of 40 days in any one year. An indication of what this involved is provided by acts passed by the Scottish government in June 1545 when organising support for a French expeditionary force commanded by Jacques de Montgomery, Seigneur de Lorges. This legislation commanded Scots to muster at Roslin Muir on 28 July 'with armour and weapons' and with victuals 'for the space of a month'.[2] A small committee was also appointed to formulate policy and tactics for the war, and a similar organisational team may well have been formed for 1547.[3]

For many medieval campaigns there is a lack of credible data on the number of combatants. This is not the case for the Scots at Pinkie. The Earl of Huntly, who commanded the Scottish rear-guard, stated shortly after the battle that Arran's army consisted of 22,000 or 23,000 men.[4] The same figure was written by Edward VI of England in his personal chronicle.[5] These estimates for Pinkie are remarkably close to the figure of 25,000 armed men, which in 1543 the French diplomat Jacques de la Brosse claimed was the total fighting strength of the Scots. De la Brosse was sent to Scotland partly to assess the Stewart kingdom's military capabilities and to determine the support needed for the Scots to attack England. He obtained information from the queen mother Mary of Guise, the chancellor of Scotland Cardinal David Beaton and the Earl of Lennox (who would subsequently side with the English). These high-ranking figures informed De la Brosse that the Scottish forces were led by the principal nobles, who each commanded their own followers, and that nobody was paid – assertions that may not have been totally accurate. De la Brosse gives the following list of nobles and the number of men they provided for war:

The Earl of Argyll	6,000 men
The Earl of Huntly	6,000 men
The Earl of Bothwell	2,000 men
Lord Erskine	1,000 men
The Thane of Cawdor	1,000 men
Lord Fleming	1,000 men
Lord Livingston	1,000 men

These findings led De la Brosse to advise that to attack England the French needed to supplement the Scottish forces with 1,500 to 2,000 hackbutters and 3,000 or 4,000 Swiss lansquenets (or other seasoned soldiers).[6]

De la Brosse's figures imply that the Scottish turnout in 1547 was impressive. However, several key nobles like Angus and Arran are not included in De la Brosse's list. The French diplomat also does not explain why the Scottish army was restricted to 25,000 men. The total Scottish population may have been approaching one million at the time of Pinkie.[7] Although many Scots would have been excluded from military service by reason of age or sex, there must have been more than 25,000 active adult males in Scotland in the 1540s. The limit on the size of the army may have related more to the constraints of arraying and manoeuvring large forces, rather than the number of available men.[8]

Wappenshaws

By the Late Middle Ages the process of creating a host in Scotland started with wappenshaws (local musters and reviews of weapons and equipment). From time to time updated instructions about wappenshaws were sent to officials across the country. In December 1540 the Scottish parliament set out detailed instructions for the training and arming of men, commands that would have remained in force in 1547. Wappenshaws were to be held 'twice in the year' throughout 'all the realm', with the responsibility for organising these events resting with regional and local officials, including sheriffs, stewards, provosts and bailies.[9] Nobles, lairds and other prominent figures were obliged to have their names, and those of their men, entered into a book alongside details of 'the manner of their harness and weapons'.[10] These entries were to be updated yearly. Unfortunately, none of these muster books seem to have survived.

Royal officials (known as commissars) were sent to the various wappenshaws to help choose a captain from each parish who was responsible for drilling a company of local men. According to the acts of 1540 these companies were to be convened at least twice every month during May, June and July.[11] If this legislation was implemented across the whole country it should have resulted in a large pool of reasonably well-drilled fighting men.

The mobilisation

On 3 August 1547, five royal messengers were sent across the country with letters of proclamation charging 'all manner of men betwixt sixty and sixteen years' to be ready 'upon eight hours warning' to come with their arms and armour to 'such places as shall be appointed' (Figure 4.1).[12] There were probably established routes for these messengers as they took the letters to local officials, who then organised their public proclamation.[13] In 1545 the Scottish government ordered sheriffs' officers to pass to market crosses and there 'by open proclamation' command 'all and sundry' to join the muster.[14] Similar procedures were followed in August 1547. Indeed, Robert Lindsay of Pitscottie (who was a teenager in the 1540s) recalled that even Orkney and Shetland were included in the summons for Pinkie.[15]

A significant challenge for the Scots in the summer of 1547 was knowing when and where the enemy would attack. Both sides depended on reports by diplomats and spies. The Earl of Arran and Mary of Guise were certainly receiving information from Adam Otterburn, the Scottish ambassador at the Tudor court.[16] Arran also counted on the services of spies (sometimes called 'advertisers') to bring him intelligence from England.[17] Other reports would have come from traders and from residents of the Borders.

On 17 August 1547, Arran had another set of letters sent out for proclamation. This time, sealed letters were also delivered to several 'great men'. Northern nobles were told 'to be in Edinburgh with all diligence possible' in accordance with 'the first warning for resisting of the Protector of England and his army'. Similar instructions to mobilise were presumably sent to great men in other regions.[18] More letters followed in the next few days, with some providing specific local instructions. For example, letters sent on 21 August to the inhabitants of Dunbar, Duns, Langton, Kelso, Jedburgh, Melrose, Hawick, Selkirk and Peebles required them to be 'ready to rise' as soon as they saw warning bale-fires (Figure 4.2).[19] Letters of proclamation were also directed to churchmen requiring them to 'come forward to the army', with clerics in the diocese of Glasgow being told to be in Edinburgh by the last day in August.[20] By 23 August messengers were being sent out with letters and 'the fire cross'.[21] Such crosses were only used in situations when the nation was in serious peril.[22]

Unfortunately, little information survives on the actual mobilisation of August 1547. Most men will have arrived on foot. In 1540 the Scottish parliament decreed that only nobles and great landed men were allowed to ride horses on campaign. The only other horses that were permitted were draught animals. The ban on horses was intended to prevent damage to crops and property *en route*.[23] Remarkably, no mention was made

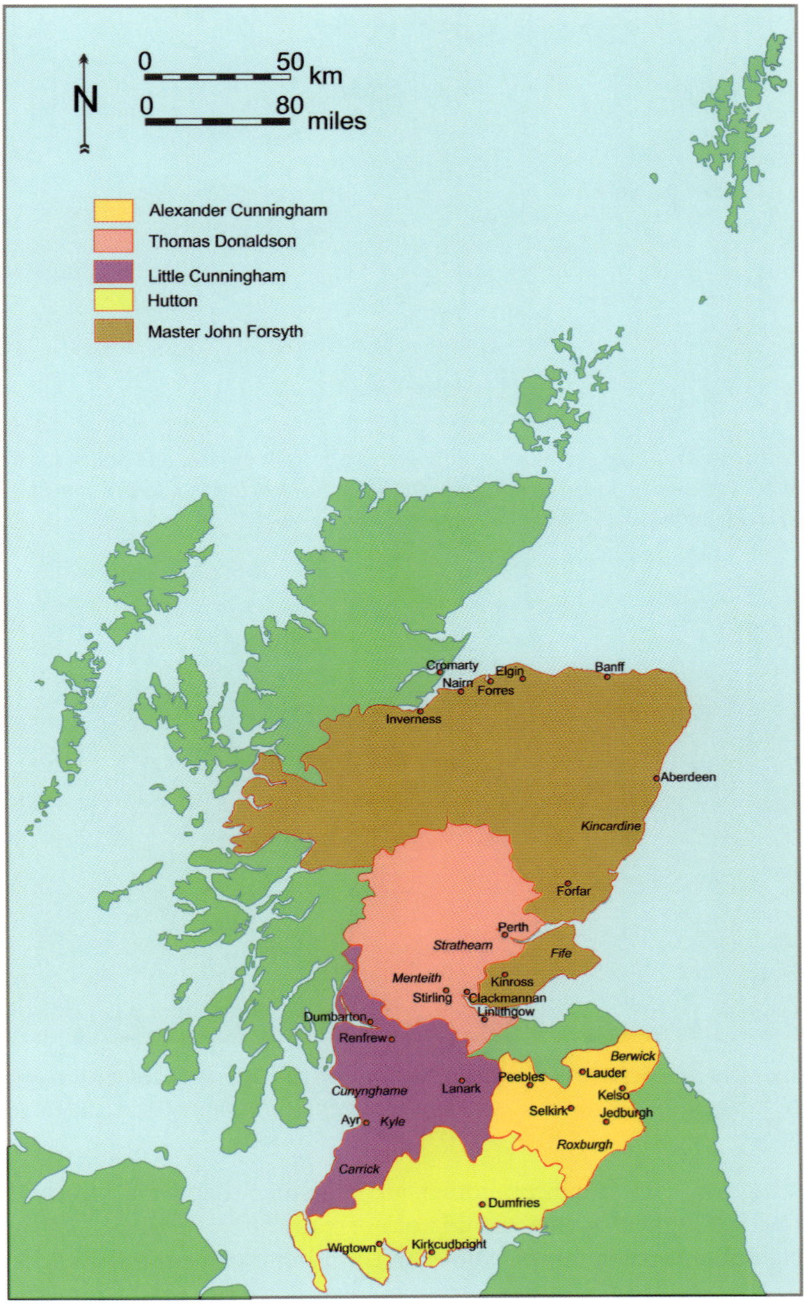

Figure 4.1: The Scottish mobilisation. Five royal messengers were tasked with delivering letters of proclamation on 3 August. The areas each covered and the centres to be visited are displayed on this map (David Caldwell)

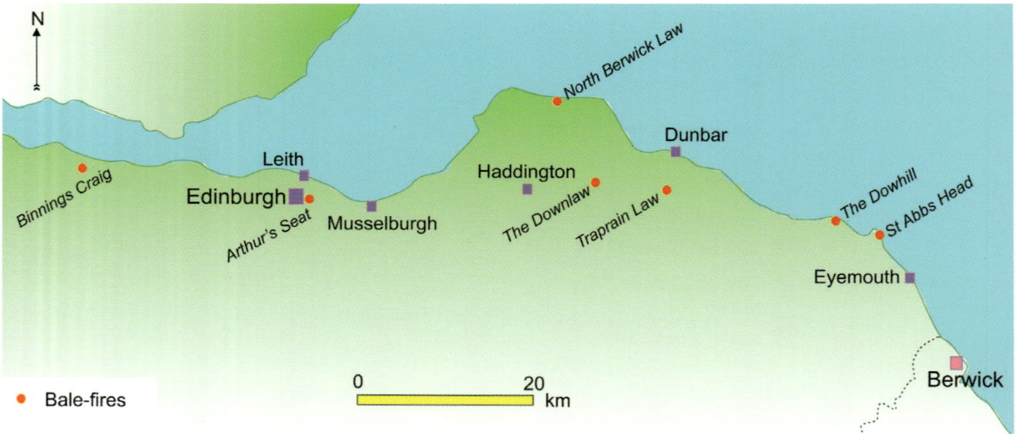

Figure 4.2: Bale fires. This map shows where fires were to be lit to warn of an English coastal invasion. It is based on a list drawn up in 1547, which also specifies the local landholders responsible for looking after them (David Caldwell)

Figure 4.3: Fala Moor from Soutra Aisle, with the Pentlands in the distance. It was probably a traditional muster place for Scottish armies, and camping place for invading forces (David Caldwell)

of the contingents who fought on horseback, but since they were mostly Borderers, perhaps it was thought that they would not normally be traversing Scottish territory.

The original Scottish muster point for the Pinkie campaign was Fala Moor in Midlothian, an area of uncultivated ground adjacent to the road from Edinburgh to Lauder (Figure 4.3).[24] The length of service was specified as 20 days, the maximum time Arran could at that point legally demand.[25] This was because the Scottish host had already been called out for 20 days in July for the siege of Langholm. Evidence from

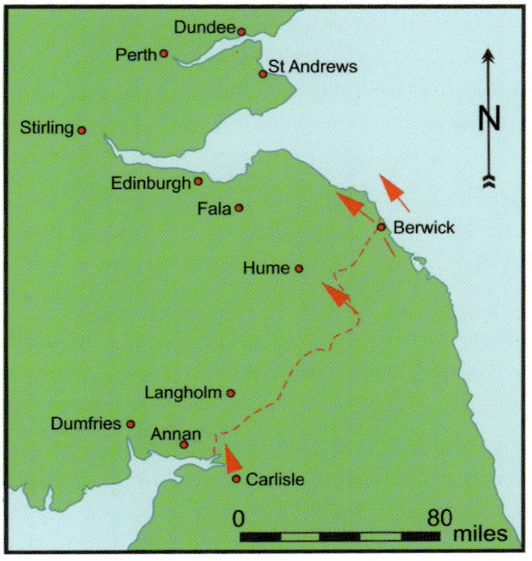

Figure 4.4: Possible invasion routes into Scotland (David Caldwell)

Figure 4.5: Edinburgh Castle, as represented on the Battle of Pinkie Roll (Bodleian Library, MS. Eng. Misc. C 13 (R))

earlier mobilisations suggests that contingents would have gathered at regional muster points before travelling to the national muster at Fala.[26]

When Arran opted to have his army gather at Fala he may have been unsure about English intentions. He perhaps thought that Fala gave him several options for movement once the main threat materialised. There were several plausible possibilities (Figure 4.4). On the east side of the country an army marching from Berwick-upon-Tweed could attack along the line of the present-day A1 near Musselburgh or go further inland along the route of the modern A68 via Jedburgh and Lauder. An attack from a fleet in the Forth was another risk. Large-scale invasion in the west was also a possibility, though perhaps less likely.

It appears that the Scots never seriously attempt to repulse a major English force at the border. Nor do they seem to have developed a clear strategy for defensive lines further north. What they did sometimes do was control where major pitched battles took place, and prepare the ground and their forces appropriately. The outstanding example of this was Bannockburn in 1314.[27]

In the run up to Pinkie, Arran made considerable preparations for his country's defence.[28] During 1546 and 1547 additional fortifications were built at Edinburgh Castle (which was both a royal residence and the base for the nation's artillery train and gun foundry). The work at Edinburgh Castle included an earth defence overlooking the town. This was designed by an Italian engineer and may have been the first *trace italienne* fortification in Britain.[29] Its construction was perhaps triggered by worries about the threat posed by English forces in 1544 (Figure 4.5).

In the late summer of 1547 Arran was moving artillery around the country. A large gun that had been at the siege of St Andrews Castle was returned to Dunbar Castle on the south side of the Forth.[30] Dunbar Castle was in the possession of the Crown and had a sophisticated artillery blockhouse (Figure 4.6). It was commanded by Robert Hamilton of the Briggs and had a team of professional gunners.[31] Such measures may have proved effective – certainly Somerset's army avoided attacking Dunbar in September 1547.

Bands of hackbutters were paid to man strongpoints, including the church steeple at Annan and Lord Hume's residence at Hume Castle.[32] The intelligence update sent to Somerset on 24 August by his commanders Lennox and Wharton reported that the fortifications at Hume Castle were being strengthened and ordnance sent there.[33] Hume Castle was regarded as a key defensive site, and it overlooked a likely route for an English invasion. It is difficult now to understand Hume Castle's design in the 1540s as most of the original structure was swept away and replaced by an eighteenth-century folly (Figure 4.7).[34]

Additional fortifications were also constructed at Leith in August 1547.[35] However, these proved rather pointless as by 2 September 1547 most of Leith's inhabitants had already left, fearing the return of the English.[36] Attempts had been made to fortify

Figure 4.6: The artillery blockhouse in Dunbar Castle with large casemates for pieces of artillery. It was constructed about 1517–23 by the Duke of Albany, Governor of Scotland who had had considerable experience as a French commander. Although Dunbar could have provided good harbour facilities Somerset avoided it, presumably assessing he could not take the castle that guarded it (David Caldwell)

Figure 4.7: Hume Castle (MacGibbon and Ross 1887–92). This folly on the site of the medieval castle does not give an adequate impression of the importance and strength of this stronghold

Figure 4.8: Leith, as represented on the Battle of Pinkie Roll. Three large ships are sheltering in its harbour, protected from enemy attack from the sea by pieces of artillery. The town itself was in two halves on either side of the Water of Leith, connected by a bridge (Bodleian Library, MS. Eng. Misc. C 13 (R))

Leith with entrenchments in 1544, but had proved ineffective.[37] Despite being Scotland's leading port, an English image from 1560 shows the harbour at Leith as being relatively small and located at the mouth of the Water of Leith. [38] This would have been how it was in 1547 when it was also described as being dry at low tide (Figure 4.8).[39] It is not known what steps might have been taken to protect Leith's harbour from enemy ships. Leith had been burned by the future Protector Somerset in 1544 and probably had not totally recovered at the time of Pinkie.[40] The burgh of Edinburgh had also been partly destroyed in 1544. However, at the beginning of September 1547 the Scots were still attempting to keep the English out of the capital, and turf defences were being constructed at the Netherbow gate.[41]

The Scottish government knew that the English were sending a fleet up the east coast, but there seems to have been no question of opposing it at sea. This is surprising as Scotland did have considerable naval resources, with access to royal, merchant and privateering ships. Recently, Steve Murdoch has argued that Scottish naval inactivity in September 1547 was attributable to poor leadership. The situation probably was not helped by the fact that Arran had recently imprisoned the Lord High Admiral, Patrick Hepburn, 3rd Earl of Bothwell, on grounds of disloyalty.[42] In 1547 some Scottish ships remained in Leith whilst others sheltered under the guns of Blackness Castle (Figure 4.9).[43]

Arrangements to deal with English shipping off the west coast, specifically victuallers for the English forces, appear to have been more successful. All vessels at Glasgow, Dumbarton, Ayr, and Kirkcudbright were put under the overall command of Captain Andrew Campbell of Glasgow and ordered to watch for the English. It was reported on 1 September 1547 that Scottish men of war had done notable damage in the Isle of Man.[44]

Many lords and lairds with lands on potential invasion routes would have looked to their own defences. Some had impressive family fortifications. The Earl of Angus had good reason to be confident about the ability of his imposing castle at Tantallon to resist attack. In 1528 James V had failed to make much impression on Tantallon with a substantial artillery train and since then its fortifications

Figure 4.9: The royal castle of Blackness, on the south coast of the Firth of Forth to the west of Leith. Scottish shipping attempted to shelter from English attack under its guns (David Caldwell)

had been strengthened (Figure 4.10).[45] As with Dunbar Castle, Somerset and his commanders appear to have deemed Tantallon too strong to tackle. The holders of other castles on the route from Berwick to Edinburgh (such as Dunglass, Thornton and Innerwick) appear to have cleared them of family and servants and manned them with small garrisons. Some private castles, such as Hailes Castle in East Lothian (which belonged to the imprisoned Earl of Bothwell), were even provided with artillery.[46]

On 2 September 1547 the pro-English Laird of Ormiston informed Somerset that Arran had left Edinburgh the day before, heading to Newbattle and then to Fala, intent on hastening his army on to the Pease.[47] The Pease (or Peaths) was a ravine on the coastal route through Berwickshire that would have been an obvious place to oppose the English.[48] The land there was held by the Earl of Angus' brother, Sir George Douglas, although ownership of it was disputed by Lord Hume.[49] Arran sent boys with letters to Sir George at Cockburnspath on 16 August.

Whether or not Arran thought on 2 September that there was time to oppose the English at the Pease is unclear, but he evidently thought by then that Fala was the

Figure 4.10: Tantallon Castle. This was one of the strongest castles in Scotland, well equipped and with updated defences. Its massive fourteenth-century walls had withstood bombardment by the artillery train of King James V in 1528 (Vicky Oleksy)

wrong place for his army and that a new position was needed if Edinburgh was to be protected. He probably knew that Somerset's main attack was going to come via the coastal route from Berwick. He presumably was also aware of the smaller English army mustering at Carlisle under Lennox and Wharton, but other than sending hackbutters to man the tower of Annan Church, he took few steps to deal with this threat (Figure 4.11).

Arran's eventual decision to focus his forces on defending the crossing of the River Esk at Musselburgh was relatively sensible. The route from Fala to Musselburgh was reasonably direct and only about 11 miles. There is no evidence that the contingents had been organised into a single army at Fala, and they probably headed off in separate groups to the new muster point 'upon the west side' of the Esk at Monktonhall, slightly south of the main settlement of Musselburgh.[50] Most of the army must have been at Monktonhalll by 8 September when Arran held a convention there to grant relief from feudal casualties to the heirs of men who died in the forthcoming military operations.[51] The choice of Monktonhall was facilitated by the fact that it belonged to Dunfermline Abbey, whose abbot, George Durie, was one of Arran's 'kitchen cabinet' of senior churchmen.[52]

Someone must have had the responsibility of laying out the Scottish camp. There is, however, a notable absence of information on this in the extant sources. It may

Figure 4.11: Annan in the aftermath of the siege by the English on 12 September. The Scottish garrison put up a spirited defence but were forced to surrender. Detail from Thomas Petit's plat of Castlemilk. The church is in ruins and its steeple has fallen and is lying on its side (reproduced with permission of the Marquess of Salisbury, Hatfield House)

have been one of the responsibilities of the master of the artillery. There must also have been enough space to assemble men into units. When the order was given for the Scots to advance across the Esk on the morning of 10 September they were already formed into battles and units ready for combat.

The Scottish commanders

At Pinkie the Earl of Arran was in overall command and had responsibility for the main battle – a reflection of his status as governor. Meanwhile the Earl of Angus was captain of the vanguard, the Earl of Huntly had the rear-guard and Lord Hume commanded the light horse. The men from Argyll and the Western Isles were led by the Earl of Argyll and the artillery train was probably overseen by either Lord Methven or Robert Hamilton of the Briggs. These men were not a ready-made team and had often found themselves on different sides in the complex politics of the time. Hume and Angus were major rivals in East Lothian and the East March, whilst Angus had in 1542 been part of the English force defeated by Huntly at Haddon Rig.

Although all the commanders had previous military experience, it is not clear how much expertise they (or their subordinates) had in drawing up and manoeuvring large pike formations. Much of the action seen by Huntly and Argyll in their own spheres of influence in the north and west probably involved smaller units largely armed with bows and axes (like Argyll's forces at Pinkie). Of the four main leaders, arguably the best was Angus. He clearly commanded military respect from both the English and his fellow countrymen. He alone came away from Pinkie with his reputation intact, having led his men into battle, defeated the English horse and avoided capture.[53] The decisions of the Scottish commanders had a significant bearing on the result at Pinkie and it is therefore worthwhile outlining their military backgrounds.

James Hamilton, 2nd Earl of Arran

Arran was appointed Governor of Scotland after the death of James V in December 1542. He was then in his early twenties and gained the governorship because he was heir presumptive to Mary Queen of Scots. On gaining power, Arran initially considered alliance with England and a more tolerant attitude to religious reform. However, he soon backtracked, leaving some Scots doubting his reliability.[54] This background of mistrust almost certainly informed some of the contemporary criticism of Arran – including allegations that he lacked personal courage.[55]

Arran led a politically and religiously divided nation. He was surrounded by factions that he could rarely rely on. Arguably, it is remarkable that he was able to mount a credible resistance to the English at all. Perhaps his ability to bring people together has been underestimated. He certainly showed a willingness to work with former opponents and to forgive past sins. A relevant example is the lengths he went to in 1546 to secure peace between the Earl of Argyll and the chief of Clann Iain Mhoir (Clan Donald South), James MacDonald of Dunyvaig and the Glynns (referred to as James

Canochson in contemporary records). Arran arranged a meeting of the Privy Council at Ardrossan on the coast of Ayrshire to which both factions could come by ship.[56] Whereas some West Highlanders had actually fought on the English side at the battle of Ancrum Moor in February 1545, thanks to the successful outcome of this diplomacy numerous soldiers from Argyll and the Western Isles fought for Arran at Pinkie.[57]

By September 1547 Arran had a degree of experience of war. Arran's guardian in his teenage years was his elder half-brother, Sir James Hamilton of Finnart, who had a great interest in guns and fortifications.[58] Arran went on as governor to use guns to besiege several Scottish castles, including Dalkeith, Glasgow, Dumbarton and Langholm.[59] All had been taken, though in the case of Dumbarton he had to admit it was by a miracle.[60] Arran did notably fail to retake St Andrews Castle for over a year, but his actions there were constrained by the complication that his son was being held hostage by the defenders.[61]

Arran's record as a commander in the field prior to September 1547 was mixed. In May 1544, when the future Duke of Somerset landed at Granton Craig (in those day a little way outside the burgh of Edinburgh), Arran was almost totally unprepared. Along with Cardinal David Beaton he hastily managed to gather an army to defend Leith and Edinburgh. Their force consisted of about 5,000 or 6,000 horse, plus footmen and artillery. The Scots opposed the English advance beside a brook (possibly the Water of Leith). However, after some sharp fighting Arran's forces withdrew, abandoning their artillery. The English did not pursue them, but made instead for Leith, which they soon entered despite some opposition from another Scottish force. Meanwhile Edinburgh was further reinforced with 2,000 Borderers under the Earl of Bothwell and Lord Hume.

When the English marched on Edinburgh two days later they had little difficulty in battering down the Netherbow Gate with a culverin (a large piece of artillery), despite the opposition of the town's guns mounted there and fire from the castle (Figure 4.12). There was some street fighting, in which the Scots are said to have come off worse, but the English withdrew in disorder having attempted to fire part of the town. Two days later the English again forced their way in through the newly refortified Netherbow Gate, and now met no effective resistance, apparently because Arran had abandoned the town to its fate. Edinburgh was burned and many other places besides, including the towns of Haddington and Dunbar.[62]

It is difficult to put a positive spin on this. Arran had avoided being drawn into a disastrous pitched battle, but being on the side-lines whilst the enemy rampaged through the country's most important urban centre was not a good look. Contemporary Scots were certainly not impressed with their governor's performance in 1544.[63] John Knox (who saw these events as divine punishment for Arran's abandonment of the Protestant cause and an English alliance) detailed how the governor and the cardinal first bragged about fighting the invaders, but then fled as fast as their horses could carry them.[64] Revenge did come early the next year in a striking Scottish victory over the English at Ancrum but, as we will see below, the credit for that belonged

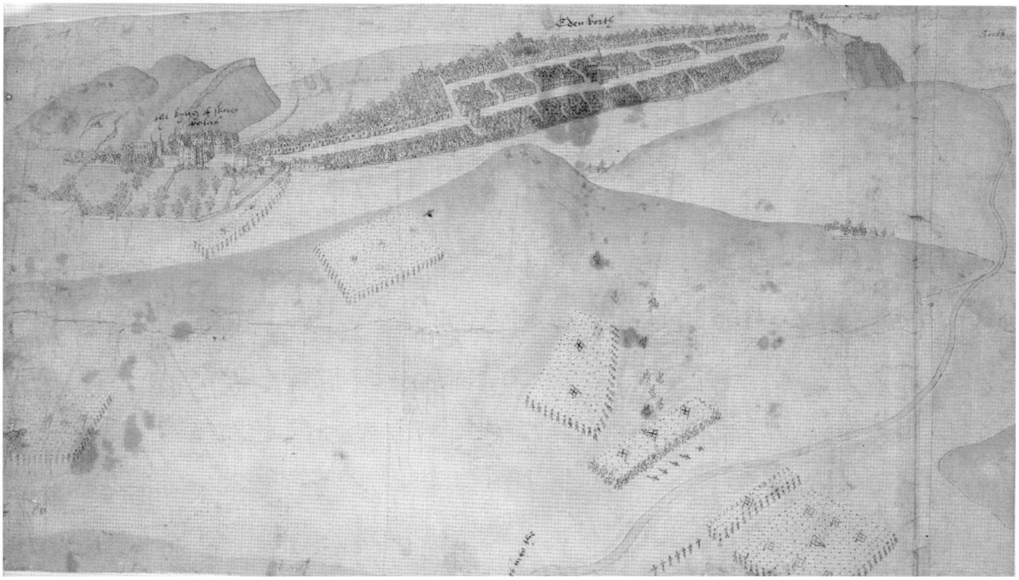

Figure 4.12: Bird's eye view of Edinburgh by Richard Lee at the time of the English invasion in 1544. The town slopes gently down from the castle at top right, with two main streets, High Street and Cowgate. Beyond the town wall High Street continues as the undefended Canongate to the king of Scots' palace at Holyrood Abbey, below Arthur's Seat (© The British Library Board, Cotton Augustus 1. ii. 56)

principally to the Earl of Angus. Later in 1545 a French military force under Jacques de Montgomery, Seigneur de Lorges (actually of Scottish descent) arrived in Scotland with money and supplies for the war against England. Although the combined French and Scottish army which moved against Wark Castle that summer saw little action, the experience may have provided Arran with an opportunity to learn about French military practice.

Archibald Douglas, 6th Earl of Angus

At the beginning of the 1540s, the Earl of Angus was an exile in England, with his extensive Scottish lands forfeited and redistributed to others (Figure 4.13). Born about 1489, Angus had aimed high in Scottish affairs, marrying Margaret Tudor, the widow of James IV of Scotland and sister to Henry VIII of England. For a time (1525–28) Angus had governed Scotland, before the young James V took control. As a result of his stepson's enmity there was for many years no place for Angus in Scotland. However, Arran chose to welcome Angus back to his homeland in 1543.[65]

Already militarily experienced before going to England, Angus gained further skills with his new masters, although he was nearly captured by Huntly in 1542 at Haddon Rig.[66] Angus remained to a large extent pro-English and Protestant, but back in

Scotland he turned his military expertise to aiding his countrymen against his erstwhile allies.

Figure 4.13: Archibald Douglas, 6th Earl of Angus, painter unidentified (Royal Collection Trust/© His Majesty King Charles III 2022)

On 27 February 1545 a Scottish army defeated an English force at Ancrum Moor (also known as Lilliard's Edge and Paniarhough). Although Arran was present, it is clear that Angus was the main Scottish leader. This Scottish victory still rankled with the English in 1547, with William Patten mentioning it twice in his book on Pinkie.[67] Early in 1545 the English sent into Scotland a force of about 5,000 men, led by Ralph Evers, Warden of the Middle Marches, and Sir Brian Layton, Captain of Norham Castle, with the intention of attacking Melrose. They were resisted by a much smaller Scottish army, although Arran had brought a small train of field guns from Edinburgh Castle. English sources are silent on what happened, and we have to rely solely on Scottish accounts, the fullest of which is that of Pitscottie. The Scots are said to have drawn up on foot on Ancrum Moor and to have waited for the English to advance. The Scots had the advantage of sun and wind, and soon had the better of the English, who were perhaps advancing too hastily. Much of the English force consisted of 'assured Scots' (so-called because they had made assurances of assistance to England) who changed sides when they saw which way the battle was going. Evers and Layton were both killed. Between 200 and 500 of the English died, and as many as 1,000 were taken prisoner. Casualties amongst the Scots were very slight.[68] The Scottish victory at Ancrum Moor led the English to desert their fort at Coldingham and caused many assured Scots to reject alliance with the Tudors.[69]

George Gordon, 4th Earl of Huntly

The 4th Earl of Huntly was in his thirties at the time of Pinkie. He held considerable power in the north of Scotland, and often represented the interests of central government administratively, judicially and militarily. Huntly was heavily involved in pacifying the clans in the northwest, for instance suppressing Clanranald and the Camerons in 1544.[70] He also organised resistance to England, being made Lieutenant of the Borders in 1542.[71] In August of that year Huntly (with a force of about 1,000 men) defeated an English raiding party (of about 3,000) at Haddon Rig in Teviotdale.[72]

At the end of October 1542, the Duke of Norfolk led an invasion from Berwick into the Merse (the area of Scotland between the River Tweed and the Lammermuir Hills). This achieved little other than burning Kelso as Huntly was well prepared for him with a force of 4,000 horse and 3,000 foot. However, Huntly was criticised for not attacking the English as they retreated across the Tweed.[73] Perhaps he should have been congratulated for his skilful handling of an enemy of greater strength. Huntly was a leading Catholic and hostile to England. He had some disagreements with Arran, but was persuaded to support him, not least by being appointed chancellor after Cardinal Beaton's murder in 1546.[74]

George Hume, 4th Lord Hume

Lord Hume led an important Border family and played a key role in the administration of southern Scotland, serving as Warden of the East March for many years. In 1529 he even had a role as lieutenant, with more general responsibilities for the Border.[75] By 1547 Hume was an experienced leader of light horsemen, with practice in skirmishing and gathering intelligence. Lord Hume was not greatly involved in central government, perhaps because his elder brother had been executed for treason in 1516. He was anti-English and pro-French in outlook.[76] Indeed, in May 1544, when hastily working out how 'best to keep and defend' the Borders against the English invasion, Hume informed Mary of Guise that he his followers would be 'true Scottish men' and never 'consent' to the English.[77] Lord Hume's residence at Hume Castle, near Kelso, held considerable strategic importance.

Archibald Campbell, 4th Earl of Argyll

The Earl of Argyll was born in 1498 and inherited his earldom in 1529. He wielded immense power in the West Highlands and Islands, and played a prominent part in national affairs, not least through his hereditary roles as Justice-General and Master of the Royal Household.[78] Argyll's experience as a military leader outside of his own local area prior to Pinkie is largely an unknown.[79] Although in later life he was a prominent Protestant, he was a supporter of Cardinal Beaton in the earlier years of Arran's administration. Arran, actually his brother-in-law, was able to bring him round to supporting him, not least through engineering a reconciliation between him and the leader of Clann Iain Mhoir, James MacDonald, his main rival for power in the west. This was the basis for Argyll, with strong MacDonald support, to field large contingents of men in the campaigns of 1547.[80]

The Master of the Artillery

In 1547 the role of Master of the Artillery should have been performed by Henry Stewart, Lord Methven, but he was either out of favour with the governor or too unwell to perform the task, which seems to have been given to Robert Hamilton of the Briggs, Captain of Dunbar Castle.[81] In June 1548 Methven wrote in a letter to the queen dowager, Mary of Guise, that he was afflicted with 'infirmity of gravel, and dolour of stone', to the extent that he could not attend upon her.[82] It was, perhaps, his close association with her rather than poor health which led to him being passed over until he was reinstated after the arrival of the French expeditionary force under D'Essé in 1548.

The structure of the army

It is not known at what point decisions were made as to the overall structure of the army at Pinkie. Scottish armies were traditionally recruited on a territorial basis and fought in large battles (battalions or formations) arrayed territorially. However, this was not always the case in the 1540s. Several sources, including the *Diurnal of Remarkable Occurrents*, provide information on the structure of the Scottish army drawn up for a battle (which ultimately did not take place) on 10 August 1545 just over the border into England in the vicinity of Wark Castle. The day before it had mustered at Fernyrig Muir near Birgham on the Scottish side of the Tweed, along with the French expeditionary force of 2,500 men led by Jacques Montgomery, Seigneur de Lorges. The Scots are said to have numbered 30,000, probably an exaggeration. They were divided into three battles. In the vanguard were the earls of Angus, Marischal, Errol, Glencairn and Cassilis, as well as the Lords Gray, Glamis and Yester. In the rear-guard were the earls of Huntly and Bothwell, and Lords Ruthven, Drummond, Borthwick, Fleming and Hume. In the middle ward was the Governor with the body of the realm and Frenchmen. There were two wings, with Lord Seton, the laird of Bass and many other gentlemen in one wing, and the laird of Buccleuch with all of Liddesdale and Teviotdale in the other.[83] It appears that, as in 1547, the commanders of the three main battles were Angus, Arran and Huntly. They would have been on foot while the two wings, consisting largely of contingents from the Borders, would have been mounted.

The lords listed as serving in the vanguard in 1545 represented lands spread across Angus and the Northeast, East Lothian and Ayrshire. The factors that seem to have united them were not territorial, but support for Angus, Protestantism and the English marriage.[84] The lords brigaded in the rear-guard with Huntly also represented a wide spread of territories in the Northeast, Perthshire, the Lothians, Lanarkshire and the Borders. It is harder to detect political or other considerations that might have bound them together. Perhaps, broadly speaking, they were moderates. It is also not clear why Lord Hume, one of the greatest of the Border Lords, should have been serving in the rear-guard rather than commanding one of the wings.

However the description of this army in August 1545 is interpreted, it appears that it was not drawn up on strict territorial lines. Possibly new military thinking in the sixteenth century encouraged a more flexible approach. Whatever the case, the August 1545 array is of significance since in several ways it prefigured that employed at Pinkie two years later with many of the same men and commanders. It must also have been done with the cooperation and advice of the French commanders. An army in which the main element was three battles was a European norm, with which the Seigneur de Lorges and his colleagues should have been very familiar. Flanking bodies of light horse would also have been a disposition they understood.[85] The horse would have been intended primarily for scouting and skirmishing and were not necessarily intended to stay in close contact with the foot units or engage in battle alongside them.

The major sources of information on the formation of the complete Scottish army at Pinkie all agree that it consisted of three large battles of footmen, the vanguard commanded by Angus, the main battle by Arran, and a rear-guard led by Huntly (Figure 4.14). There was also a force of light horse under Lord Hume, a unit of archers led by Argyll, and a train of artillery. The intention would have been that the three battles of footmen would be arrayed alongside each other, the vanguard to the right and the rear-guard to the left of the main battle.

Understanding of the role of the Scottish horse at Pinkie, and how it was drawn up in relation to the battles of footmen, has been prejudiced by Charles Oman's opinions on the subject. Oman believed that the Scottish cavalry was not a viable fighting force on the Saturday as a result of its defeat the day before.[86] There is no solid basis for this interpretation in early sources. William Patten actually indicated that on the Saturday there was a force of 400 Scottish horse adjacent to their vanguard and that a force of 500 Scottish horse mounted an attack on the English guns positioned on Falside Hill. Both of these positions or events are shown in the contemporary Battle of Pinkie Roll (sheet 2).[87]

Several early sources mention archers commanded by Argyll, but they cannot readily be identified in any of the illustrations or tables, and there are apparent

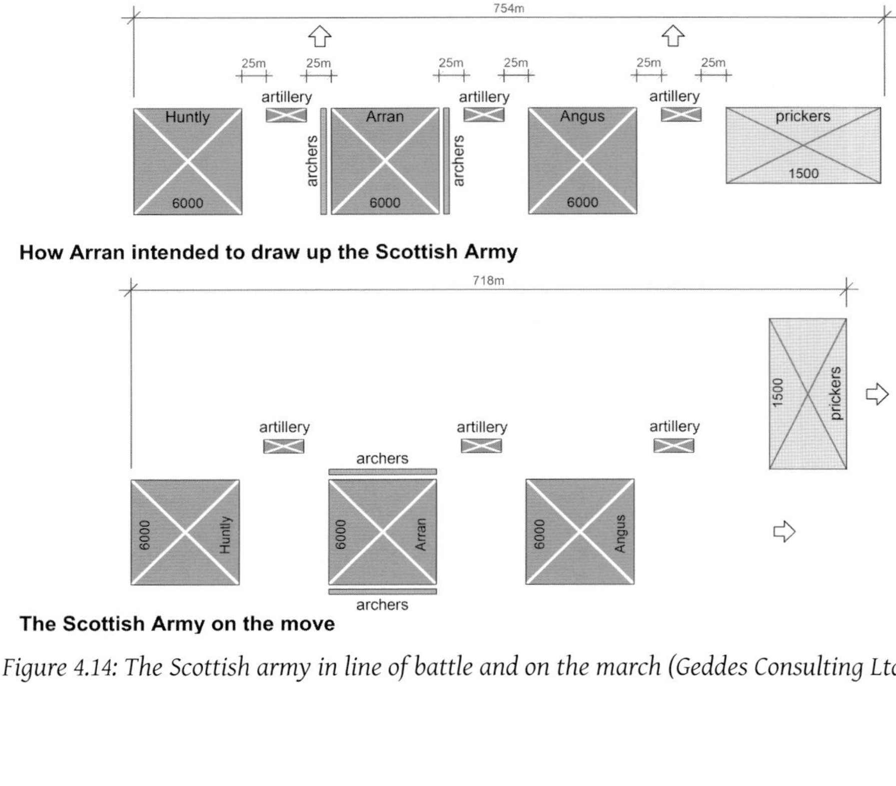

Figure 4.14: The Scottish army in line of battle and on the march (Geddes Consulting Ltd)

inconsistencies as to their position and role. Patten describes how the English galley shot and killed the Master of Graham along with 25 near him, and so scared the 4,000 'Irish archers' brought by the Earl of Argyll that, instead of being a wing to their vanguard as planned, they could not 'be made to come forward'.[88] In contrast, Holinshed and Knox both seem to indicate that Argyll, and therefore the archers, were brigaded with Arran's battle.[89] This is also what is to be learned from Bishop Leslie's history, although in describing Arran's command as the third battle he created the impression that it was the rear-guard.[90] Pitscottie wrote how the Earl of Argyll was on the right hand and wing with a force of West Highlanders, whilst MacLean, MacLeod and Mackenzie were on the left hand with a force of Islesmen (meaning men from the Hebrides).[91] A possible explanation that accommodates all these pieces of information is that Argyll's command was amalgamated with Arran's. This would be the reason why the archers cannot be identified as a separate unit in the early illustrations and might allow us to interpret Pitscottie's description (his wings of Hebrideans being positioned to left and right of Arran's battle, not the whole army). Importantly, none of the early accounts of the battle say that Argyll's men were actually hit by the gun fire from the galley, and in any case, at the time of the bombardment, not all Scottish units were necessarily in position in line of battle. As we will show below, there is ample evidence that Argyll's men did take part in the battle.

Only William Patten provides any detail about the disposition of the Scottish artillery on 10 September. He described how there were four or five pieces to the right of the vanguard and the rest were divided between the main battle and the rear-guard.[92] The conclusion that may be drawn from this information is that Arran did not keep all his guns together in one battery, but shared them out so they could provide support to different divisions in his army. It is known that horses were provided to transport the guns from Edinburgh Castle to Musselburgh, but Patten states that when the Scottish army was on the move on 10 September they had their guns pulled by men.[93] This enabled the guns to be manoeuvred and fired more quickly than would have been the case if teams of horses had to be hitched and unhitched.

The footmen

If we accept that the Scottish army had about 22,000 to 23,000 men in total, it is probable that the number of footmen (excluding Argyll's archers) was in the region of 15,000 to 18,000 men. It is probable that Arran's original intention was to have three battles of equal size, which is how two reasonably reliable Scottish sources described the arrangements.[94] Some confusion on the size of the battles may relate to a decision after the initial deployment on the Saturday morning to relocate Argyll's archers to form sleeves to the main battle. Battles of 6,000 men may have been deliberately planned by Arran and his advisers in 1547. Formations of that strength equated with the legions into which Francis I of France had reorganised his national force of infantry in 1534.[95] It is possible that in 1545 the Seigneur de Lorges, the commander of the French forces in Scotland and himself the colonel of the legion of Normandy, could have tried to persuade the Scots that the creation of legions on the French model was a path worth taking.[96]

Lindsay of Pitscottie claims that at Pinkie the main battle included contingents from Lothian, Fife, Angus, Strathearn, Stirlingshire and the burghs. The Earl of Huntly, in command of the rear-guard, led men 'from the north parts'.[97] A later history of the Douglases by Hume of Godscroft says that Angus' command included contingents from Kyle, Carrick and Cuninghame (the three districts of Ayrshire), Stirlingshire and Strathearn.[98]

There were complications caused by the defection to the English of the Earl of Lennox, one of the main magnates of the realm, whose lands and supporters were mostly in the Lennox, Renfrewshire and Ayrshire. Arran may have been unclear to what extent the fencibles of those areas would turn coat in support of Lennox or perhaps decide to remain at home to protect their property from the westerly attack Lennox and Wharton were launching from Carlisle. A Lennox supporter, the Earl of Glencairn, confidently predicted in the first week of September that many in his own and Lennox's sphere of influence were determined to live and die with Lennox. However, lists of known casualties on the Scottish side in the battle show that some men from those parts did turn out to fight for Arran.[99] It is possible that some lairds mustered in person for Arran but left many of their men behind to defend their property. This may explain why Alexander Dunbar of Cumnock in Ayrshire was present at Pinkie and yet 26 tenants, inhabitants and indwellers from about Cumnock, were prosecuted for staying away.[100] Patrick Hepburn, 3rd Earl of Bothwell, was another major Anglophile magnate who did not take part in the Pinkie campaign, as he had been imprisoned by Arran not long before (his name having been found in the register of English supporters left in St Andrews Castle).[101] Bothwell's lands and interests lay largely in East Lothian, of which he was sheriff, and in the Border region of Liddesdale, where he held the important administrative and military post of keeper.[102]

It was normal practice in the 1540s for units of footmen to be drawn up in square formations (and this is shown in early images of Pinkie). Each man required a space of one pace on each side of him and three paces to front and rear, resulting in a ratio of 3:7 in terms of creating a square formation.[103] On that basis a battle of about 6,000 men (actually 6,018) could have had a front line of 118 men, stretching a distance of 107.91 m, and been 51 rows of men in depth. It thus consisted of 51 ranks by 118 files (Figure 4.15). The Scottish army probably had a complex command structure with units led by junior officers and a system of signals and commands, perhaps largely in the hands of heralds and trumpeters, to communicate orders from the general to the rest of the army.

Instructions on how to wage war were described in detail in a book published in Paris in 1548 by the distinguished French soldier, Raymond de Beccarie, Baron de Fourquevaux.[104] Fourquevaux's methodology for how to draw up and arrange units of different sizes was presumably describing French practise as it was in the 1540s. Fourquevaux's instructions were not exactly designed for the Scottish situation, but

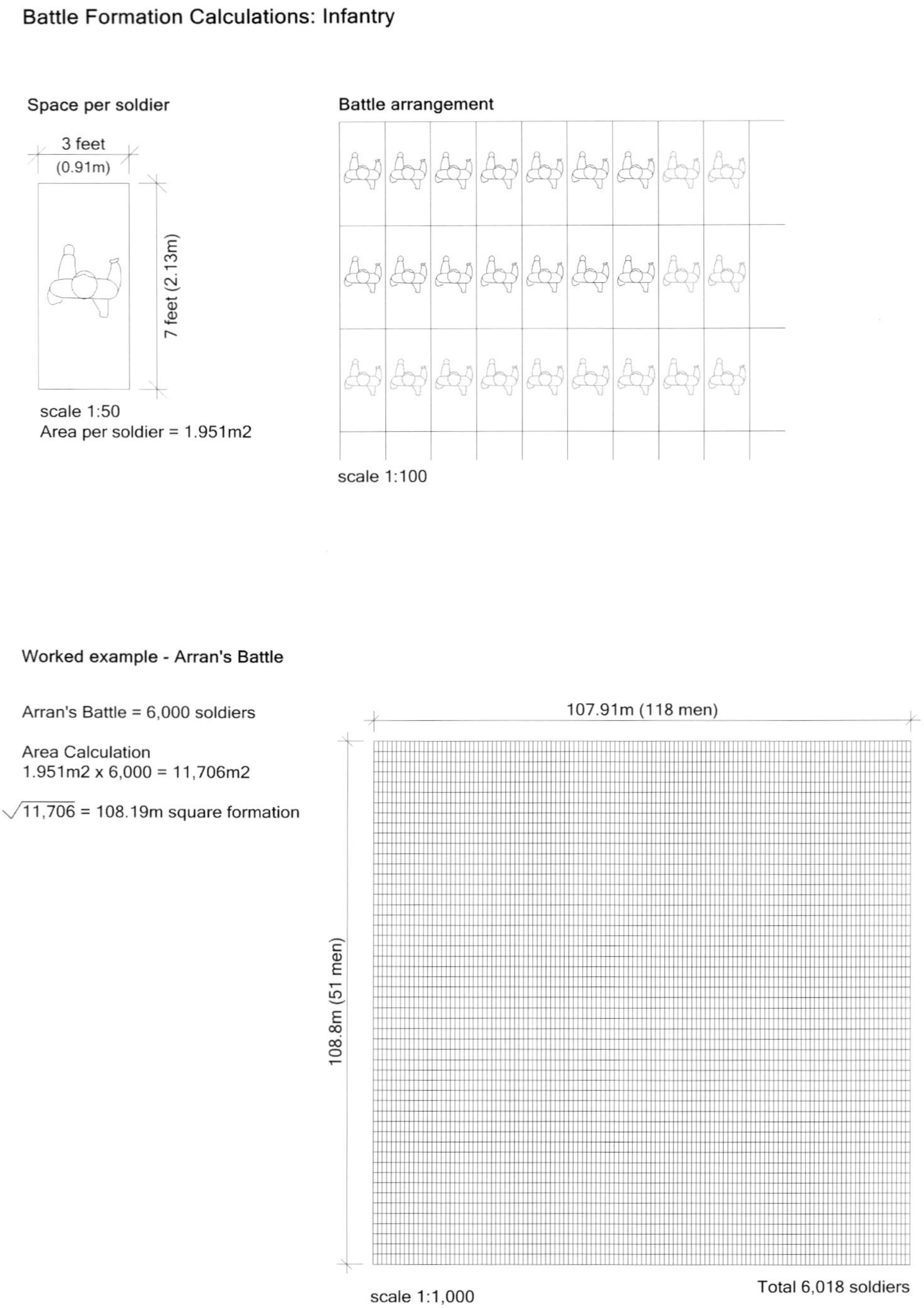

Figure 4.15: Diagram of one of the Scottish battles of footmen showing how its size has been calculated (Geddes Consulting Ltd)

key to them was a complex system of command, detailed in his fifth chapter. Arran might well have learned from French advisors that a battle of 6,100 men should be formed of 12 bands, each commanded by a captain supported by a lieutenant and other officers. Each band should then be sub-divided into six companies, each led by a corporal. Each company was sub-divided into four squadrons of 20 men, each headed by a junior officer. Each squadron was further subdivided into two units, each led by a decinier.

Some information on junior officers can be gleaned from the employment by Arran of bands of mercenaries or professional men of war in the years prior to Pinkie. In January 1544 the Lord Treasurer's accounts list fees for two bands, one of 300 and the other of 525 men. They served together under one captain, and there were also four principal quartermasters, 12 sergeants, a lieutenant and a provost, and three drummers.[105] This may have been a more professional command structure than for most of the national army. There was in 1540 legislation requiring the appointment of a captain in each parish to lead and drill the parish company of men, but little indication of the structure beneath that.[106]

With the exception of the horsemen, most of the forces that advanced from the Scottish camp on the morning of Saturday 10 September had not previously been arrayed as an army. It would have been no small task for the commanders to order, manoeuvre and position their battles to form an effective line of battle on the higher ground to the east of Inveresk Church, overlooking Pinkie Cleugh. As we will show below, this operation was successfully achieved, despite a crossing having to be made of the River Esk.

The arms and armour of the footmen

The 1540 army legislation included a detailed listing of appropriate, and acceptable arms and armour. Nobles, great landed men with £100 of yearly rent, and dwellers in burghs with £100 worth of possessions, were required to have plate armour. Amongst the protective clothing deemed appropriate for those of lower degree were jacks of plate along with protective head gear, especially steel bonnets.[107] No steel bonnets of the period have survived in Scotland, but they were presumably fairly simple head pieces without added protection for the face and neck. The main English account of Pinkie by William Patten identified them as 'skulls' and described how kerchiefs were wound around the neck, twice or thrice, as a defence against cutting.[108]

Here we should pay particular attention to jacks since that is what caught Patten's attention. He described how all – lords, lairds and commoners – were clad alike in jacks covered with white leather, doublets of the same or fustian (a type of cotton cloth), and most commonly with white hose. Several had chains of latten (a copper alloy) wound four or five times around their thighs and the sleeves of their doublets as a defence against cutting.[109]

Jacks seem to have been preferred by the Scots to plate armour for their flexibility and probably cheapness. Because they were reinforced with small plates of iron, they still provided a considerable amount of protection against enemy weapons. Some surviving sixteenth-century examples are sleeveless doublets with the iron plates sewn between quilted linen (Figure 4.16).[110]

Arran had a lot of attention paid to his jack in the weeks prior to the battle, presumably because he intended to wear it on campaign. He had it covered with purple taffeta, but not being content with that, had it replaced with purple velvet. The same velvet was used to cover metal splints (arm defences) and a plate apron (skirt) that went with the jack. An embroiderer was paid to cover the cross (a saltire?) on the jack with gold.[111]

Figure 4.16: Jack padded with iron plates, a type of protective garment worn by many on both sides at Pinkie (© National Museums Scotland)

While even Arran seems to have been clad in a jack at Pinkie, Huntly was picked out because he was wearing a complete harness (suit) of plate armour, described, possibly with some exaggeration, as gilt, enamelled.[112] Portions of such a garniture by the Nuremberg based armourer, Kunz Lochner, are in the Kuntshistorisches Museum in Vienna. It was made about 1555 and belonged to Prince Nicholas Radziwill.[113] It is known that French armourers were working in Scotland in the reign of James V, some, at least, based at Holyrood Palace. It is possible that they made such armour as well.[114]

The 1540 legislation required that every man should have a sword. Patten praised the Scottish swords, noting that they were broad and thin, exceedingly well tempered and 'made to slice'.[115] He also mentioned that they had bucklers, a small type of shield.[116] This may mean that the front ranks of the footmen were provided with bucklers as an extra defence when under attack. It is also possible that men with swords and bucklers, but without pikes, were positioned behind the pikemen, ready to come forward when the latter were locked together in combat with enemy pikemen and break their way through. This was a tactic at which contemporary Spanish armies were adept.[117]

It is probable that not every footman in the Scottish battles was provided with a pike because there were not enough to go around. An influential early mathematical book by the Englishman Leonard Digges and his son Thomas posed a question for

Figure 4.17: Grave slab of the early or mid-sixteenth century at Keills in Knapdale with a sword and buckler, flanked to the left by a battle-axe and a bow to the right (David Caldwell)

sergeant majors: how should they work out how to draw up a square shaped battle including several units of men with a mixture of pikes and halberds, so that all sides of the battle, seven ranks deep, consisted of pikemen (Figure 4.18).[118] Two points need to be made about this. First, as we will deal with more thoroughly in the next chapter, it is known that Digges fought on the English side at Pinkie. Second, it appears that he was presenting this problem as a typical one of his time. In the case of the Scottish battles, the alternative to pikes is more likely to have been a mixture of weapons rather than just halberds.

Patten observed that the Scots had few or no hackbutters, that is men armed with long guns, and the French diplomat, Jacques de la Brosse, reported in 1543 that the Scottish army would need to be strengthened with a force of

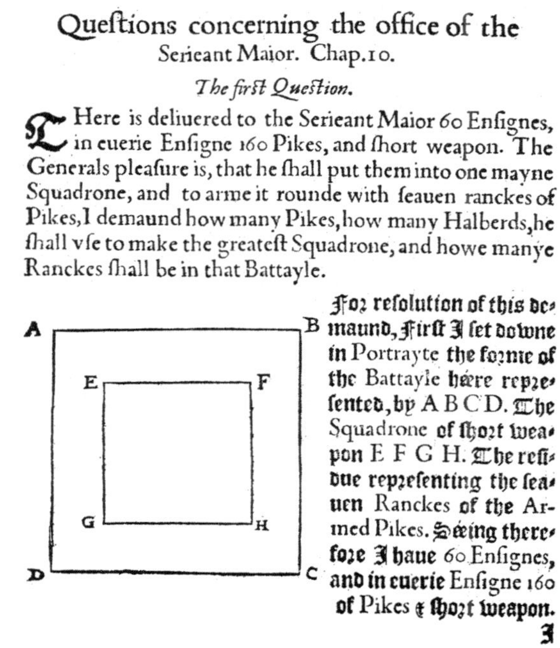

Queſtions concerning the office of the Serieant Maior. Chap.10.

The firſt Queſtion.

THere is deliuered to the Serieant Maior 60 Enſignes, in euerie Enſigne 160 Pikes, and ſhort weapon. The Generals pleaſure is, that he ſhall put them into one mayne Squadrone, and to arme it rounde with ſeauen ranckes of Pikes, I demaund how many Pikes, how many Halberds, he ſhall vſe to make the greateſt Squadrone, and howe manye Ranckes ſhall be in that Battayle.

For reſolution of this demaund, First I ſet downe in Portrayte the forme of the Battayle heere repreſented, by A B C D. The Squadrone of ſhort weapon E F G H. The reſidue repreſenting the ſeauen Ranckes of the Armed Pikes. Seeing therefore I haue 60 Enſignes, and in euerie Enſigne 160 of Pikes & ſhort weapon. I

Figure 4.18: How to marshall a unit of footmen composed of pikemen and halberdiers. From Digges, Stratioticos

1,500 to 2,000 hackbutters provided by France, thus implying they were not then available in Scotland.[119] Unlike the English, the Scots do not seem to have had units of men armed with guns. Carrying a gun as well as a pike would no doubt have been very inconvenient. There is, however, contemporary evidence of a Scottish interest in manufacturing and using firearms in warfare.[120]

Patten said that all the Scots were provided with knives and made a disparaging remark about the recovery from the battleground of rattles – bags filled with stones mounted on long shafts, for frightening enemy horses. Their use in battle in Scotland is implied by other sources, and perhaps they did work in some circumstances.[121] Undoubtedly the key weapons in use at Pinkie were pikes, that is spears with very long shafts (Figure 4.19).[122] The 1540 legislation decreed that they should be 6 ells (5.64 m) in length. They were not asked for to the exclusion of other weapons, including spears, axes, bows and culverins (handguns).[123] It was probably the case that very few had a house or other property where a weapon over 5 m long could conveniently be stored, and perhaps very few individuals had their own pikes. In a study of Scottish preparations for the war against the English in 1513, it was surmised that pikes were imported by James IV from the Continent and stock-piled in Edinburgh Castle, ready to be handed out when battle seemed imminent or inevitable. They may have been transported on campaign in carts.[124] All this may still have been the practice in 1547. On 21 August that year letters were sent out asking all carriage men to bring forth weapons.[125] Probably it was pikes that were meant. The French fleet that arrived at Dumbarton in October 1543 with money and supplies for the Scots to wage war against England included in its cargo 11,088 pikes.[126] These pikes were probably wielded at Pinkie.

Figure 4.19: Woodcut by Hans Burgkmair the Elder (1473–1531) of a fight between pikemen and billmen, actually the Scots and English at Flodden in 1513

The eye-witness account of the Scots pikemen at Pinkie by Patten allows a thorough understanding of how the pikes were deployed and the effectiveness of using them in battle. First of all, he described their use in attacking mode. In the front rank the pikemen stood shoulder to shoulder, pikes held level in both hands. The pikemen at their backs laid their pikes over the shoulders of the men in front.[127] On the march pikes were held over the shoulder, a relatively simple task which required limited strength or concentration. Yet, having a whole battle lower their pikes and march forward in unison, while holding them steady, was a feat achievable only through training and discipline.

Patten also described how the Scottish foot fought defensively, in the context of Pinkie, to ward off attacking forces of cavalry. The front ranks thrust their shoulders close to each other. They had bucklers in their left hands and positioned the butts of their pikes against their right feet so that the points projected towards their enemy at breast height. They also stooped low in order to allow the men behind to thrust their pikes forward, crossing with the pikes of those in front to give the appearance of an angry hedgehog.[128] The Scottish pikes were long enough for the five front ranks to be engaged when an enemy attacked. An early Scottish source backs up this description by describing how the vanguard 'footed their spears' when attacked.[129]

The horsemen

Horsemen, able to scout and harass English units on the march, were a key part of the Scottish forces. They were Borderers, men inured to raiding and warfare. They relied on horses, supposedly despising those who went on foot.[130] The Scottish mounted forces are, however, the least well known and understood component in the Scottish army (Figure 4.20). Contemporary English illustrations of Pinkie, namely the Pinkie Roll in the Bodleian Library and a copperplate engraving perhaps related

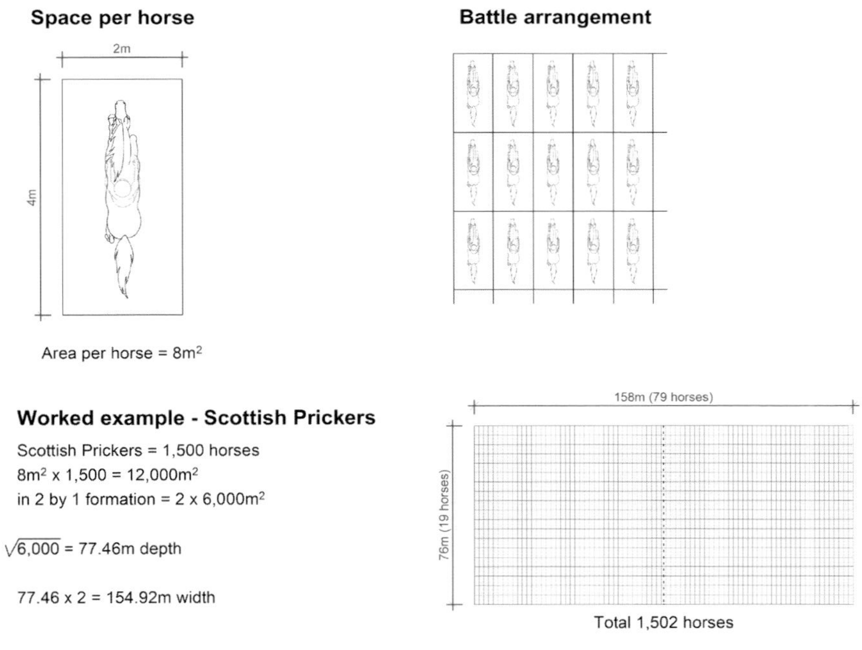

Figure 4.20: Diagram showing how the size of the formations of light horsemen have been calculated (Geddes Consulting Ltd)

to it (see Figures 1.1, 5.8), show them armed with long spears or lances. Presumably protective clothing, especially jacks and steel bonnets, were worn. A body of 60 Scottish horsemen that almost managed to capture the Earl of Warwick on the march into Scotland from Berwick were described as being armed with lances, a type of spear specifically designed for use by mounted troops.[131]

The horses would have been small and unarmoured. The Scottish historian, John Major, writing in 1521, described how Border chiefs could gather a force of mounted men to oppose a large English invasion within 12 hours.[132] Reiving, mounting raids into England and against neighbours, was a way of life extending back long before the sixteenth century. That explains this particular contribution to national armies. It is also perhaps worth pointing out that many of the horsemen who turned out to fight for the national army in 1547 had probably been the target, as thieves and robbers, of royal military and judicial expeditions in previous years. Estienne Perlin, a French student who visited Scotland in 1553, describes the men as being clad in jacks of plate (*iacques-de-maille*) and being armed with lances.[133]

There are no reliable figures for the numbers of Scottish horse. It is clear that the Scots had fewer horsemen than the English, and that their numbers on 10 September had been reduced as a result of loses the day before. There might have been 4,000 turned out for the campaign, but only 900 available by the Saturday. Patten informs us that the Scots, by their own admission, had 1,500 horsemen engaged in skirmishing on Friday 9 September, of whom not 800 returned to base.[134]

Lord Hume was in command of the light horse, but he himself was not present on 10 September as he had been wounded in the fighting on the day before. His son, the Master of Hume, had then been taken prisoner.[135] A remarkable document preserved in the Buccleuch Muniments records how there was a meeting to the west of Cousland, immediately after the fighting on 10 September, at which two parties, both consisting of lairds from the Middle March, agreed to remain loyal to their queen and oppose the English. On the one hand there was Sir Walter Scott of Branxholm, Walter Kerr of Cessford, John Kerr of Fernihurst, Gilbert Kerr of Greenhead and Mark Kerr of Littledean, with their servants and friends, and on the other hand there was Branxholm's son and heir apparent, William Scott, Robert Scott of Howpasley, Robert Stewart of Tracquair, Robert Scott of Wamphray, Walter Scott of Synton and Patrick Murray of Falahill, with their friends and servants.[136] Not included in this list was one 'Dandy Car' (Andrew Kerr), described as a captain of horsemen when he was engaged in skirmishing on 7 September.[137]

It is possible that the two parties in question were the two units of horse depicted on sheets 2 and 4 of the Battle of Pinkie Roll in the Bodleian Library (see Figures 5.7 and 5.9) with Branxholm in charge of one of them and his son the other. The lack of mention of contingents from the East and West Marches raises a question about the level of their participation on 10 September. Perhaps the Humes, from the East March, suffered the bulk of the losses on 9 September, and with both their leaders injured or captured, failed to make a showing the following day.

The West March chiefs of the Maxwells and Johnstones, respectively Robert, 6th Lord Maxwell and John Johnstone of Johnstone, were at that time prisoners in England.[138] Whether or not there was then strong leadership of both kin groups, it would have been understandable if West March fencibles were reluctant to abandon their home territory in the face of the invasion force mustering in Carlisle under Wharton and Lennox. Nevertheless, it is believed that a son of the Laird of Johnstone died at Pinkie and Patten described how one Richard Maxwell was wounded and captured in a skirmish between the horse of both sides on Wednesday 7 September.[139]

With Bothwell imprisoned by Arran, there was nobody to raise and lead the men of Liddesdale. It is noteworthy that Patten recorded how the Laird of Mangerton with 40 gentlemen joined the English army at Berwick on Sunday 28 August.[140] Mangerton is in Liddesdale and the laird was chief of the Armstrongs, one of the most notorious of the Border reiving families. The Armstrongs had suffered greatly from the efforts of James V to pacify the Borders and already in September 1543 had agreed to serve the English.[141] The horsemen who turned out to fight on 10 September may thus essentially have been contingents from the Middle March, mostly Scotts and Kerrs.

Argyll's Highlanders and Islanders

Argyll's men are likely to have included a large contingent of MacDonalds from Islay and Kintyre under James MacDonald of Dunyvaig and the Glynns, who took part in the raid to Langholm several weeks earlier. Pitscottie also mentions Islesmen led by MacLean, MacLeod and MacKenzie.[142] The MacLeans, largely based in Mull, were within Argyll's sphere of influence. The MacLeods and Mackenzies had lands further north in Harris, Lewis, Skye and the northwest mainland, but were nevertheless, presumably also part of Argyll's overall command. Argyll is claimed to have brought 12,000 Highlanders ('Irishmen') and 2,200 carriage horses to join the national army in November 1542.[143] It appears he had considerably fewer men in 1547. For the raid of Langholm that year he is said to have landed 4,000 near Glasgow and to have expected another 2,000.[144] At Pinkie his command seems to have been smaller than that of the main battles of pikemen, so perhaps 4,000 at most, the number given by Patten.[145]

These men were described as archers, although they were presumably also armed with axes, and some with swords. No Scottish bows of the period survive but one is shown on a grave-slab at Keills in Knapdale, along with a buckler and sword (Figure 4.17).[146] Argyll's contingents were present again at the siege of Haddington in July 1548 and there they caught the attention of a French commentator, Jean de Beaugué. They were dressed in jacks, and each held a large bow in his fist; a quiver, sword and buckler slung about them. Many others (without jacks) were clad only in dyed shirts and light woollen blankets of several colours (*couvertures legeres faites de laine, de plusieurs couleurs*) but carried the same weapons as the others.[147]

'The jacks' worn by some of these Highlanders were probably aketons (Scots, 'actouns'), a type of padded, protective coat (Figure 4.21).[148] The dyed shirts of the

Figure 4.21: Grave slab of the mid-sixteenth century at Finlaggan, Islay, showing Donald MacGillespie, a gentleman of Clan Donald, wearing an aketon (R. C. Graham)

rest of these Highlanders would have been coloured yellow with saffron and worn long. Their coloured blankets can be identified as tartan plaids. De Beaugue's account is the earliest reasonably certain reference to tartan plaids being worn by warriors in Scotland.[149] He also described how Argyll's men at the siege of Haddington incited themselves to battle by the sound of their bagpipes. This is the earliest evidence for Scots using bagpipes in this way. It is more than likely that these men also marched to the sound of their pipers at the battle of Pinkie.[150]

English commentators were (arguably unfairly) quite disparaging of these men. Patten says they were so scared by gunshot from the English galley that they could not be persuaded to come forward, and later he noted that they were the first in the Scottish army to run away.[151] According to another early source they were the first to falter.[152] It needs, however, to be understood that of all the forces in the Scottish army these warriors were likely to have been the most experienced and professional, many having participated in campaigns in Ireland against the English administration there. The Western Isles had a long tradition of supporting a warrior caste that provided mercenary services.[153] De Beaugué admired Argyll's warriors for their enthusiasm and courage. However, he noted they were put out by the English artillery, throwing themselves to the ground when it was fired.[154] This would have seemed remarkable behaviour to de Beaugué, for whom steadiness under fire was the crowning military virtue. Yet presenting less of a target to gunshot made a lot of sense, and should not automatically be interpreted as a sign of cowardice. According to the Scottish historian, George Buchanan, when the Scottish army disintegrated at Pinkie the '*Scoti prisci*' (literally, the old fashioned or venerable Scots, presumably a reference to the Gaelic speakers or Highlanders) formed into a circle in good order and retreated without loss, unassailed by the English.[155] This sounds like the behaviour of a truly professional force.

The artillery train

A significant, albeit numerically small, element in the Scottish army in 1547 consisted of a number of professionals, workmen and volunteers, tasked with transporting and operating the artillery train. In Scotland artillery was primarily the concern of the national government. Guns, and the specialists who looked after them, became a separate establishment, an early use in Scotland of professionals in warfare, and a forerunner of the standing military units of the present day. Edinburgh Castle had become the main royal arsenal in the reign of James IV, and here a gun foundry was established in 1510 or 1511, and a number of craftsmen based there made, repaired and looked after the munitions, all under the supervision of a Master of the Artillery (Figure 4.22).[156]

It is clear that the gunners, smiths and wrights based in Edinburgh Castle were working hard for some time beforehand preparing guns and related equipment and supplies for the Pinkie campaign. There were about 15 of them, some of whom took part in the campaign, along with an extra 15 gunners employed on a temporary basis.[157] One of the royal messengers or pursuivants, Adam MacCulloch, had a special responsibility as clerk or servant of the Master of the Artillery and many of the duties of organising the artillery train for expeditions seem to have been delegated to him.[158] In December 1543, Alexander Guthrie was appointed searcher and provider of horses, oxen and other things necessary for transporting the artillery, munitions and victuals.[159] He also had the task of paying the gunners and workers in Edinburgh Castle, for which he received 20 merks a year. His servant, William Stewart, was clerk of the pioneers, also described as clerk and payer of the workmen and gadmen (ox-drivers).[160] One hundred and forty pioneers were hired for the campaign and 132

Figure 4.22: Two early seventeenth-century panels carved with guns, now built into the outer gatehouse of Edinburgh Castle. The largest guns used by the Scots at Pinkie probably had a calibre of less than 100 mm (RCAHMS)

horses specifically to pull the artillery, as well as others for the gunners and the pavilions. Twelve carts, each pulled by four horses, were taken on to carry equipment for the guns, no doubt including shot and powder.[161]

The Scottish artillery train, captured by the English after the battle, included about 30 pieces mostly of small size, suitable for use as field guns or anti-personal pieces.[162] Pitscottie says there were 12 pieces of artillery and a further 20 small field guns, while the Treasurer's accounts supply fascinating detail including the fact that the artillery core had its own banner.[163] The French had sent the Scots 12 pieces of artillery, well provided with powder, shot and other supplies, in 1543, but the guns actually taken to Pinkie clearly included several already in the nation's artillery train (Figure 4.23).[164]

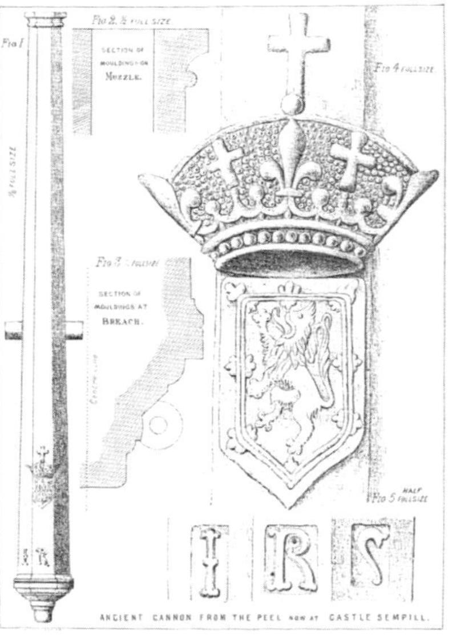

Figure 4.23: Cast bronze gun (a small falcon) with the arms and initials of King James V of Scotland, probably made in Edinburgh Castle in 1526. Guns like this with a bore of 46 mm and a range of about 1 km were probably present at Pinkie. It is now in the collection of Glasgow Life (Archaeological & Historical Collections of County Renfrew, vol. 1 (1885), pl. VII)

Other specialists who took to the field with the army included four trumpeters, presumably employed to give signals that could be heard above the noise of battle. Pitscottie wrote that the order for the men in the vanguard to lower their pikes against the onslaught by the English cavalry was given by trumpet blast. There were also heralds, presumably mounted, to convey messages from Arran to his other senior commanders.[165]

Non-combatants

Sixteenth-century armies were accompanied by large numbers of non-combatants. Their presence may explain some of the exaggerated figures for the sizes of armies. The bulk of these consisted of the servants of the nobles and also boys and young men who looked after the horses and baggage. On 24 August Arran had a messenger deliver letters to Musselburgh, Haddington, Dunbar, Lauder and Jedburgh, charging them to provide victuals for the army.[166] This was directed at merchants with food and drink for sale. These summonses would have resulted in a veritable market with attractive opportunities for those ill supplied with comestibles brought from home. There could well have been a significant number of others, including merchants and tradesmen selling their wares, women and spectators. Altogether these non-combatants could have amounted to several thousand. The army that came to grief at Flodden in 1513 possibly had a fighting strength of 20,000, plus 15,000 non-combatants.[167]

There may have been a similar ratio of combatants to non-combatants with the army in September 1547.

The French soldier, Jean de Baugué, who wrote about his service in Scotland in 1548 and 1549, found it strange that the 700 or 800 Scots horsemen that joined a French force for a campaign into Tweeddale all had either a horse or a valet to carry their own baggage and supplies of food. The French evidently expected to rely on food being supplied by sutlers hired for that purpose. This expedition ran into difficulties because the Scots were forbidden to carry food with them and the hired food vendors failed to deliver in a countryside ruined and deserted.[168]

Scottish battlefield successes

A brief overview is offered here of Scotland's military effectiveness in an attempt to explain how this small, relatively poor country used its limited resources to deal with military incursions and invasions by its much larger and more powerful southern neighbour. The Scots were often adept in mounting small-scale raids and could take the view that major pitched battles were best avoided. With the breakdown of the marriage negotiations with England in 1543 much of the war effort of Scotland and England was directed into raids. In a study of the years from 1543 to 1550 Marcus Merriman has shown that the average raiding party was 400 to 500 strong; though it could be as small as 100 or as large as the 2,000 that went to burn Coldingham and district on 18 February 1544. Along the East Marches alone, during the two years from June 1544 until the Treaty of Camp in June 1546, 159 raids are known to have been made.[169] This raiding was one of the main manifestations of war, a substratum over which the more prestigious campaigns and sieges were conducted.

Many men in the army at Pinkie would have been justifiably concerned about fighting a pitched battle with the English. A proportion had previous experience of doing so. There would have been some older men in the ranks, like John Mackenzie of Killin, who had been at Flodden in 1513, which was not unreasonably reckoned to be the country's worst military disaster.[170] The arms and armour used on that occasion, the battle formations and methods of fighting, were not dissimilar to those of the 1540s, except for one quite significant difference. At Flodden all the units from all parts of the country fought on foot with pikes. At Pinkie, the forces brought from Argyll and the Isles by the earl of Argyll fought with their traditional weapons and kit, and the Borderers reverted to their role of harrying the enemy forces from horseback. Although Flodden was a major defeat, one of the Scottish battles had routed the English one that opposed it and many others fought long and bravely. The two armies probably only managed to disengage when darkness fell.[171]

Later encounters with large English forces had also produced mixed results. In August 1542 about 1,000 Scottish footmen, plus some horsemen, had successfully seen off 3,000 (mostly) English raiders in the confrontation at Haddon Rig.[172] However, later that year a much larger Scottish army (perhaps over 10,000 men) suffered a humiliating defeat on 24 November at Solway Moss at the hands of a much smaller English force.[173] In May 1544 the Earl of Arran and Cardinal Beaton (with about 5,000 to 6,000 horse, plus some footmen) had made a very poor showing against the future Duke of Somerset near Granton Craig.[174] The engagement at Ancrum Moor in February 1545 was, from a Scottish perspective, a happier experience, with Angus and Arran having seen off a much larger English force. Against this background, it was not unreasonable for some Scots in 1547 to think that they might be successful in a pitched battle against a significantly smaller English force. On the morning of Saturday 10 September 1547 the outcome at Pinkie was very hard to predict.

Notes

1 Dalrymple 2, 362–63. Compare George Buchanan's discussion of this in G. Buchanan, *The History of Scotland*, trans. J. Aikman (Glasgow and Edinburgh, 1827–29), vol. 2, 387–90.
2 RPS, A1545/6/7.
3 RPS, A1545/6/3.
4 Selve, 219.
5 Jordan, *Chronicle and Political Papers*, 7.
6 J. de la Brosse, *Two Missions of Jacques de la Brosse*, ed. G. Dickenson (Edinburgh, 1942), 43, 45.
7 A. Grant, *Independence and Nationhood Scotland 1306–1469* (London, 1984), 72–75; J. Wormald, *Court, Kirk, and Community Scotland 1470–1625* (London, 1981), 166.
8 One of the authors (Caldwell) has discussed this topic of the size and composition of Scottish medieval armies in other recent publications, especially D. H. Caldwell, 'How Well Prepared Was James IV To Fight By Land And Sea in 1513?', *Journal of the Sydney Society for Scottish History* 14 (2013), 33–75; D. H. Caldwell, 'Bannockburn: the Road to Victory', in M. Penman (ed.), *Bannockburn 1314–2014: Battle and Legacy* (Donington, 2016), 15–35.
9 RPS, 1540/12/28.
10 RPS, 1540/12/32.
11 RPS, 1540/12/34.
12 *TA* 9, 106.
13 *TA* 9, 106.
14 RPS, A1545/6/7.
15 Pitscottie 2, 91.
16 *MLSC*, no. CXLI (pp. 192–94).
17 *TA* 9, 34, 35, 43, 61. For the creation of an intelligence network in England by the Scots in the 1530s and 1540s see A. Blakeway, 'Spies and Intelligence in Scotland, *c.* 1530 – 1550', in S. M. Butler and K. J. Kesselring (eds), *Crossing Borders: Boundaries and Margins in Medieval and Early Modern Britain* (Leiden, 2018), 83–104.
18 *TA* 9, 107–8.
19 *TA* 9, 109.
20 *TA* 9, 110.
21 *TA* 9, 109, 110.
22 Patten, f. 16r–v.
23 RPS, 1540/12/29.
24 One of the authors (Caldwell) has undertaken a detailed study of the mobilisation of the Scottish army that fought at Flodden in September 1513, including a review of likely routes, ferries and bridges that would have been used by contingents from all parts of the country. Much of this is

as relevant for 1547 as 1513. A summary of it can be found in D. H. Caldwell, 'Scottish Ways to War 1513 – The Mobilisation for the Flodden Campaign', in *Flodden Legends & Legacy. The findings of the Flodden 500 Project* (The Flodden 1513 Ecomuseum, 2016), 81–86.

25 *CSP Scot* 1, 18 (no. 40).

26 For mobilisations in 1523 see *ADC*, 178–80, 185, and for another in July 1547, *CSP Scot* 1, 8 (no. 19), 9 (no. 23). See also N. Murphy, 'The Duke of Albany's Invasion of England in 1523 and Military Mobilisation in Sixteenth-century Scotland', *SHR* 99/1, no. 249 (Apr. 2020), 1–25.

27 D. H. Caldwell, 'The Defence of the Scottish Border', *Journal of the Sydney Society for Scottish History* 12 (2010), 61–82; Caldwell, 'Bannockburn: the Road to Victory'.

28 *TA* 9, 99–106.

29 D. H. Caldwell and G. Ewart, 'Excavations at Eyemouth, Berwickshire, in a mid 16th-century *trace italienne* fort', *Post-Medieval Archaeology* 31 (1997), 61, fig. 30.

30 *TA* 9, 103.

31 I. MacIvor, 'Artillery and Major Places of Strength in the Lothians and the East Border, 1513–1542', in D. H. Caldwell (ed.), *Scottish Weapons & Fortifications 1100-1800* (Edinburgh, 1981), 107–119; B. Coombs, 'John Stuart, Duke of Albany and his contribution to military science in Scotland and Italy, 1514–36', *PSAS* 148 (2019), 231–266. For accounts of royal expenditure on the castle see *TA* 9.

32 *TA* 9, 99–106.

33 *CSP Scot* 1, no. 34 (p.15).

34 Canmore, site 58561 (accessed 29 January 2022).

35 *CSP Scot* 1, no. 34 (p.15).

36 *Hertford Exp*, 9; *CSP Scot* 1, no. 40 (p.18).

37 *Hertford Exp*, 5.

38 C. Fleet and D. MacCannell, *Edinburgh, Mapping the City* (Edinburgh, 2014), 8–11.

39 *CSP Spain* 9, 168.

40 *Hertford Exp*, 9; *CSP Scot* 1, no. 40 (p.18).

41 *CSP Scot* 1, no. 40 (p.18).

42 S. Murdoch, *The Terror of the Seas? Scottish Maritime Warfare, 1513-1713* (Leiden, 2010), 49–50, 59–60. Marcus Merriman's biography of Bothwell gives the impression that he was not highly rated by his contemporaries. See M. Merriman, 'Hepburn, Patrick, third earl of Bothwell (c. 1512 – 156)', *ODNB*.

43 Patten, f. 125r–v.

44 *CSP Scot* 1, nos 37, 39 (pp. 16, 17).

45 MacIvor, 'Artillery and Major Places', 122–24, 132–33.

46 Patten, ff. 45v–53r.

47 *CSP Scot* 1, no. 40 (p.18).

48 *CSP Scot* 1, no. 40 (p.18).

49 After more than one session the Privy Council found in favour of Sir George on 24 July (*RPC* 1, 76).

50 Pitscottie 2, 92.

51 RPS, A1547/9/1–3.

52 *Dunfermline Reg*, 430ff; Buchanan, *History* 2, 366.

53 Angus' reputation as a soldier amongst his contemporaries, Scots and English, is dealt with by M. Merriman, 'Douglas, Archibald, sixth earl of Angus', *ODNB*.

54 For more discussion of Arran's politics see M. Merriman, 'Hamilton, James, second earl of Arran, and duke of Châtelherault in the French nobility', *ODNB*. Recently there has been an important reassessment of Arran by Blakeway, *Regency in Sixteenth-Century Scotland*, especially pp. 236–37.

55 Buchanan, *History* 2, 344; Pitscottie 2, 30; Patten, f. 101r.

56 *RPC* 1, 30. For the background to the falling-out between Argyll and MacDonald see D. H. Caldwell, *Islay. The Land of the Lordship* (Edinburgh, 2017), 82–86.

57 Torquil, chief of the MacNeills of Gigha, obtained a precept of remission for his part in the battle. It is probable that he was not the only West Highlander there. See K. A. Steer and J. W. M. Bannerman, *Late Medieval Monumental Sculpture in the West Highlands* (Edinburgh, 1977), 148.
58 J. Cameron, *James V* (East Linton, 1998), chapter 9 (pp. 191–227); MacIvor, 'Artillery and Major Places', 94–152. Compare C. McKean, 'Craignethan: the castle of the Bastard of Arran', *PSAS* 125 (1995), 1069–90.
59 Information on gun movements, calling out of the host, etc, for these and other sieges can be found in *TA* 8. Other detail is provided by early histories, for example *Diurnal*, 36–44.
60 *ADC*, 553; *L&P* 21/2, no. 6.
61 *L&P* 21/2, no. 380. The mine dug by Arran as a means of taking the castle, and the countermine dug by the defenders, survive till this day.
62 *L&P* 19/1: nos 472, 483, 518, 533, 534; *Hertford Exp.*
63 Merriman, 'Hamilton, James, second earl of Arran', *ODNB.*
64 J. Knox, *History of the Reformation in Scotland*, ed. W. C. Dickinson, vol. 1 (Edinburgh, 1949), 56–58.
65 Merriman, 'Douglas, Archibald, sixth earl of Angus', *ODNB.*
66 *L&P* 17, nos 662, 673; HES, Haddon Rig Battlefield Research Report, https://historicenvironment.scot/archives-and-research/publication/ (accessed 3 August 2022).
67 Patten, ff. 68v, 106r.
68 *TA* 8, 348, 351; *L&P* 20/1, nos 129, 285; Pitscottie 2, 34–41; Dalrymple 2, 285–86; Buchanan, *History* 2, 346–48; *Diurnal*, 38. See also HES Portal, https://portal.historicenvironment.scot/designation/BTL2 (accessed 3 August 2022).
69 *Diurnal*, 38.
70 D. Gregory, *History of the Western Highlands and Islands of Scotland* (Edinburgh, 1836), 159–63; A. Cathcart, *Kinship and Clientage. Highland Clanship 1451-1609* (Leiden, 2006), 181–82.
71 A. White, 'Gordon, George, fourth earl of Huntly', *ODNB.*
72 *L&P* 17, nos 662, 673; HES, Haddon Rig Battlefield Research Report. Other recent accounts of this battle have given much larger figures for the forces involved and have drawn attention to the involvement on the Scottish side of the internationally experienced soldier, Walter Lindsay, Preceptor of the Knights of St John. See, for instance, G. Phillips, 'In the Shadow of Flodden: Tactics, Technology and Scottish Military Effectiveness, 1513–1550', *SHR* 77 (1998), 167–68.
73 *L&P* 17, no. 1100.
74 Merriman, *Rough Wooings*, 213.
75 T. I. Rae, *The Administration of the Scottish Frontier 1513-1603* (Edinburgh, 1966), 237–38, 254.
76 M. M. Meikle, 'Hume [Home], George, fourth Lord Hume', *ODNB.*
77 *MLSC*, 80.
78 J. E. A. Dawson, 'Campbell, Archibald, fourth earl of Argyll', *ODNB.*
79 Contrast the sympathetic, supportive outline of his career by a clan historian, A. Campbell of Airds, *A History of Clan Campbell Volume 2 From Flodden to the Restoration* (Edinburgh, 2002), 15–44, with the cutting opinion of another recent historian, J. Wormald, *Lords and Men in Scotland. Bonds of Manrent 1442-1603* (Edinburgh, 1985), 108, that the earl was a muddler and ditherer, inefficient and weak.
80 *RPC* 1, 30.
81 Methven's replacement by Hamilton is based on an analysis of contemporary documents given in D. H. Caldwell, Guns in Scotland. The manufacture and use of guns and their influence on warfare from the fourteenth century to c.1625, 2 vols (University of Edinburgh PhD, 1982) vol. 1, 181, 191; vol. 2, 575, 589–90.
82 *MLSC*, 242–43.
83 *Diurnal*, 39–40. Compare the accounts of the expedition by this army given by Pitscottie 2, 46–47; Buchanan, *History* 2, 349–50; and Dalrymple 2, 288.

84 Clues to this can be detected in Merriman, *Rough Wooings*, 21, 113, 118.
85 Oman, *History of the Art of War*, 34–35.
86 Oman, 'The Battle of Pinkie', 12, 13, 16; Oman, *History of the Art of War*, 363, 364.
87 Patten, ff. 88v, 103r. The Battle of Pinkie Roll is discussed and interpreted in the next chapter.
88 Patten, f. 80r–v. Argyll's archers did not come from Ireland. They are called 'Irish' because they spoke Gaelic. It was quite usual in the sixteenth century for people from the Highlands and Island to be called Irish.
89 Holinshed, *The Firste Volume*, 468; Knox, *History* 1, 99.
90 Dalrymple 2, 299.
91 Pitscottie 2, 96.
92 Patten, f. 88v.
93 *TA* 9, 115, 117; Patten, f. 81r.
94 Buchanan, *History* 2, 367; Master David Hume of Godscroft, *The History of the Houses of Douglas and Angus* (London, 1648), 271–73.
95 T. Arnold, *The Renaissance at War* (London, 2001), 54–56; D. Potter, *Renaissance France at War. Armies, Culture and Society, c.1480–1560* (Woodbridge, 2008), 112–17.
96 Potter, *Renaissance France at War*, 116.
97 Pitscottie 2, 96.
98 Hume, *Douglas History*, 271–73.
99 *CSP Scot* 1, 18 (no. 41); Caldwell, 'The Battle of Pinkie', 91, n.35.
100 *CSP Scot* 1, 18 (no. 41); *ADC*, 574; *RSS* 3, no. 2769.
101 *CSP Scot* 1, no. 33 (p. 14). See Merriman, *Rough Wooings*, 226–27 for more information on this register.
102 Merriman, 'Hepburn, Patrick, third earl of Bothwell', *ODNB*.
103 Arnold, *The Renaissance at War*, 70–71. Compare L. Digges and T. Digges, *Arithmeticall militare treatise named Stratioticos* (London, 1579, reprinted by Da Capo, Amsterdam and New York 1968), 53–55.
104 Fourquevaux *Instr*.
105 *TA* 8, 249–51. For information on similar junior officers in contemporary French armies, on whom these Scottish roles may have been modelled, see Potter, *Renaissance France at War*, 190–99.
106 RPS, 1540/12/34.
107 RPS, 1540/12/30.
108 Patten, f. 86r.
109 Patten, f. 107r.
110 A. V. B. Norman, *Arms and Armour in the Royal Scottish Museum* (Edinburgh, 1972), 15–16; A. R. Duffy, *European Armour in the Tower of London* (London, 1968), pl. CXXIII; T. Gabra-Sanders, 'Part of a 16th century quilted jack of plate found at Craigievar Castle, Aberdeenshire', *Journal of the Arms & Armour Society* 14 (1993), 147–52.
111 *TA* 9, 97–98, 112.
112 Holinshed, *The Firste Volume*, 469.
113 https://www.khm.at/en/objektdb/detail/371792/ (accessed 27 April 2023).
114 D. H. Caldwell, 'Royal Patronage of Arms and Armour Making in Fifteenth- and Sixteenth-century Scotland', in D. H. Caldwell (ed.), *Scottish Weapons & Fortifications 1100-1800* (Edinburgh, 1981), 86–87.
115 RPS, 1540/12/30; Patten, f. 86r.
116 Patten, f. 86r.
117 C. W. C. Oman, *The Art of War in the Middle Ages* (Ithaca and London, 1968), 108–10; Oman, *History of the Art of War*, 52.
118 Digges and Digges, *Stratioticos*, 52–53.

119 Patten, ff. 85v–86r; Brosse, *Two Missions*, 43.
120 Caldwell, 'Royal Patronage of Arms and Armour Making', 79–82.
121 Patten, f. 114r–v; *DSL*, https://dsl.ac.uk/entry/rattle (accessed 20 September 2020).
122 It appears from contemporary Scottish documentation that 'speir' (spear) was often used as a synonym for pike. It should also be noted that there is potential confusion or uncertainty in some cases as to whether pikes or picks are meant, spears or spars, all equipment required for military operations. Normally the context is a reasonable guide.
123 RPS, 1540/12/30.
124 Caldwell, 'How Well Prepared Was James IV', 41–42.
125 *TA* 9, 109.
126 Potter, *Henry VIII and Francis I*, 105–06, n. 77.
127 Patten, f. 86r–v.
128 Patten, f. 86v.
129 *Diurnal*, 45. Compare D. Eltis, *The Military Revolution in Sixteenth-century Europe* (London, 1995), 45, for contemporary use of pikes in European armies.
130 Dalrymple 1, 99.
131 Le Sieur de Berteville, *Recit De L'Expedition En Ecosse L'An MDXLVII Et De La Battayle de Muscleburgh Par Le Sieur Berteville Au Roy Edouard VI* (Edinburgh, 1825), 10–12.
132 J. Major, *A History of Greater Britain as well England as Scotland compiled from the ancient authorities*, trans. A. Constable (Edinburgh, 1892), 29–30.
133 M. E. Perlin, *Description Des Royaulmes D'Angleterre et D'Ecosse* (Paris, 1558), 29.
134 Patten, ff. 68v–6r.
135 Patten, f. 69r.
136 Sir W. Fraser, *The Scotts of Buccleuch*, 2 vols (Edinburgh, 1878), vol. 2, 185–86.
137 Patten, f. 57r.
138 J. Balfour Paul (ed.), *The Scots Peerage*, 9 vols (Edinburgh, 1904–14), vol. 1, 244; vol. 6, 481.
139 C. L. Johnstone, *History of the Johnstones 1191–1909* (Edinburgh, 1909), 343; Patten, 41.
140 Patten, f. 37r.
141 Cameron, *James V*, 77–83; *L&P* 18/2, no. 137 (pp. 74–75).
142 Pitscottie 2, 96.
143 *L&P* 17, no. 1100 (p. 610).
144 *CSP Scot* 1, no. 23 (p. 9).
145 Patten, f. 88v.
146 D. H. Caldwell, 'Having the right kit: West Highlanders fighting in Ireland', in S. Duffy (ed.), *The World of the Galloglass* (Dublin, 2007), 159–63.
147 I. de Beaugué, *L'Histoire de la Guerre D'Escosse* (Paris, 1556), 22v. For an inexpert translation into English see M. Beague, *The History of the Compagnes 1548 and 1549*, trans. Dr [Patrick] Abercromby (Edinburgh, 1707), 19. De Beaugué describes these men as from Orkney, but their presence under the Earl of Argyll is noted in contemporary reports. See *CSP Scot* 1, 136–37.
148 Caldwell, 'Having the right kit', 151–59.
149 D. H. Caldwell, 'The Origins of Plaid Wearing', *SHR* C3 (2021), 448–49, 453–54.
150 Beaugué, *L'Histoire de la Guerre D'Escosse*, f. 54v.
151 Patten, ff. 80r–v, 101r.
152 BL, Harleian MS 540, ff. 70–71.
153 D. H. Caldwell, 'The Sea Power of the Western Isles of Scotland in the Late Medieval Period', in J. H. Barrett and S. J. Gibbon (eds), *Maritime Societies of the Viking and Medieval World* (Society for Medieval Archaeology monograph 37, 2015), 350–68.
154 Beaugué, *L'Histoire de la Guerre D'Escosse*, f. 23–24.
155 Buchanan, *History* 2, 368.
156 Caldwell, 'Royal Patronage of Arms and Armour Making', 74–78.

Table 5.1: Data on army sizes, numbers of casualties and prisoners, derived from early sources

	Scottish Army	Scottish Dead	Prisoners	English Army	English Dead
Italian letter	40,000	15,000			800
Van Der Delft	24,000	15,000			
De Selve	40,000	13,000		16,000	600
Ribault	24,000	7,000		16,000	
Huntly	23,000	6,000			
Hooper		15,000			
Patten	32,000	14,000	500	16,800	
Berteville	36,000			15,300	
Harleian MS		10,400	2,000	18,000	
Edward VI	36,000	10,000	1,000	18,000	
Grafton	30,000	14,000	1,500	18,100	
Diurnal		7,000		7,000	600
Leslie		8,000	1,000		
Pitscottie	40,000	10,000			

about four miles, whilst only 400 English soldiers were killed.[23] He also stated that the English had captured the Scottish artillery and baggage.

De Selve clearly had reservations about the reliability of Paget's claims and quickly searched out other informants, who told him that the Scots had about 13,000 dead, whilst between 2,000 and 3,000 Englishmen had fallen. The French ambassador further noted that the Earl of Warwick was being given credit for capturing the Scottish artillery and commented on the resistance the Scots had given to an attack by the English cavalry. He also remarked on naval activity alongside the land invasion, claiming that two Scottish ships had been captured and one English vessel sunk.[24] As more news about Pinkie emerged in the following weeks, De Selve sent additional despatches to the French king. The evidence De Selve gathered indicated that Pinkie was a remarkably close-run thing. Indeed, the French ambassador alleged that had it not been for Somerset's leadership the English would have fled the field.[25]

In the middle of October 1547, De Selve's understanding of what happened at Pinkie was enhanced by conversations with the Earl of Huntly (who had been captured by the English at Pinkie) and the French mercenary Jean Ribault (who had fought in Somerset's army). Although Huntly was a prisoner, he had a degree of freedom at the Tudor court, and De Selve was soon tapping him for information. According to Huntly, the blame for the Scottish defeat at Pinkie lay with the Earl of Arran. Supposedly, Huntly had argued that the Scots should remain in their camp and play for time but

Arran had pushed to attack the English – with fateful consequences. De Selve reports that Huntly claimed the Scottish army numbered around 23,000 men, of whom 6,000 had been killed in the fighting.[26]

A more detailed analysis of the events of the battle was provided by Jean Ribault – a Huguenot soldier and maritime expert who would ultimately be killed on an expedition to colonise Florida in the 1560s.[27] Ribault fought with the English cavalry at Pinkie, and a few days before the main battle had helped prevent the Earl of Warwick from being captured in an ambush. In his conversation with the French ambassador, Ribault recalled how on Saturday 10 September the Scottish vanguard had advanced at speed towards high ground. The English cavalry found it impossible to break the advancing Scottish ranks and were repulsed. Ribault claimed that for about an hour it looked as though the Scottish army was winning, but then unknown persons shouted 'they flee, they flee' and the Scots dropped their pikes and ran. The English cavalry then gave chase.

Ribault noted five major mistakes made by the Scots. Firstly, they left crops in the fields, enabling the English to feed their horses. Secondly, they failed to launch surprise attacks to disrupt the English march into Scotland. Thirdly, Ribault reckoned that if the Scots had played for time food shortages might have forced Somerset's forces to withdraw. Fourthly, on 10 September the Scots put themselves at a disadvantage by racing towards the hill. Finally, the Scottish army engineered their own defeat by their unnecessary flight.[28]

Whilst the French ambassador was clearly sceptical about the English government's reports on the Pinkie campaign, the Imperial ambassador, Francis van der Delft, appears to have accepted most of the information William Paget relayed to him. This difference in outlook probably reflects the relatively cordial relations between England and the Holy Roman Empire, as well as the differing characters of the two diplomats. Van der Delft had extensive and often remarkably open discussions with Protector Somerset, both before and after the campaign. His ambassadorial despatches provide an extraordinary insight into Somerset's war aims, as well as indicating how the English protector portrayed his expedition upon his return.[29]

Van der Delft wrote several letters regarding the Battle of Pinkie. On 19 September he sent the Emperor Charles V and Queen Mary of Hungary (then regent of the Netherlands) information gained from William Paget about the 'great and glorious' victory against the Scots.[30] He noted that by 9 September the English had 'penetrated so far' into Scotland that they were 'only four miles away from Edinburgh'.[31] Realising that a Scottish army of 24,000 men was approaching Somerset 'decided to be beforehand' and occupy 'a mountain which stood between the two armies'. To check out the high ground Somerset despatched 2,000 light horse, who 'came into contact' with the enemy 'some of whom were killed and some captured'.[32]

According to Van der Delft, on 10 September the English set out to take 'the mountain', but the Scots also advanced 'in order of battle' and Somerset sent his cavalry to skirmish with them. As the English cavalry approached, the Scottish advance guard (who were riding) dismounted, crossed their lances and stood 'in such close order' that the English cavalry 'could not do them much harm'. Whilst this was taking place, the rest of the two forces continued 'marching towards each other' until 'they were so close that they exchanged shots'.[33] Warwick then led 'a good body of horse' to attack the Scottish rear-guard.[34] The English had 'some smoky fires lit' to conceal their movements, enabling Warwick successfully to surprise the Scots, many of whom fled. When the rest of the Scottish army saw the rear-guard in 'full flight' they followed the same 'example'.[35] Van der Delft alleged that some of the first Scots to flee had 'an understanding' with Somerset.[36] Echoing the information Paget also gave to the French, Van der Delft noted that 15,000 Scots had been killed or captured, including the Earl of Huntly.

The Imperial ambassador continued to send updates on the Scottish campaign throughout the autumn of 1547. Many of these discussed the progress of the war after Pinkie. However, on 21 October Francis van der Delft wrote to the future Philip II of Spain again describing the events of Pinkie itself.[37] This letter provides some different details from the despatches sent on 19 September – presumably reflecting how the information available at the Tudor court had evolved in the intervening weeks. Van der Delft informed Prince Philip that Somerset's army 'pushed on' until they were four miles from Edinburgh, where they 'took a stand' so close to the Scots that 'there was only a brook between them'.[38] The Scottish army apparently crossed the brook 'in order to occupy the two hills which flanked both armies'.[39] The Scots gained the first hill, but the English 'were before them' on the second, and it was here 'the two armies met'. The fighting was quite brief as the Scots 'without any need' panicked and fled. According to the October letter the Scots lost over 10,000 men (a noticeably lower figure than Van der Delft had given in September).[40]

Yet Francis van der Delft was not the only person from whom the Habsburgs got information. The Spanish government archive at Simancas has preserved an anonymous letter from London, dated 18 September 1547, sharing 'the good news received from Scotland'.[41] The letter is in Italian, but was clearly written by an Englishman, or someone who identified closely with the English cause. It describes how on 10 September Somerset's forces 'encountered' a Scottish army of 40,000 men. The English army 'gained the victory', wreaking 'great destruction' on the Scots', 15,000 of whom were supposedly 'left dead upon the field'. The letter claims that 'the greater part' of the Scottish nobility were 'killed or taken', although the Earl of Arran escaped. The letter then gives a rather confused account of the English army's actions after Pinkie, claiming that the Earl of Warwick was besieging Edinburgh and that the English would fortify Leith. The anonymous informant also maintained that there was 'a severe fight' between the Scottish and English fleets, but 'our side proved the stronger'.[42] The letter is clearly not an accurate record of the conduct of Somerset's campaign, but it does provide an insight into how the news of Pinkie was first received in southern England, and then communicated to governments across Western Europe.

Another letter written fairly soon after the battle, is the message from the English churchman John Hooper (later Bishop of Worcester and Gloucester) to Heinrich Bullinger, then leading the Protestant community in Zurich.[43] Hooper's letter is not dated, but appears to be from the period between Protector Somerset's return to London at the beginning of October and the assembling of the English Parliament in early November 1547.[44] During the autumn of 1547 Hooper was on the Continent, so his account was presumably itself derived from other people's letters. Nevertheless, he makes several interesting points. Hooper claims that on 10 September Lord Grey and the English cavalry charged 'the Scottish front' but were 'forced to retreat', with the loss of 48 horsemen. Seeing the cavalry 'give way' the Earl of Warwick advanced with 4,000 archers and attacked the Scottish artillery and baggage. The English 'cannon-balls and volleys of arrows' caused the Scots to 'fall back' into a position where they had 'the enemy both in front and rear' and the sun shining in their eyes. The English cavalry then made a second attack on the flank, causing the Scottish forces to be 'thrown into disorder'. The Scots then 'betook themselves to flight'. According to Hooper 15,000 Scots were killed and 2,000 taken prisoner. Hooper also notes how 'the English ships' sailed into 'various Scottish harbours' where they captured 'vessels which were adapted either for trade or naval warfare' and burned the rest. Finally, Hooper incorrectly states that the queen (probably a reference to Mary of Guise) 'gave herself up to the protector upon his own terms'. Somerset then supposedly took hostages 'for the fidelity of the queen' and left five garrisons behind in Scotland. In a postscript Hooper also adds that the English at Pinkie had 17,000 soldiers, whilst the Scots had 30,000.

The letters written about Pinkie in the autumn of 1547 by men such as Odet de Selve, Francis van der Delft, or John Hooper were composed close in the immediate aftermath of the fighting. They record initial understandings of the battle, and the conflicting reports that filtered down to southern England, and across Western Europe. However, these letters were almost entirely written by men who were not in Scotland at the time of Pinkie. The extant newsletters and diplomatic despatches are contemporary records, but they are still second-hand accounts.

Accounts by eye-witnesses and close relatives of combatants

At least two detailed eye-witness descriptions of the battle have survived. There are also a small number of accounts written by people whose close relatives fought at Pinkie. The earliest and longest memoir regarding Pinkie is William Patten's *Expedition into Scotland* (completed in January 1548).[45] Patten was part of the team of administrators assisting the English high command during the 1547 invasion, where he served as one of the judges of the Marshalsea.[46] The Court of the Marshalsea handled disputes that arose within a radius of 12 miles of where the monarch or regent was residing.[47] Whilst on campaign Patten had 'liberty to ride to see things that were done' and sufficient 'leisure to note occurrences', although he did complain that in hindsight there were details regarding 'the situation of towns, castles and churches', 'the lying of hills' and 'the course of rivers' that he wished he had 'more perfectly' recorded.[48]

Patten was a Londoner and served as parish clerk of St Mary-at-Hill, Billingsgate (finishing his book at the parsonage there). Yet Patten also had previous military experience. He was part of the invasion of France in 1544 and may have served with the English in France in 1546 and Scotland in 1544.[49] His book on the 1547 invasion is a remarkably fine campaign diary, providing considerable detail about the activities of Somerset's forces. Patten is noticeably uncritical of the English high command. Whilst some contemporary observers expressed reservations about Somerset's choices, Patten's book praised 'the special invincible virtue and valiant policy of my lord Protector's grace'.[50] Other high-ranking officers, including the Earl of Warwick (who secured Patten his appointment on the Marshalsea Court) and Lord Grey of Wilton, likewise received positive depictions. Patten's account may have been intended as a semi-official commemoration of the campaign and was dedicated to Sir William Paget.

After a preface explaining in highly Protestant and Anglo-centric terms the causes of war, Patten's *Expedition into Scotland* provides a day-by-day break-down of the campaign. The main narrative begins with the arrival of the Duke of Somerset at Newcastle on Saturday 27 August 1547, before tracing the Protector's journey to Berwick-upon-Tweed, and the subsequent crossing of the English army into Scotland on Sunday 4 September. Patten then outlines the English route north to Pinkie, travelling up the coast via Reston, the Peaths (or Pease), the castles of Dunglass, Thornton and Innerwick (all of which the English took), Tantallon Castle (which the English merely camped near), East Linton, Longniddry and Prestonpans.[51] The movements of the English fleet are occasionally described, but this is mainly a story about Somerset's land forces. At the heart of the book (and taking up over a third of its length) are the events of Friday 9 and Saturday 10 September.[52] The final few pages provide a hurried overview of the movements of the English forces after Pinkie, with the main narrative ending when Protector Somerset crossed back into England on Thursday 29 September, before a brief afterword summarises the achievements of the campaign.

Patten's *Expedition into Scotland* provides by the far most detailed account of what happened on 9 and 10 September. It is mostly from an English perspective. However, some information (such as the comments on the death of the Master of Graham and 25 others by gunshot from the English galley) was presumably acquired from Scottish sources.[53] According to Patten, at Pinkie the English had a fighting force on land of 16,800 men (including 4,000 heavy cavalry and 2,000 light horsemen), plus 15 great guns.[54] Meanwhile the Scottish army consisted of 26,000 footmen, 4,000 'Irish' archers (the term Irish then often being used for Gaelic-speaking Scots), 2,000 light horsemen, and 30 pieces of artillery.[55]

Patten describes how on the morning of Friday 9 September the English army was encamped near Prestonpans (which he calls 'Salt Preston').[56] He states that the

English camp had the Firth of Forth to the north and the slopes of Falside Brae to the south, and was about two miles from the Scottish camp, which was located to the west of the River Esk.[57] Somerset's army spent Friday morning unloading supplies from their fleet. However, in the afternoon the English sent 'a band of light horsemen and a troop of demilances' to oppose the Scottish prickers which had been 'pranking up and down' Falside Brae. In the ensuing skirmish the Scottish cavalry commander Lord Hume was 'sore hurt' and over 1,300 Scots were killed. Supposedly nine Scots were captured, including Lord Hume's eldest son. On the English side a Spanish hackbutter was wounded, whilst three captains of light horse were taken prisoner.[58] The English clearly got the better of the engagement, and shortly afterwards Somerset and Warwick, accompanied by Patten and a 'small guard', went to 'view' the Scottish camp from the high ground at Falside Brae.[59] On the way back a Scottish herald and trumpeter approached Somerset, but the English commander showed little inclination to negotiate, claiming that the Earl of Arran had already 'refused' generous offers of peace and 'therefore let him look for none'.[60]

On Saturday 10 September the English 'dislodged' their camp near Prestonpans before 8 am.[61] According to Patten, Somerset's army 'marched straight toward' the church at Inveresk, intending to place artillery on the rise there. However, the Scottish army had crossed the River Esk and had almost reached the church, while the English were 'half way to it'.[62] The Scots drew up in line of battle between two 'hillocks', located 'betwixt' the English and the church.[63] As the Scots were mustering, the English galley fired on them, killing the Master of Graham and several others and making the Irish archers 'so scared' they could not 'be made to come forward'.[64] The Scots then headed south towards Falside Brae, apparently seeking to win the high ground and also gain an advantage regarding the wind direction. This movement was noted by the English cavalry officer Sir Ralph Fane, who 'quickly advertised' it to Somerset.[65] Patten states that the Scots were in such 'haste' they moved their artillery southwards 'by draught of men'.[66] Soon the Scottish guns were able to fire on the English army.

In response, Somerset ordered Lord Grey and 1,800 horsemen to attack the Scots. By this stage the vanguard of the English infantry was also on the slopes of Falside Brae, whilst the main battle and rear-guard were on the slightly lower ground beside it. According to Patten, the Scottish and English vanguards were now only two 'flightshot' (i.e. bow-shot) apart.[67] The Scots carried on moving 'fast' towards the high ground, looking as if they would get there before the English infantry, although Somerset's master of ordnance did manage to get some artillery weapons (including two or three cannons) 'well nigh upon the top' of the hill, where the Scottish horse unsuccessfully sought to capture them.[68] Somerset himself apparently rode up 'to tarry by the ordnance' where he could 'survey' the movement of the forces as well as 'by his presence be a defence to the thing that stood . . . most in danger'.[69]

All of a 'sudden' the Scottish army stopped in a fallow field. At this point Lord Grey's cavalry had almost reached the Scots. However, there was 'a cross ditch or slough' which impeded the English horsemen's progress.[70] Many of the horses leapt across it, but some got stuck. The English cavalry attacked the Scottish vanguard, which was armed with pikes and commanded by the Earl of Angus. The Scottish vanguard repulsed Grey's horsemen, who then 'made a soft retire up toward the hill'.[71] Several of the English cavalry (including Lord Grey himself) had been wounded, and others killed.

In the meantime, the English footmen had been drawn up in line of battle, with the vanguard totally on the hillside, just beside 'a square plot enclosed with turf', the main battle partly on the brae and partly on the plain, and the rear-guard wholly on the plain.[72] The English now sent their hackbutters to fire on the Scots from the slough which had impeded the cavalry charge. Archers and artillery were also deployed. The English cavalry was then brought forward for another effort. This time the Scottish forces broke and fled.

Patten claimed that Arran was the first to flee, taking 'hastily his horse', soon followed by Angus and 'other chief captains'.[73] Also among the early departures were 'the Irishmen' (that is the men from Argyll and the Western Isles). The whole army then cast down their weapons and ran off towards Edinburgh, sparking a bloody

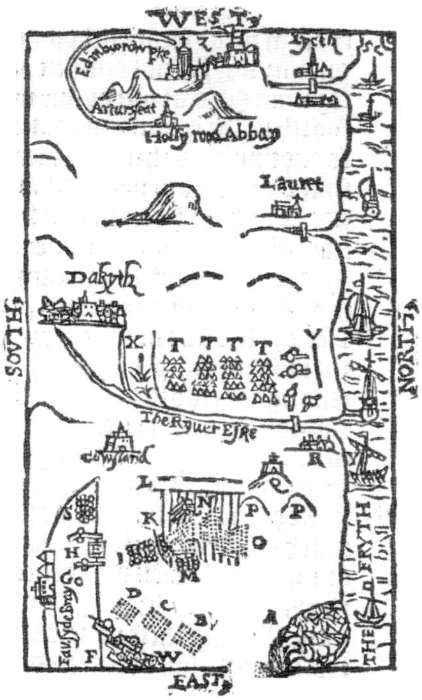

Figure 5.1: William Patten's first table. For Patten's key to symbols and letters see Figure 5.4. In the bottom part, the English cavalry (J) is attacking the Scottish vanguard (M) while the rest of the English army is still advancing

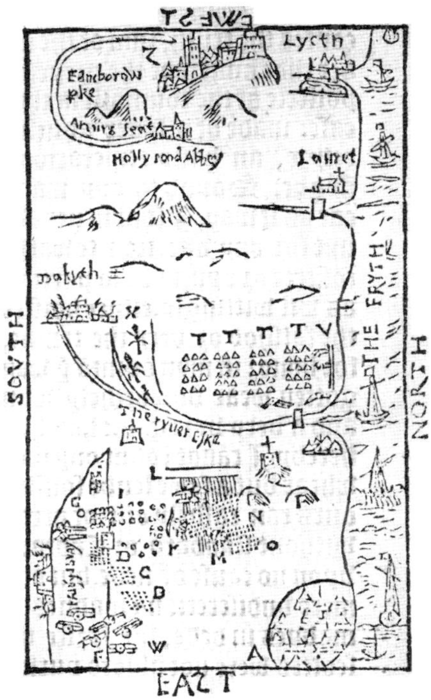

Figure 5.2: William Patten's second table. The Scots have repulsed the English cavalry attack but the English army is now drawn up in line of battle and there are English pieces of artillery on Falside Brae

'race' to escape the English. According to Patten, so many 'staves' were 'strewed on the ground' they seemed like 'rushes in a chamber'.[74] More gruesomely 'dead corpses' were also 'dispersed abroad', with Patten estimating that 14,000 Scots lost their lives, whilst the River Esk 'ran all red with blood'.[75] Towards the end of the day the English also set fire to Falside Castle, before eventually making camp at a place called Edgebuckling Brae, just near the ravine known as Pinkie Cleugh.

To aid his readers in following the complicated events of 10 September, Patten also provided three woodcut diagrams or 'tables', showing different phases of the fighting. In table 1 (Figure 5.1) the three English units of foot are advancing, whilst the Scottish battles are standing in the field. In table 2 (Figure 5.2) the English foot are in their final position, whilst the Scots have just seen off Grey's cavalry. Table 3 (Figure 5.3) shows the Scots in total flight. The diagrams were probably sketched out by Patten himself and then turned into woodcuts by a blockmaker called S. Cromes

Figure 5.3: William Patten's third table. The rout of the Scottish army

The exposicio[n] of y[e] letters of this table.
A. Signifieth the place we camped in before the battaile.
B. Our rerewarde.
C. Our battaile.
D. Our forewarde.
E. The square close.
F. The foot of the hylles syde.
G. My lorde Protectours grace.
H. The master of the ordinaunce.
I. Our horsmen.
K. The slough.
L. The lane and the .ii. turf walles.
M. Their forewarde & horsme[n] by y[e] same.
N. Their battaile.
O. Their rerewarde.
P P. The .ii. hillockes before the church.
Q. Saint Mighels of vndreske.
R. Muskelborowe.
S. Their horsmen at the ende of fauxside Bray.
TTTT. Their rewes of tentes.
V. The turf wall toward the frith.
VV. Our cariages.
X. the marish.
Y. Our galley.
Z. Edinborow castell.
The significacio[n] of certein other notes.
Signifieth a footman.
A horsman.
A hakbutter a foot.
A hakbutter on horsback.
An archer.
A footman slayn.
A horsman slayn.
The fallowe felde, wheaton their armye stode.

Figure 5.4: Patten's key to the symbols and letters on his three tables of the battle on 10 September

(a name which appears on the third diagram).[76] The woodcuts are early examples of overhead plans of a battle. The main fighting units, and some landscape features, are identified by letters for which a key is provided (Figure 5.4). The names of other places are spelled out.

The River Esk flows through the middle of the tables, running south to north. On the west bank is the Scottish camp, represented as four blocks of tents with some pieces of artillery to the north. Towards the sea there is a turf wall, and at the other end of the camp a marsh. Dalkeith, Edinburgh, Leith, Musselburgh and Inveresk Church are all represented, as is Falside Brae. The 'fallow field' is prominently marked, and features such as the 'slough' and the 'square close' are also noted. In the main, Patten shows a good understanding of the local geography, but there is at least one notable error, the church identified as 'Lauret' seems more likely to actually be Restalrig collegiate church. Like so much of Patten's work, the diagrams of the Battle of Pinkie are an invaluable but sometimes flawed record of the events of September 1547.

Apart from Patten's book, the other detailed eye-witness description of Pinkie is an account by the French Protestant mercenary Jean de Fontenay, Sieur de Bretteville (often called Sir John Berteville by English-speaking historians).[77] During the 1547 invasion of Scotland, Berteville served under the Earl of Warwick. He commanded a force of eight mounted hackbutters and was wounded 'in the buttock' in skirmishing on Wednesday 7 September, when he helped prevent Warwick being captured in an ambush.[78] Berteville was knighted by Warwick in Berwick-upon-Tweed just after the end of the Pinkie campaign.[79]

Berteville's memoir was dedicated to the 'very triumphant and magnanimous King Edward VI'.[80] It is in French and covers the whole of the Pinkie campaign. Yet despite being an eye-witness account it has several notable errors – including dating the main fighting to 6 September 1547. Berteville's knowledge of Scottish geography is also much less good than Patten's. It is possible that these errors indicate that Berteville did not discuss his work with other people.

Berteville stated that the English had about 12,000 footmen, 800 men-at-arms and 2,500 light horsemen, plus artillery weapons and a baggage train.[81] He summarises the English army's journey from Berwick up towards the River Esk, where the Scots were supposedly guarding the bridge over the river.[82] Berteville describes how on 'the Friday' there was a three-hour long skirmish between the English light horse and perhaps 1,000 or 1,200 Scottish horsemen.[83] The Scots were driven off, losing about 800 men. The English commanders were then able to gain a good view of the Scottish camp and a 'long' hill that overlooked it.

On Saturday the English army set out in its usual marching order to take up position on the hill. The Scots then abandoned their camp in an effort to secure the high ground first. The Scottish army consisted of about 35,000 or 36,000 men, with 15,000 in the vanguard, and the others split equally between the main battle and the rear-guard. Seeing the Scottish movements, the English high command changed their plan, expecting now to fight. According to Berteville, the English wanted to take up position on another hill near the Scots. In the meantime there was skirmishing between the two armies. Then, thanks to the 'will of God', the Scots abandoned their hill and marched straight towards the English.[84] This put them in an unfavourable position relative to the English, who were able to use their artillery to fire down on the Scots.

Berteville notes that Warwick organised the English infantry into a line of battle, riding personally between the battalions.[85] Meanwhile Lord Grey of Wilton and the men-at-arms attacked the Scottish vanguard. This cavalry charge was driven off by the Scots and Grey was wounded.[86] The English vanguard, led by Warwick, then marched straight towards the Scots, whilst Somerset rallied the defeated men-at-arms. Having regrouped the cavalry, Somerset then led them in another charge against the foremost Scottish battalion. This time the Scots gave way. The rest of the Scottish army also broke, with even their captains 'losing courage', whilst the governor (Arran), the lieutenant (possibly a reference to Angus) and the master of the artillery all fled from the battlefield.[87] The English forces gave chase and many Scots were killed. Eventually Somerset and Warwick stopped the pursuit (seeking to avoid needless bloodshed) and that night the English camped on the battlefield. Berteville ends his account with a brief summary of the subsequent English achievements in Scotland, including the establishment of garrisons on an 'island near Edinburgh' (presumably Inchcolm) and a 'castle near to Dundee' (presumably Broughty Ferry). In his final sentence Berteville remarks that he hoped to see 'the end of the superstition of the Scots' – a reminder of the French exile's own beliefs and of the religious aspect to the 1547 campaign.[88]

Berteville's account is problematic, but it was seemingly read with enthusiasm by the young Edward VI. The brief description of Pinkie that Edward included in his personal chronicle (the boy king's own history of important events in his reign) is heavily influenced by Berteville.[89] Indeed, Edward actually mentions Berteville by name, noting his role in preventing Warwick being captured.[90] Like Berteville, the English king incorrectly dates the main fighting at Pinkie to 7 September. Edward also crossed out an estimate that the Scottish army consisted of 36,000 men and replaced it with 23,000, perhaps because he had heard that, directly or indirectly, from Huntly.

Edward VI's description of Pinkie is one of a small number of accounts written by people whose close relatives fought in the battle. Yet it is unclear how much of Edward's summary is attributable to his uncle Somerset's own remarks. Edward does state that on the day of the battle 'the Lord Protector thought to get the hill, but the Scots seeing [this], crossed the bridge over the River Musselburgh, and strove for the higher ground and almost got it'.[91] This comment might reflect information from Somerset, but it could equally well be from Berteville or another witness. What is clear is that even the young king was informed that the Battle of Pinkie did at times seem to hang in the balance, with Edward noting how the English horsemen were initially 'stayed' and the English forces had to be 'gathered together again' by Somerset and Warwick.[92] Edward's casualty claims are interesting (if probably inaccurate).

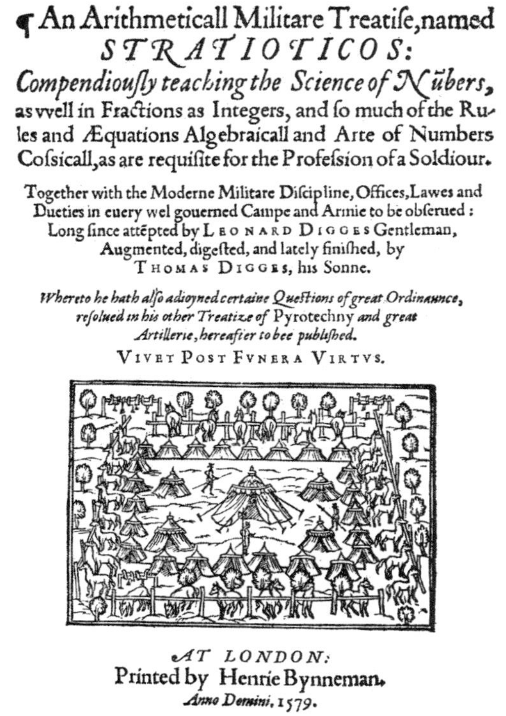

¶ An Arithmeticall Militare Treatiſe, named
STRATIOTICOS:
Compendiouſly teaching the Science of Nũbers,
as vvell in Fractions as Integers, and ſo much of the Rules and Æquations Algebraicall and Arte of Numbers Coſsicall, as are requiſite for the Profeſsion of a Soldiour.

Together with the Moderne Militare Diſcipline, Offices, Lawes and Dueties in euery wel gouerned Campe and Armie to be obſerued: Long ſince attẽpted by LEONARD DIGGES Gentleman, Augmented, digeſted, and lately finiſhed, by THOMAS DIGGES, his Sonne.

Whereto he hath alſo adioyned certaine Queſtions of great Ordinaunce, reſolued in his other Treatize of Pyrotechny *and great Artillerie, hereafter to bee publiſhed.*

VIVET POST FVNERA VIRTVS.

AT LONDON:
Printed by Henrie Bynneman.
Anno Domini. 1579.

Figure 5.5: Title page of Stratioticos, *a mathematical treatise for use by the military, published in London in 1579. Its author, Leonard Digges, fought at Pinkie*

He states that 10,000 Scots died at Pinkie, but on the English side only 51 horsemen and one footman were killed. The English infantry almost certainly had higher losses than this, but the king's comments may reflect a valid impression that the cavalry had heavier casualties than other parts of the English army.

Edward VI's account of Pinkie was probably composed not long after the battle and was definitely written before the summer of 1550. Our other accounts by relatives of combatants at Pinkie were compiled rather later. In 1579 the mathematician and politician Thomas Digges published *An Arithmetical Military Treatise named Stratioticos* (Figure 5.5).[93] This work provided methods of calculating things like the range of guns, the area of ground necessary to encamp an army, and how to draw up units of fighting men. Thomas Digges' book seems to have been influenced by the ideas of his similarly mathematically minded father Leonard, an English surveyor who fought at Pinkie.[94] Indeed Leonard Digges is mentioned by Patten as playing a role in the English cavalry attack on the Scottish vanguard.[95]

Thomas Digges' 1579 treatise contains an interesting (if very brief) reference to 'Musselburgh Field', which implies that at Pinkie the English used 'corrupted spies' to spread a 'rumour' among the Scots that 'their General was slain or some part of them defeated or flying away', false news which led the Scottish army to sway and break.[96] It is possible that this interpretation reflects a view that circulated among the junior officers and ordinary soldiers in the English army.

A more detailed discussion of Pinkie is given by the son of another veteran, namely Arthur, 14th Baron Grey of Wilton, whose father William, 13th Baron Grey, had commanded the English cavalry at Pinkie.[97] The younger Lord Grey wrote a detailed account of his father's career, paying particular attention to the events of 9 and 10 September 1547.[98] This biography was produced at some point between 1562 (when the older Lord Grey died) and the publication of the first volume of Holinshed's *Chronicles* in 1577 (which draws heavily on this account of Pinkie). The younger Lord Grey's description of Pinkie appears to have been based on his father's own recollections. Indeed, Lord Grey (junior) ends his discussion of Pinkie stating that this was as 'much' as he knew from his father's 'own mouth concerning the battle'.[99]

There are some notable inaccuracies. For instance, Grey's biography claims that the Earl of Huntly was captured on Friday 9 September, when most other sources indicate that he was taken on the Saturday. It also gives the impression that the cavalry engagement on the Friday took place whilst the English army was still on the march. This does not fit with other evidence that suggests the English were already in their camp at Prestonpans by the evening of Thursday 8 September. Nevertheless, the account has interesting details about the discussions of the English leaders and the cavalry tactics employed by the elder Lord Grey – perhaps described in the commander's own words.

At the start of the Scottish expedition Lord Grey (senior) supposedly brought over from Boulogne the garrison's men-at-arms, his own 'band of lances' (demilances), and a band of 'Italian' hackbutters (perhaps in reality the Spanish hackbutters led by Pedro de Gamboa).[100] On the march towards Musselburgh tensions arose between Grey and Somerset about whether the English cavalry should respond to harassment from the Scottish light horsemen or 'prickers'. Matters came to a head at supper on Thursday 8 September, when Grey and Warwick both argued for attacking the Scottish light horse, whilst Somerset felt such a wish stemmed more from 'a jollity of courage than knowledge of the enemy'.[101] Eventually, Somerset agreed to the English responding to provocation from the Scottish horse, on the condition that Grey just used the men he had brought from Boulogne.

On Friday 9 September Grey's men engaged the Scots. According to his son's account, the elder Lord Grey arranged his forces with two troops of demilances at the front (one in front of the other), the Italians as a wing to the second troop, whilst the men-at-arms brought up the rear.[102] This description differs from Patten's recollection of a force of light horse and demilances being deployed on the Friday.[103] Grey told 'the leaders of his troops' that when the Scots came near they should not be drawn into skirmishing, but wait until 'the enemy's wheeling about' at which point the troop that had initially been approached should charge, supported by the next troop, keeping in formation. This tactic was successfully implemented against a force of about 1,500 horsemen on the Friday afternoon, leading to 'the greatest part' of the Scottish cavalry being 'overthrown'.[104]

The next day Grey and Somerset again disagreed about how the cavalry should be used. The Scots were seen marching 'in great haste' towards 'the hill'.[105] According to the account of Grey's son, at this point Somerset was not certain that the Scots would fight. However, as the Scots looked as if they would take the high ground, the English decided to intervene, with Grey advocating for the 'adventuring of some horsemen to stay the enemy's march' and enable the English infantry 'to get the hill'. This was clearly a risky endeavour and Grey asked Somerset to be 'good to my wife and children' if he fell. Grey then led a cavalry force, consisting of the men-at-arms from

Boulogne, 'his own band of lances', and 'a few' gentlemen pensioners and courtiers, and charged 'the whole' of the Scottish 'battle'.[106] This supposedly changed the tide of the battle as the Scots were 'stayed and shaken' whilst 'in the meantime' the English 'recovered the hill and presently after the victory'.[107] However, in the charge Lord Grey 'received a great wound in the mouth with a pike'. Supposedly he 'notwithstanding' continued in 'the chase', but nearly suffocated 'with the abundance of blood, heat of the weather, and dust of the press', until eventually the Earl of Warwick saved him by lifting 'a firkin of ale to his head'.[108]

Importantly, there is at least one account of Pinkie written by a close relative of a Scottish survivor of the battle. David Hume of Godscroft's history of the houses of Douglas and Angus includes a description of Pinkie.[109] Hume's history was published around 1630 but was composed a few years earlier.[110] The author's father, David Hume of Wedderburn, had fought for the Scots at Pinkie.[111] Hume of Godscroft was also secretary to the 8th Earl of Angus, whose great-uncle had commanded the Scottish vanguard on 10 September 1547. Although Hume's history was written a long time afterwards, it may preserve stories told by Scottish veterans of the battle. Notably, the account provides several details about the actions of Angus – perhaps derived from the earl's own family.

According to Hume, when Arran heard that Somerset was invading by land and sea, he mustered an army at Edinburgh and then marched to Musselburgh. Meanwhile the English army had camped at Preston with their fleet in view. Like several other Scottish histories (discussed further below), Hume recounts how Somerset made overtures of peace to the Scots, but Arran was persuaded by a small group of Catholic churchmen to contemplate battle.

On the Saturday, both armies were split into three battles. The Scottish vanguard was led by the Earl of Angus and had contingents from Carrick and Cunninghame, Kyle, Stirlingshire and Strathearn. The Earl of Arran had command of the main Scottish battle and the Earl of Huntly was in charge of the rear-guard. Hume states that a planned withdrawal by the English was halted by the Scottish vanguard marching uphill towards them. Angus initially went slowly but was commanded twice by Arran to speed up, which he did, being assured that the other Scottish battles would provide support. Angus then moved forward so fast that it appeared to the English that his men were riding.

According to Hume, Lord Grey's cavalry were sent to stop the Scottish advance. Angus advised his men to use their pikes to stab the English horses in the belly. This tactic was successful, resulting in 200 of the English attackers being killed. Somerset ordered Lord Grey to charge again, but he answered that he might as well command him to run against the walls of Boulogne. At this point Somerset resolved to retire and called for some Scots in his army to act as his guide. One of them was Thomas Lorraine, a tenant of the Laird of Redbraes in the Merse, 'of whom many have often heard this report'. Warwick, however, suggested sending in Gamboa and his men to attack the Scottish vanguard's flank. Recognising this danger, Angus turned his battle 'softly' towards them, a manoeuvre that was interpreted by Arran as fleeing. As a consequence, the main battle ran away, followed by the men of Huntly's division. The vanguard was left without support and was overthrown. As an excuse for not assisting the vanguard, Huntly and Arran supposedly pointed out that the Scottish rear-guard had been unsettled by gunfire from an English galley and two pinnaces that had come close to shore. The Earl of Angus escaped from the battlefield and rode to Calder. Others, including David Hume of Wedderburn (the father of the writer), sought refuge in Dalkeith Castle, but were taken prisoner when the castle surrendered after a short siege.

Visual sources

One of the exceptional features of Pinkie is the number of early visual depictions. As well as the diagrams created for Patten's book, there survives a sixteenth-century copperplate engraving of the battle, and a set of birds-eye views now in the Bodleian Library (hereafter called the Battle of Pinkie Roll, or the Roll), discovered in their collections in the 1890s. The link to Pinkie was noted by Charles Oman in the 1930s.[112]

Oman thought the Roll was the work of a man named John Ramsay, as that name appears on the manuscript. From this, and the fact that Ramsay is a common Scottish surname, Oman speculated that Ramsay was one of the Scots who joined the English army at the beginning of the campaign. There is, though, no guarantee that the Ramsay note relates to the drawing's creator, and little reason to assume that the artist was Scottish.

It seems more likely that the Roll is the work of a military engineer or artist on the staff of the English army. The style of the Roll is remarkably similar to a bird's-eye view of the assault on Edinburgh in 1544, now in the British Library in London.[113] The Edinburgh illustration was created by the military engineer Richard Lee, who also accompanied Somerset on the Pinkie campaign. There are also similarities between the Battle of Pinkie Roll and a map of the 1560 siege of Leith (originally in the Petworth House archives, and now in the West Sussex Record Office).[114] The Leith drawing may also be the work of Richard Lee, who apparently sent Elizabeth I a map of Leith to inform her about the siege.[115] If the Roll was created by Richard Lee (or indeed one of his close colleagues), that would suggest that it was made for official purposes by Somerset's team. A certain amount of roughness in the execution of the Roll may indicate that it was an initial draft, rather than being a finished presentation piece.

The Roll is composed of six sheets of paper, numbered by us for convenience of description as 1 to 6 (reading from left to right). They are joined together to form a roll 2.12 m (7 ft) long. Five of the sheets are about 395 mm (15½ inches) wide, but the left hand one is only 165 mm (6½ inches). The sheets have been pasted together, each with a narrow overlap. Slight mismatches of ink lines indicate that the drawings were completed prior to the roll being created. Each sheet has a watermark of a lidded flagon surmounted by a crown, with a band round its belly containing the initials CM.

Figure 5.6: The Battle of Pinkie Roll, sheet 1, showing the cavalry engagement on 9 September. St Michael's Church is in the foreground with Pinkie House to the left and Musselburgh to the right. The castle in the background is Cousland. The English can be distinguished from the Scots by their flags and on the original by the use of a pink wash for their horses (Bodleian Library, MS. Eng. Misc. C 13 (R))

This watermark is consistent with paper made in Normandy in the 1540s.[116] Most of the drawing on the Roll is linear, in black ink, but there is also limited use of colour washes in red, brown and black. There are three brief (probably) Latin inscriptions on the Roll, all in a different hand to the Ramsay text. The inscriptions are in the sky at the top of the Roll. The two left-hand inscriptions are hard to interpret, whilst the right-hand one is an abbreviated form of 'Deus perdidit' (a comment that God has destroyed them).

In the clouds over the battlefield there is an image of God wearing a papal triple tiara. God has a large sword in his right hand, and thunderbolts in his left – presumably indicating his just punishment of the Scots. The papal tiara may seem surprising given Somerset's Reformist sympathies but reflects traditional ways of depicting God the Father. To the right of God there is an image of the sun (with a human face) shining through the clouds. The wind is also personified and shown blowing towards the Scots.[117] Beneath these Heavenly figures the movements of the Scottish and English armies play out – with their manoeuvrings best explained by an analysis of each section of the Roll.

Sheet 1 (Figure 5.6)

The first sheet is the narrowest and may now be missing its left-hand portion. The image that survives shows the cavalry engagement on Friday 9 September. In the foreground is a representation of Inveresk Church, shown with a spire on a piece of rising ground. To the left of the church is a tower and a few smaller buildings (probably Pinkie House). To the right is Musselburgh – depicted as several houses and one spire. Behind Inveresk Church there is a turf-walled lane. On the hill in the background units of mounted troops are seen in action whilst dead bodies already lie on the ground.

Sheet 2 (Figure 5.7)

Sheet 2 clearly depicts the events of Saturday 10 September. The hill, strewn with bodies from the day before, can be seen in the background. Inveresk Church, the lane, Pinkie House and Musselburgh appear as on the previous sheet. The River Esk is also shown, crossed by a two-span bridge. On the sea there are several English ships (six sailing vessels, and two rowing vessels, at least one of which appears to be a full-sized galley). A small group of tents is shown on the left-hand edge of the sheet, presumably depicting the English camp.

The English army is shown in marching order, relatively near the coast. The three battles of footmen are flanked by sleeves of archers on their left and hackbutters on their right. Three units of horse are shown further inland. Two horsemen with plumes on their helmets may represent Somerset and Warwick. The English baggage train can be seen on the left flank of their rearguard. The artillery is represented by three guns in front of the vanguard with smoking barrels. Meanwhile the large galley is also firing onto land.

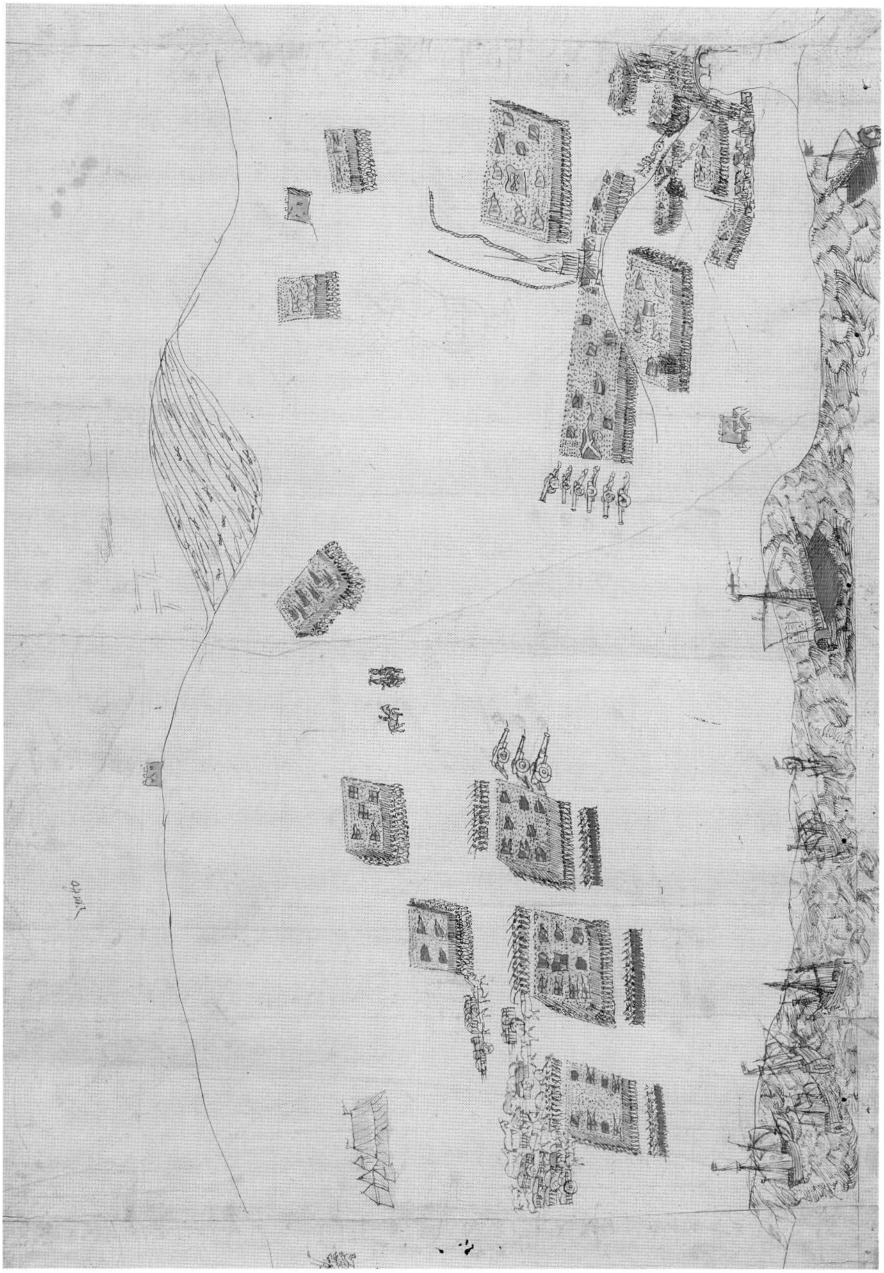

Figure 5.7: The Battle of Pinkie Roll, sheet 2. The English army is shown in marching order. Two horsemen with plumes on their helmets represent Somerset and Warwick, engaged in talk with a third commander. The Scottish army, approaching from the right, is manoeuvring into battle order. Their vanguard and rear-guard lag behind the main battle. The English galley in the foreground is firing on the Scots (Bodleian Library, MS. Eng. Misc. C 13 (R))

The Scottish army is depicted moving into battle order close to Inveresk Church. In front of the Scottish army are six pieces of artillery. Further inland, near a tower house (probably Cousland Castle), are two units of Scottish horse. Other Scottish units are still crossing the River Esk.

Sheet 3 (Figure 5.8)

The main development on this sheet is an attack by English horsemen on the Scottish foot. The latter is shown as one large rectangular formation – presumably because the vanguard, main battle and rear-guard have merged together. The top left corner of the Scottish foot has pikes levelled to fend off the enemy attack. There is a large dent in the other end of the Scottish formation and bodies are shown strewn on the ground – which may be the aftermath of Grey's initial attack on the Scottish vanguard. The Scottish artillery is positioned inland of the footmen. The two units of Scottish horse shown on the previous sheet appear to have moved round to the back of the high ground.

The English infantry are now in three battles, with some hackbutters to the front interspersed with pieces of artillery. The archers are behind the main units of footmen. Other pieces of English artillery and the baggage train are now on the summit of the hill, near a tower representing Falside Castle. Over the brow of the hill can be seen spears and a flag – probably the Scottish horse preparing to attack the English artillery.

Sheets 4 to 6 (Figures 5.9–5.11)

These three sheets form one long diorama depicting the rout of the Scottish forces. The English army is shown with a wide gap between its vanguard and main battle, which groups of horsemen are riding through. These are probably Grey's cavalry troops retreating in disorder.

The Scottish pikemen are also depicted as running away, with lots of individuals heading westwards across the River Esk. There are bodies strewn on the ground. English horsemen are riding the fugitives down, and some English footmen (identifiable by their flags) are also in pursuit. The Scottish camp on the bank of the River Esk is being looted. Two settlements appear to be on fire.

The English camp after the battle is represented as a group of tents to the southeast of Leith. The town and haven at Leith are depicted, with three ships in the harbour. In the background is a view of Edinburgh and Holyrood Abbey.

Whilst the Battle of Pinkie Roll has a sketch-like quality, another early image of the battle, the copperplate engraving, is definitely a finished work (see Figure 1.1). The engraving is titled 'THE ENGLISH VICTORY AGAINST THE SCOTS BY MUSSELBURGH'. An original of this engraving has recently been acquired by the British Library.[118] The image was probably produced soon after the battle, and certainly before the English defeat in 1549.[119] It is the earliest known impression of a British copperplate print. The artist may have been Thomas Gemini (alias Lambrechts), an engraver and printer who received payments from Henry VIII and Edward VI.[120] Gemini printed two books by Leonard Digges, who of course served at Pinkie.[121] Another possible artist

Figure 5.8: The Battle of Pinkie Roll, sheet 3. The English army is shown in line of battle. Some of its artillery and the baggage train are adjacent to Falside Castle while a large force of horse attacks the Scottish foot, now merged into one very large rectangular formation (Bodleian Library, MS. Eng. Misc. C 13 (R))

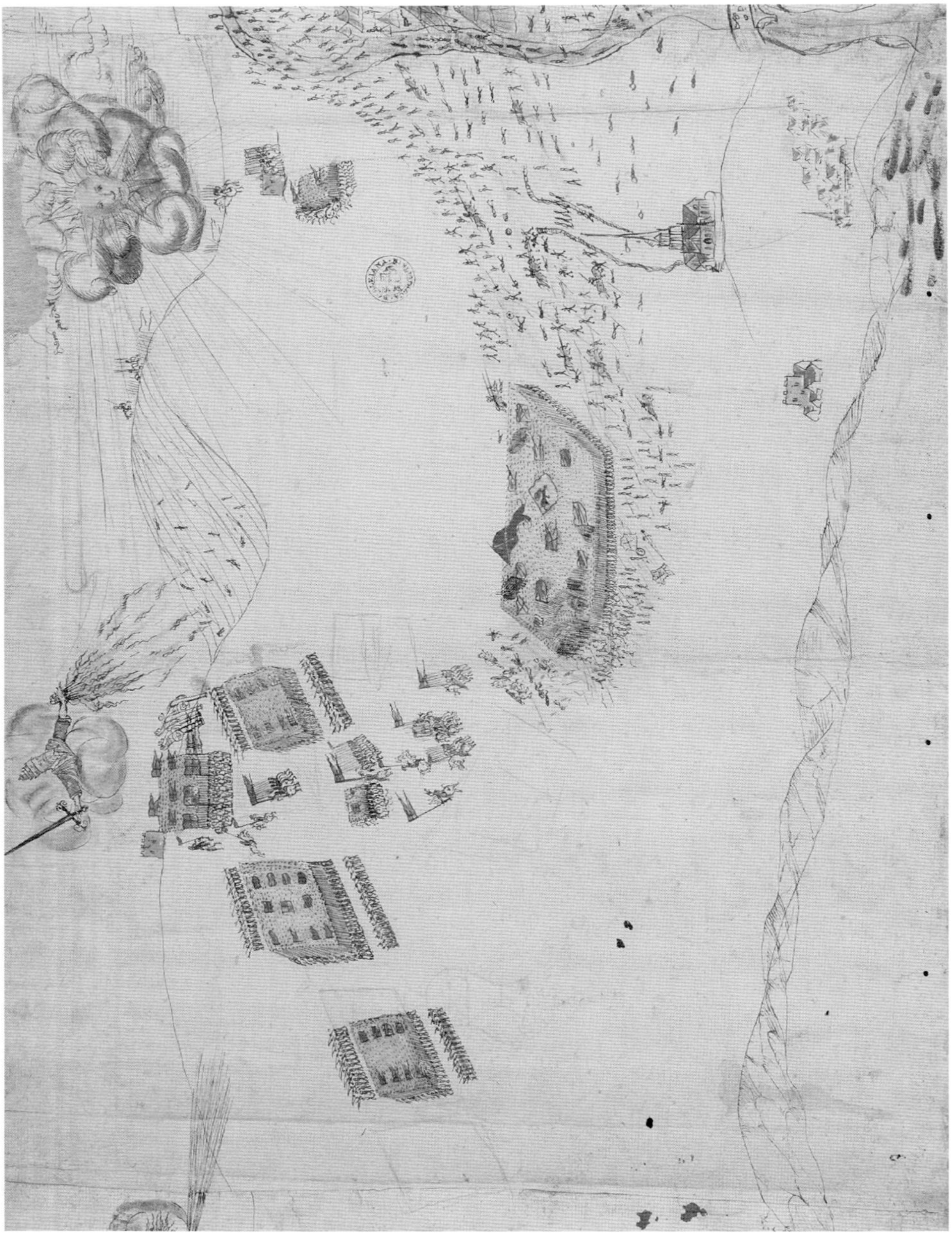

Figure 5.9: The Battle of Pinkie Roll, sheet 4. The Scottish army is beginning to break up and English horsemen are pursuing the fleeing Scots (Bodleian Library, MS. Eng. Misc. C 13 (R))

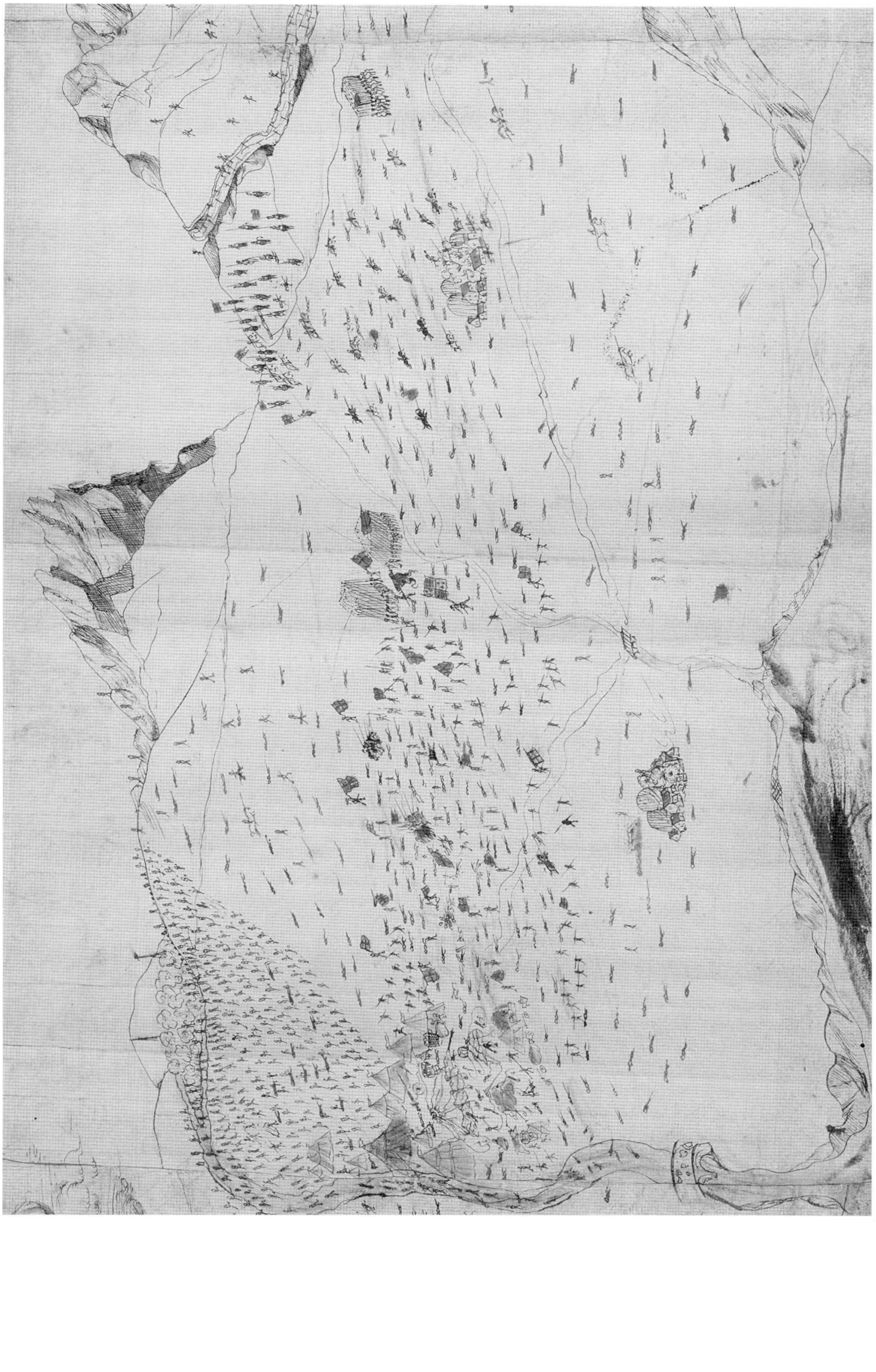

Figure 5.10: The Battle of Pinkie Roll, sheet 5. The Scots are in full flight, chased by English horsemen and footmen. The Scottish camp is to the left (Bodleian Library, MS. Eng. Misc. C 13 (R))

Figure 5.11: The Battle of Pinkie Roll, sheet 6. A view of Edinburgh, partially obscured by Calton Hill, the castle to the right, Holyrood Abbey to the left beneath Arthur's Seat. The English camp is in the centre near the port of Leith (Bodleian Library, MS. Eng. Misc. C 13 (R))

and printer is Reyner Wolfe (also based in London). In 1547 Wolfe received a royal appointment from Edward VI for printing and selling books.[122] He had previously printed an account of Somerset's 1544 invasion of Scotland.

The copperplate engraving derived information from the Battle of Pinkie Roll. There are, however, differences that indicate some additional input. Particularly interesting is the representation of Inveresk Church, which on the Roll is an Anglicised generic image of a church, but on the engraving is a more believable example of Scottish ecclesiastical architecture. There is also extensive (and helpful) labelling on the engraving.

In geographical terms the engraving covers the area from the English camp near Prestonpans on the left, to Leith and Edinburgh on the right. The Firth of Forth is along the bottom of the page, with several English ships and a galley firing inland. The top of the engraving includes Falside Hill (described as the 'hill of Musselburgh') and Arthur's Seat (labelled 'the hill').

The units of the English army are shown already being deployed, and some are fighting the Scots. Each of the English battles has a contingent of hackbutters on the right and archers on the left. English cannon are deployed in several places, including on the slope of Falside Hill. Somerset is identified on a horse in front of the main battle. A group of English light horsemen are shown mounting a charge on the Scottish rear-guard. Horsemen are also shown attacking the Scots' main battle (perhaps a later phase of the same action). English 'carters' are depicted with bills raised near Falside Castle. Much of the baggage train is still making its way to the hilltop. Some Scottish cavalry is attacking the English transport teams. Other Scottish horsemen are shown 'running away' to the back of a castle (almost certainly Cousland). The Scottish infantry are shown in line of battle, opposite the English army. The three battles are massed close together. The Scottish artillery is positioned to the left and right of the footmen. The Scottish camp is shown as three groups of tents on the west bank of the Esk. There are additional pieces of Scottish artillery facing across the river, and two large guns on a mound to the south of the camp. There is also a battery of guns being fired beside Inveresk Church. Adjacent to the stone bridge over the Esk is what may be a temporary wooden bridge. The English camp outside Leith is also shown, and in the distance lots of armed men (presumably Scots) are entering Edinburgh. A large unit of Scottish horse is labelled as running away. The Scottish infantry are shown on the verge of collapse. Columns of men are already streaming towards the River Esk and dead bodies are strewn across the countryside.

English chronicles, ballads and other histories

The English public were for a time clearly interested in Pinkie. The battle became the subject of at least one ballad, now known as 'Musselburgh Field'. A fragment of this ballad was published in the nineteenth century in Francis Child's monumental *English and Scottish Popular Ballads*.[123] However, in the twentieth century the full text of the ballad was discovered.[124] It is believed to have been published originally as a broadsheet in 1548. The ballad's primary value to historians is what it shows about popular perceptions of Pinkie.

The ballad recounts how the armies 'met on a plain'. The two hosts camped all night, with the Scots playing cards. Subsequently, the Scots were defeated when they heard the English 'great guns crack' and 'cast down their weapons and turned their backs'. The Scots are described as being beaten back to Edinburgh, whilst less than 200 Englishmen were lost. The ballad has many inaccuracies, but it is interesting that elements such as the role of artillery and the Scottish rout had entered English popular culture.

Pinkie was also discussed in more serious sixteenth-century English histories. There survives in the British Library a work titled 'Two Warlike Voyages into Scotland', which describes Somerset's invasion of 1547 and Elizabeth I's intervention on behalf of Scottish Protestants in 1560.[125] It is sometimes known as the Harleian MS on account of its catalogue reference (Harleian MS 540). We do not know who wrote 'Two Warlike Voyages'. The section dealing with Pinkie was probably not written by an eyewitness, but it may have been composed quite soon after the battle as there is a comment that the 1547 invasion was in 'September last'. The author of 'Two Warlike Voyages' is one of the few sources (other than Patten) that recounts the English journey into Scotland in any detail, including mentioning the English taking the castles of Dunglass, Innerwick and Thornton.

According to 'Two Warlike Voyages', at Pinkie the English army was split into three wards or battles, with Somerset in command of the main battle, the vanguard under Warwick, and the rear-guard under Dacre. Meanwhile Grey of Wilton was captain of the men of arms and demilances. There were also additional units of light horsemen, hackbutters and artillery.

The Scottish army had a vanguard led by Angus, the middle ward was led by Arran, and the rear-guard was led by Huntly. There is also a reference to Argyll's 'Irishmen'. The Scottish artillery included 14 iron bases and 12 pieces of brass. Before the battle the Scottish army supposedly had three camps beside 'Musselburgh River'. The English meanwhile were camped at Buckling Braes 'a mile and half' from the Scottish army.

The preliminary cavalry engagement (which the anonymous author misdates to 8 September) is described as going on for six hours and about 800 Scots were 'slain or taken' by the English. On the Saturday, Somerset set out with his army intending to camp at 'Henderuke' (Inveresk) Church, but the Scots foiled this plan by marching towards the English. When the two armies were within range the Scots fired a piece of artillery. The English fired back, also using guns from their fleet. The two sides continued to fire at each other for three hours, before the Scots tried to occupy a hill on the English army's left side. The English prevented this manoeuvre by taking the top of the hill themselves. Supposedly the English cavalry then attacked the Scottish vanguard and were forced to retire. As they did so, the Scots approached the English, their three wards joining into one. The 'Two Warlike Voyages' is the only written source that describes the three Scottish battles combining into one at the height of the fighting, although it appears to be shown in the copperplate engraving. Indeed, it is possible that this text was meant to explain the engraving.

The Scots soon halted about an arrowshot from the English line, being fired upon by the English artillery, archers and hackbutters. The Earl of Argyll's Irishmen were the first to falter and soon the whole Scottish army was fleeing. The English horsemen, and many of their footmen, followed the chase for six miles to the gates of Edinburgh. On the next day, after rounding up the Scottish artillery, the English advanced to Leith, which had been abandoned by its inhabitants.

The 'Two Warlike Voyages' appears to have only circulated in manuscript in the sixteenth century. However, Pinkie also made its way into major printed chronicles of the period. Pinkie is included in Richard Grafton's *A Chronicle at Large*, which was first published in London in 1569 by Grafton's son-in-law Richard Tottel.[126] The chronicle contains a relatively full account of the Battle of Pinkie, described as 'Musselburgh field, near unto a place called Pinkie slough'. However most of the information appears to be copied from Patten. A few details, including a reference to the Scottish camp being in a valley by the River Esk, may be derived from otherwise unknown eyewitness statements. In the main though (like much of the rest of Grafton's *Chronicle at Large*) the description of Pinkie is highly derivative.

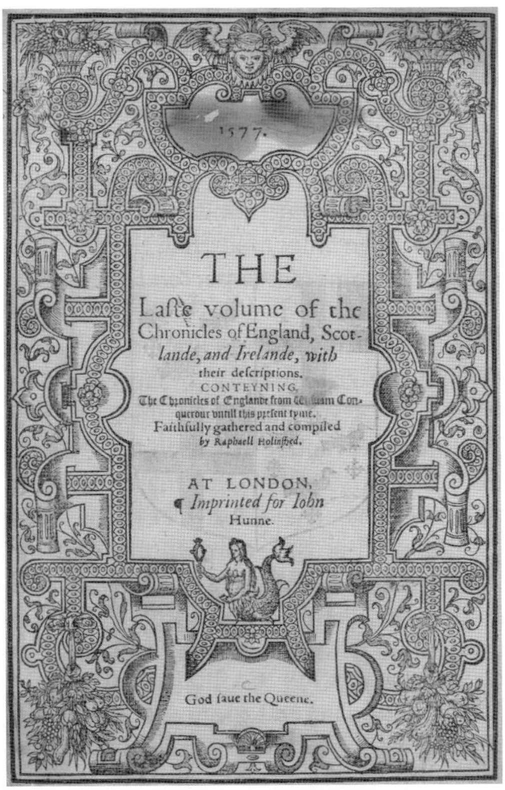
1577.
THE
Lafte volume of the
Chronicles of England, Scotlande, and Irelande, with
their defcriptions.
CONTEYNING,
The Chronicles of Englande from William Conquerour untill this prefent tyme.
Faithfully gathered and compiled
by Raphaell Holinfhed.
AT LONDON,
Imprinted for Iohn
Hunne.
God faue the Queene.

Figure 5.12: Raphael Holinshed, Chronicles, *1577 edition, title page of the second volume*

A description of Pinkie was also published in Raphael Holinshed's famous *Chronicles of England, Scotland and Ireland*. This work has gone through many editions, but the most relevant regarding Pinkie is the original 1577 edition.[127] There are actually two accounts of Pinkie in the 1577 edition. The first volume, chronicling events in Scotland, includes a description of the battle largely derived from the younger Lord Grey of Wilton's biography of his father, although Holinshed may have also used the history compiled by the Scottish historian John Leslie (discussed below).[128] In the second volume (Figure 5.12), which provides a reign by reign history of England, there is a full account largely derived from Patten.[129] There is little

the *Diurnal*, the two armies advanced. Both Scots and English were arrayed in three battles. Lord Grey with the English 'barded' cavalry attacked the Scottish vanguard, who 'footed their spears'. They killed 60 of the English horsemen and the rest fled. The Scots (who were facing English cannon fire) approached the enemy, but all of a sudden fled. In total 7,000 Scots were killed, and 600 English.

A much lengthier account is provided by the Fife chronicler Robert Lindsay of Pitscottie, in his *History and Chronicles of Scotland*.[136] Pitscottie's history was not printed until 1728, but several sixteenth-century manuscripts survive and seem to have had a wide circulation.[137] Pitscottie was born about 1532 but probably did not fight at Pinkie. He perhaps obtained information about the battle from his kinsman, the Lion Herald, Sir David Lindsay of the Mount.[138] Sir David may have been present at Pinkie, and certainly worked closely with men who were. Sir David's heraldic perspective on military procedures is possibly reflected in details such as the handing to Arran of lists of those who had mustered at the Scottish camp. As a herald, Sir David may have been particularly well placed to know about the negotiations between Somerset and Arran before Pinkie – a key feature of Pitscottie's account.

Pitscottie provides a firmly Protestant take on Pinkie. In his eyes it was not just the English who were the enemy. For Pitscottie, another enemy was just as dangerous, namely Arran himself, and his Catholic advisors: the Archbishop of St Andrews (John Hamilton), the Abbot of Dunfermline (George Durie), Mr Hugh Rigg and Archibald Beaton. In pursuing a Catholic agenda they misrepresented the willingness of the English to come to terms and were responsible for bringing disaster upon the Scots.

Pitscottie's account is in places confused and he seems to have had limited geographical knowledge of the area where the battle took place. Nevertheless, his account provides an interesting perspective on how later Scots perceived the events of 1547. According to Pitscottie, when news of the planned English invasion filtered north, the Scottish government issued a proclamation requiring military service by all men between 16 and 60. On the appointed day the Scottish army was mustered on the west side of the Esk.[139] The English army meanwhile camped above Preston. When the English viewed the Scottish army they saw that it was larger than they had anticipated and so tried to open negotiations, but Arran and his council rejected a peaceful resolution. Nevertheless, the English attempted again the next morning to initiate negotiations, this time suggesting a compromise over how long Queen Mary should remain in Scotland, but this offer was kept secret by the governor and his councillors.[140]

The English, disappointed by the response to their overtures and doubtful of a good outcome in battle, decided to turn for home. This was reported to the governor who, based on advice from his four problematic councillors, determined to attack the English.[141] The Scottish army was arrayed in battle order. The Earl of Angus was leader of the vanguard with 10,000 men, Governor Arran led the great battle with 20,000 men from Fife, Angus, Strathearn, Buchan, Stirlingshire and the burghs, and the Earl of Huntly led the rear-guard with 12,000 men from the north parts. The Earl of Argyll was on the right of the main battle with a force of West Highlanders, whilst a force of Islesmen (men from the Hebrides) were on the left.[142]

According to Pitscottie, Angus was ordered to march the vanguard over the Esk, but initially refused to do so, only moving when Arran sent a herald charging him to obey on pain of treason. Arran then crossed over to the west of Inveresk Kirk and arrayed his battle within sight of the English and awaited the governor and the rest of the army crossing the Esk by the bridge.[143] The English now realised they could not safely head for home and so Protector Somerset commanded Lord Grey to mount an attack with his great horsemen and demilances on the Scottish vanguard. Angus and the vanguard stood their ground. An order was given by trumpet blast for the Scots to lower their spears, which were long enough to dismount the English cavalry, killing 200 of them. The rest fled back to Somerset, reporting that it would be easier to break through 'a stone wall' than the Scots.[144]

Whilst Angus and the vanguard then advanced, some Highlanders broke ranks in order to pillage. Pitscottie alleges that someone in the main Scottish battle raised a cry of treason and the (Scottish) master gunner fired a shot from a great piece of artillery which killed the master gunner of England. The noise of the gun unsettled the Highlanders who started to flee. Because the army was passing through fallow land the dust was so great that visibility was poor. A more general Scottish flight then followed. Some of the English footmen, who were only a quarter of a mile away, also turned and fled.[145]

Figure 5.15: John Leslie, bishop of Ross, painting by an unknown artist, after 1580 (National Galleries of Scotland. Purchased 1922)

Both armies were thus in flight. However, Somerset and Warwick restored some order among the English and a cry went up that 'the Scots are fled; they are all our own'. The trumpets were sounded for an attack on the Scottish vanguard. Angus, seeing this, tried to manoeuvre his battle to stand with the remnants of the main battle and rear-guard. By this stage the weather was wet and misty, and poor visibility led Huntly to fear that Angus and his men were English, causing further chaos. The English foot and horse were by now attacking the Scots, and soon many of the latter threw away their weapons and ran away. About 10,000 Scots died, many from drowning in the river.[146] The fallen Scots included Lord Fleming, as well as the Masters of Erskine, Graham, Buchan, Livingston and Ogilvie. Some said the Scots were betrayed by their own countrymen, others that it was their own arrogance that let them down.[147]

Whilst Knox and Pitscottie's accounts of Pinkie have a firmly Protestant slant, John Leslie's analysis of the battle has a rather different religious perspective. Leslie was a committed Catholic cleric who continued working for the Roman Church even after the Scottish Reformation (Figure 5.15). He was appointed as the Catholic Bishop of Ross in 1566.[148] Leslie initially discussed Pinkie in his *History of Scotland*.[149] This work was written in Scots and presented to Mary Queen of Scots in 1571.[150] Leslie then wrote about Pinkie again in his Latin account of the Scottish people, *De Origine, Moribus, Et Rebus Gestis Scotorum*, published in Rome in 1578.[151] Leslie's Latin text was in 1596 translated into Scots by Father James Dalrymple (a monk living in the Scottish monastery at Regensburg in Bavaria), although this translation was not published until the late nineteenth century.[152]

There are minor, but significant, differences in the information provided in the 1571 and 1578 texts. Dalrymple also makes some emendations not supported by Leslie's Latin. One variation of interest is the statement only found in the 1571 text that on the morning of 10 September several of the Scots, especially the 'Irishmen', were killed by shot from the English galley, which had been rowed close to shore along with its pinnaces.[153] A detail only provided by the 1578 text (and Dalrymple) is the erroneous claim that the English camp before the battle at Salt Preston (Prestonpans) was beside 'Loreta' (the chapel of Our Lady of Loretto, Musselburgh).[154]

In 1547 Leslie was a canon at Aberdeen Cathedral, and probably did not take part in the fighting. Leslie may have subsequently discussed Pinkie with his patron, the Earl of Huntly and, as a life-long supporter of Mary Queen of Scots, would have also known other survivors of the battle.[155] Leslie spent some time in England and may have been aware of Patten's book. That would explain how Patten and Leslie have an identical list of leading Scottish casualties (Table 5.2). Leslie did not have a detailed knowledge of the location of the battle. For instance, he believed that Pinkie Cleugh was a hill and he did not have a name for the hill (Falside) that the two armies aimed to take. Unlike other Scottish chroniclers, Leslie expressed sympathy for Arran. He is also the only early source that claimed the English killed certain prisoners in cold blood.

Table 5.2: Pinkie casualties recorded in two or more early histories

	Patten	*Harl. MS*	*Leslie*	*Pitscottie*
Gordon of Lochinvar	x	x	x	
Ruthven, Master of	x	x	x	
Erskine, Master of	x	x	x	x
Fleming, Lord	x	x	x	x
Shelley, Edward	x		x	
Avondale, Master of	x		x	
Graham, Master of	x		x	x
Ogilvy, Master of	x		x	x
Livingstone, Master of			x	x

According to Leslie, after the English entered Scotland, there was significant skirmishing. However, Arran and the Scottish nobles were reluctant to offer battle and only intended to act defensively. The English, getting word of this, decided on 9 September to try and draw the Scots into battle by sending out a large force of horse backed up by footmen. They were met by a force of Scottish horse commanded by Lord Hume and some infantry. In the fierce fighting that followed, over 1,000 men were slain on both sides. Lord Hume was incapacitated by a fall from his horse and the Master of Hume was captured. Amongst the English taken by the Scots were three captains of light horse.[156]

Early the next morning, on 10 September, the English struck camp, intending to take a hill called Pinkie Cleugh and place artillery there. The Scots hastily arrayed their army in three battles, the vanguard led by Angus, the rear-guard commanded by Huntly and the great battle led by Arran, along with Argyll and other noblemen. Their speed was such that they almost became disordered. Meanwhile the English galley rowed close to shore and shot at them, killing many (especially the 'Irishmen') and causing fear throughout the army. The English, seeing the Scots on the march, placed their ordnance and their whole army on the head of the hill, awaiting the arrival of the Scots. The latter, tired by the weight of their armour and their hasty crossing of the Esk and marching, were already out of breath before joining with the enemy. Nevertheless, Angus and the vanguard attacked the English horse with great courage, killing over 500 of them, including Captain Shelley, Captain Ratcliffe, and the heir of Sir John Clarence. Lord Grey of Wilton was dangerously wounded in the mouth by a spear and the English standard was allegedly captured. The English retreated in disorder but were rallied by Warwick. Meanwhile some of the Scots had left their ranks so they could slaughter the English. According to Leslie, this confusion gave the English time to recover.

In the meantime the English great guns on the hill and in the ships wreaked havoc, whilst the English hackbutters (both horse and foot) fired so hotly that the Scottish vanguard was forced to retire.[157] This relatively disorderly manoeuvre brought the vanguard towards the main battle and was interpreted by many Scots as a sign that all had been lost. They suddenly turned and fled, giving the victory to the English, who pursued them with great fury. Some gentlemen who were taken prisoner, including the Masters of Erskine, Graham and Buchan, were killed after they had handed over their armour and been promised life. Other Scots who died in the fighting and the chase included Lord Fleming, the Masters of Ogilvy, Avendale, Methven and Ruthven, and the laird of Lochleven. The English also took nearly 1,000 prisoners, including Huntly and Lord Yester. Arran escaped, set the Earl of Bothwell free from Edinburgh Castle, and went on to Stirling where the queen was kept. The day after the battle the English gathered up all the spoil and marched to Leith. There they remained until 18 September, keeping their prisoners in Leith parish church although many of them were badly wounded.[158]

According to Leslie, the Earl of Huntly agreed to stand caution for the payment of the ransoms of most of the Scottish prisoners. Huntly is supposed to have owed a great deal to his own following, about 100 of whom had stayed with him on 10 September as the rest of the Scots fled. Several others fought and died around Huntly before he was forced to capitulate, partly exhausted by the weight of his armour.[159]

Another Latin account of Pinkie by a Scottish author is George Buchanan's *Rerum Scoticarum Historia*, first published in 1582.[160] Buchanan (Figure 5.16) was one of the leading academics of his day, and at the time of the battle was teaching in Portugal. He later returned to his homeland, eventually becoming tutor to the young James VI.[161] Buchanan was a committed Protestant and bitterly opposed Mary Queen of Scots after her abdication.

Figure 5.16: George Buchanan, a portrait attributed to Arnold Bronckorst, 1581 (National Galleries of Scotland. Purchased 1985)

Buchanan noted that the French fleet had scarcely departed from the siege of St Andrews Castle when news was brought that the English had gathered a great naval and military force to invade Scotland. Governor Arran assembled a considerable army at Edinburgh, which then marched to the mouth of the Esk to await the English. The Scottish horsemen annoyed the English on their march and attempted to provoke them to battle, but the English commander was at first reluctant to be drawn. He at last permitted Grey, the commander of his horsemen, to challenge the Scots with some troops of heavy cavalry and the Scots were put to flight. Many of the English, from their over eagerness in the pursuit, were taken captive.[162] Seeing there were more Scots than they had expected, the English prepared to negotiate rather than fight, but Somerset's letters were delivered to Arran, who only showed them to the Archbishop of St Andrews, the Abbot of Dunfermline, Archibald Beaton and the lawyer Hugh Rigg. Despite their lack of knowledge of military affairs, these advisors were confident of victory over the English forces and so ignored the English offer of peace.[163]

Like many other sources, Buchanan states that the Scots were divided into three battles, commanded by Angus, Arran and Huntly. However, a sudden rumour arose that the English were fleeing as a result of a shortage of supplies.[164] Governor Arran was impatient of delay and ordered Angus forward. Angus initially advanced slowly but was ordered to speed up. Eventually Angus crossed the river, the other two battles following at distance.[165] The English had been on the point of leaving when they saw the Scots advancing. Grey was sent forward with horsemen to delay Angus, until the English infantry took possession of a nearby hill. Most of the English cavalry were heavily armed and did not think the Scots could resist their charge. However, the Scots stood in close order with their spears projecting like a rampart. The first rank of the English was received on the points of the Scottish spears, whilst the next rank retreated. Like Pitscottie, Buchanan alleges that the English cavalry claimed breaking the Scottish ranks would be as hard as riding through a stone wall. The English horse were ready to take flight and order was only re-established with difficulty.[166]

The Scots were prevented from advancing against the English, largely due to the Spaniard Gamboa coming down on them with mounted hackbutters. This caused the Scottish vanguard to veer away. Seeing this, the Scots in the main battle thought their vanguard was turning to flee and themselves broke and ran. English horsemen then cut down the fugitives. The English were supposedly especially hard on the monks and priests who had fought. Interestingly, though, Buchanan claims that the 'Gaels' or Highlanders moved into a circle in good order and retreated without loss.[167]

Buchanan (and perhaps Leslie as well) may have influenced the account of Pinkie in the memoirs of John Maxwell, 4th Lord Herries.[168] Although Herries was born in the 1510s he does not appear to have been at Pinkie. Herries was a Protestant who remained loyal to Mary Queen of Scots after her deposition, and commanded Mary's cavalry at the battle of Langside in 1568. He was the author of a set of memoirs of his own times which survives in a seventeenth-century abridged version.[169] However, his description of Pinkie appears quite derivative. Perhaps Herries' most interesting contribution is his comment that 360 women of Edinburgh were made widows as a result of the battle. Herries also notes that the Protestant and Catholic factions each blamed the other for the defeat – suggesting that even in the immediate aftermath of Pinkie there was disagreement about what actually happened.

Overview

As might be expected, there are variations in the accounts of Pinkie. Nevertheless, some key points are repeated across a lot of sources. It seems there was a cavalry engagement a day or so before the main battle. The English won this skirmish but experienced some losses. On the night of Friday 9 September, the English were camped near Prestonpans, whilst the Scots were by the River Esk. On the morning of Saturday 10 September, both armies were on the move quite early, with the Scots crossing the Esk to approach the English. The English and Scottish infantry were each arranged in three battles. At some point the English galley (and perhaps other vessels) fired on the Scots from the sea. There followed a phase when both Scots and English were heading for high ground overlooking the battlefield. The Scots in particular were moving at speed. The English managed to get some cannons up the hill, but much of their infantry were being outpaced by the Scots. The English then launched a cavalry charge. This was repulsed by Scots with pikes. In the aftermath of this attack, and whilst under fire from artillery and other projectile weapons, the Scottish army embarked on some manoeuvres which went wrong (possibly not helped by poor visibility). Part of the Scottish army broke and ran. Panic spread and a rout ensued in which the English cavalry cut down large numbers of Scots, whilst others drowned in the Esk. This is the core narrative that emerges from the written evidence. Yet to understand the battle properly we need to relate the textual sources to the topographical and archaeological record.

Notes

1 W. Patten, *The Expedicion into Scotlande of the most worthy fortunate Prince Edward, Duke of Soomerset* (London, 1548). In this book folio references for Patten are given in relation to the original 1548 edition. We have assigned folio numbers beginning with the title page. There are also later reprints of Patten available online at https://archive.org. One was published in Edinburgh in 1798 by W. Dalyell in his *Fragments of Scotish* [sic] *History* (Edinburgh, 1798). The other is included in *Tudor Tracts 1532-1588* published under the name of A.F. Pollard (Westminster, 1903). Of these Dalyell's edition is closer to the original 1548 text. There is also a later Latin version of much of Patten's text by Ralph Starkey (died 1613). The manuscript is in the Bibliothèque Nationale in Paris (C. V. Colbert 35). It has been published as 'De expeditione in Scotiam commentarius' in Teulet 1, 124–58. See also Caldwell, 'The Battle of Pinkie', 63, 90, notes 6 and 7.

2 Patten, ff. 7v, 11v.

3 NRS, PC1, Register of Acts.

4 *RPC* 1, 59–82.

5 *RPC* 1, 75.

6 *TA* 9, 115–23.

7 *TA* 9, 116.

8 *TA* 9, 119.

9 *TA* 9, 113.

10 *TA* 9, 123.

11 RPS, A1547/9/1–3.

12 Many of them are listed in *ER* 18, pp. lxviii–lxx.

13 NRS, Notarial Protocol Book of Thomas Kene (NP1/2A), f. 123.

14 *APC* 2.

15 A. Clifford (ed.), *The State Papers and Letters of Sir Ralph Sadler, Vol. 1* (Edinburgh, 1809), 355–64.

16 See for instance: *CSP Scot*; *CSP Edward VI*; *CSP Dom. Add.*

17 For an example of some of the issues with the calendared texts see the discussion of the manuscript recording the Earl of Glencairn's advice to the English government in the summer 1547 in Chapter 2 of this book.

18 See *HP* 2 for published texts of many of the letters relating to the 1544 campaign.

19 *CSP Spain* 9, 168.

20 BL, Lansdowne MS 1236, f. 16.

21 BL, Harley MS 5087, ff. 16v, 17v–18r.

22 Selve, pp. xi–xiv.

23 Selve, 203–4 (no. 227).

24 Selve, 203–4 (no. 227).

25 Selve, 206 (no. 229).
26 Selve, 218–19 (no. 242).
27 M. A. F. Gorman, 'Jean Ribault's Colonies in Florida', *Florida Historical Quarterly* 44, no. 1/2 (July–October 1965), 51–66.
28 Selve, 221–23 (no. 242).
29 For more discussion of these aspects see Chapters 2 and 8 of this book.
30 *CSP Spain* 9, 151.
31 *CSP Spain* 9, 151.
32 *CSP Spain* 9, 151.
33 *CSP Spain* 9, 151.
34 *CSP Spain* 9, 151.
35 *CSP Spain* 9, 152.
36 *CSP Spain* 9, 152.
37 *CSP Spain* 9, 181–82.
38 *CSP Spain* 9, 181.
39 *CSP Spain* 9, 181.
40 *CSP Spain* 9, 181–82.
41 *CSP Spain* 9, 150.
42 *CSP Spain* 9, 150.
43 *Original Letters*, 43–44 (letter XXIV).
44 This dating is derived from internal evidence in the letter itself.
45 Patten, f. 153r.
46 Patten, f. 150v.
47 D. G. Greene, 'The Court of the Marshalsea in Late Tudor and Stuart England', *American Journal of Legal History* 20/4 (October 1976), 267–81.
48 Patten, ff. 148v, 151r.
49 P. Sherlock, 'William Patten (*d.* in or after 1598)', *ODNB*. Brian O'Kill's claim that Patten was the author of the report on the 1544 invasion of Scotland (*Hertford Exp*) has now been shown to be mistaken. See B. O'Kill, 'The Printed Works of William Patten (c. 1510 – c. 1600), *Transactions of the Cambridge Bibliographical Society* 7/1 (1977), 29–30; and H. Summerson, 'Sources: 1587', in P. Kewes, I. W. Archer and F. Heal, *Oxford Handbook of Holinshed*, 76.
50 Patten, f. 7r.
51 Patten, ff. 43v–64r.
52 Patten, ff. 64v–121v.
53 Patten, f. 80r.
54 Patten, f. 35r–v.
55 Patten, ff. 17r, 88v, 122r.
56 Patten, f. 64r.
57 Patten, ff. 66v–67r.
58 Patten, ff. 67r–69r.
59 Patten, ff. 69r–70v.
60 Patten, f. 72.
61 Patten, f. 79r.
62 Patten, f. 79r.
63 Patten, f. 80r.
64 Patten, f. 80r–v.
65 Patten, f. 80v.
66 Patten, f. 81r.
67 Patten, f. 82v.

68 Patten, f. 83r.
69 Patten, f. 83v.
70 Patten, f. 88r.
71 Patten, f. 91r.
72 Patten, f. 95v.
73 Patten, f. 101r.
74 Patten, f. 101v.
75 Patten, f. 104r–v.
76 Patten, f. 100r.
77 Berteville.
78 Patten, f. 57v.
79 Potter, *Henry VIII and Francis I*, 268; Patten, f. 146r.
80 Berteville, 1.
81 Berteville, 8–9.
82 Berteville, 12.
83 Berteville, 12–13.
84 Berteville, 14.
85 Berteville, 15.
86 Berteville, 15.
87 Berteville, 16.
88 Berteville, 18.
89 Jordan, *Chronicle and Political Papers*, p. xix.
90 Jordan, *Chronicle and Political Papers*, 7.
91 Jordan, *Chronicle and Political Papers*, 7.
92 Jordan, *Chronicle and Political Papers*, 8.
93 Digges and Digges, *Stratioticos*.
94 S. Johnston, 'Digges, Leonard (c. 1515 – c. 1559), mathematician', *ODNB*.
95 Patten, f. 93r.
96 Digges and Digges, *Stratioticos*, 158.
97 Grey, *A Commentary*.
98 Grey, *A Commentary*, 10–15.
99 Grey, *A Commentary*, 15.
100 Grey, *A Commentary*, 10.
101 Grey, *A Commentary*, 11.
102 Grey, *A Commentary*, 12.
103 Patten, f. 67v.
104 Grey, *A Commentary*, 13.
105 Grey, *A Commentary*, 14.
106 Grey, *A Commentary*, 14.
107 Grey, *A Commentary*, 15.
108 Grey, *A Commentary*, 15.
109 Hume, *Douglas History*, 271–73.
110 P. M. McGinnis and A. H. Williamson, 'Hume, David, of Godscroft (1558 – 1629 x 31), political theorist and poet', *ODNB*.
111 Hume, D. *De Familia Humia Wedderburnensi Liber* (Abbotsford Club, 1839), 42; G. H. Johnston, *The Heraldry of the Johnstons* (Edinburgh and London, 1905), 30; NRS, CS7/3/1 fol 239v.
112 The manuscript of the Pinkie Roll is catalogued as Bodleian, MS. Eng. Misc. C 13 (R). For Oman's discussion of the manuscript see: Oman, 'The Battle of Pinkie', 1–25.
113 Cotton MS Augustus I ii 56. For a good reproduction see Fleet and MacCannell, *Edinburgh*, 4–7.

114 West Sussex Record Office, PHA 4640.
115 Fleet and MacCannell, *Edinburgh*, 10.
116 The watermark is like Briquet's no. 12712 ('pot à couvercle surmonté d'une couronne fleuronné'). C.-M. Briquet, *Les filigranes; dictionnaire historique des marques du papier dès leur apparition vers 1282 jusqu'en 1600* (Leipzig, 1923).
117 Much of this paragraph is derived from ideas kindly offered by Dr Thomas Tolley of Edinburgh University.
118 British Library, CC.5.a.409.
119 When one of the authors (Caldwell) published a previous account of Pinkie in 1991 he underplayed the importance of this work. The only version of it known to the writer at that time being in the National Army Museum (accession no 7102-33-296). He was advised that it was printed on paper much later in date than the sixteenth century. However, the watermark on the version of the engraving in the British Library is similar to Briquet 13526 (paper from the Auvergne region found in England from about 1510). Caldwell, 'The Battle of Pinkie', 64–65.
120 This information on the map is derived from its BL catalogue entry. The underlying research and identification was published by P. Barber, 'Putting Musselburgh on the map: Two recently-discovered cartographic documents from the "Rough Wooing"', in P. van Gestel-vanhet Schip and P. van der Krogt (eds), *Mapæ antiquæ: liber amicorum Günter Schilder* (Houten, Netherlands, 2007), 327–38.
121 P. M. Jones, 'Gemini [Geminus, Lambrit], Thomas (*fl.* 1540–1562)', *ODNB*.
122 A. Pettegree, 'Wolfe, Reyner [Reginald, Reynold] (d. in or before 1574)', *ODNB*.
123 *English and Scottish Popular Ballads*, 5 vols, ed. F. J. Child (Boston, 1882–98), vol. 3, 378–79 (no. 172).
124 A. B. Friedman, 'A New Version of "Musselburgh Field"', *Journal of American Folklore* 66, no. 259 (January–March 1953), 74–77.
125 BL, Harleian MS 540, ff. 70–71; *Catalogue of the Harleian Manuscripts*, vol. 1 (London, 1808), 345.
126 R. Grafton, *Chronicle or History of England to which is added his table of the Bailiffs, Sheriffs and Mayors of the City of London from the year 1189 to 1558 inclusive*, 2 vols (London, 1809), vol. 2, 500–4; M. G. Ferguson, 'Grafton, Richard (1506/7–1573)', *ODNB*.
127 Holinshed, *The Firste Volume*; and *The Laste Volume of the Chronicles of England, Scotlande, and Irelande, with their descriptions* (London, 1577). See also P. Kewes, I. W. Archer and F. Heal (eds), *The Oxford Handbook of Holinshed's Chronicles* (Oxford, 2013), for detailed analyses and information on this and later editions.
128 Holinshed, *The Firste Volume*, 467–69. A. Blakeway, 'A New Source for Holinshed's 1577 Hystorie of Scotland', *Notes & Queries* 62/1 (2015), 53–56.
129 Holinshed, *The Laste Volume*, 1619–29.
130 Holinshed, *The Laste Volume*, 1626, and *The Firste Volume*, 473. For the Drumlanrig ambush see Phillips, *The Anglo-Scots Wars*, 214–17.
131 E. Hodnett, *Image & Text. Studies in the illustration of English literature* (Aldershot, 1986), 38–40.
132 Knox, *History*, vol. 1, p. xi; R. A. Mason, 'Writing Scotland's History', *SHR* 76 (1997), 55, 65.
133 Mason, 'Writing Scotland's History', 58–63.
134 Knox, *History* 1, 98–101.
135 *Diurnal*, pp. v, 44–45.
136 Pitscottie 2, 91–101.
137 F. L. Mackay, Reading Pitscottie's Cronicles: a case study on the history of literacy in Scotland, 1576–1814 (Glasgow University PhD Thesis, 2016), 34–47, 54–108.
138 W. W. Scott, 'Lindsay, Robert, of Pitscottie (c. 1532 – c. 1586), historian', *ODNB*; J. K. McGinley, 'Lyndsay (Lindsay), Sir David (c. 1486 – 1555), writer and herald', *ODNB*.
139 Pitscottie 2, 91–92.
140 Pitscottie 2, 92–94.

141 Pitscottie 2, 95–96.
142 Pitscottie 2, 96.
143 Pitscottie 2, 96–97.
144 Pitscottie 2, 98.
145 Pitscottie 2, 98–99.
146 Pitscottie 2, 99–100.
147 Pitscottie 2, 101.
148 R. K. Marshall, 'Lesley [Leslie], John (1527 – 1596), bishop of Ross, historian, and conspirator', *ODNB*.
149 Lesley, J., *The History of Scotland, from the death of King James I in the year MCCCCXXXVI to the year MDLXI* (Edinburgh, 1830), 195–203.
150 Lesley, *The History of Scotland,* 195–203.
151 J. Leslaeus, *De Origine, Moribus, Et Rebus Gestis Scotorum* (Rome, 1578), lib. X, pp. 461–65.
152 J. Leslie, *The Historie of Scotland, written first in Latin by the most reverend and worthy Jhone Leslie, Bishop of Rosse, and translated in Scottish by Father James Dalrymple 1596,* 2 vols (STS, 1888–95), vol. 2, 296–301.
153 Lesley, *The History of Scotland*, 197–98.
154 Dalrymple 2, 296.
155 Marshall, 'Lesley [Leslie], John', *ODNB.*
156 Lesley, *The History of Scotland*, 197.
157 Lesley, *The History of Scotland*, 198.
158 Lesley, *The History of Scotland*, 199.
159 Lesley, *The History of Scotland*, 200.
160 Buchanan, *History*, vol. 2, 364–68.
161 D. M. Abbott, 'Buchanan, George (1506 – 1582), poet, historian, and administrator, *ODNB.*
162 Buchanan, *History*, vol. 2, 364–65.
163 Buchanan, *History*, vol. 2, 365–67.
164 Buchanan, *History*, vol. 2, 367–69.
165 According to a footnote in a later edition of Buchanan's history this message from Arran was delivered to Angus by Archibald Douglas, sergeant at arms. Angus, who was being accused of treason, is said to have written on the back of it, for return to Arran, 'If you be as free of cowardice as I shall be of treason we shall have a good day of it'. G. Buchananus, *Rerum Scoticarum Historia* (Aberdeen, 1762), 449, n.2.
166 Buchanan, *History*, vol. 2, 367.
167 Buchanan, *History*, vol. 2, 368.
168 G. R. Hewitt, 'Maxwell, John, fourth Lord Herries of Terregles (c.1512–1583)', *ODNB.*
169 J. Maxwell (Lord Herries), *Historical Memoirs of the reign of Mary Queen of Scots and a portion of the reign of King James The Sixth* (Edinburgh, 1836), 19–21.

6

Pinkie Battlefield: topography and archaeology

Landscapes influence the outcomes of battles. A knowledge of the landscape of a battlefield is, therefore, vital to understanding the actions taken by competing armies (Figure 6.1). At Pinkie, some key landscape features which influenced the course of the battle, like Falside Brae, Carberry Hill and the River Esk, are largely unchanged. Other aspects of the landscape, such as the coastline at Musselburgh, have altered considerably since 1547. A number of the built structures mentioned by early sources are also still present, including Falside Castle, the 'Roman' bridge at Musselburgh and St Michael's Church at Inveresk, though they have all been considerably modified or rebuilt (Figure 6.2). Other built features may still survive, but the contemporary descriptions of them and their locations require some interpretation.

The archaeological record has thus far provided limited information about the action of the battle, meaning that detailed landscape analysis, combined with historical study, is essential. This chapter draws on the locational, directional, and distance information provided by historical sources, to examine the movement of the armies through the landscape, the positions of the army camps, and the location of the ultimate clash between the English and Scottish forces.

What's in a name?[1]

The sixteenth-century names given to the battle we now call Pinkie are of more than passing interest for understanding where the opposing armies were positioned on 10 September 1547. According to William Patten, the English and Scots did not use the same names for the confrontation. Patten states that the English called it 'Musselburgh Field' as that was 'the best town' near the 'meeting' of the two armies.[2] This term was used in a number of other sixteenth-century English sources, including in a note that William Cecil made in his family chronicle about his involvement in the battle.[3]

Yet Patten asserts that other names were also used. He claims that some Scots called it 'Seton' to suit an alleged prophecy about many being slain near there.[4] This comment reflects a knowledge of the poetic prophecies by then attributed to the thirteenth-century Thomas of Ercildoune (Thomas the Rhymer), which circulated in both Scotland and England in the sixteenth century.[5] Further names Patten notes include: 'Falside Brae' (because the English vanguard stood 'upon the side' of that hill), 'Inveresk Field' (reflecting the name of the fallow fields where the Scots stood

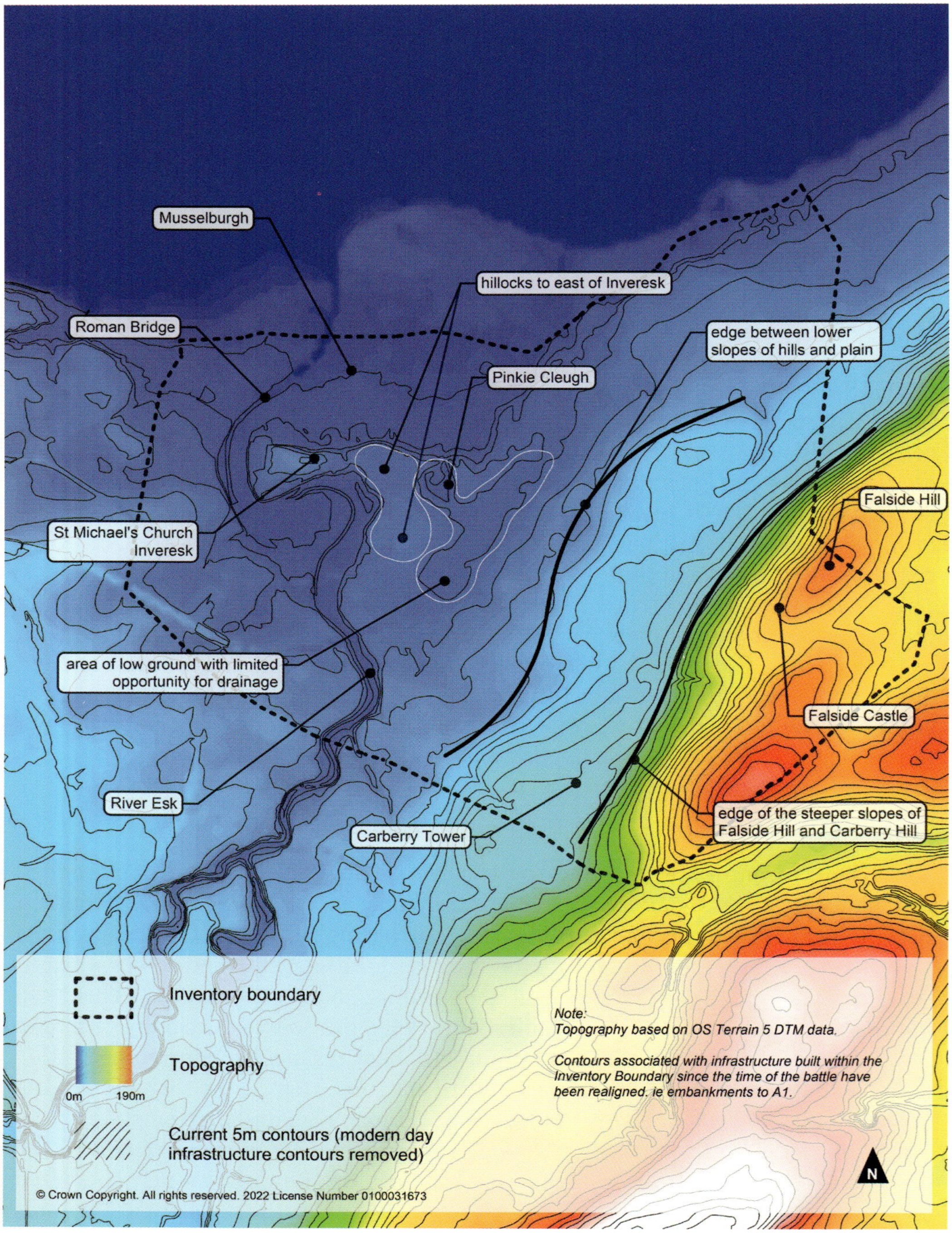

Figure 6.1: Topographical analysis of Pinkie Battlefield and surrounding area (Geddes Consulting Ltd)

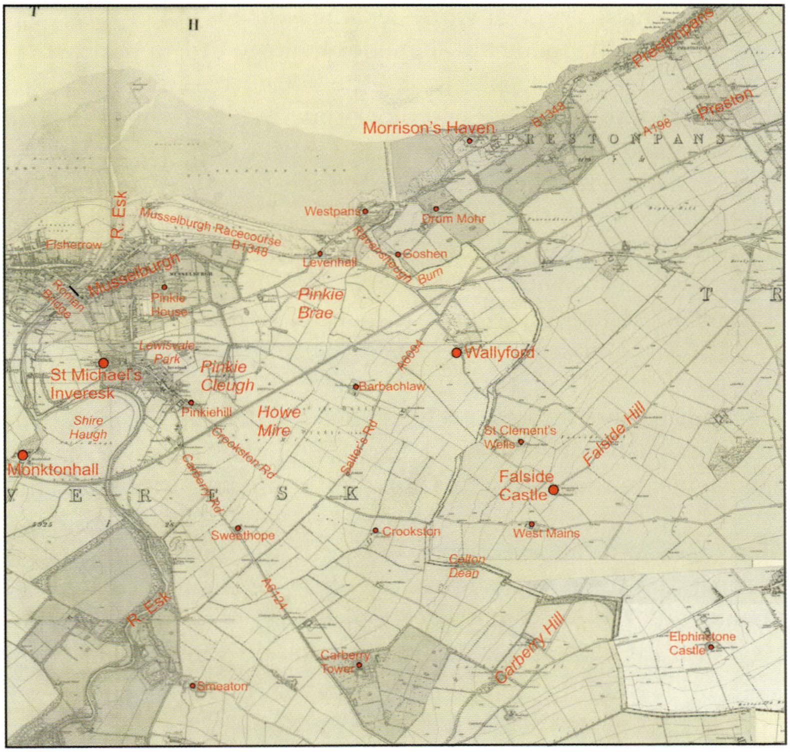

Figure 6.2: Map of area of battlefield showing places and features mentioned in the text; based on 1st edition Ordnance Survey maps through CC-BY licensing (courtesy of the National Library of Scotland)

Figure 6.3: Pinkie Cleugh, now the location of Edenhall Hospital, surrounded by trees, which hide its extent and depth. Only a tall chimney provides a clue to the presence of the hospital. Viewed from the Crookston Road, where it crosses the Edinburgh–Berwick railway line

and the two armies 'met'), and Wallyford (a name which is not properly explained by Patten, but is of course the name of the modern village just to the east of Inveresk). Patten's account of the varying names for the battle therefore implies that at the climax of the confrontation on 10 September the Scots were lined up on the arable lands of Inveresk while the English vanguard was on the side of Falside Brae.

So why do we now use the term 'Pinkie' or 'Pinkie Cleugh'? From an early date this name was given in many Scottish records. The phrase 'the field of Pinkie Cleugh' was already being used in the autumn of 1547 by the Scottish government clerks compiling financial records associated with the campaign.[6] Similarly, the Scottish Privy Council referred to 'the Field of Pinkie', whilst the name of Pinkie was also employed in the official register of acts and deeds when dealing with the consequences of the battle.[7] The term Pinkie or Pinkie Cleugh was used by sixteenth-century Scottish chroniclers.

Pinkie Cleugh is the hollow now occupied by the Edenhall Hospital (a nineteenth-century house previously known as Pinkieburn) (Figure 6.3). 'Cleugh' is a Scottish word for a gorge or ravine. In their progress from their camp towards Falside Hill the Scots would presumably have avoided this place, which was probably more of a topographical impediment in 1547 than is apparent now. As we will show below, however, it was Pinkie Cleugh that separated the two armies at the effective commencement of hostilities on 10 September, and the Scots may have looked over it for some considerable part of the day. It is drained northwards by a small burn, the Pinkie Burn.

Topographical overview

The general area in which the Battle of Pinkie took place is a coastal plain defined to the west by the River Esk, to the north by the Firth of Forth and to the south and southeast by a low range of hills, including Falside Hill rising to a height of 144 m above sea level. Its northwest facing flank or brae is reasonably steep, almost 1 in 5 (20%). The width of this coastal plain at the River Esk is approximately 4 km; at Prestonpans, about 6 km; and to the northeast of the mouth of the Esk, it narrows to less than 2 km before broadening out again eastwards. To the west of the Esk the land is relatively wide and flat on the approach to Edinburgh, some 10 km away. Within the area of the battlefield several landscape zones can be recognised. First, an area of blown sand (or links) adjacent to the Firth of Forth, now occupied by Musselburgh Racecourse. Second, a series of raised beaches, from about 7.6 m to about 30 m above sea level. The 30 m contour runs very approximately southwest to northeast on the line of Salter's Road, the A6094. Third, between these raised beach deposits and the foot of Falside Brae, there is a broad gently sloping area, the Fore-brae. Most of the landscape inland from the sandy area of Musselburgh Racecourse is, or was prior to modern developments, prime agricultural land (Figure 6.1). In the 1790s it was noted that the soil in the area varied 'according to its distance from the sea'. The 'flat' land around Musselburgh was naturally 'sandy', but 'having been for ages in a high state of cultivation for gardens and small fields' had become 'abundantly fertile'. The 'fields above Inveresk' apparently had 'better quality soil' and were highly fertile. Meanwhile, the land 'towards the hill' to the southeast (e.g. Falside Brae) had 'more of a clay soil', which if properly managed could produce 'great crops of grain'.[8]

The coastal plain has always been a significant line of communication between Edinburgh and Berwick (and ultimately London). The East Coast main line and the A1 dual carriageway that now cut through it are the present-day articulations of this important route. The River Esk is of course an obstacle to transport along the coastal plain. At the time of the battle the bridge at Musselburgh was the only dry way to cross it. However, on 10 September 1547 the Esk was apparently shallow enough for much of the Scottish army to wade across it to take up position on Pinkiehill.

The Esk flows northwards from Dalkeith and loops westwards round higher ground at Inveresk before entering the Firth between the neighbouring settlements of Fisherrow (to the west) and Musselburgh (to the east). The course of the river has probably changed since 1547, especially in the areas around Shire Mill and Shire Haugh, to the south of Inveresk. The nineteenth-century antiquarian, James Paterson, believed that in the 1620s it flowed above Inveresk in a more westerly direction, leaving the Shire Haugh almost wholly on the eastern side'.[9] Shire Haugh today is located to the west of the river and occupied by Musselburgh Golf Club.

The coastline at Musselburgh has also altered significantly since 1547. There is evidence for coastal erosion between Musselburgh and Prestonpans since at least the eighteenth century, possibly earlier.[10] In addition, the Levenhall Links reclamation scheme has pushed the shoreline out over half a kilometre, northwards from the links now occupied by Musselburgh Racecourse.

The harbour arrangements have probably also changed. Today there is a tidal harbour for small boats at Fisherrow but this does not appear to be of great age. It is possible that at the time of Pinkie some boats were brought into the mouth of the Esk (which is now unnavigable). However, it appears that even during the early modern period only smaller vessels could access Musselburgh from the sea. In the 1650s, Thomas Tucker reported to the English government that at Musselburgh there was 'an open harbour on the outside of their town', which was an 'opportune place' for 'the carrying out and bringing in of goods unto or from any ship that shall be lying in the road' – implying that goods were off-loaded from ships in deeper waters further out in the Forth and then ferried back to the shore.[11] In the early eighteenth century, Daniel Defoe remarked of Musselburgh that 'they call this a sea-port town', but as the river was 'not navigable' the residents did 'not meddle much with trading by sea'.[12]

There were few ports between Berwick and Leith that would have been usable by the larger English ships in 1547, with only Eyemouth and Dunbar being deemed in the 1650s as having 'good' harbours.[13] In the 1650s, Tucker specifically noted that from Musselburgh to Leith 'the shore being open upon a flat sand with some rocks before it, nothing can either safely or commodiously be landed'.[14]

There is sixteenth-century evidence for a small port to the east of Musselburgh at Preston Grange (Morrison's or Acheson's Haven).[15] However, it is not clear whether this had been constructed by 1547. A striking feature of the English progress into Scotland is the lack of evidence for Somerset being able to maintain regular contact with his fleet.

If there had been harbour facilities at Preston Grange when the English camped there or very close by on 8 September they would surely have used them. Instead, Patten merely notes that Somerset signalled for his admiral to come ashore to discuss tactics and report on the Scottish dispositions on 8 September. The next day English transport vessels did come 'to the shore' and victuals and munitions were unloaded, whilst the 'great' ships remained further out.[16] Interestingly, contemporary English accounts also do not mention the fort at Morrison's Haven, which was allegedly erected in the late 1540s by John Acheson, an officer in the King of France's Scots Guards.[17] The absence of any reference to this structure probably indicates that it was not there in September 1547.

Another major change to landscape around Pinkie is of course the extent of building and development. The area is now part of the commuter belt for Edinburgh, and the settlements towards the coast, such as Fisherrow, Musselburgh, Inveresk and Wallyford are now contiguous small towns. Further inland, smaller villages like Cousland and Elphinstone are scattered across the landscape, interspersed by farms. Some significant areas of farmland, including arable cultivation, do remain. Development in the area is

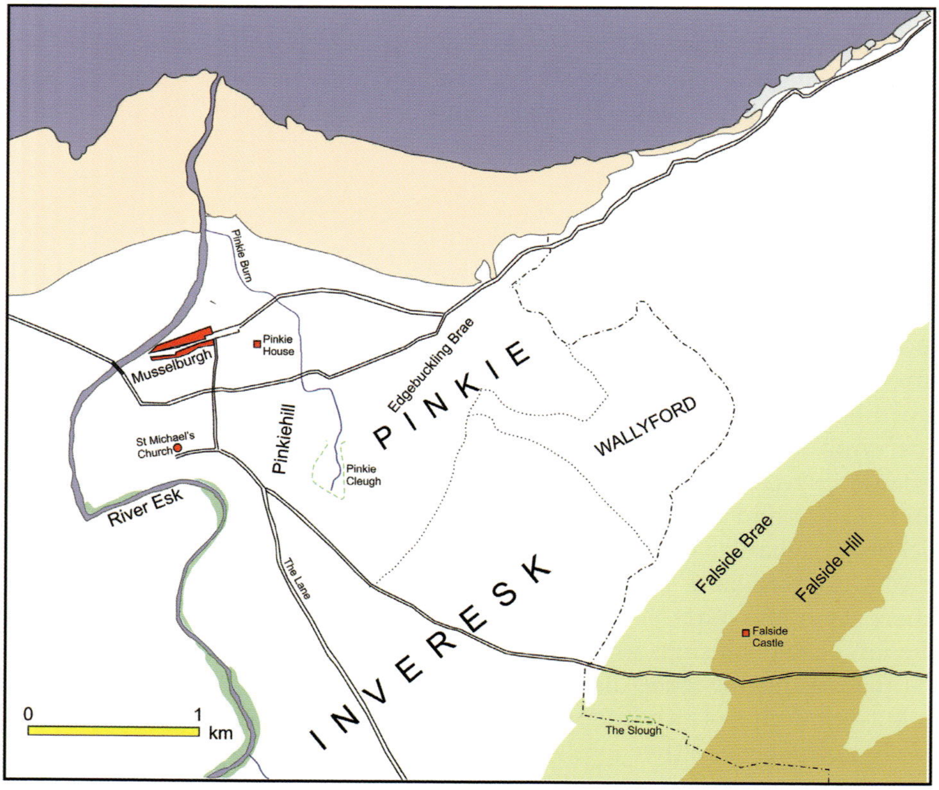

Figure 6.4: Map of area of battlefield in 1547. The estate boundaries are based on eighteenth- and nineteenth-century maps. Tree coverage was probably largely restricted to the banks of the Esk. 'The slough' (Colton Dean) is shown on the county boundary between Mid and East Lothian

ongoing, with new buildings being constructed at Wallyford at the time of writing. It seems likely that the landscape of Pinkie will become more densely occupied in the coming decades, distancing us further from the landscape of the 1540s.

Lordships and lands

Patterns of land use and holding, and associated boundaries, may well have influenced the movements of the two armies in 1547. The sixteenth-century property records for the area are patchy. However, when supplemented by later documentation and maps, an impression of the local tenurial structures, and the agricultural and industrial activities that were probably taking place in the area in the sixteenth century, can be obtained (Figure 6.4).

Much of the land around Pinkie was part of the Lordship of Musselburgh, which had long belonged to the important Benedictine abbey at Dunfermline in Fife (Figure 6.5). The lordship was contained within the county of Midlothian and extended to the boundary with East Lothian. The lands of the lordship of Musselburgh lay on both sides of the Esk. On the west bank they encompassed Monktonhall, and to the east included the burgh of Musselburgh, as well as the lands of Smeaton, Carberry, Wallyford, Pinkie and Inveresk.

Inveresk

Despite owning the land at Inveresk, the abbots of Dunfermline do not appear to have maintained a residence there. The estate centre was instead the parish church of St

Figure 6.5: Dunfermline town and abbey, Fife, from John Slezer's Theatrum Scotiae, *1693. The Benedictine abbey was an important, wealthy royal foundation, which owned the lands of Pinkie, Inveresk and Monktonhall. The Commendator, George Durie, was a close adviser to the Earl of Arran (The Trustees of the National Library of Scotland)*

Michael, served by a vicar appointed by the abbey.[18] It may have been at St Michael's that the abbey's officials received payments of rents and teinds (the traditional Scottish term for tithes).

At the time of the battle, the Abbey of Dunfermline still had not feued its lands at Inveresk. (Feuing was a form of perpetual lease which gave tenants much more security of tenure, in exchange for what was originally a relatively high fixed annual payment.) Instead, the land appears to have been farmed by 'kindly' tenants – in other words families who had some limited rights because of generations of occupation, but who could be more readily removed from their holdings than those with feu-charters. Most of the families farming at Inveresk appear to have had relatively limited holdings. According to a charter from 1563 the lands of Inveresk amounted to 41 oxgangs. These were occupied by 10 tenants, each holding from two to eight oxgangs.[19] An oxgang was nominally the area of land that one plough team could plough in a year, perhaps, typically, 13 Scottish acres (each about one and a quarter times an English acre).[20] At least two of these tenants, John Frog and Edward Merchanistoun, appear still to have been at Inveresk in 1581, when no less than 140 kindly tenants from Inveresk, Monktonhall and Smeaton, who were under threat of eviction, appealed to the Scottish Privy Council, claiming that they had occupied their holdings for several generations.[21]

In the 1750s the formerly open fields of Inveresk were divided and enclosed. A detailed measured map was created by Thomas Phinn at this time.[22] This map not only provides an overall plan of the land of Inveresk, but also named neighbouring properties. On this evidence Inveresk was historically bounded on the northeast by Wallyford, to the east it went up to Falside Brae, in the south it marched with the land of Carberry and on the west it was bounded by the Esk. The northern boundary was more complex. Part of it was bordered by Pinkie Fields, whilst the north-western corner stretched up to the high ground occupied by St Michael's Church.

Pinkie

Pinkie is first recorded as an estate in the twelfth century. The name appears to mean 'valley-wedge', as in the opening out of the Esk from Pinkie towards the sea.[23] Two pillars erected in 1770 at the original end of Musselburgh High Street mark the division between the town itself and the lands of Pinkie.[24] Placenames still current today (including Pinkie Cleugh, Pinkie Burn, Pinkie Brae, Pinkie Mains and Pinkiehill) show that the lands of Pinkie occupied an area east of the town of Musselburgh, north of Inveresk Fields and west of Wallyford.

In the sixteenth and seventeenth centuries Pinkie was often paired in documents with 'the Carse of Pinkie', sometimes just called 'the Carse' – a term used for fertile agricultural land, especially along a river. The Carse is not indicated on later maps, meaning there is doubt about its extent and location. It may have covered a relatively small area. In a document of 1617 the Carse is described as lying to the east of the orchard and yards of Pinkie House, and being bounded on the south, north and east by the commonty (common pasture land) of Musselburgh.[25] There is also a tantalising thirteenth-century reference to the Carse, which indicates that it included a saltworks claimed by Newbattle Abbey that was located in the lordship of Musselburgh.[26]

In 1547, the estate of Pinkie was leased from Dunfermline Abbey by George Douglas, brother of the Earl of Angus. When Arran besieged and captured the Douglas stronghold of Dalkeith Castle in 1543, he also sent a detachment to take Pinkie House from George Douglas and return it to the commendator of Dunfermline.[27] Nevertheless, George was given a 19 year tack of Pinkie and the Carse by the commendator, George Durie, in the following year.[28] This, however, specifically excluded the house and principal fortalice of Pinkie (also known as the Dow Inche) which Durie reserved for use by himself and subsequent commendators. It is therefore unlikely that Douglas actually resided at Pinkie. The land was probably occupied and farmed by the abbey's existing kindly tenants.

Wallyford

The lands of Wallyford stretched from the fields of Inveresk to the march with East Lothian. In the 1540s they were still part of the estates of Dunfermline Abbey but were subsequently feued. A charter of 1627 noted that the lands of Wallyford then had a manor and extended to about 11 oxgangs.[29] However, Wallyford was perhaps best known as a centre of coal production.[30]

Falside

The land of Falside lay to the southwest of the land of Inveresk, the boundary between the two also marking the dividing line between East Lothian and Midlothian. It is more than likely that this significant boundary would have been defined by a march dyke. It also marks a clear break of slope, the base of Falside Brae. In 1547 it is probable that the arable cultivation of Inveresk stopped at it and that the brae itself, which was too steep to be conveniently tilled, was pastureland.

Musselburgh, burgh lands

Another significant open space was the burgh lands of Musselburgh. These appear to have been located towards the sea, although it is difficult to ascertain their exact boundaries in the 1540s. By the late eighteenth century the common lands of the burgh extended eastwards to the Ravensheugh Burn, and the border with East Lothian. They would have been bound to the west by Pinkie Cleugh. In the 1790s the 'territories' of the burgh were described as extending 'along the sea-coast' for the whole width of the parish of Inveresk, and stretching inland for a distance of between half and a quarter of a mile.[31]

Settlements

The only settlements of any size in the general area of the battle in 1547 were Musselburgh and Prestonpans. The size of their populations in the 1540s is a matter of conjecture. Perhaps each were in the range of 1,000 to 3,000 occupants.

Musselburgh

The origins of Musselburgh, as a regional centre, extend back well beyond the early fourteenth century when it is recorded as a burgh dependent on Dunfermline Abbey.[32] The Battle of Pinkie Roll shows it as a single, straight street extending east–west, but not lined up with the bridge over the Esk (Figure 5.6). There is a tower with a steeple at its east end, possibly representing St James's Chapel, and what appears to be the tower of the tolbooth is shown half-way along.[33] The tolbooth tower still survives, although much of the rest of the building has been rebuilt (Figure 6.6). There are houses on both sides of the street. These have gable-ends and seem to be either of one or two storeys. The roofs are picked out in red but are more likely to have been covered with slates or shingles than ceramic tiles or thatch. The copperplate engraving represents the town of Musselburgh as two or three substantial houses, at least one of which had two storeys and crow-stepped gables. It may only have been after 1547 that the town expanded along the east bank of the Esk to the south of the bridge, as is represented on a sketch showing the meeting at Carberry Hill on 15 June 1567 between Mary Queen of Scots and the lords who opposed her.[34]

Figure 6.6: Musselburgh tolbooth. Only the tower pre-dates 1547 (David Caldwell)

Prestonpans

In the sixteenth century, Prestonpans was commonly known as Saltpreston. That name remained in use until the early eighteenth century.[35] Salt works are first recorded there in the thirteenth century and survived well into the twentieth century.[36] Coal mining dates back to at least the early thirteenth century.[37] The copperplate engraving shows the tents of the English camp behind the houses of this coastal settlement, which did not then have the status of being a burgh. There is no sign, however, of the Hamilton tower-house, Preston Tower, still standing, but much altered. It, or a predecessor, was destroyed by the English in May 1544 and it may still have been in ruins three years later.[38]

Other settlements

There were several estate centres and elite residences in the countryside around Musselburgh. The residence of the abbots of Dunfermline at Pinkie can be seen on the Battle of Pinkie Roll, where it is depicted as a tower-house surrounded by houses, near the coast to the east of Musselburgh. This structure was later incorporated into Pinkie House (now Loretto School), off the extended Musselburgh High Street.[39] It is not known if it was occupied or defended in September 1547. There is no specific record of it suffering damage at that time.

Two laird's houses figure in accounts of the battle, namely Cousland Castle and Falside Castle. Cousland Castle, is shown and labelled on the first and third tables provided by Patten (Figures 5.1, 5.3). It is also represented as a tower-house on the Battle of Pinkie Roll (Figures 5.6, 5.9) and the copperplate engraving (see Figure 1.1). On the latter it is in ruins, presumably as the result of destruction by the English. It is not known who occupied it at the time of the battle, but it seems to have been a possession of the Ruthvens.[40] The ruins of a tower-house, probably of sixteenth-century date, still survive above ground (Figure 6.7).

Falside Castle is now a heavily restored sixteenth-century L-planned castle and is a prominent landmark on the summit of Falside Hill (Figure 6.8). In 1547 the core of the castle consisted of a rectangular, four storey tower-house, and it was the home of the Falsides of that ilk.[41] The copperplate engraving shows it surrounded by other buildings, some 10 or so houses, according to Patten.

Two other nearby laird's houses, Elphinstone Castle and the tower-house at Carberry, are not mentioned in descriptions of the campaigning, although both are likely to have been within the range of troop movements on 9 September. Elphinstone

Figure 6.7: Cousland Castle, probably incorporating the remains of a tower house destroyed by the English in 1547 (David Caldwell)

was the home of the Johnston family and had a substantial fifteenth-century tower-house.[42] The tower-house at Carberry is believed to date to the sixteenth century, and in 1547 the land of Carberry was possessed by the advocate Master Hugh Rigg, supposedly one of the advisors who encouraged Arran to confront Somerset.[43] When the lands of Carberry were feud to Hugh Rigg in 1543 by the Commendator of Dunfermline there was no mention of any castle or tower.[44] Possibly it was not erected until after 1547.

Figure 6.8: Falside Castle in the late nineteenth century, in a drawing by the architectural historian, Thomas Ross. In 1547 the castle consisted only of the tower-house to the right of a later wing in this view. The castle was restored in the late twentieth century (MacGibbon and Ross 1887–92)

Another local landmark was St Michael's Church at Inveresk, less than a kilometre inland from Musselburgh. Inveresk is now a substantial village, however, the Battle of Pinkie Roll depicts only the church, with no adjacent settlement. It is possible that there were in 1547 few dwellings in the vicinity. Unfortunately, we have little information on the houses in the smaller rural settlements around the battlefield. There will have been a number of cottages, barns and yards for the tenants and labourers who worked and lived on the land. None of them are likely to have been an obstacle to a determined army on manoeuvres. A plan of the fort at Eyemouth made by an English spy soon after it was re-occupied by the French in 1557 shows a street of houses adjacent to it, most of which appear to be small single storey structures with hipped roofs.[45] Many of the dwellings around Pinkie may have been of a similar type.

Communications

The way taken into Scotland by the English army in 1547 was by Cockburnspath and East Linton, along what later became known as the great post road, nowadays the A1 (see Figure 1.2).[46] Important coastal settlements and castles at Dunbar and Tantallon were by-passed, as was the burgh of Haddington, the main town to the east of Edinburgh. To the west of East Linton, the way diverged from the A1 route on to, what is now, the A198 by Seton (Figure 6.2). It passed along the street of Preston village, past Prestongrange and Drum Mohr, to the coast just west of Westpans. It then went on the line of the later B1348 via Levenhall to Musselburgh old bridge, going to the north of Pinkie Cleugh and by-passing Musselburgh itself. West of the bridge the line of the road was basically that of the old A1, round the north of Arthur's Seat to

Canongate and Edinburgh. The road itself is not mentioned by Patten or in any other early texts, nor is it shown on the Battle of Pinkie Roll or the copperplate engraving, although the Roll does sketch in roads to the west of the Esk.

It is probable that the present 'old bridge' at Musselburgh contains significant elements of the medieval bridge that was there by 1547.[47] The Battle of Pinkie Roll and the copperplate engraving (see Figure 7.8) depicted it as a two-arch structure, though this need not be taken too literally. It presently has three arches, a length of over 75 m, and a width between its parapets of about 3.5 m (Figure 6.9). The relatively recent steps at both ends, which replaced earlier ramps, give a misleading picture of the accessibility of a structure across which it was possible to ride horses and wheel carts and gun carriages. In 1547 there was no other way to get vehicles across the Esk and no obvious detour to avoid it. The Scots had it defended by pieces of artillery. Patten's estimate that it was about 12 score paces (that is 240 paces = about a quarter kilometre) from the Firth is either plain wrong, and a warning of the inexactitude of some of his estimates of distance, or else this is more evidence of the shift in the coastline northwards since 1547.[48]

Another routeway that was of significance in the context of the battle is what Patten called a lane or a street, shown on his tables as running south from Inveresk

Figure 6.9: The old ('Roman') bridge over the River Esk. It has been destroyed and rebuilt more than once but probably incorporates much of the stonework of the bridge there in 1547 (David Caldwell)

Church towards the western end of Falside Brae (Figures 5.1–5.3). It is described as being 30 ft (about 9 m) wide and banked on either side by walls of turf and ell (about 1 m) high. By it, Somerset, Warwick and a small party approached within two flight shots of the Scottish camp on the afternoon of 9 September. The Battle of Pinkie Roll also depicted this lane running directly south from the church (see Figure 5.6). These sources support the interpretation that this road was the Carberry Road, the A6124, which was an extension of Inveresk Main Street and the modern Double Dykes Road, which leads north-eastwards towards the Scheduled Roman settlement of Catherine's Lodge.[49] It was probably a well-established road long before 1547, branching off from the Roman Dere Street, which passed through the Borders via the Roman fort at Newsteads and all the way to Crammond, the other side of Edinburgh. The Carberry Road would have provided access to the Roman fort and settlement at Inveresk.[50] More to the point, as far as 1547 is concerned, is that we can recognise that this lane was a loan or loaning, an enclosed track through cultivated land for driving animals. It was first recorded in a thirteenth-century Dunfermline Abbey charter as 'le Loning' connecting Inveresk with the wood of Carberry and Smeaton.[51]

According to Patten, Somerset gave orders on the evening of 9 September that artillery should be planted in this lane early the next morning to fire into the Scottish camp.[52]

Land use

Arable farming

At least some of the land on which the battle was fought appears to have been used for arable farming. In the 1540s, Scottish arable land was typically laid out in systems of rigs farmed as runrig, that is with the individual rigs of tenants interspersed and swapped from time to time in an effort to ensure that good and bad land was fairly distributed. There is a significant clue, however, that this was not the case in the region of the battlefield. Both Patten and Pitscottie state that at the climax of the battle the Scottish army was drawn up in a fallow field. Since both of these sources also commented on the dust raised, either by the Scots themselves or the English horse, it might also be reasonable to suppose that the fallow land in question had been ploughed.[53] Certainly, at the end of the eighteenth century fallow land in Midlothian might be ploughed as early as September for seeding with wheat.[54] The presence of a fallow field large enough to contain the Scottish army in 1547, implies that the holdings of the tenants were at that time consolidated – otherwise there would probably have been a patchwork of rigs, with some still fallow, some with crops and others harvested. A 1563 charter of the lands of Inveresk lists the dues to be provided each year by the 10 tenants.[55] Significantly, as well as money and capons, each tenant owed quantities of wheat, an indication of the high quality of the ground.

It is likely that much of the landscape from the Esk eastwards, inland from the coastal links and up to the lower slopes of Falside Hill, was dominated by systems of rigs and furrows, some enclosed with turf dykes, especially where they bordered pastureland. There were probably few trees, apart from along the banks of the Esk and other water courses. Aerial photographs show some rig systems of unknown date surviving as crop marks at Barbachlaw, east of Pinkie Cleugh, and in the area between Sweethope and Barbachlaw (Figure 6.2).[56] However, examination of aerial photographs and LiDAR data failed to provide any evidence of a boundary between cultivated ground and pastureland (Figure 6.13). That no clear division was discernible is likely a result of the intensive modern cultivation of land in this area, which has now extended up to the tops of Falside and Carberry Hills.

Commonty

Commonty was pastureland retained for use by the community as a whole. In 1547 it largely consisted of Edgebuckling Brae (Figure 6.4), land now known as Pinkie Brae. Either the tenants of Pinkie, or possibly the burgesses and indwellers of the burgh of Musselburgh, would have enjoyed access to it. Edgebuckling Brae is marked on John Adair's 1682 map of East Lothian.[57] In topographical terms the name related to sloping ground rising to a height of over 15 m above sea level, extending north-eastwards from Pinkie Cleugh. Edgebuckling Brae was clearly not land under cultivation since it was selected as the muster place for a Scottish army on 5 September 1548.[58] A curious tradition recorded in 1845, which noted that it was the furthest east which the archer guards of the Scottish kings were required to accompany their monarch, may just contain some memory that it was a recognised muster point.[59]

Mining

In the sixteenth century coal mining was a significant industry in the area between Musselburgh and Prestonpans and it likely shaped the landscape around Pinkie in 1547. There are no specific mentions of mine workings in the early accounts of the battle, but Patten provided a description of an incident on 8 September when a group of Scots were deliberately burned or suffocated in a 'cave' near Prestonpans.[60] The cave was clearly a mine working with at least three vents. However, Patten did not appear to understand this, nor show any other awareness of the importance of local coal production.

In March 1549, the burgh of Edinburgh supplicated the Lords of Council about the drastic rise in coal prices causing dearth and hardship. Since the Battle of Pinkie, they had more than doubled. The suppliers of coal that were cited in the document were all landholders from the general area of the battle, including Lord Seton, Newbattle Abbey and the lairds of Elphinstone and Falside. The 'potes' (pitheads) where the coal was sold included Tranent, Elphinstone, Edmonstone, the Grange (Prestongrange) and Wallyford. The Lords of Council did decide to try to regulate prices.[61] All this suggests that coal mining around Pinkie in 1547 was a significant industry that had experienced considerable disruption as a result of the English invasion.

Wallyford was a centre of coal production in the sixteenth century.[62] In 1543 the Earl of Arran had sought to raise tax revenue from 'the coal-pits of Wallyford and Preston'.[63] The coal industry clearly had challenges in the decade or so after Pinkie. At the time of the Reformation it was noted by Dunfermline Abbey that 'large expenses were made' in the 'winning' of the coal of Wallyford in 1556, 1557 and 1558.[64] Interestingly, in 1559 Arran's son apparently 'wasted' the coal at Wallyford in such a way that 'no profit' could be 'had thereof without great expense in time coming'.[65] In charters from the 1580s it was noted that the coal-works at Wallyford, as a result of long-standing practice, actually comprised all the pits and mines in the lands of Inveresk and Pinkie and those belonging to the burgh of Musselburgh.[66]

Coal mining must have had a considerable effect on the landscape in terms of pits, spoil heaps and water courses. This might particularly have presented challenges to horsemen. The extent of such workings in 1547 is not known, but when the English launched their cavalry attack against the Scottish vanguard on 10 September, it may have suited them to sweep round by Falside Hill, avoiding mine workings, growing crops and rigs and furrows on the lower ground.

Clues regarding the impacts that the coal extraction industry had on the landscape are provided by an indenture drawn up in 1532 between the abbeys of Dunfermline and Newbattle relating to the drainage and operation of their adjacent coal workings. Newbattle had significant coal workings on their land at Prestongrange, while Dunfermline had coal extraction on their estates of Pinkie and Inveresk. The agreement between the two abbeys mentions open stairs (ramps, shafts), levels (underground workings), dams and mills.[67]

A series of aerial photographs show extensive pitting, just to the east of Pinkie Cleugh and north of the main line railway[68] as well as coal sinks extending in two broad lines between Sweethope and Barbachlaw and the Howe Mire.[69] These can reasonably be interpreted as early mine workings but are largely of unknown date. They are on ground identified as part of Howe Mire on Phinn's 1756 map of Inveresk Fields.[70]

Howe Mire

In recent times, considerable attention has been paid to Howe (or How) Mire, supposed by Sir James Fergusson to be a morass that might in some way have affected the development of the fighting in 1547.[71] Howe Mire appears southeast of Pinkie Cleugh on Ordnance Survey maps. It is presently a field where crops are grown (Figure 6.10). It is not, and has not been for some considerable period of time, a marsh or bog. The area has been modelled along with Pinkie Cleugh and Barbachlaw as an area of low ground with limited opportunity for drainage (Figure 6.1).[72]

Howe Mire did not feature by name in early accounts of the battle, nor do they indicate a mire or bog as being relevant to the progress or position of either of the opposing armies on 10 September. In 1991 Caldwell, like others, assumed that it would have been of reasonable antiquity, and, if anything, more of an obstacle prior

Figure 6.10: Howe Mire, looking south-eastwards from the Crookston Road where it crosses the main railway line towards Falside Hill. It is now well drained arable land (David Caldwell)

to modern improvements in agricultural land.[73] The local minister in the 1790s, the well-informed Dr Alexander Carlyle, described how the Scottish army, after passing Inveresk Church, would have been sheltered from gunshot from the English fleet as the ground slopes from thence down to Howe Mire, in his time drained and cultivated but formerly a morass. From there the ground rises gently to the bottom of the hills of Carberry and Falside.[74]

In the Stirling University report on Pinkie battlefield, Ross noted that Howe Mire occurred as a placename in estate-papers extending back to 1717, but its location was not clear. His suggestion that it might originally have been an artificial drainage channel seems etymologically unlikely.[75] Elsewhere in the same report Richard Tipping described Howe Mire as a relict glaciofluvial channel, the source of the Pinkie Burn, which flows northwards through Pinkie Cleugh and is separate from the Esk. Phinn's 1756 map of Inveresk Fields showed four adjacent fields named as Wester, Middle, West part of East and Easter How-myre. The land in question stretched from the Crookston Road along the north side of where the railway line now runs.[76]

From his research in estate papers Ross identified that the first record of sustained flooding on the fields of Inveresk and Pinkie was in the 1790s, and this resulted in the estate deciding to deepen and widen an existing drainage ditch running westwards to the Carberry Burn.[77] An existing bridge over the burn was strengthened to cope with the increased flow of water. Ross speculated that the flooding might have been caused by an increased amount of sediment flowing off Falside Hill and Carberry Hill after the rig and furrow on them had been flattened.[78] A core from Howe Mire did provide evidence for poor drainage, probable peat accumulation in the past, but none of this amounts to clear evidence that Howe Mire was a marsh in 1547, which would need to be avoided. The best interpretation of the evidence appears to be that boggy ground in this area was the unintended consequence of much later agricultural improvements.[79]

On manoeuvres, September 1547

There are few precise timings for the troop movements during the battle. We have some clues regarding what time key events happened on 10 September. As noted in Chapter 5, there is a Scottish last will and testament that was witnessed at the Scottish camp at Monktonhall at 8 o'clock that morning. Patten also notes that some sections of both armies were already on the move at that time. There is evidence that the initial standoff between the two armies, before they moved inland, lasted three hours. Meanwhile the chase by the English cavalry is said to have lasted some five hours before it was recalled by Somerset ordering the sounding of a trumpet at 5pm. In September 1547, especially with the weather described as overcast turning to rain, options for noting time accurately were probably limited. The Musselburgh Tolbooth, however, is believed to have had a clock by this time and that might have provided some guide to both sides (Figure 6.8).[80]

The Scottish camp, 7–10 September

Early sources use a variety of place names to describe where the Scots camped before the battle. Patten states that the Scottish camp was about a mile square and located at Edminston Edge near Gilberton, a place belonging to the Laird of Brunstane, half a mile beyond Musselburgh.[81] Seemingly reinforcing this identification, a Scot named Bartholomew Balfour, killed on 10 September, had a document drawn up at Gilberton three days earlier.[82] Gilberton is an older name for Brunstane, located about a mile west of the old bridge over the Esk (see Figure 7.6).[83] In the 1790s the minister of Inveresk claimed that before Pinkie 'the Scottish army were encamped on that large field west of the Esk, which went by the name of Edminstone Edge'.[84] Unfortunately, the minister's account does not indicate if this place name was still used in the eighteenth century, or if the information came from Patten, with whose work he was clearly familiar. John Knox comments that on the morning of 10 September the Scottish army had 'betwix them and the English army the Water of Esk', whilst Pitscottie also notes that the army mustered on the west side of the river.[85] Patten's battle tables show the Scottish camp on the west side of the Esk (Figures 5.1, 5.2), as does the Battle of Pinkie Roll (Figure 5.10). There is therefore a significant body of evidence that places the Scots on the west side of the river, although Bishop Leslie of Ross did describe the Scottish camp as being at Inveresk.

It is possible that there was more than one Scottish camp. The Harleian MS 540 mentions three camps on the north (*recte* west) side of the river. Similarly, the sixteenth-century copperplate engraving of the battle also appears to represent three camps. Whether or not it was officially divided into three sites, the Scottish camp must have extended over a large area. As well as the fighting force, and in some cases their horses, there will have been the artillery train and waggons for food and supplies. There will also have been camp followers. In a detailed study of the Scottish army at Flodden in 1513, Caldwell suggested that there may have been 15,000 non-combatants along with a fighting force of 20,000, as well as 5,000 horses ridden on campaign along with a further 1,000 for baggage.[86] There is every reason to think that the proportions of fighting men to non-combatants and horses involved in 1547 would have been comparable, so on the basis of a fighting force of 22,000 to 23,000, there were perhaps about 39,000 men, plus 8,000 or more horses.

The size of camp for all of them would have been enormous. More research is needed on medieval and later military camps, but it is known that military strategists of the sixteenth century, for example Leonhard Fronsperger, looked back to ancient Roman models for inspiration.[87] The legionary fortress at Inchtuthil in Scotland, erected in the late first century AD, had an area of 21.5 ha (53 acres) for a force nominally 5,400 strong.[88] On that basis the Scottish camp in 1547 could well have been in excess of 150 ha, or to put it another way, might have occupied an area about 1 km by 1.5 km.

Digges' *Stratioticos* presented camp masters with formulae for calculating the area required for armies of different sizes and composition.[89] He noted that from his own experience an area 550 paces square (a pace probably being roughly equivalent to a yard) was necessary for either 1,000 horsemen or 10,000 footmen, which might suggest a Scottish camp somewhere in the region of a square mile, as estimated by Patten. The French military expert, Fourquevaux, described in 1548 how to layout camps. His estimate for a legion of 6,000 men was an area 660 paces square, apparently a more generous provision than that made by Digges.[90]

Patten's statement that to the east of the Scottish camp there were high and steep banks down to the river might indicate that the forward edge of the camp was positioned on the present day Monktonhall Terrace on the lands of Monktonhall, now a housing estate. This location is also indicated by contemporary Scottish documents. First are three related acts of a convention held by the governor at Monktonhall on 8 September granting relief from feudal casualties to those who should die fighting the English.[91] The second is the last will and testament of Master Thomas Slimon (Sluthman) of Edinburgh witnessed on the lands of Monktonhall about 8am on 10 September.[92] There is no evidence that there was an actual house at Monktonhall at that time that would have been large enough or prestigious enough to contain a parliamentary convention (Figure 6.2). Monktonhall here must refer to the location of the camp, and a meeting in the open air or under canvas.

The camp is said to have been protected on the seaward side by a turf wall mounted with two field guns and some hackbuts of crok (small pieces of artillery with hooks instead of trunnions for mounting them).[93] Patten's tables also show this wall and that access from the bridge was included within the area of the camp. Two assumptions that might reasonably be made are, first, that it would not have been feasible for English forces to pass round the north side of the camp, and second, that the turf wall was intended as protection from guns mounted on the English ships. These points might suggest that the north boundary of the Scottish camp was on the edge of the shore, where Fisherrow was later to develop.[94]

The east side of the camp was obviously protected by the River Esk – Patten described it as not very deep, but with high and steep banks that could readily be defended against an assault (Figure 6.11). His comparison with the Pease ravine, however, for whichever stretch of the Esk he had in mind, was an obvious exaggeration.[95] The copperplate engraving shows eight large pieces of artillery spread out along the riverbank, mounted to fend off attack from the other side. It would have been some of these guns that fired on Somerset's party after the cavalry engagement on 9 September as they made their way along the lane towards Inveresk Church. There were also pieces of ordnance positioned to defend the bridge.[96]

Figure 6.11: View from the River Esk westwards up the slope of Haugh Park to Monktonhall Terrace, the forward edge of the Scottish camp (David Caldwell)

According to Patten the camp was protected on the south by a great marsh, which is also depicted on his tables. In 1991 Caldwell thought that this would have been the low-lying ground known as the Shire Haugh, on the west bank of the Esk and due south of St Michael's Church, by then the well-drained Musselburgh Golf Course.[97] More recently, Richard Tipping has cast doubt on whether this could have been boggy ground in 1547. In a detailed scientific study, he concluded that the most likely location for an extensive marsh in 1547 would have been on the Dean Burn, a tributary of the River North Esk at Lugton Bogs, about 2 km to the west of Dalkeith (see Figure 7.6).[98] This may well represent the remains of the marshy ground through which the majority of the Scots fleeing towards Dalkeith are said to have sought safety when the battle turned into a rout, but it is much further from the coast than might have been anticipated for the right flank of the camp, approximately 5 km.[99]

That the Scots were camped this far south may be supported by other evidence. There is the statement by Patten that on 9 September the English horse chased the Scots for three miles (almost 5 km) from the summit of Falside Hill, almost to the furthest point of the Scottish camp on its south side.[100] If, as argued below, the chase passed by Cousland Castle, then the camp stretched on the west bank of the Esk well to the south of Monktonhall. Later on 9 September, when Somerset and his party viewed the Scottish camp from Falside Brae they were only about half a mile (0.8 km) to the southeast of it.[101] If we take into account that Patten nowhere uses the placename Carberry or Carberry Hill, and seems to have applied the name Falside to all of the higher ground hemming in the coastal plain, this observation is also consistent with a camp well south of Monktonhall.

The Stirling University team have also drawn attention to a placename, Camp End, on the A68 to the west of Dalkeith, and have speculated about it relating to events in 1547. They also suggested that Patten's description of the camp being at 'Edminston Edge near Gilberton' might relate to the present-day settlements of Gilmerton and Edmonstone, some 5 km to the west of the Esk.[102]

Clearly the information available on the location of the Scottish camp presents challenges. Was it further south than hitherto supposed or of really enormous size? On the one hand, it might be expected that the Scots would have positioned themselves to prevent the English crossing the bridge unopposed. On the other hand, some Scottish commanders might have recalled how the Scottish patriot William Wallace allowed only part of an English army to cross Stirling Bridge unchallenged before attacking and decisively defeating it in 1297.[103]

Perhaps the best way to resolve the contradictions about the location of the camp are to recall how Harleian MS 540 mentions three camps on the north [*recte* west] side of the river, and three camps may be what is represented in the copperplate engraving of the battle (see Figure 1.1). In that case, we might suppose that the fighting force was in one camp, nearest the bridge, and the other two camps, further to the south, were reserved for camp followers, animals, supplies, etc.

While there seems generally to have been agreement that the main Scottish camp was in a position of some strength, there were obvious weaknesses, especially the fact that it was overlooked by the hillock occupied by the parish church of Inveresk. This high ground rises to a height of about 30 m above sea level and forms a level summit to the west of the church, now a burial ground. In assessing its strategic significance, it is worth pointing out that it was the site of a major Roman fort in the mid-second century AD, with an area estimated as about 2.7 ha (146 m by 187 m).[104] In 1549 the French expeditionary force in Scotland also built a fort here, perhaps not of dissimilar size, as part of their strategy to clear the English out of Scotland.[105]

The present St Michael's, parish church of Inveresk, dates to the beginning of the nineteenth century and is presumably on the site of its medieval predecessor.

Patten's battle diagrams, the Battle of Pinkie Roll and the copperplate engraving all show the church on top of a hill. The Roll depicts it as a cruciform church with a tower and spire at the crossing (see Figures 5.6–5.9). On the copperplate engraving it takes the form of an aisled church with a rectangular west tower and a projecting rectangular south aisle (see Figure 1.1). John Slezer's 1693 view of the coast of Lothian from Stoneyhill shows it as a cruciform church with a tower and steeple at the west end.[106] A painting of 1805 indicates that the steeple had, by then, been removed but the tower remained (Figure 6.12).[107] Its minister, a few years beforehand, described it as being 102 ft (about 31 m) long and 23 ft (about 7 m) wide internally, but with four aisles, two each side.[108] Such a building could provide shelter for a considerable detachment of troops and the tower was a readymade lookout post, if not a platform for mounting pieces of artillery. Harleian MS 540 noted it was the English intention to camp at the church, and Patten adds that Somerset wanted to mount his guns on the hill in order to fire into the Scottish camp.[109] Perhaps he intended to shelter his army to the east of the church from retaliatory Scottish fire.

Patten describes the (main?) Scottish camp as having four rows of tents, arranged east–west, about a 'prickshot' apart. A prick in this context was a target for archery practice. English legislation of 1512 required men of 24 years or more to shoot at a mark of at least 220 yards (c. 201 m).[110] Whatever the exact distance between the rows of tents, the impression provided by Patten's text, backed up by his tables, is one of orderliness and spaciousness. It is legitimate to wonder if he provided such detail because the layout of this camp was markedly different from his own experience of the English one.

Figure 6.12: The medieval church of St Michael at Inveresk (from a painting reproduced in 1857 by Paterson, History of the Regality of Musselburgh*)*

The Scottish commanders would have had their men camped in the units and order in which they would be deployed in the forthcoming campaigning. In that case, three of the rows would have been for the battles of footmen. Perhaps the fourth would have been for Argyll's archers and the prickers. Huntly apparently described the camp as a fort when he was quizzed after the battle by the French ambassador, de Selve. He believed that it was a sound option to remain in it rather than advance towards the English army.[111]

Patten's tables show tents, represented as triangles, each row with three to four columns and four rows, amounting to 48 or 50 tents, a total not to be taken literally (see Figures 5.1–5.2). The Battle of Pinkie Roll depicts a scattering of large conical pavilions, held in place with guy ropes and with pennons fluttering at their tops (see Figure 5.10). The copperplate engraving also has an assortment of other tents, some smaller and some rectangular (see Figure 1.1). The governor's pavilions were kept in Edinburgh Castle. There were seven in all taken to the camp at Musselburgh, requiring 22 horses to carry them and a specialist group of 14 men to look after and erect them. When they were repaired or replaced the following year, yellow and red buckram was required to decorate their ridges.[112]

It is probable that other great men, and also burghs, supplied pavilions for themselves and their followers. Patten describes simple little tents consisting of a sheet of canvas stretched over two inverted V frames of sticks stuck into the ground. They were lined with straw for warmth.[113] Many, no doubt, would have created for themselves modest little shelters of wood, foliage and turf, like the shieling huts erected on the moors in summer in many parts of the country until relatively recent times. They were so common and ubiquitous as only very rarely to require any comment, like those of the Scots army at Otterburn in 1388, or the common soldiers in the Scots army camped out on Duns Law in 1639.[114]

The English camp (before the battle), 8–10 September

Patten wrote that on the nights of 8 and 9 September the English camped near Salt Preston by the Firth of Forth, and about a mile (1.6 km) from Falside Hill.[115] The representations of this camp in his tables show rather a jumble of tents in comparison to the orderly rows of tents in the Scottish camp (see Figures 5.1 and 5.2). On the basis of Patten's third table (see Figure 5.3), the English camp appears to have been in an oval enclosure abutting the shore, beside the Ravensheugh Burn.

Fearing a night-time attack Somerset made a late decision on the evening of 9 September to defend his camp by entrenching it, using his waggons and artillery to create a 'waggenboorowe'. Such defences had been created for English armies campaigning in Flanders earlier in the 1540s, like one at Englefontaine to the north of Landrecies in August 1543. The ditch around it is said to have been at a distance of about a pike and a half.[116] Patten's representation of the English camp erected close by on the evening of 10 September, after the battle of Pinkie, shows it as such a defended encampment (see Figure 5.3).

The copperplate engraving shows the tents of the English camp inland of Prestonpans (see Figure 1.1). Harleian MS 540 names the place as Buckling Braes; Knox describes it as Preston and about Prestonpans; Pitscottie places it above Preston under Tranent; Leslie describes it as at Saltpreston beside Loret; Buchanan says Preston.

Buckling Braes is an earlier form of the name Edgebuckling Brae, but this is where the English army is said to have camped on the evening of 10 September (see below), and so it is not unreasonable to assume that the writer of the Harleian manuscript is confusing days and events.

Leslie's mention of 'Loret' is misleading. He intended Loretto, a chapel dedicated to Our Lady of Loretto. Its location has been claimed to be at the entrance to Loretto School (Pinkie House) in Musselburgh north of the main road[117] and alternatively south of the main road in a piece of waste land.[118] It was clearly a well-known church, a place of pilgrimage. James V made a pilgrimage to it in 1536[119] and Mary of Guise walked there on foot in 1543 to pray for peace amongst her nobles and with England. In 1544 it was burnt or destroyed by the English army on its progress home from Edinburgh.[120] It was not near Saltpreston. Nor was it located to the west of a river mouth with a bridge, between Musselburgh and Leith, as shown on Patten's tables. The river in question is probably the Brunstane Burn, known to have been spanned by the Magdalene Bridge at an early date.[121] In that case Patten's 'Lauret' would be a misidentification for the collegiate church at Restalrig.

The English camp, like the Scottish camp, must have occupied a large area. Although Patten says it was in the vicinity of Prestonpans, he described it as being within sight of the Scottish camp and guessed that it was a little more than two miles distant from it. If this were true, it would indicate that it was further to the southwest than Prestonpans, perhaps extending from Preston Grange to Drum Mohr and Goshen. It might, then, have included the harbour facilities at Morrison's Haven.

Cavalry manoeuvres on 9 September

Patten wrote that the Scottish horse were 'pranking' up and down along Falside Hill on 9 September. A force of English light horse and demilances were sent to oppose them on even ground. Some of the action that ensued took place on the highest, and well-nigh nearest of the hills to the Scottish camp. This was clearly the summit of Carberry Hill (Figure 6.2).[122] John Knox's *History*, in the context of the encounter here in 1567 between Mary Queen of Scots and the Rebel Lords, described how there were ramparts erected by the English in 1547. The remains of a multivallate fort, obviously of Iron Age rather than sixteenth-century date, are being referred to, but it is reasonable to suppose that the fort was re-occupied by the English at some stage on 9 September 1547. Knox himself may not have been directly responsible for this part of his history, but perhaps David Buchanan who had it printed in 1644.[123] Hume of Godscroft has Somerset looking down from Carberry Hill on the Scottish camp on the 9th, after the cavalry engagement, and making the discovery that the Scottish army was bigger than he had expected.[124]

The initial sheet of the Battle of Pinkie Roll represents this military action on 9 September (see Figure 5.6). It is taking place on a hill in the background, at the top of the sheet. The hill is partially covered with rig and furrow, though only to the south of the Falside and Carberry summits where the land slopes more gradually away to the south. It appears already strewn with dead bodies. The rigs depicted would have been on the neighbouring lands of Elphinstone. The Lords of Council were later required to judge the liability of the holders of Elphinstone to pay teinds to the Abbey of Holyrood since their crops had been destroyed and taken away by the English and Scottish armies.[125] There is a tower-house below and to the right of the summit of this high ground. This was Cousland Castle, named and represented on Patten's tables although it is not mentioned in his text. It stood less than a mile south of Carberry Hill.

A large body of Scottish horse streams across the hill, perhaps in flight from smaller units of English horse approaching from the left. The brow of the hill is lined with the upright spears and English flags of other units. It is perhaps also of relevance to note an agreement drawn up on 10 September, in the immediate aftermath of the Scottish defeat, between the Scotts, Kerrs and others – that is Borderers who supplied much of the force of Scottish horse. This agreement that they should carry on the struggle against the English was made to the west of Cousland, presumably where these forces had withdrawn after their attack on the English.[126]

The castle is shown with a large force of Scottish horse around it, probably the same force already shown on the hill. This is a later phase of the fighting with English horse closing in from the back of the hill and some small groups of Scottish horsemen riding off to the right. Patten further tells us that the chase carried on almost to the south side of the Scottish camp, but does not indicate if any of the English forces crossed the Esk.

The Scottish army draws up in line of battle on the morning of 10 September

When the English advanced from their camp first thing on the morning of 10 September they soon discovered that the Scots had crossed the Esk and were arrayed in line of battle. The identification of this piece of ground is key to our understanding of how the battle developed.

It must have been selected by Arran as a strong position, perhaps failing to perceive that there might be a risk that some of it could be within range of guns on English ships. The English galley was able to get close enough to fire its artillery, killing (Robert) the Master of Graham, along with 25 others near him.[127] It is reasonable to suppose that Graham, with landed interests mostly in the northeast, would have been placed in the rear-guard under Huntly. Estimates of the range of guns of the period, even when based on contemporary manuals and treatises, vary greatly. It is the view of Caldwell that few pieces of artillery in use in 1547 are likely to have had an effective range of more than about 2,000 yards (1829 m), but others, for example Arnold, have suggested ranges up to 4,000 paces (that is yards?).[128] A great deal depends on what is meant by 'effective'. Assuming the English ships were very close in, and making allowance for the reclamation of land to the north of Musselburgh Racecourse, it is possible that some of their guns could have mounted an effective bombardment of the Scots, but only if they were not any further south than the ground between Inveresk Church and Pinkie Cleugh. In sheet 2 of the Battle of Pinkie Roll (see Figure 5.7), a large gun mounted in the bow of the large galley is shown in the act of firing. An ink line traces its shot between Pinkie House and the town of Musselburgh, ploughing into one of the Scottish units.

There was clearly not enough room on the high ground immediately adjacent to St Michael's Church for the full deployment of the Scottish army, but there was ample space further to the east, on ground now occupied by the village of Inveresk and Lewisvale Park and identified as an area of high ground in the topographical analysis shown in Figure 6.1. Early writers did not know of a convenient name for the high ground in question. Holinshed calls it 'Pinkhill', while Leslie (as translated by Dalrymple) gives it as 'the hill of the place named Pinkincleuch'. Pinkiehill is the name of a farmhouse on the road extending south-eastwards from Inveresk village towards Crookston and Falside Hill (see Figures 6.2 and 6.4 for the location of Pinkiehill).

According to Patten, what the English perceived as they approached from the east, was two hillocks between them and Inveresk Church where the Scots were mustered 'somewhat brim in our eyes'.[129] These two hillocks have caused much confusion because they are not at all apparent in the present day, largely built over, landscape. In the middle of the nineteenth century the minister of St Michael's Church thought that Patten was referring to two mounds in his churchyard. One, to the northeast of the church, had been removed, the other, to the northwest, still appears as a low spreading mound, called Oliver's Mound after a local belief that it was originally the site of a gun battery erected in the 1650s by Oliver Cromwell. The minister, however, noted that in his time it was also known as 'Dessé's Wark'; a much more apposite name since we believe that the mounds are most likely to represent the remains of the French fort erected here in 1549, perhaps specifically two of its bastions. The Dessé in question was André de Montalembert, sieur d'Essé, then commander of the French forces in Scotland.[130]

Even if these mounds were of earlier date than September 1547, they are neither in the right location nor on a large enough scale to answer the description provided by Patten, who marked them on his tables to the east of, and separate from the hill surmounted by St Michael's Church. To understand what Patten saw it is necessary to remove, digitally, the modern infrastructure at Inveresk, as in modelling undertaken in 2015 by Geddes Consulting in collaboration with AOC Archaeology Group (Figure 6.1).[131] This reveals an area of higher ground, separate from the church and immediately to the west of Pinkie Cleugh. The northern portion of it is now a broad level hilltop, much of it taken up by a cricket ground. The summit area extends to include a nursery and much of the area of the village of Inveresk. Its edges are defined by a steepish slope facing eastwards towards Pinkie Cleugh and westwards down to the River Esk. This would have been one of Patten's hills. The other, Pinkiehill itself, lies to the south, between the roads leading from Inveresk to Carberry ('the lane') and another heading towards Crookston. In 1547, viewed from the east of Pinkie Cleugh, it would have been obvious that there were two separate summits, but also a potential length, north–south, of over 1 km for a battle front.

The English army heads for Inveresk

Somerset's plan for 10 September, according to Patten, was to take the high ground at Inveresk and shoot his artillery into the Scottish camp. His route would likely have been along the main road, skirting to the north of Pinkie Cleugh and then through or around Musselburgh to the bridge over the Esk. The question is, how far did the English army get before it was brought to a complete standstill by the awareness that the Scots were in battle array ahead of them?

As we have seen, there is a lack of absolute clarity as to where their camp lay, and there are no detailed estimates of time that might allow a calculation of progress. There are only two clues from early accounts that provide some help. First, the armies were close enough that artillery was fired by both sides. The only early sources for this are the Battle of Pinkie Roll and Harleian MS 540, but if the range had been short enough for the shooting to be effective, surely it would have developed into a sustained battery that would have been reported by other sources. Second, when the Scots advanced southwards, news of this manoeuvre had to be brought to Somerset by Sir Ralph Fane, Lieutenant of the men-at-arms and demilances.[132] The explanation for this must be that the two armies were so far apart and positioned in such a way that there was no effective line of sight for the English high command. Balancing these two clues together suggests the English army was brought to a halt somewhere in the region of Levenhall (Figures 6.2 and 7.9), perhaps well over 1 km from the Scottish position.

Manoeuvrings in Inveresk fields

Both armies next turned inland. The English discerned, Patten reported, that the Scots meant to take the high ground of Falside Hill, and early sources are agreed that both armies vied for this advantage. It would have been relatively simple for the Scottish high command to order their battles to turn about clockwise and march in the same order, the vanguard first, towards that destination. Early accounts only speak of them progressing through a fallow field, the obvious route between the River Esk and Pinkie Cleugh taking them along the line of a road that may or may not have been present in 1547. This is now an unlisted road (Figure 6.2 – 'Crookston Rd') heading southeast from Inveresk to Crookston and then eastwards up to the summit of Falside Hill to the south of Falside Castle, where the slope is gentler than further along the brae.

To prevent the Scots gaining the high ground ahead of his own forces, Somerset launched a cavalry attack that was intended to stop them in their tracks. The key piece of information, provided only by Patten, is that the Scots were in 'a fallow field', the furrows of which lay side-on to the English attack. Adjacent to these furrows, and about a 'stones cast' from the Scots' vanguard, was a cross ditch or slough that the English had to cross. Those who could not leap over it 'stuck' in it, to 'no small danger of themselves and some disorder to their companions'.[133] It is only a guess, but perhaps a distance of about 100 m should be factored in for the 'stones cast'.

A slough is defined by the *Oxford English Dictionary* as a piece of soft, miry or muddy ground; also a ditch, dike or drain.[134] Patten also describes his slough as a cross ditch, which might be taken to mean one that ran at right angles to the adjacent agricultural rigs – except that is not what his tables show. They represent something linear, approximately on the same orientation as the rigs, which in reality would have been aligned with the slope of the ground, however slight (Figures 5.1 and 5.3, feature 'K'). It appears to have been straight and narrow with distinct edges, a feature that could be leapt over by some of the English horsemen, but in the bottom of which others got stuck.

We have already commented on Patten's awareness of the prophecies of Thomas of Erceldoune in connection with a supposed battle at Seton. His choice of the word 'slough' to describe a feature he also called a cross ditch must be seen as relating to his knowledge of these prophecies, which foresaw a battle at a place called 'Spynkarde cloughe'. The earliest surviving manuscript (The Thornton MS) that included this prophecy and placename is believed to date to about 1430–40. Another fifteenth-century manuscript (The Sloane MS) described the place as 'Spankard slough'.[135] It is possible that 'slough' had much more currency in England in general, and sources available to Patten, than 'cloughe'.

Patten, however, missed identifying 'Spynkarde Cloughe' as Pinkie Cleugh. This interpretation appears in the earliest known printed version of the prophecy, produced by Robert Waldegrave in Edinburgh in 1603 and was subsequently reprinted many times. Whereas the Thornton, Sloane and other pre-1547 manuscripts indicate that the Scots won a victory over the English in the battle in question, reinterpreted as Pinkie Cleugh, printed versions only mention much blood being spilled.[136]

Taking Patten's tables literally, this slough was a ditch that defined the south edge of the rig and furrow cultivated zone, which stretched southwards from Inveresk. In 1991 Caldwell suggested that the slough or ditch might now be represented by a small burn, a tributary of the Esk, which flows from near Colton Dean and to the south of Crookston (see Figure 1.11). He erroneously named it the Crookston Burn, a name that, he is now informed, is not known locally.[137] Although estate records indicate that it was widened and deepened at the end of the eighteenth century it does not appear now to be a major obstacle to determined horsemen, and, in any case, raises the issue of why Patten would have called a stream of running water a slough.[138]

Caldwell's 1991 identification of the slough was rejected in 2014 by Ryan McNutt in a thesis attempting to model the Pinkie battlefield. Instead, McNutt suggested it might have been one of several possible linear depressions (identified from LiDAR data) in the fields between Inveresk, Wallyford and the slopes of Falside Hill, or else the former Ravensheugh Burn (Figure 6.13). He did not comment or elaborate further

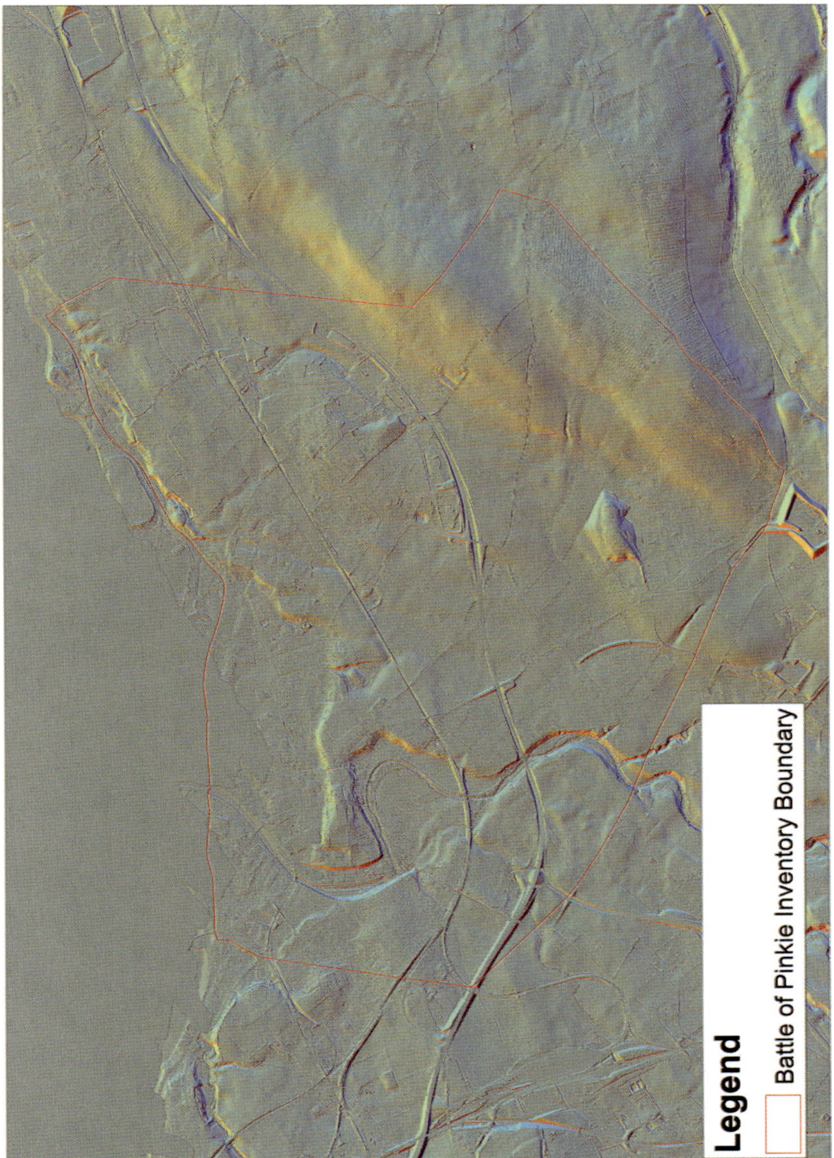

Figure 6.13: LiDAR analysis of the Pinkie battlefield using Multi-Hillshade x 16 Directions (AOC Archaeology Group). LiDAR was examined to identify somewhat ephemeral features that are not necessarily visible on the ground. At Pinkie, examination of LiDAR was undertaken in the hopes of identifying the boundary between land previously planted out as rig and furrow and that further up the hillslope that would have been used for grazing. Identification of such a boundary would help in narrowing the search for the slough and the square turf banked enclosure mentioned by Patten

on these linear depressions but focused attention on the Ravensheugh Burn, which LiDAR data indicated flowed parallel to, and north of the present day A1 before turning south-westwards towards Crookston.[139] The Ravensheugh Burn is depicted on eighteenth- and nineteenth-century maps as the boundary between the counties of Midlothian and East Lothian. It appears to have risen on Falside Hill to the south of West Mains and just to the east of Colton Dean, through which it flowed before turning north-eastwards and passing between Wallyford and St Clement's Wells.[140]

The stream supposed by Caldwell in 1991 to be the slough (see Figure 1.11) no longer appears to us to be a likely candidate. Even now, after it was widened and deepened at the end of the eighteenth century, it does not look much of an obstacle to a determined force of horsemen. The same would probably have been true of the Ravensheugh Burn where it passed between Wallyford and St Clement's Wells. Colton Dean, itself, however, does represent a serious obstacle to horsemen. It is a deep ravine, some 20 m wide and 5 m deep, encumbered with trees and is on the boundary between the lower and the steeper slopes of Falside Hill. It would make sense if it marked the usual limit, on its southern edge, of cultivation in 1547 (Figure 6.14). It is labelled as the slough on Figure 6.4 and features on Ordnance Survey maps as a wood, southeast of Crookston and southwest of West Mains (see Figures 1.12 and 7.11).

Figure 6.14: Aerial view of Colton Dean from the southeast, the direction from which the English cavalry would have approached it, assuming it was the slough described by William Patten (view from drone per Howard Wallace)

The extent to which Colton Dean may have changed or been altered since 1547 presents a challenge to this interpretation, especially given issues with drainage in this area from the 1790s mentioned above, and the disappearance of the Ravensheugh Burn. It is now relatively dry, but that is clearly due to a substantial piped drain that runs its length. The environmental archaeologist, Richard Tipping, also concluded, cautiously, in 2008, that Colton Dean could represent the location of Patten's slough.[141]

Identification of the location of the slough, may have proved easier, if the direction of the English attack was known, but that is not spelled out by Patten or other early written sources, and it is not possible to extrapolate it from the early visual sources. It can be pointed out that the English units of horse lay on the left flank of the battles of foot as the army was on the march, and so for a large force to be sent off to attack the Scottish vanguard the logical route would have been round the head of the marching foot units. This would have taken them up Falside Brae before descending down again to confront the Scots as they came towards them. Colton Dean would have been in the path of such a route.

If our analysis is correct, then we can envisage that the Scottish army, at the point that it was attacked by the English horse, was still in marching order, stretched out from about the position of the present-day steading of Crookston ESE for a distance, perhaps, of about 0.7 km, almost to Colton Dean.

Meanwhile, the English army was also heading inland towards Falside Hill. As it advanced, it appears that the distance between it and the Scottish army was getting less and less, so that, at the point that the English cavalry attack was launched, the vanguards of the two armies were, according to Patten, two flightshots apart.[142] A flightshot is the distance to which an arrow could be shot.[143] This might be supposed to be rather further than a 'prickshot', a term also used by Patten, seemingly to describe the distance of up to about 201 m over which an archer shot when firing at a prick (target).[144] Experimental work with long bows of the type found on the English royal warship the *Mary Rose*, sunk in 1545, demonstrates that they could be shot distances in excess of 300 m.[145] So, assuming Patten's eye for distances was reasonably reliable, that would suggest that the two vanguards came as close to each other as between 400 m and 600 m. Pitscottie's estimate that the two armies were a quarter of a mile apart (about 483 m) compares very well.[146]

The cavalry attack on the Scots gave time for the English foot battles to be turned around to form a battle line. Using Patten's figures for the size of the English force and making the same sorts of estimates as for the Scottish, it can be envisaged that when the English forces were drawn up to face the Scots, their front line would have been rather shorter than the Scottish one. No doubt, if a full-scale clash had developed between the two armies the English commanders would have attempted to use their superiority in mounted troops to stop their foot battles being outflanked.

Again, we are very reliant on Patten's text for a description of the location of the English deployment. He says that their forward had the full advantage of the hillside of Falside, but was, nevertheless, unable to stand full square in array because of a square, turf-banked enclosure to the west of them, 'upon their right hand' (*sic*), and towards the enemy. The main battle was next in order, partially on the hillside and partially on the plain. Then came the rearward, totally on the plain.[147] This plain was the gently sloping land previously described in this chapter as the Fore-brae, also occupied by the Scottish army.

Patten's tables show the turf banked enclosure close to the foot of Falside Brae, somewhat further west than Falside Castle (see Figure 5.1, feature 'E'). These diagrams also clearly indicate that one side of it coincided with the bottom of the hill, and it extended up slope from there. It was therefore in the county of East Lothian, over the boundary with the lands of Inveresk. It has been suggested to the authors that this enclosure may have related to the now Scheduled West Mains fort[148] located immediately southwest of Falside Castle. The fort, which is now identifiable through cropmarks only, represents the remains of a probably Iron Age, prehistoric defended settlement. Whilst now only surviving as subsurface remains it is possible that in 1547 some form of earthworks survived; its current condition, at least in part, likely to have resulted from modern ploughing.[149] However, the fort was circular in shape, rather than square like the enclosure described by Patten, and it is located just off the summit of Falside Hill rather than near the intersection of the hillslope and the plain as indicated by Patten's tables. For these reasons the authors feel it unlikely that the fort represents the remains of the enclosure described by Patten.

An enclosure at Sweethope was also noted to the authors as a possibility for the turf banked enclosure described by Patten. However, upon investigation, which included review of historic maps, aerial photographs and LiDAR data, the authors consider that the cropmarks visible to the west of Sweethope appear to coincide with field boundaries shown on the first edition Ordnance Survey map. Beyond the structures at Sweethope itself, now a hotel (marked as such on the bottom left of Figure 7.10), no convincing evidence of any enclosure has been identified. Furthermore, and in contrast to West Mains, Sweethope's location is fully on the plain with the hillslopes only beginning to rise in earnest south of the modern-day route of Salter's Road. The authors, therefore, are unconvinced that Sweethope could be the location of the enclosure described by Patten.

Based on Patten's description and topographical analysis, a reasonable interpretation is that the enclosure was a predecessor of the settlement at St Clement's Wells (see Figure 6.2). If that marked the position of the English forward, then it was about half a kilometre or a bit more away from our best estimate of the position of the Scottish vanguard. If the army had turned inland, as we suppose, from the region of Levenhall, we might expect that it ended up stretching from St Clement's Wells northwards through Wallyford.

The rout

Patten says that the Scots downed weapons and made variously for Leith, Edinburgh and Dalkeith. He noted that most of them headed for Dalkeith and the Battle of Pinkie

Roll seems to concur with this (Figure 5.9–5.11). He describes how the English chased the fleeing Scots for some five miles in length towards Edinburgh and Leith and four miles in breadth from the Firth towards Dalkeith, though he also wrote that, given the marsh towards Dalkeith, the horse could not effectively follow those that fled in this direction. He noted that the chase lasted some five hours before the cavalry were recalled to the Scottish camp where the tents were plundered.

Figure 6.15: The inscription on this simple monument in Lewisvale Park claims that it marks the site of Somerset's camp on 9 September. It was erected between 1761 and 1804, east of its present position (David Caldwell)

The English camp after the battle

Patten tells us that the English camped on the evening of 10 September at Edgebuckling Brae (Figure 6.4), about a mile from the previous campsite, while Berteville says they camped on the battlefield. This camp is shown on the third of Patten's tables, still on the coast but extending as far as the two hillocks. The drawing is not detailed enough to show Pinkie Cleugh. In contrast to Patten's representation of the earlier English camp on tables 1 and 2, this new camp is shown as being defended by a circuit of waggons interspersed with pieces of artillery, except where it bordered the shore (see Figure 5.3). It is probable that this camp extended over the field at Pinkie Mains where there were infantry barracks from 1803 to 1814.[150]

Some confusion as to the exact location of this camp is caused by a stone monument ('pillar') in what is now Lewisvale Park, to the west of Pinkie Cleugh, recording Somerset having camped there in 1547 (Figure 6.15). It dates to the eighteenth century but is not in its original location.[151]

The archaeology of the Battle of Pinkie

There has been increased interest in battlefield archaeology since the early 2000s. Much of this work has been interdisciplinary, relying on improving technology, such as Geographic Information Systems (GIS) and LiDAR, which allow for more detailed and accurate analysis of terrain, incorporating review of historical records and cartographic information. Such studies have aimed to identify areas of fighting and thus areas of archaeological potential.[152] Pinkie has been no exception as evidenced in work by archaeological contractors, the University of Stirling and individual researchers.[153] Given the nature of battles, archaeological recovery has largely been focused on finds, particularly those recovered through metal detecting (Figure 6.16).

The National Record of the Historic Environment (NRHE) records historic finds that it attributes to the Battle of Pinkie[154] and the East Lothian Historic Environment Record records over 130 archaeological investigations within the Battlefield (that is within the Battlefield boundaries as indicated by Historic Environment Scotland's Inventory). These will be discussed in detail here with an aim of understanding what archaeological recovery has already contributed to an understanding of the Battle of Pinkie and what potential it has for further contribution (Figure 6.17).

The battlefield area was already an extensively used landscape when the battle took place, one that contained significant areas of both agricultural and mining activity. These activities have carried on into the modern period, causing significant amounts of soil movement as have the construction of roads and railways. Modern and continuing development at Inveresk, Pinkie and Wallyford have rendered significant portions of the battlefield archaeologically sterile.

Clues within Patten's text point to a number of features that could potentially survive within the archaeological record. These include the remains of trenches

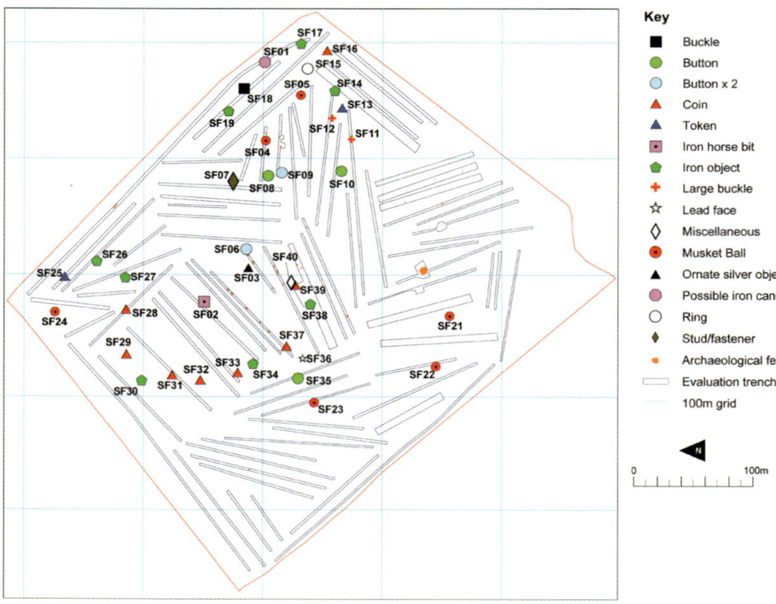

Figure 6.16: Plan of trial trenches excavated at Gula Flats (Area 3) with significant small finds marked. With the exception of a possible example of composite round shot, none were found to be demonstrably related to the Battle of Pinkie (AOC Archaeology Group). Provided here as an example of the extent of investigation undertaken in certain areas of the battlefield

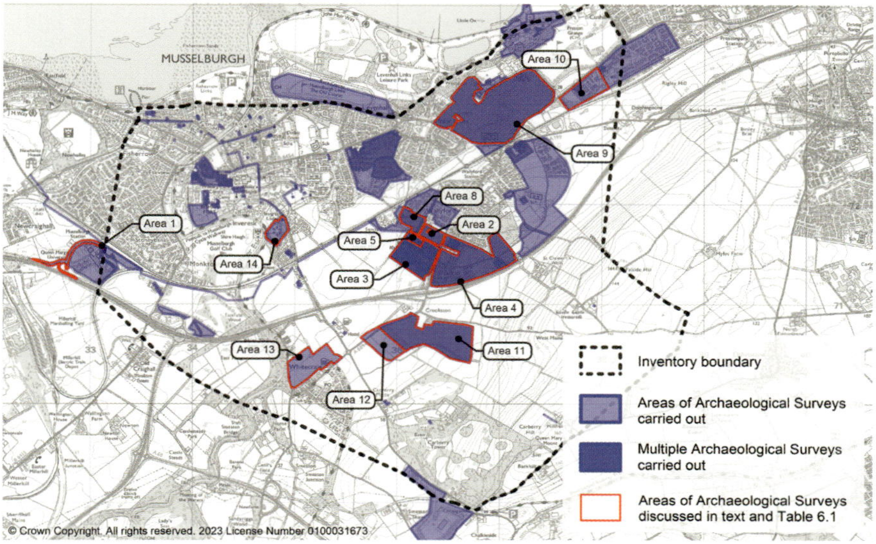

Figure 6.17: Map showing the extent of archaeological surveys within the Inventory area of the battlefield (Geddes Consulting Ltd)

dug around the English camp on the night of 9 September, the turf enclosure which inhibited the array of the English forward, and indeed the burial pits for the fallen English soldiers whom Patten indicates were buried the day following the battle. None of these features, as yet, have been identified.

In his 2008 study, the late Alasdair Ross, from an examination of estate records, identified changes that could have had a significant impact on the landscape and thus the archaeological potential of the battlefield. In the 1680s when a new field system was created on the Pinkie Estate, the work involved shifting around cartloads of earth, removing undulations and digging drains. Ross concluded that the documentary evidence pointed to a massive redistribution of the topsoil on both the Pinkie Estate and the fields of Inveresk prior to 1700. He also noted that leases issued after 1710 specified that all old traces of mining were to be filled in and levelled.[155]

It can be anticipated that the very makeup of the ground will have been affected by landscaping and other agricultural activities. The practice of farmers in earlier times, in an area extending for a distance of about five miles around Edinburgh and Leith, purchasing cartloads of 'street dung' to spread as manure on their fields, also has the capability of providing misleading evidence.[156] It is certain that this muck would have contained artefacts, including some that could be confused as battle losses from 1547.

Excavations at Wallyford Expansion encountered buried topsoil, beneath the current topsoil, the latter perhaps being redeposited from work on the A1 road.[157] Historic photographs of the construction of the A1, in the vicinity of the River Esk crossing, indicate the huge amount of earthmoving involved (Figures 6.18 and 1.13).

Figure 6.18: Photograph taken about January 1985 during the construction of the A1 dual carriageway, showing the extent of ground disturbance associated with building the road (photo by Ronnie Weir)

On this basis the original provenance of any finds recovered via metal detecting and from the topsoil in a wide area on either side of the road is questionable.

The identification of military equipment is, in any case, fraught with difficulties. Almost all the weapons and armour shed on 10 September 1547, including thousands of pikes, would have been gathered up straightaway. Only some small items like buckles and other clothing and harness mounts are likely to have eluded those scavenging the fields for anything of value in the immediate aftermath of the fighting. Pieces of shot and arrowheads fired on the day would have been recognised as having a worth, but were generally more likely to be missed since many would have thudded into the earth. So far, no arrowheads have been recognised amongst the archaeological material recovered within the battlefield area, but several pieces of shot have attracted attention and are considered further below.

Loss in battle is only one of several scenarios for explaining the recovery of pieces of shot. Small metal cannonballs were used in the game of bullets or henching in which competitors attempted to throw or roll them nearest a target. Shooting game, legally or otherwise, has been popular since the advent of handguns in the late fifteenth century and no doubt explains the presence of many pieces of lead shot commonly found during metal detecting exercises on greenfield sites throughout Lowland Scotland, whether or not a battle has taken place in the vicinity. This observation is based on the experience of one of the authors (Caldwell) dealing with stray finds submitted to the National Museum of Scotland for identification.

There are yet further challenges peculiar to Pinkie in interpreting artefacts that might be judged to be of the right type and date for events in the mid-sixteenth century. The area was traversed or fought over by Scottish, English and French forces on several occasions from 1544 to 1560. Many men were involved in more than one of these campaigns. These other military events include the passage home from Leith of the English army, shadowed by Scottish forces, on 15 May 1544, when Musselburgh was partially destroyed, and the occasion in September 1548 when the English army sent to relieve the siege at Haddington deployed in readiness to give battle to a combined French and Scottish force. The latter were protected by their fort, perhaps including the 'two hillocks' where Arran had arrayed his army a year earlier on the morning of 10 September, and the English were probably located approximately where Somerset halted his army at that time.[158] All of these events may have left artefacts similar to those which would have resulted from the battle. Barracks of the Napoleonic Era which occupied the area northeast of Pinkie Cleugh are likely to have contributed to the shot deposited in this landscape.

Historical finds

The NRHE records the Battle of Pinkie[159] and places it to the south of the current location of the Ordnance Survey 'cross-swords' and to the east of the Howe Mire within the area known as Gula Flats. The NRHE assigns to this location an entry in the Ordnance Survey Name Book, which, the NRHE claims, attributes a number of finds to the battle. These primarily comprise human remains and some metal artefacts related to weaponry and horses, including pieces of spears, swords, horse-shoes and officers' epaulettes. However, a review of the Ordnance Survey Name Book of 1852–53 itself indicates that that entry for the Battle of Pinkie describes a much wider area and that the finds recovered did not in fact come from Gula Flats. The entry states:

> The Battle of Pinkie encompassed a large extent of ground ranging from near the foot of the Pinkes to the farms of Falside and Carberry by Howe Mire, here the Scots came in close contact with the English. The Battle now commenced and raged with the greatest fury extending through the lands of Wallyford and Barbachlaw, until at last the Scots, were forced to fly, some towards Edinburgh and others in the direction of Dalkeith. From time to time large quantities of human bones have been found, in the tract of land described and at present, some are finding in a quarry at the foot of Pinkie Brae. Also pieces of spears, swords, Horses shoes and officers epaulettes have been found in a flat piece of land, then a moss lying immediately south of Pinkie Burn House.[160]

The finds referenced in NRHE as coming from Gula Flats are clearly stated as coming from a mossy area immediately south of Pinkieburn House (Edenhall Hospital). While this largely corresponds with the area now known as the Howe Mire, the description of the proximity to Pinkieburn House suggests that these were recovered from the north-western corner of the area, which has come to be known as the Howe Mire and not the eastern edge, as the NRHE point data suggests. The entry in the Name Book for 'Howe Mire' itself makes no mention of the battle or these finds.

None of these finds can now be traced and there has to be considerable doubt as to whether they have been correctly identified or could even be of the right date. Epaulettes would be most unlikely to date any earlier than the eighteenth century.

In addition, the human remains are noted as coming from Pinkie Brae to the north of the point data given by the NRHE, not from any low-lying mossy or boggy ground. The entry for Pinkie Brae records that human remains had been dug up there from time to time along the top of the brae. The surveyor, completing the entry in the Name Book, wrote that he himself observed upwards of 20 coffins being recovered from the quarry at the northeast end of the brae.[161] The First Edition Ordnance Survey map indicates that this quarry was in the vicinity of Levenhall, about 1.4 km to the north of the NRHE data point.

The bodies being recovered from Pinkie Brae and Levenhall quarry are described in the Ordnance Survey Name Book as including coffins; while the New Statistical Account notes in particular that they were recovered from stone coffins.[162] Stone coffins clearly indicate that these bodies were of a significantly earlier period, probably representing late prehistoric or early historic cist burials.

Such burials are relatively common throughout the coastal areas of southeast Scotland and examples are known locally at Newton near the junction of Salter's Road at the A68.[163] Indeed, the NRHE lists the human remains found at Pinkie Brae as long cists found at Musselburgh Links[164] and quotes the very same entries from the Name Book and the Statistical Account that are quoted for Howe Mire and the battle. The eminent archaeologist Audrey Henshall lists the Levenhall site in her body of work on Scottish long cist cemeteries.[165] On this basis, no case can be made that any of the finds historically related to the Battle and recorded by the NRHE are of the right type and date to have been lost on 9 or 10 September 1547.

Recent archaeological investigations

Since the early 2000s, the potential for encountering battle-related remains in the area between the Esk and Wallyford has been considered a possibility. This has led to investigations at a number of greenfield sites identified for future development within what is now the Inventory Boundary and these sites have been subject to archaeologically rigorous metal detecting surveys as well as, in some cases, geophysical survey and intrusive investigation as well as post-excavation analysis.[166] These areas are shown in Figure 6.17 and the relevance and significance of each area's finds in relation to the Battle of Pinkie are summarised in Table 6.1.

Table 6.1: Summary of finds possibly associated with the Battle of Pinkie

Report/Investigation	*Finds possibly associated with the Battle of Pinkie*
Whitecraig, East Lothian: Metal Detecting, Trial Trenching and Excavation (Wallace and O'Connell 2019) (Area 13 on Figure 6.16)	A total of 193 metal objects were recovered during the metal detecting survey. These included seven coins, two finger rings, multiple decorative objects, including buckles, an axe head and various agricultural objects. Initial examination has not identify any objects which can definitely be related to the Battle of Pinkie.

(Continued)

Table 6.1: (Continued)

Report/Investigation	*Finds possibly associated with the Battle of Pinkie*
Crookston Metal Detected Assemblage (Engl 2016 and McLaren 2017) (Area 11 on Figure 6.16)	Items which potentially relate to the Battle of Pinkie include four lead shot. On initial inspection one of these was thought to represent composite exploding shot, damaged as the result of use and/or impact. On the basis of further examination this was dismissed. Other finds possibly related to, or contemperaneous with the battle include a possible cast bronze, spherical sword pommel and two copper alloy mounts.
Crookston: Finds Recovered from Metal Detecting Survey (Caldwell 2016) (Area 11 on Figure 6.16)	These finds include 12 lead shot, five of which were flattened by impact; a silver badge with a red enamelled Tudor rose design (Figure 6.21), two copper alloy mounts (Figures 6.20 and 6.22); three copper alloy scabbard mounts; iron fragments, possibly of armour.
Land at Dolphingstone Farm, Prestonpans, East Lothian: Archaeological Works (Engl 2016) (Area 10 on Figure 6.16)	No artefacts directly related to the Battle of Pinkie were encountered.
Victory Lane, Barbachlaw, Wallyford (Oleksy and Wilson, 2016) (Area 2 on Figure 6.16)	No finds related to the Battle of Pinkie.
Gula Flats Metal Detecting Survey (Oleksy and Wilson, 2016) (Area 3 on Figure 6.16, part of Gula Flats)	No finds related to the Battle of Pinkie.
Wallyford Expansion Area 4 (Engl, 2015) (Area 4 on Figure 6.16)	The metal detecting survey recovered four pieces of lead shot (unfired musket, sprigged shot, two impacted musket balls) which may be broadly contemporary with the Battle of Pinkie. These finds have not yet undergone any post-excavation analysis and their dates cannot be confirmed.
Victory Lane Car Park (Engl and McLaren 2014) (Area 5 on Figure 6.16, part of Gula Flats)	No finds related to the Battle of Pinkie.
Inveresk Lodge: Metal Detecting Survey, Trial Trenching and Test Pitting (Franklin 2013) (Area 14 on Figure 6.16)	No finds related to the Battle of Pinkie.
Goshen Farm, Wallyford, East Lothian: Archaeological Metal Detecting Survey Interim Report (Hills and Anderson 2012), Goshen Farm, Wallyford, East Lothian: Archaeological Metal Detecting Survey: Final Report (Anderson and Neighbour 2012); Goshen Farm Musselburgh, East Lothian: Archaeological Evaluations (Savory and Glendinning 2016) (Area 9 on Figure 6.16)	Finds considered as possibly contemporary with the Battle of Pinkie include 22 pieces of lead shot, three round shot, one of which was composite, lead/iron, and a fragment of iron grenade. Only the composite round shot could confidently be dated to the period of the battle.

Small finds evidence

Table 6.1 and the discussion below refer to a number of different munition types. Lead shot refers generally to munitions of lead or lead alloy shot from firearms – hand held guns. From the late fifteenth to the nineteenth century smooth bore firearms were in use, which were loaded with small lead balls. The variety of these guns, their efficacy and the lock mechanisms that fired them improved over the years, but at present there is not enough detailed information on calibres or other scientific analyses to allow individual pieces of shot to be dated other than by the context in which they have been discovered. No pistols are specifically mentioned in the context of Pinkie in early sources, but it is probably the case that a few men on both sides would have been armed with them. Pistols of the period generally had smaller calibres than long guns like hackbuts. Most gun owners would have expected to cast their own shot using whatever metal came to hand and simple moulds.

Round shot refers to larger munitions which would have been fired from the pieces of artillery by both armies at the Battle of Pinkie (Figure 6.19). These might be of iron, lead or stone. Composite shot comprised an iron cube or stone encased in lead. This type of shot is considered to be particularly relevant to discussions of the Battle of Pinkie, as it is believed to date mostly to the sixteenth century. It is known to have

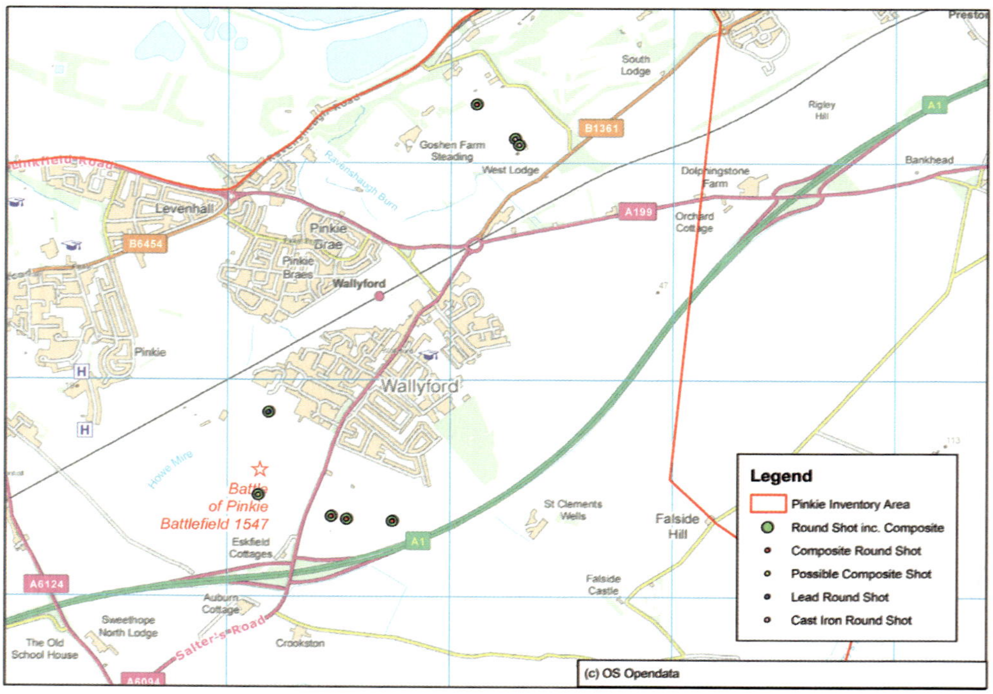

Figure 6.19: Distribution map of round shot recovered from the Inventory area of the battlefield (AOC Archaeology Group)

been used by the Scots as early as 1496 and has also been recovered from the 1545 wreck of the English warship, *Mary Rose*.[167] It is, however, not understood how late it remained in service. Case shot was also used with artillery and comprised a number of small lead shot or pieces of metal enclosed in a canister for firing. Cylindrical and conical wooden canisters of case shot have been recovered from the *Mary Rose*.[168]

Finds identified as possibly relating to the battle and which were recovered from the surveys at Wallyford Expansion (Area 4, Figure 6.17) and Gula Flats (Area 3, Figure 6.17), as outlined in Table 6.1, were subject to post-excavation analysis to determine whether they were associated with the Battle of Pinkie.[169] In addition, land at Barbachlaw (Area 8, Figure 6.17) was subject to metal detecting in 2005–2006.[170] While no resulting report is available for the survey, the finds recovered were also analysed. The results of the post-excavation analysis for the sites at Wallyford Expansion, Gula Flats and Barbachlaw (Areas 3, 4 and 8 on Figure 6.17) are discussed below.

Analysis of the finds recovered from Barbachlaw (Area 8, Figure 6.17) indicates that a total of 25 early modern lead bullets were recovered, 16 were provided for analysis. All were lead balls, with one bullet that might have represented firing as case shot. One lead round shot was also recovered. It is of a calibre which is compatible with firing from a small artillery piece such as a sixteenth-century falconet.[171]

Analysis of the finds from Wallyford Expansion (Area 4, Figure 6.17) identified shot which could be contemporary with the battle. These were stated to be four pistol balls, and four carbine balls. Three impacted examples lacked banding, which would be expected on shot fired directly from a gun barrel; leading to the interpretation that they may have been used as case shot. These shot were of lead with small amounts of tin likely resulting from the recycling of scrap metal. Two complete lead/iron composite shot were recovered along with one possible fragment. These were noted to provide evidence for the use of small artillery of two different calibres.[172]

Assessment of the finds from Gula Flats (Area 3, Figure 6.17) indicated that 10 lead bullets of early modern type were recovered, two of which may have been fired as case shot from artillery. It was hypothesised that if this was case shot, then several other pieces should be expected within 100 m to 200 m of the location.[173] More intensive surveys were undertaken at Gula Flats in 2014 (Area 5, Figure 6.17) and 2016 (Area 3, Figure 6.17) but recovered no further lead shot.

It was initially hoped that comparison of the finds from Gula Flats (Area 3, Figure 6.17) with the finds from Barbachlaw and Wallyford Expansion, taken together as a whole would help build a broader picture of potential battle-related remains. Altogether, the finds that may be attributable to the period of the battle amounted to a total of 41 lead shot from across the three sites.[174] However, only two composite round shot from the Wallyford Expansion Site (Area 4, Figure 6.17), a possible composite round shot from Gula Flats (Area 3, Figure 6.17) and the one lead round shot from Barbachlaw (Area 8, Figure 6.17) can be said potentially to be contemporary with the battle.

Survey prior to 2016 had been limited to discreet areas north of the A1. While areas such as Gula Flats (Area 3, Figure 6.17) and Wallyford Expansion (Area 4, Figure 6.17) have been subject to detailed surveys, no baseline had been established for the wider Inventory area. Additionally, the lack of comparable assemblages of artefacts recovered from battle sites contemporary with the Battle of Pinkie has also prevented a secure interpretation of the extent of the battlefield or movement across it from the finds alone.

In more recent years, since 2014, work by archaeological contractors has sought to increase the sample of surveyed areas south of the A1 and also to the north at Goshen. Previously surveyed areas have also been re-examined to test whether there might be potential for the recovery of more artefacts to support hypotheses on the location of the fighting in 1547.

Additional metal detecting survey was undertaken in 2014 at Victory Lane Car Park, part of Gula Flats (Area 5, Figure 6.17), and upon the rest of the land at Gula Flats (Area 3, Figure 6.17) in February 2016. The intensive metal detecting surveys did not recover any lead shot or other artefacts thought to be associated or contemporary with the Battle of Pinkie.[175] Further metal detecting at Wallyford Expansion (Area 4, Figure 6.17) only recovered four lead shot.[176]

Between 2012 and 2016 CFA Archaeology Ltd examined an area proposed for development at Goshen Farm. Goshen has traditionally been considered to have been the area of the English camp on 9 September and therefore had the potential to contain remains related to the encamped army and traces of the trenches dug for the protection.

Metal detecting within the area recovered 25 pieces of lead shot, including three pieces of round shot, one of which was composite. There was also a fragment of a cast iron grenade, and a further three pieces of lead shot were found during metal detecting which directly preceded trial trenching.[177]

Land at Crookston (Areas 11 and 12, Figure 6.17), to the south of the A1, has been subject to three metal detecting surveys since September 2016. A total of 19 ha have been surveyed to date, including a 13 ha field surrounding Crookston House (Area 11, Figure 6.17) and a further 6 ha field to the west (Area 12, Figure 6.17). The larger field was initially surveyed by experienced amateur metal detectorists and subsequently subjected to further archaeological metal detecting survey.[178] The adjacent 6 ha field was also surveyed by archaeologists.

The amateur metal detectorists submitted 307 metal items (133 copper alloy, 59 lead, 116 iron) for consideration by the Treasure Trove Unit. The majority of these are clearly, or probably, of eighteenth- to twentieth-century date. They include lead waste, copper alloy and iron fittings and pieces associated with harness, horses, carts, iron tools and nails, and some pieces of domestic origin, for instance five broken copper alloy spoons and a fragment of an iron cooking pot. Sporting activity is suggested by three trigger guards for guns, a bullet and a cartridge case.[179]

The surveys at Crookston undertaken by archaeological contractors led to the recovery and examination of over 1,000 items of metal, most of which could readily be identified as of eighteenth-century or more recent date. Some finds, at the time of writing, have proved difficult to identify or date in a meaningful way. They include buckles, possible fragments of armour, and six pieces of lead shot, three of which have been flattened by impact. A sherd from the rim of a cast bronze laver with a handle mount in the form of a human bust (Figure 6.20) is from a well-known late medieval type. Probably of similar date, is a bronze lid from a nest of weights. Neither a laver nor a set of weights are obvious items of equipment to have been carried on military campaign or to have normally been in a rural house or steading. A more likely explanation for both is that the pieces from Crookston got there in a cartload of midden from the streets of Edinburgh or Leith.

Figure 6.20: Part of the rim and handle mount, in the form of a human head, from a late medieval cast bronze laver, found at Crookston (David Caldwell)

Interest at this stage must focus on three mounts that can be interpreted as English military accoutrements of the sixteenth century. Two of them are of copper alloy, one in the form of an imperial crown (Figure 6.21), and the other a crowned flower design (Figure 6.23). The third mount is of silver, and has a rose design, originally enamelled red (Figure 6.22). Other copper alloy mounts, one for a strap and the other cross-shaped, could also date to the time of the battle, as could four pieces of lead shot, three of them distorted by impact.[180]

Figure 6.21: Copper alloy mount in the form of an imperial crown, found at Crookston (David Caldwell)

On the basis of the above, it is not possible to accurately define the extent or character of the action that took place during the battle based solely on the evidence of small finds. Despite extensive survey across considerable areas of the supposed battlefield, the conclusion from this archaeological effort must be that too few

Figure 6.22: Broken silver badge in the form of a rose, with traces of red enamel, found at Crookston (David Caldwell)

Figure 6:23: Broken copper alloy badge in the form of a crowned flower, found at Crookston (David Caldwell)

small finds, broadly datable to the sixteenth century, have been found in quantities or contexts which indicate that they can be demonstrably related to the battle. Potentially the most significant items are the eight pieces of round shot from the area of the battlefield (Figure 6.19) and the mounts with designs of roses and crowns from Crookston. The two cast iron pieces of shot from Goshen could reasonably be of any date from the late fifteenth to the nineteenth century. The piece of lead shot and the five composite shots are likely to date to the sixteenth century, but we do not have enough understanding to say whether they are English or Scottish, or to reconstruct their trajectories before they ended up in the ground – even supposing they are in, or close to their original place of deposition. If, however, the mounts from Crookston are accoutrements – English? – lost during the battle, they are more likely to give a clue as to where the fighting took place. They could be supposed to have been dropped to the ground where fighting took place.

Archaeological features

Given the evidence for soil movement in the years since 1547 it is possible that only archaeological features, now buried, will provide secure evidence for the battle. Such features could include the entrenchments around the English Camp and the turf banked enclosure on the lower slopes of Falside Hill, which interrupted the English array. A key discovery might also be the burials of the English dead made the day after the battle.

Human remains were discovered beyond the Inventory Boundary during the construction of Queen Margaret's University (Area 1, Figure 6.17). The bones were found by a member of the public during construction and the pit later identified by archaeologists. Dating of the bones indicates they are broadly of the sixteenth century and thus could relate to the rout after the battle.[181].

Archaeological investigations at Gula Flats (Area 3, Figure 6.17), Wallyford Expansion (Area 4, Figure 6.17), Barbachlaw (Area 2, Figure 6.17) and Goshen (Area 9, Figure 6.17) included not only rigorous metal detecting surveys but also trial trenching. At Goshen investigations were particularly aimed at identifying evidence for the entrenchments of the English camp occupied on 8 and 9 September 1547. No evidence of entrenchments was found and it was concluded that there was no archaeological evidence for the English camp having been at Goshen.[182] Whilst archaeological remains were found on the other three sites and included evidence of Roman, medieval and post-medieval occupation and agricultural activity, no archaeological features associated with or used during the battle were identified.

Intensive examination at sites such as Goshen and Gula Flats, including a number of follow up surveys at Gula Flats aimed at testing theories on shot recovery, failed to uncover any definitive evidence.

Despite a substantial number of archaeological investigations across the battlefield, including those at Wallyford Expansion, Gula Flats and Goshen designed specifically with a view to collecting archaeological evidence for the Battle of Pinkie, the results have effectively been negative. Whilst negative evidence can rule out the association of certain locations with the battle, it is considered that there remains the potential for the archaeological recovery of battle related finds and features elsewhere. The recovery of the three mounts (Figures 6.21–6.23) from Crookston that can be interpreted as likely English military accoutrements of the sixteenth century, indicates the potential for non-projectile metal finds to further contribute to our understanding of the battle. Further finds of this type may help to determine more precisely the location of the cavalry charge as well as providing more personal information with regard to the cavalry. Whilst a considerable amount of caution should be applied in associating certain finds and features recovered from the battlefield area to the Battle of Pinkie itself, the potential for the archaeological record to contribute to the understanding of the battle remains.

Notes

1 For more information on the early sources cited in this chapter, see Chapter 5.
2 Patten, f. 15r.
3 Hatfield House, CP 140/13.
4 Patten, f. 15r–v.
5 Thomas of Erceldoune, *Romance and Prophecies*, ed. J. A. H. Murray (London, 1875), pp. lxxviii–lxxix.
6 *TA* 9, 112, 115.
7 *APC* 1, 98. NRS, Register of Acts and Decreets, 1st series, CS7/3/1, CS7/3/2 passim.
8 *OSA* 16, 10.
9 J. Paterson, *History of the Regality of Musselburgh* (Musselburgh, 1857), 45.
10 CFA, *Pinkie Report*, 17–18.
11 T. Tucker, *Report by Thomas Tucker Upon the Settlement of the Revenues of Excise and Customs in Scotland, A.D. MDCLVI* (Edinburgh, 1824), 27.
12 Defoe, *A Tour*, 36.
13 Tucker, *Report*, 26–27.
14 Tucker, *Report*, 27.
15 A. Graham, 'Archaeological Notes on Some Harbours in Eastern Scotland', *PSAS* 101 (1971), 200–85; Canmore: https://canmore.org.uk/site/53652 (accessed 22 May 2019).
16 Patten, ff. 60v, 64r, 67r–v.
17 Canmore: https://canmore.org.uk/site/53664 (accessed 22 May 2019).
18 I. B. Cowan, *The Parishes of Medieval Scotland* (Edinburgh, 1967), 88.
19 *RMS 1546–1580*, no. 1475.
20 R. D. Connor and A. D. C. Simpson, *Weights and Measures in Scotland* (Edinburgh, 2004), 641–42.
21 *Register of the Privy Council of Scotland, vol. III, A.D. 1578–1585*, ed. D. Masson (Edinburgh, 1880), 396.
22 NLS, MS.5115, 04. Available at: https://maps.nls.uk/estates/rec/8023 (accessed 19 January 2023).
23 N. Dixon, The Placenames of Midlothian (Edinburgh University PhD Thesis, 1947), 133.
24 E. P. Dennison, S. Eydmann, A. Lyell, M. Lynch and S. Stronach, *Painting the Town. Scottish Urban History in Art* (Edinburgh, 2013), 360.
25 *Yester Writs*, nos 618, 1168.
26 *Newbattle R*, 186; *Holyrood Lib*, 48, 186.
27 *L&P*, 18/2: nos 353, 364.
28 *Yester Writs*, no. 618.
29 *RMS 1620–1633*, no. 1182.
30 For more discussion of coal production see later in this chapter.
31 *OSA* 16, 26; Hay's New Plan of Musselburgh, 1824: maps.nls.uk/towns/rec/7504 (accessed 3 Jul. 2020); *Great Reform Act Plan of Musselburgh* (London, House of Commons, 1832): maps.nls.ul/view/74491914 (accessed 29 June 2020).
32 G. S. Pryde, *The Burghs of Scotland, a Critical List* (Oxford, 1965), 44–45.
33 Paterson, *History of the Regality of Musselburgh*, 83–84, 94.
34 TNA, MPF 1/366/2.
35 *OSA* 17, 61.
36 *Holyrood Lib*, 48, 85; Canmore: https://canmore.org.uk/site/53734/prestonpans-salt-works (accessed 21 June 2020).
37 *Newbattle R*, 53.
38 Canmore: https://canmore.org.uk/site/53671 (accessed 29 May 2019); *Hertford Exp*, 11.
39 Canmore: https://canmore.org.uk/site/53873 (accessed 29 May 2019).
40 Canmore: https://canmore.org.uk/site/53403 (accessed 28 May 2019); *RMS* 2, no. 2986.

41 Canmore: https://canmore.org.uk/site/53666 (accessed 28 May 2019); C. H. Bedford, 'Notice of the Fawsydes of the ilk', *PSAS* 24 (1889), 370–78.
42 Canmore: https://canmore.org.uk/site/53340 (accessed 22 May 2019).
43 Knox, *History*, vol. 1, 99.
44 Canmore: https://canmore.org.uk/site/53362 (accessed 22 May 2019); *Dunfermline Reg*, 391–92.
45 British Library, Plan of Fort Point, Eyemouth (Cotton Augustus 1.i.60): https://imagesonline.bl.uk/077537 (accessed 11 July 2020).
46 See Graham, 'Archaeology on a Great Post Road', 318–47 for a detailed examination of this route.
47 Canmore: https://canmore.org.uk/site/53885 (accessed 28 May 2019). It is often called 'Roman' but there is no reason to think it is of such an age.
48 Patten, f. 70r.
49 HES Portal: http://portal.historicenvironment.scot/designation/SM3612 (accessed 27 December 2022)
50 M. Cook, *'Howe Mire: excavations across the cropmark complex at Inveresk, Musselburgh, East Lothian', PSAS 134 (2005), 150.*
51 *Dunfermline Reg*, 102 (no. 180); *DSL:* https://dsl.ac.uk/entry/dost/loning (accessed 2 July 2020).
52 Patten, f. 76v.
53 Patten, f. 100v; Pitscottie 2, 99.
54 G. Robertson, *General View of the Agriculture of the County of Midlothian* (Edinburgh, 1793), 15.
55 *RMS 1546–1580*, no. 1475.
56 Canmore: https://canmore.org.uk/site/82098 (accessed 17 Jun. 2020); ELHER: https://www.johngraycentre.org/collections/getrecord/ELHER_MEL2031/ (accessed 9 September 2022); ELHER: https://www.johngraycentre.org/collections/getrecord/ELHER_MEL95/ (accessed 9 September 2022).
57 NLS: https://maps.nls.uk/counties/rec/65 (accessed 6 May 2019).
58 R. Pitcairn, *Ancient Criminal Trials in Scotland, Volume First* (Edinburgh, 1833), 345.
59 *NSA* 1, 246.
60 See Chapter 7 of this book for further discussion of this incident.
61 *ADC*, 584–85.
62 *Dunfermline Reg*, 446, 456, 482.
63 *RPS*, 1543/3/40.
64 J. Kirk (ed.), *The Books of the Assumption of the Thirds of Benefices* (Oxford, 1995), 40.
65 Kirk, *Books of the Assumption*, 40.
66 *RMS 1580–1593*, no. 291.
67 *Dunfermline Reg*, 362–63.
68 Canmore: https://canmore.org.uk/site/77640 (accessed 18 June 2020).
69 ELHER: https://www.johngraycentre.org/collections/getrecord/ELHER_MEL95/ (accessed 9 September 2022)
70 NLS, MS.5115, 04. Available at: https://maps.nls.uk/estates/rec/8023 (accessed 19 January 2023).
71 Fergusson, *The White Hind*, 18.
72 V. Oleksy, B. Salter and R. Miller, *Battle of Pinkie 1547: Heritage Assessment* (AOC and Geddes Consulting, Report, 2015), figs 4.1–4.3.
73 Caldwell, 'The Battle of Pinkie', 81, fig. 6.
74 *OSA 16, 7.*
75 CFA, *Pinkie Report*, 19.
76 T. Phinn, *Plan of the Fields of Inveresk as distinguished by the valuators and division of the same among the several heritors* (1756); J. Laurie, *A Plan of Edinburgh and Places Adjacent* (Edinburgh 1766); and R. Kirkwood and Son, *A Map of the Environs of Edinburgh* (Edinburgh, 1817).

77 'Carberry Burn' is apparently a name not now in use locally. The burn in question flows westwards and south-westwards to the south of Crookston Farm.
78 CFA, *Pinkie Report*, 18.
79 CFA, *Pinkie Report*, 15–19, 21, 29. Writing in 2014, R. K. McNutt, Finding Forgotten Fields: A Theoretical and Methodological Framework for Historic Reconstruction and Predictive Modelling of Battlefield Locations in Scotland, 1296–1650 (Glasgow University PhD thesis, 2014), 314, appears to have been unaware of the work by Alasdair Ross and his colleagues, and suggested that a depression in this location inferred from LiDAR data might represent a prehistoric marsh, at most a soggy patch of ground by 1547.
80 Paterson, *History of the Regality of Musselburgh*, 83–84. We are grateful to Dr Alison Morrison-Low for the suggestion that the clock might have provided the timings noted or implied by Patten for events on 10 September.
81 Patten, f. 100v.
82 *RMS 1546–1580*, no. 160.
83 Dixon, The Placenames of Midlothian, 136.
84 *OSA* 16, 7.
85 Knox, *History*, 1, 99.
86 Caldwell, 'Scottish Ways to War 1513', 81–86, at p. 82.
87 Arnold, *The Renaissance at War*, 74–75.
88 Canmore: https://canmore.org.uk/site/28592/inchtuthil (accessed 6 May 2019).
89 Digges and Digges, *Stratioticos*, 57–60.
90 Fourquevaux *Instr*, especially the diagrams on fols 21r and 27r.
91 RPS: https://www.rps.ac.uk/A1547/9/1–3 (accessed 30 March 2019).
92 NRS, Notarial Protocol Book of Thomas Kene (NP1/2A), fol. 123.
93 Patten, f. 69v.
94 Archaeological evidence from Fisherrow suggests that settlement dates only from the sixteenth century at the earliest. See M. Kimber, *Archaeological monitoring in the streets of Musselburgh* (Edinburgh, 2009), 15, https://doi.org/10.5284/1017938 (accessed 18 Jun. 2020).
95 Patten, f. 69v.
96 Patten, f. 70r.
97 Caldwell, 'The Battle of Pinkie', fig. 6.
98 CFA, *Pinkie Report*, 25–28.
99 Patten, f. 102r–v.
100 Patten, f. 68r.
101 Patten, f. 69r.
102 CFA, *Pinkie Report*, 34–35.
103 They could have learned this from Hary's *Wallace*, a fifteen-century poem printed in Edinburgh about 1508–9 by Chepman and Myller.
104 Canmore: https://canmore.org.uk/site/53919 (accessed 17 June 2020).
105 Merriman, *Rough Wooings*, 336. In April 1550 the keeping of this fort was to be transferred to George Durie and Sir George Douglas. See *RPC* 1, 84.
106 J. Slezer, *Theatrum Scotiae* (1693): https://maps.nls.uk/view/91169162 (accessed 29 June 2020).
107 R. McD. Stirling, *Inveresk Parish Lore from Pagan Times* (Musselburgh, 1894), illus. 5.
108 *OSA* 16, 24.
109 Patten, f. 76v.
110 M. Strickland and R. Hardy, *The Great Warbow* (Stroud, 2005), 393, 414.
111 *Selve*, 218–19 (no. 242).
112 *TA* 9, 79, 117, 215.
113 Patten, ff. 109v–110r.

114 J. Froissart, *Oeuvres De Froissart*, ed. K. de Lettenhove (Brussels, 1867–77), tome XIII, 213; R. Baillie, *Letters & Journals* (Edinburgh, 1841), vol. 1, 211.
115 Patten, f. 64r.
116 Potter, *Henry VIII and Francis I*, 143.
117 Dixon, The Placenames of Midlothian, 136. See also https://canmore.org.uk/site/53850 (accessed 6 May 2019). For a survey of the documentary evidence for it see Paterson, *History of the Regality of Musselburgh*, 94–108.
118 E. P. Dennison, *Historic Musselburgh: the archaeological implications of development* (Edinburgh, 1996), 24.
119 Dennison, *Historic Musselburgh*, 24.
120 *Diurnal*, 30; *Hertford Exp*, 11.
121 Canmore: https://canmore.org.uk/site/149732 (accessed 24 January 2019).
122 Patten, f. 67r.
123 Knox, *History*, vol. 1, pp. xciii–xciv; vol. 2, 211. For the fort, and an inscribed stone commemorating events in 1547 see the entry on Queen Mary's Mount in the Canmore Database: https://canmore.org.uk/site/53384/queen-marys-mount (accessed 13 July 2020).
124 Hume, *Douglas History*, 271.
125 NRS, CS7/3/2 fols 239v, 346r.
126 Fraser, *The Scotts of Buccleuch*, vol. 2, 185–86.
127 Patten, f. 80r.
128 See, for instance, the table of gun sizes in D. H. Caldwell, Guns in Scotland. The manufacture and use of guns and their influence on warfare from the fourteenth century to c.1625 (Edinburgh University PhD, 1982), vol. 1, 60; Arnold, *The Renaissance at War*, 40–41.
129 Patten, f. 80r.
130 *NSA* 1, 275–77; Canmore: https://canmore.org.uk/site/53743 (accessed 29 Jun. 2020). Merriman, *Rough Wooings*, 307, 336.
131 Oleksy *et al.*, *Battle of Pinkie 1547: Heritage Assessment*, figs 4.1–4.3.
132 Patten, f. 80v.
133 Patten, f. 88r.
134 *OED* 15, 740.
135 Thomas of Erceldoune, *Romance and Prophecies*, 32–33. According to A. Fox, *The Press & The People, Cheap Print & Society in Scotland 1500-1785* (Oxford, 2020), 64, Thomas' prophecies may already have been in print around 1520.
136 Robert Waldegrave in Edinburgh in 1603 in *The Whole Prophesies of Scotland, England, Ireland, France and Denmark* (Edinburgh, 1603) and subsequently reprinted many times. See Thomas of Erceldoune, *Romance and Prophecies*, 48–51 for a 1615 printed version.
137 Caldwell, 'The Battle of Pinkie', fig. 6 and p. 83. This water course, however, does appear previously to have been known as Carberry Burn.
138 CFA, *Pinkie Report*, 18–19.
139 McNutt, Finding Forgotten Fields, 308, fig. 10.15.
140 For instance, J. Knox, *Map of the Shire of Edinburgh* (Edinburgh, 1816).
141 CFA, *Pinkie Report*, 31.
142 Patten, f. 82v.
143 *OED* 5: 1057.
144 *OED* 12: 457.
145 Strickland and Hardy, *The Great Warbow*, 393, 414.
146 Patten, f. 82v.; Pitscottie 2, 99.
147 Patten, f. 95r–v. Patten apparently confuses right and left in his text, but not on his tables, in describing the juxtaposition of the English vanguard with the turf banked enclosure.

148 Canmore: https://canmore.org.uk/site/53667/west-mains (accessed 28 December 2022).
149 The nearby Scheduled Queen Mary's Mount, Fort (SM6204) survives as earthwork ramparts within the wooded portion of Carberry Hill but is only identifiable through cropmarks in the arable fields to the east.
150 They are shown on J. Hay's *New Plan of Musselburgh and its environs* (Edinburgh, 1824): https://maps.nls.uk/view/216390366 (accessed 29 June 2020).
151 Andrew Coulson personal communication (8 December 2022).
152 A. Hodgkins, 'Reconstructing Rebellion: Digital Terrain Analysis of the Battle of Dussendale (1549)' *Internet Archaeology* 38 (2015), available online at: https://doi.org/10.11141/ia.38.3 (accessed 28 December 2022).
153 See for example McNutt, Finding Forgotten Fields.
154 Canmore: https://canmore.org.uk/site/53680/battle-of-pinkie-howe-mire (accessed 28 December 2022).
155 CFA, *Pinkie Report,* 17.
156 The practice is recorded in Robertson, *General View*, 46–47. It is likely to have originated in medieval times.
157 R. Engl, *Wallyford Expansion (Areas 1 & 4), East Lothian: Archaeological Works Data Structure Report* (AOC Report 2014).
158 *Hertford Exp*, 9, 11; Holinshed, *The Laste Volume*, 1638.
159 Canmore: https://canmore.org.uk/site/53680/battle-of-pinkie-howe-mire (accessed 28 December 2022).
160 Midlothian Ordnance Survey Name Book vol. 8, p.12, available online on the ScotlandsPlaces website: https://scotlandsplaces.gov.uk/digital-volumes/ordnance-survey-name-books/midlothian-os-name-books-1852–1853/midlothian-volume-08/12 (accessed 27 April 2022).
161 Midlothian Ordnance Survey Name Book vol. 8, p.27, available online on the ScotlandsPlaces website: https://scotlandsplaces.gov.uk/digital-volumes/ordnance-survey-name-books/midlothian-os-name-books-1852–1853/midlothian-volume-08/27 (accessed 28 December 2022).
162 *NSA* 1, 266.
163 Canmore: https://canmore.org.uk/site/53479/newton (accessed 28 December 2022).
164 Canmore: https://canmore.org.uk/site/53674/musselburgh-links (accessed 28 December 2022).
165 A. Henshall, 'A Long Cist Cemetery at Parkburn Sand Pit, Lasswade, Midlothian', *PSAS* 89 (1958), 279.
166 The text below aims at synthesising the results of work done on the Pinkie Battlefield post-2000. This includes work undertaken largely by commercial archaeological companies including AOC Archaeology Group, CFA Archaeology Ltd and Headland Archaeology. Analysis of finds recovered was undertaken in-house by these companies' finds specialists and also by experts such as Glenn Foard and staff at the Royal Armouries.
167 D. H. Caldwell, 'Tantallon Castle, East Lothian: a catalogue of the finds, *PSAS* 121 (1992), 344; G. Foard and R. Morris, *The Archaeology of English Battlefields* (York, 2012), 68–69; Hildred, *Weapons of Warre*, part 1, 348–70.
168 Hildred, *Weapons of Warre*, part 1, 370–81.
169 G. Foard, *A report on the metal finds from investigation of Pinkie battlefield by AOC Archaeology* (Unpublished Report for AOC Archaeology, 2008); G. Foard, *Report on CFA 2008 Lead munitions and other metal finds from the CFA Investigation at Wallyford* (Report for CFA, 2008).
170 B. Simpson, 'Land to the South-West of Barbachlaw', *DES* 8 (2007), 73.
171 G. Foard. *Pinkie Battlefield Report on survey undertaken in 2005–6 by B Simpson for East Lothian Council* (Report for East Lothian Council, 2008).
172 D. Starley and G. Rimer, *Lead Shot from Pinkie Battlefield* (Royal Armouries Report No. AM 2089, 2008).

173 Foard, *A report on the metal finds.*
174 Foard, *A report on the metal finds.*
175 V. Oleksy and S. Wilson, *Gula Flats Metal Detecting Survey* (AOC Data Structure Report, 2016).
176 Engl, *Wallyford Expansion (Areas 1 & 4), Data Structure Report.*
177 C. Hills and S. Anderson, *Goshen Farm, Wallyford, East Lothian: Archaeological Metal Detecting Survey* (CFA Report No. 2070, 2012).
178 D. McLaren, *Crookston Farm, Wallyford, East Lothian. Report on metal detected finds assemblage* (AOC Report, 2017); D. H. Caldwell, *Preliminary metal detection finds from fields around Crookston* (Unpublished Report, 2016).
179 Caldwell, *Preliminary metal detection fines from fields around Crookston.*
180 McLaren, *Crookston Farm.*
181 Canmore: https://canmore.org.uk/site/281623/musselburgh-mucklets-road-a1-craighall-link (accessed 28 December 2022).
182 G. Savory and B. Glendinning, *Goshen Farm, Musselburgh, East Lothian: Archaeological Evaluations* (CFA Report No. 3497, 2016).

7

A new interpretation of the Battle of Pinkie

The evidence for the Battle of Pinkie is at times confusing and contradictory. The source material is also far from balanced – we have far more information about the actions and attitudes of the English than we do for the Scots. However, by integrating the seemingly most reliable textual, topographical and archaeological data we can gain an overview of what probably happened in the fighting on Friday 9 and Saturday 10 September 1547, and in the days just before that bloody confrontation. This chapter seeks to provide a fresh interpretation, arguing that Somerset's victory was far from inevitable. It also strives to locate more accurately than hitherto the movements of the Scottish and English forces and to consider how the appearance of the landscape in the 1540s might have shaped the behaviour of the two opposing armies.

The English advance into Scotland

Preparations for war had been taking place in Scotland and England throughout the summer of 1547. However, it was on Friday 2 September that the die was finally cast, when the English navy set out from their east coast base at Berwick-upon-Tweed in the direction of Scotland.[1] Two days later the main part of the English army crossed into Scottish territory and headed northwards up the east coast.[2] At the same time, the English were also readying a smaller force to attack Scotland's West March (now part of Dumfries and Galloway). This western force was led by Lord Wharton and the treasonous Scottish nobleman the Earl of Lennox, who eventually crossed into Scotland on Friday 9 September with 2,000 foot and 500 horse (200 of whom were Scots in English service).[3] Wharton and Lennox's venture appears to have been intended as a feint, with the limited objectives of recruiting disaffected Scots and establishing a forward base in the west, which they did by putting a garrison at Castlemilk (Figure 7.1).[4] The intervention in the west put extra pressure on the Scottish government, but as the campaign was mostly conducted separately from Somerset's eastern attack it will not be discussed in detail here.

During late August the main English army gathered at Newcastle-upon-Tyne and in the heavily fortified town of Berwick (once a part of Scotland, but consistently in English hands since the 1480s). The mustering of the English army was overseen by the Earl of Warwick, with the assistance of Sir Ralph Sadler – who together ensured that the land forces 'were in good order and well supplied'.[5] Meanwhile the naval

Figure 7.1: A plat of Castlemilk made in late 1547 by the English surveyor, Thomas Petit, to show the achievements of the expedition under Lennox and Wharton. Castlemilk is placed centrally with other named places of significance round about. It is not to scale but distances between castles and other settlements are marked. South is to the top with Carlisle at top left (reproduced with permission of the Marquess of Salisbury, Hatfield House)

forces were prepared by Lord Clinton, who spent much of late August on board his flagship *Pauncy* in the waters around Berwick and Lindisfarne, which the English navy was using as a supply depot.[6]

Somerset met up with his forces relatively late on, joining the English cavalry at Newcastle on Saturday 27 August.[7] After a hectic weekend in which Somerset attended a civic reception, met with Lord Wharton to discuss the invasion of the West March, inspected the English demilances and light horsemen, accepted the allegiance of 40 'Scottish gentlemen of the east borders' and hanged an English soldier 'for quarrelling and fighting', the Lord Protector and his horsemen departed from Newcastle early on Monday morning.[8] They passed that night at Alnwick Castle, before arriving at Berwick on the afternoon of Tuesday 30 August.[9]

The next day the English commanders spent mostly 'in consultation about orders and matters' concerning the invasion, whilst much of the wider English army were preoccupied with sorting out supplies, Somerset having given an order that every soldier should make 'private provision' for four days of 'victual'.[10] As the English army continued their preparations on Thursday 1 September, the Duke of Somerset and a small group of horsemen made a brief excursion into Scotland and inspected the settlement and river estuary at Eyemouth, where it was determined to construct a fort and harbour.[11] Over the course of the campaign other strong points would be identified, garrisoned and fortified. The establishing of modern artillery forts at strategic locations was one of Somerset's key aims. To implement this policy the protector was assisted by the experienced military engineer Sir Richard Lee and the commander of the pioneers John Brende (who had previously advised on the redesign of the English military defences at Carlisle).[12]

Somerset also hoped to exploit religious divisions in Scotland and win over hearts and minds. To this end, an English herald had announced at Berwick that Somerset came as 'a friend and conservator of Scotland' and that his army 'pretendeth a force in appearance' but 'not in deed'.[13] In particular, the English emphasised that they would welcome to their camp Scots who supported the 'Godly purpose' of a marriage between Edward VI and Mary Queen of Scots, or who were willing to 'bring any kind of victual'. This proclamation was also printed and efforts were made to have it distributed within Scotland.[14] On 25 August Arran sent letters to towns in southern Scotland forbidding Scots from reading it on pain of death.[15]

Somerset clearly intended for the Pinkie campaign to be perceived as a less punitive intervention than previous Tudor invasions of Scotland. According to his proclamation the English would avoid 'devastation of any man's goods or cattle' with the telling exception of those 'who shall declare themselves repugnants'.[16] It is unknown how most Scots regarded Somerset's promises. There clearly were some who were willing to collaborate with the invaders, but after years of intermittent warfare many Scots were understandably suspicious of their southern neighbours. It is likely that the passage of the English forces through the Scottish countryside in 1547 did not further endear them to many local residents. Although Somerset did not apparently set out to cause widespread devastation, there clearly was significant damage to crops. This is documented in legal cases brought before the Lords of Council for non-payment of teinds (tithes), rents and other dues.[17]

Such losses were still in the future on Friday 2 September when the English fleet set sail towards Scotland and the army at 'sound of trumpet' marched out of Berwick.[18] The army did not go very far on that day, making camp two 'flight shots' away from the town 'on the sea side, and toward Scotland'. [19] This allowed the English forces to gain experience setting up camp in a controlled environment before they faced the challenges of camping in enemy territory. The camp that was established on Friday 2 September was probably on the Magdalene Fields, land now occupied by a golf-course, or else between the sea and the eastern medieval walls, perhaps defended to the north by an earthwork known as Spades Mire. There would have been sufficient space here to get the army in order ready for its entry into enemy territory and a source of water for horses in Tapee Loch (just to the northeast of Berwick Castle). On Sunday 4 September the army marched out in proper order, ready to be formed into a line of battle if the Scots threatened to fight. They were preceded by a force of light horse to establish a safe route, whilst the baggage train was tucked in for protection on the seaward-side of the main units.[20]

There is some information on the English progress from Berwick to Pinkie in the British Library's Harleian MS 540.[21] However, the most detailed account of the route is provided by William Patten. The first day's march was a distance of about 10 miles through relatively easy country (see Figure 1.2). This would have been a good opportunity to check that command structures and signalling were functioning. That night camp was established at Reston where the Eye Water would have provided access to water.[22]

On Monday 5 September the army marched on 8 miles to the Pease, a deep and broad ravine that was known to be a major obstacle on the way to Edinburgh (see Figure 3.9). It was anticipated that the Scots might intend to resist here, and there was evidence of them having recently dug trenches, but no active opposition was encountered.[23] The crossing was only finally achieved after sunset and camp was set up on the other side. Meanwhile Somerset sent a herald 'to summon' Dunglass Castle, a stronghold belonging to George Douglas. Its captain, Matthew Hume, requested to speak with Protector Somerset personally.[24] After a conversation in which Somerset apparently reiterated many of the points in his previous proclamation Hume returned to speak to his men.[25] The castle's garrison of 21 men then surrendered without a fight. Whilst these negotiations were taking place the English could spy their fleet sailing towards the Firth of Forth.[26]

After taking control of Dunglass Castle, Somerset gave orders for its destruction. About 300 English pioneers (who had just exerted considerable effort creating a route across the Pease for the artillery and supply train) set out to render the castle unusable by digging out the foundations and then blowing it up with gunpowder – a task that went on into Tuesday 6 September.[27] Before the process of destruction began the English stripped Dunglass Castle of weapons and supplies, killed a number of 'brood geese and good laying hens', but apparently left the town of Dunglass 'unspoiled and unburnt'.[28]

On the Tuesday two other castles, Thornton and Innerwick, were attacked. They stood either side of the Thornton Burn, here in a deep ravine, only a 'stone's cast' apart according to Patten.[29] There is now no trace of Thornton Castle (Figure 7.2) but it was probably not quite so close to Innerwick as implied by Patten. The former was a possession of the Humes, the latter of the Hamiltons (Figure 7.3). At each castle the small garrisons put up a spirited resistance, but were no match for the superior numbers and guns of the English.[30] Both were destroyed, with Thornton being 'blown up with powder' whilst Innerwick 'was burned'.[31] From a strategic point of view it made sense for Somerset to destroy these three castles since they were positioned on a difficult, unavoidable part of the route to Edinburgh and he had to be careful to maintain communications back to Berwick. Somerset may have believed he was

Figure 7.2: A fanciful representation of the taking of Thornton Castle on 6 September from the 1577 edition of Holinshed's Chronicles. *The garrison put up a stout resistance but were eventually taken and executed, the English having refused to accept their surrender. The castle was blown up*

showing moderation to win Scottish hearts and minds by only demolishing these three strongholds and not destroying wide swathes of country on either side of his path.

On the same day the army continued on its march, passing round Dunbar, a royal fortress, burgh and port. Clearly Somerset had no intention of attempting to take it. That night Patten indicates that they camped near the Earl of Angus's residence at Tantallon Castle (see Figure 4.10), which if true would have involved a considerable detour.[32] Somerset may have been particularly interested in Tantallon because of its deserved reputation as an impregnable stronghold. It is probably more likely that the camp was a couple of miles to the east of the River Tyne

Figure 7.3: Innerwick Castle in 1790. The castle was attacked by the English on 6 September and the garrison of nine killed despite having offered to surrender. The castle was then burned

Figure 7.4: The bridge across the River Tyne at East Linton possibly incorporates some stonework of the bridge used by the English army in their march towards Pinkie (David Caldwell)

where it was crossed by the Linton Bridge (Figure 7.4), the remains of which may be incorporated in the surviving historic stone bridge in the village of East Linton.

The first real signs of active opposition to the invasion came in the vicinity of Dunbar. Not only were the English fired upon by the castle's guns, but they now found they were being shadowed by a force of Scottish horsemen. That night there was a 'blind alarm' and reports were received that the Scottish army was camped at Inveresk.[33] The English commanders would have been aware of the risk that the Scots might attempt an attack when they were vulnerable, making the crossing of the Tyne at East Linton on Wednesday 7 September. It appears that the footmen got over the bridge without any mishap, while the horsemen and carriages crossed by a ford.[34] The army then marched onwards, passing close enough to the Earl of Bothwell's castle at Hailes for the garrison to fire their guns at them (Figure 7.5). The Scottish horsemen were now emboldened to skirmish, and the Earl of Warwick was almost captured in an ambush in 'a very thick mist'.[35] Following this incident the army continued on towards the village of Longniddry, where they made camp, having completed a journey of about 10 miles from the bridge at East Linton. The major burgh of Haddington, then Scotland's fifth richest urban centre, was avoided.[36]

Whilst the English were preparing to leave Longniddry on the morning of Thursday 8 September, Somerset signalled for Admiral Clinton to come ashore to share intelligence and discuss the deployment of the English ships, then mostly opposite Leith.[37] Clinton appears to have been brought into shore by the *Galley Subtle*, a reflection of that vessel's greater manoeuvrability close to land. Somerset and Clinton agreed that the 'smaller vessels that were victuallers' would be brought close in to land to resupply the army, meanwhile the 'great ships should remove from before Leith and lie before Musselburgh'.[38] After making these plans Clinton returned to sea, whilst Somerset and his land forces set out in the direction of Prestonpans. As the English army marched along the coast a large force of Scottish horsemen on the higher ground to the south shadowed it – the two opposing sides were starting to come dangerously close together.

Figure 7.5: Hailes Castle, the residence of the Earl of Bothwell (Vicky Oleksy)

Scottish preparations

The end of August and the beginning of September 1547 saw the Earl of Arran and the wider Scottish government preparing to deal with one or more English invasions. Initially, Arran opted to muster the Scottish army at Fala, about 11 miles southwest of Musselburgh (see Figure 4.3).[39] This decision was taken in August, when Arran was unsure, or perhaps even misinformed, about the route of the English army into Scotland. Even in the first few days of September Arran was still perhaps encouraging his forces to meet him at Fala. Certainly, there is an entry in Arran's expenditure for September 1547, noting a payment of 10 shillings to the messenger Alexander Cunningham for informing 'all manner of man to pass forward to Fala to my lord governor'.[40] Yet, by the time the English army was passing Dunbar on Tuesday 6 September, and probably a little before this, it had become obvious that Fala was the wrong place for the majority of Arran's forces.

We unfortunately do not have much evidence for the decisions Arran took during the critical days between Sunday 4 September and Thursday 8 September. However, some contemporaries believed that he was surprised by the speed of the English invasion. The Imperial diplomat Francis van der Delft, who admittedly got most of his information from English sources, claimed that Somerset entered Scotland 'before they expected him'.[41] It is possible that tentative Scottish plans to oppose the English army at the Pease (where some trenches were in fact dug) were abandoned because of lack of time to move troops and prepare defences.[42]

What is clear, is that as the English were nearing Longniddry on Wednesday 7 September, the Scots were running out of space in which to confront Somerset's forces. The River Esk was one of the last major barriers before the English reached Edinburgh. As governor, the Earl of Arran had a responsibility to protect Scottish lives and property, and to see off foreign threats. He had failed to protect Edinburgh in 1544, when he fled after a brief confrontation with the future Duke of Somerset's forces near Leith.[43] Leaving the Scottish capital to its fate once again would have had serious political consequences, quite apart from the likely human and economic costs. In September 1547 it would have been difficult for Arran to implement any strategy that did not prevent the English from reaching Edinburgh – hence his decision to confront the English in the vicinity of Musselburgh.

We do not know exactly when Arran and his army arrived in the Musselburgh area, but by the evening of 7 September the Scottish forces seem to have been encamped on the west bank of the River Esk.[44] The Scottish army, and its transport and other support services, will have taken up a considerable area. Indeed, it is possible that there were in fact three camps, one of which was in the area around Monktonhall.[45] In terms of stopping the English advance, the position taken up by the Scots was a good one. Arran's forces were controlling the route to Edinburgh and the river crossing. At Musselburgh there was only one bridge for getting guns, equipment and supplies across the Esk, which Arran had successfully ensured that the Scots held.

The only way the English could have crossed the river without confronting the Scots would have been to take a long detour along the east bank of the Esk via Carberry to Dalkeith, skirting extensive areas of marshy ground. This would have exposed the English flank to artillery fire from the Scots. Indeed, the sixteenth-century copperplate engraving of 'The English Victory Against the Scots by Musselburgh' depicts pieces of Scottish artillery spaced out along the Esk to provide protection from any attempted crossing by the English (see Figure 1.1). These guns did in fact see use, firing across the Esk on Friday 9 September.

There were two notable weaknesses to the Scottish position. One was the proximity of the camp to the mouth of the River Esk and the shore at Fisherrow, meaning that the English ships, and in particular their galley, could potentially fire on the Scottish camp. It is unclear how serious a threat this posed. The Scots had taken precautions against attack from ships by protecting their camp's seaward side with turf defences mounted with guns.[46] These guns and defences may well have presented their own hazard to the English fleet, especially when combined with the tricky sandbanks and rocks that characterised the coast from Musselburgh up to Leith. Significantly, on 10 September the Scots do not seem to have feared an attack from the rear by a landing force from the English fleet, and there no evidence that Somerset or Clinton ever considered this to be an option.

The other significant threat was the high ground around St Michael's Church, at Inveresk, which could potentially serve as a gun platform. Guns to threaten the Scottish camp could also be positioned along the turf walled lane leading southwards from the church. The Copperplate engraving shows two Scottish guns by the church, perhaps an indication that Arran had hoped to retain control of this area of high ground. According to the same engraving Scottish guns were also positioned on a hillock to the west of the river. It is possible that this was at Mucklets, a little to the west of Monktonhall.

Thursday 8 and Friday 9 September

On Thursday 8 September the Scottish leaders were gathered at Monktonhall, a place that is best known today as the home of Musselburgh Golf Club. At Monktonhall the Earl of Arran held a convention. There is some debate about the precise role that conventions held, but broadly speaking they were gatherings of important figures in Scottish society, who were summoned together to advise the monarch (or in this case the regent) about a particular issue or event. They were often used to gain consensus on difficult issues, and arguably helped provide a sense of collective responsibility for controversial decisions.[47] At the convention, the Scottish leaders agreed that the heirs of anyone 'slain, mortally wounded or taken [fatally] sick' in the army 'gathered for the defence of this realm' would not have to pay the usual charges for inheriting property.[48] It is likely that this is also when Arran discussed plans for how best to confront the approaching English army.

Unfortunately, there is no list of attendees for this convention. Some Scottish chroniclers who were critical of Arran's actions at Pinkie subsequently accused him of listening too much to a small, militarily inexperienced group of advisors, including the Archbishop of St Andrews (Arran's half-brother), the Abbot of Dunfermline (a notable landlord in the Pinkie area), the advocate Master Hugh Rigg and Archibald Beaton (a relative of the recently deceased Cardinal Beaton).[49] However, the convention will have consisted of more than just these men. Looking back, the Scottish nobleman Lord Herries claimed that Arran's army 'was composed of two contrary factions', who after Pinkie each attributed 'the loss of the day to the opposite party'.[50] Yet comments about divisions among Arran and his colleagues pre-date the defeat, with an English intelligence report from Tuesday 6 September noting 'great division' amongst the Scottish nobles.[51]

Despite internal divisions, a strategy for the next few days will have had to be determined. It is possible that on Thursday 8 September the Scottish high command were still hoping to avoid a pitched battle and to keep most of their forces within the protection of the camp. Indeed, Bishop Leslie asserts that while the Scots were 'in their camp at Inveresk' Arran and the nobles decided that it would be 'far contrary to their utility and profit' to confront 'so strong an enemy'.[52] However, notwithstanding such reservations, it is likely that at some point on the Thursday it was agreed that the Scottish light horsemen's ongoing campaign of harassing and spying on the approaching English forces should be escalated.

Whilst the Scots were in conference at Monktonhall on 8 September, the English army was making slow progress westwards to Prestonpans. Supposedly 'the way was somewhat narrow' with the Firth of Forth on the north and 'certain marshes' close by on the south.[53] The Scottish horsemen 'kept always pace' with the English, until eventually Protector Somerset ordered two 'field pieces' to be turned towards the Scots and 'shot off twice'.[54] Supposedly these shots successfully 'struck off the leg of a black horse' and 'killed a man', after which the Scots withdrew until the English made camp at Prestonpans, or Salt Preston as it was then known on account of the local salt industry.[55]

As the English approached Prestonpans they came across further evidence of industrial activity, almost certainly coal mining. One of the commissioners in charge of transport, George Ferrers (who had previously served in the household of Thomas Cromwell before attending on Henry VIII) came across what he regarded as 'a cave', the mouth of which was 'worn' with footprints.[56] Ferrers ventured inside and was 'received' with shots from one or two hackbuts. Supposedly Ferrers then asked if the people sheltering inside 'would be content to yield', which they refused to do. The situation was reported to Somerset, and Ferrers obtained permission 'to do with them as he could'.[57] He returned with a party of pioneers as well as William Patten, who appears to have gone along out of interest as he 'happened' to be present.

The English were aware of three 'vents' from the cave or mine workings. One of the vents they blocked up, another they 'filled full of straw and set it afire', and a third they left open to encourage the people inside to negotiate.[58] After failing to drive anyone from the mine in this fashion the open vent was 'stopped' up by Ferrers and his men. The burning and smoke then 'continued with so great a force and so long a while' that the English were 'sure' that anyone inside must be dead. [59] We do not know who or how many people were sheltering in the mine, but the likelihood is that they were local residents, possibly from the mining community.

Whilst Ferrers and Patten were setting fire to the mine, the English fleet had sailed from Leith back towards Musselburgh. On the way they shot at the Scottish camp, apparently doing no damage.[60] By this point on the evening of Thursday 8 September, the Scottish and English armies will have been less than two miles apart. Two enemy armies encamped so close together presented a situation where conflict was an increasingly likely outcome (Figure 7.6). Yet a full pitched battle was perhaps still not inevitable.

On the morning of Friday 9 September neither side brought matters to a head. Somerset spent the morning in 'consultation' with his council of war.[61] There seems to have been some differences of opinion among the English leaders around this time, although Patten does not report them. Instead, it is from the version of events Lord Grey of Wilton recounted to his son that we learn that Grey had advocated using the English cavalry to drive off the Scottish light horse who were 'pricking' and 'shouting', and otherwise 'egging' (i.e. provoking) the invading forces.[62] Throughout the march north Somerset had been opposed to such a policy, having at the start of the campaign given a blanket commandment 'that no offer of skirmish by Scottish horsemen should be taken'.[63] However, at dinner on the evening of Thursday 8 September the Earl of Warwick appears to have supported Grey's proposal for the English cavalry to respond to the Scottish skirmishing. Somerset was still doubtful, stating that he thought the proposal came from 'more of a jollity of courage than knowledge of the enemy', but eventually he consented to Grey's request.[64]

Whilst the English high command were discussing tactics, more junior officers took the opportunity of ensuring their men had sufficient food and weapons, some of which they unloaded from the ships (Figure 7.7).[65] This was the first time since leaving Berwick that the English were able to use their fleet to resupply the army. There is still some doubt as to the exact location of the English camp, but as supplies were unloaded from the ships it is reasonable to suppose that it included access to the coast about Preston Grange.

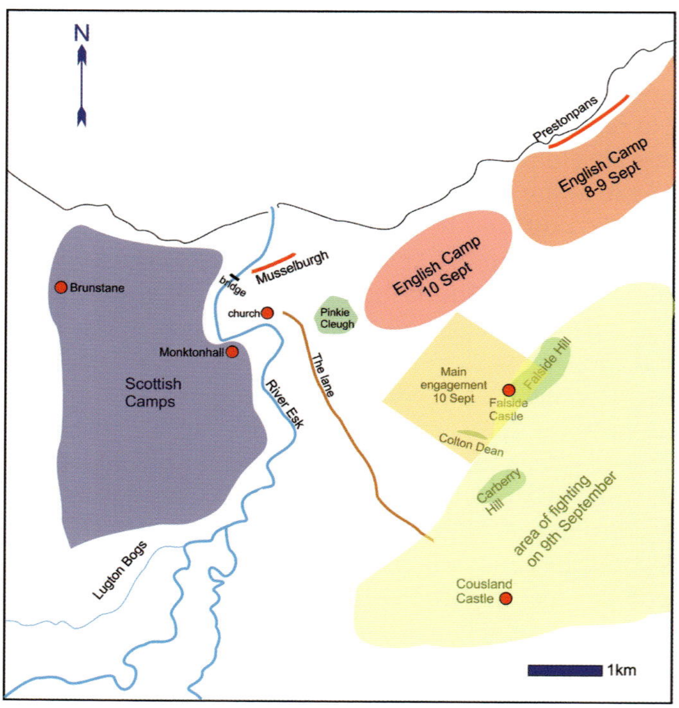

Figure 7.6: Plan of the Pinkie battlefield showing the approximate locations of the camps of the opposing sides and the areas where fighting took place on 9 and 10 September (David Caldwell)

Figure 7.7: Supplies and equipment being unloaded from the English ships to the English camp before the battle. Detail from the Copperplate Engraving of the English victory at Musselburgh (Reproduced in Berteville 1825)

Figure 7.8: The English galley shown positioned near the mouth of the River Esk and firing at the Scots. Detail from the Copperplate Engraving of the English victory at Musselburgh (Reproduced in Berteville 1825)

As the English were sorting out supplies on Friday 9 September, the Scottish horse once again showed themselves to the English 'pranking up and down' on Falside Hill.[66] This time the Scots had sent out a considerable force, as many as 1,500 men, led by Lord Hume. The manoeuvres of Hume's horsemen on Falside Hill were presumably intended to be provocative, and that afternoon triggered a response from the English. At long last Lord Grey of Wilton was able to lead his horsemen against the Scots who had so annoyed him. Berteville characterises Grey's force as consisting of light horsemen, yet evidence from the stories Lord Grey passed on to his son suggests that it also included some of the men-at-arms and demilances from Boulogne, all marshalled into troops.[67] There were also the Spanish and Italian mounted hackbutters who formed a wing with instructions to guard the hindmost troop of horsemen. Grey is said to have ordered his troop commanders when attacked to hold back their men until the Scots had wheeled away. At that point, not only the troop which had been confronted was to give chase, but also the adjacent one, or as Lord Grey's son recounted 'upon the enemy's wheeling about' both the attacked troop and 'the next troop' should 'give it in the face' to the enemy. Grey stressed how 'each troop' should 'hold together without breaking'.[68] These instructions recognised the danger for the English of being dispersed and led too far into enemy territory. However, they also reflect the skill and discipline of Grey's cavalry.

The main part of the engagement took place on Carberry Hill, spilling over to Cousland (Figure 7.6). The Scots at first held their ground as the English advanced towards them, but then adopted their usual tactics of pricking and whooping. This involved dashing up to within a stave's length of the English troops before wheeling away. No doubt this would have been very intimidating for an inexperienced adversary but many of the English force had seen service in France. The turning point is said to have come when a troop of Lord Grey's men-at-arms from Boulogne, under the command of Nicholas Gainford, responded to one such manoeuvre by 400 or 500 Scots, charging them as they wheeled away.[69]

The Scots certainly came off worse, and were chased away, presumably back across the River Esk and round the south of the marshy ground to their camp. They suffered several hundred casualties, and Lord Hume was badly hurt in a fall from his horse, leaving him unable to take any further part in the campaign. His son, the Master of Hume, was one of a handful of significant prisoners the English captured that day. The Scottish dead may have included 300 men from a force of 500 Borderers on foot, there in the hope of plunder.[70] However, the losses were not all on the Scottish side. The fact that the Scots captured three of the English captains of light horse, namely Sir Ralph Bulmer, Thomas Gower (Marshal of Berwick) and Robert Crouch, indicates that there was a price to pay. Meanwhile the Scottish author of the so-called *Diurnal of Remarkable Occurrents*, claims that many English men of lesser rank were also taken in this engagement.[71]

A consequence of this cavalry action was that it enabled Protector Somerset, along with the Earl of Warwick and 'a small guard' of men, to ride out along Carberry Hill to view the Scottish camp and the lane leading up towards Inveresk Church.[72] If Somerset had any doubts about the size and preparedness of the Scottish forces these were now dispelled.[73] Somerset's excursion enabled him to firm up plans for how to tackle the Scots the next day. He seems to have assumed that they would stay in their positions and that he would have to move his forces forward, taking the high ground at St Michael's Church and mounting guns there, and in the lane, to bombard the Scottish positions.

While the English had good reason to see the events of Friday 9 September as a success, the Scots must have been despondent. Even if the cavalry engagement was not quite as one-sided as it has been presented, the English had clearly come off better. The wounding of the Scottish cavalry commander, Lord Hume, was also a considerable blow. This was clearly a time for Arran to review whatever plans he had in place and possibly make changes. A key question is whether there might have been at this stage serious last-minute attempts by either side to come to an agreement rather than fight. After all, Somerset claimed that he had come to seek a resolution to outstanding issues between the two nations, not to defeat and conquer the Scots. Arran had at one time supported Somerset's aims and perhaps could be persuaded to look at them again. The consequences for either general of a defeat in battle were catastrophic and neither, whatever spin they had to put on their situation for the benefit of others, could be that confident that they would prevail.

Patten was in Somerset's party on the Friday as it viewed the Scottish camp. He tells how as the English rode away 'the Scots did often shoot' but that, shortly after, a Scottish herald and trumpeter came for a meeting with Somerset and Warwick. He claims not to have heard the herald's message, but states that Somerset's response in a 'louder voice' was to reject any further discussion. Supposedly, Somerset declared that he meant 'no more hurt to the Realm of Scotland' than to England, but as Arran had previously 'refused' generous offers of peace then 'let him look for none'.[74] There is no need to take seriously now, just as it was not seen worthy of consideration at the time, Huntly's subsidiary offer that the quarrel between the two countries should be decided by a few picked men from each side, or even by a fight between Huntly and Somerset alone.[75]

Several of the Scottish accounts say that the English proposed negotiations prior to the fighting on Saturday 10 September. According to Pitscottie, Somerset was prepared to relax the terms of the Treaties of Greenwich which Arran had rejected. Mary Queen of Scots would now remain in Scotland until of lawful age to marry, when she could decide for herself who to marry, and peace would be restored between the two realms and reparations made for loss and damage. Pitscottie clearly believed the Scottish Lords should have accepted the proffered deal, but that knowledge of it was kept from them through the influence of Arran's cabal of high-ranking churchmen. They were thus the chief cause of Scotland's undoing, not the English.[76] Buchanan also accuses Arran of dishonestly keeping secret from the Scottish lords the favourable terms for peace being offered by the English. He is quite scathing of Arran, describing him as an imbecile, naturally indolent and lacking any understanding of military affairs, inconstant, and changeable in his purpose at every rumour.[77]

We cannot reach a firm conclusion on the basis of this information as to whether either side was actually prepared to contemplate peace. Somerset is hardly likely to have trusted Scottish good faith if he wheeled his army away to go back the way he came. Arran might have had challenges in spinning a negotiated settlement at this late stage, particularly as some of Scotland's elites were deeply opposed to any compromise with England. Indeed Lord Hume had in 1544 stated that it was 'better to die with honour' than live with the 'perpetual shame of all Christian regions' by submitting to the English – a comment that casts an interesting light on his actions on the afternoon of Friday 9 September 1547.[78]

Since we are not aware of what plans Arran had in place prior to Hume's cavalry engagement we do not know how that setback affected his thinking. We likewise have little information about what discussions took place in the Scottish camp on the evening of 9 September, but there are clues that divisions among the leaders may have continued. During his captivity after Pinkie, Huntly indicated to the French ambassador in London that Arran over-ruled the advice of his commanders and deliberately set out to engage the English in battle.[79] Meanwhile, the highly partisan John Knox claims that Arran was incited by his half-brother, Archbishop John Hamilton of St Andrews, to fight 'the English heretics' on religious grounds.[80]

The Scottish camp on 9 September was on land held by the Abbey of Dunfermline, whose estates extended eastwards towards where the English had camped. Did leading churchmen, in particular the Archbishop of St Andrews and the Abbot of Dunfermline, use their influence to push for an advance partly to protect ecclesiastical estates? Less cynical reasons may have also encouraged church leaders to counsel Arran to attack the English. Scots of all ranks must have been aware that they were facing a Protestant commander who had in 1544 attacked major churches, including Holyrood Abbey and the monastic houses in the Borders. Resisting Somerset was for some Catholic Scots a Christian duty.

Although there were many Scots with Reformist religious sympathies, the Scottish army at Pinkie seems to have had a proudly Catholic element. According to Patten some of the Scots fought under a banner showing a woman representing the Catholic Church kneeling before a crucifix with the Latin motto 'AFFLICTAE SPONSAE NE OBLIVICARIS', which translates as 'Do not forget your afflicted wife'.[81] Contemporary English accounts, including a letter sent by Somerset to the young Edward VI, assert that there were many Catholic priests and monks killed at Pinkie.[82] Meanwhile John Knox alleged that at Pinkie 'no men were stouter than the priests and canons with their shaven crowns and black jacks'.[83]

According to some of Arran's detractors his decision to leave the Scottish camp and advance on 10 September was also motivated by a belief in the superiority of his own forces, coupled with an expectation that Somerset was about to turn and go back home. Patten claims that Arran put a very particular spin on recent events and what was going to happen next in order to buoy the morale of his men. Supposedly Arran declared that the English horse were obviously a force to be reckoned with but the rest of the English army, which was smaller in size than their own, consisted of young, inexperienced men. The withdrawal of the English fleet from Leith back to the coast adjacent to the English camp was to facilitate shipping these men back home, thus freeing up the horse to make their return journey expeditiously. Arran was expecting the imminent arrival of a French fleet of 12 galleys and 50 ships to help deal with the English ships.[84]

Patten claims that the Scots readily fell for this reassuring analysis, and it is not impossible that propaganda along these lines was circulated in the Scottish camp on the Friday evening and Saturday morning. Certainly, the writings of Buchanan and Pitscottie indicate that this may have been the case. Indeed, according to Pitscottie, Arran got news that the English intended to depart home because they lacked supplies of food.[85] It may seem incredible today that anyone could have seriously believed that the English were about to depart without fighting and that a Scottish advance from their camp would encourage the English to go. Nevertheless, almost exactly one year later two opposing armies were to face each other on this same ground at Pinkie, a combined French and Scottish force versus an English army. The latter turned away without offering battle.[86] This would appear to show that a Scottish belief in September 1547 that the English could, and might backdown was not totally absurd.

Saturday 10 September

It seems that most of Saturday 10 September was a dry but overcast day. Pitscottie describes 'a great stoor' (cloud of dust) enveloping the Scottish army and limiting visibility.[87] This was presumably caused because the fallow ground the army was moving across was bone dry. If any credence should be paid to the celestial images of wind and sun on the Battle of Pinkie Roll there may have been a wind which favoured the English, blowing towards the Scots. Rain would fall later in the afternoon after the fighting had ended.

The English were ready to advance early, before 8am according to Patten, their plan being to march straight towards St Michael's Church. There was no intention to return to this camp and so everything was packed up and moved out. Now that it was clear that battle was a likely and immediate outcome every man would have been ready with his arms and armour and not encumbered with food or other supplies. The order of march that can be deduced from the Battle of Pinkie Roll (see Figure 5.7) was the artillery followed by the vanguard, main battle and then the rear-guard, each with sleeves to right and left of gunners and archers, and three units of horse inland, to the left. The foremost of these, presumably light horse, was well ahead of the artillery and foot soldiers to act as scouts. The baggage train was tucked in behind the left flank of the rear-guard.

Meanwhile, two miles or so to the west, the Scottish army was also on the move. Some units were wading across the River Esk, some were crossing the bridge, while others were marching through Musselburgh (presumably by this time a ghost town with everything of any value that could be removed taken away by its owners). Bishop Leslie believed that Arran only resolved to advance his army that morning when he received reports that the English were approaching, intending to take the high ground between Pinkie Cleugh and St Michael's Church and bombard the Scottish camp from there.[88] It seems more likely that the Scots' decision to leave camp and cross the Esk was in fact made on the Friday, not least because of the apparent efficiency with which the move was executed. It would have required a considerable amount of planning and coordination to ready all the units, agree which were crossing the bridge and which were wading through the water, where and in what order, and ensure that all fell into line in the right place. If the advance was made as the consequence of a last-minute decision it might have resulted in a certain amount of confusion that would have been obvious to English observers.

Pitscottie describes how, when the time came to take action that morning, heralds passed through the camp to call all men to take up their arms and join their units in line of battle. Unlike the English, the Scots did not abandon or dismantle their camp, though Patten noted that their tents had been collapsed to prevent them giving shelter to deserters.[89] It would seem that Arran expected to return to this camp with his forces that evening. Once across the river the Scots lined up on the higher ground (Pinkiehill) to the east of the church that is now occupied by the village of Inveresk and Lewisvale Park. Their battle line stretched for about a kilometre, facing east on the brim of a steepish slope overlooking the ravine of Pinkie Cleugh with the Pinkie Burn flowing through it (see Figures 6.1 and 6.4). Viewed from the east by the English it appeared that they were arrayed on two separate hillocks but there is no reason to think that the topography adversely affected the integrity or unity of the line of battle.[90]

Based on our analysis of the Scottish army in Chapter 4, the three battles of pikemen were placed in line alongside each other, the vanguard, commanded by Angus, to the right and the rear-guard, commanded by Huntly, to the left of the main battle led by Arran. Each of these battles had a nominal strength of 6,000 men and a front line of 100 or more men, and it appears that Angus, Huntly and Arran all positioned themselves on foot in their commands. Argyll's archers, no more than 4,000 in number, were placed as wings to the right and left of the main battle. The artillery train seems to have been divided into three units, each assigned to one of the main battles.[91] This may just have been the smaller, wrought iron pieces, mounted on carts, designed as field guns or anti-personnel devices. They would have been placed in the gaps between the battles. The larger cast bronze guns may have been positioned to defend the camp and Pinkiehill. The horse, considerably depleted in numbers as a result of its mauling the day before, only mustered 400 or 500 men. They took up position to the right of the vanguard, but some distance away, ready to undertake scouting and skirmishing duties (see Figure 4.14).[92]

So when Somerset marched out from camp that Saturday morning what did he expect to happen? It is clear that Somerset had not anticipated that the Scots would advance and take up position on Pinkiehill (Figure 7.9). This situation caused him to halt his army, still in line of march and to the east of Pinkie Cleugh. His vanguard was over a mile from the Scottish front. Since he does not appear to have turned his army about to form a battleline he presumably had fairly quickly come to the conclusion that, on the one hand, Arran would not give up his position to get mired and disorganised in Pinkie Cleugh, just as, on the other hand, he must have seen it was not a viable option for him to mount an attack across the cleugh and up the slope beyond it in face of the full Scottish army. With neither commander prepared to take the initiative the standoff across Pinkie Cleugh lasted, according to the author of Harleian MS 540, for three hours.

It appears that it would have been a good strategy at this stage for the Scots to sit tight and wait for the English to make the first move. Shots were fired by the artillery on both sides. The account of the battle supplied to John Hooper, which refers to the artillery being silenced prior to further actions, could be taken to mean that there was a significant artillery duel, but it was probably apparent to both the Scottish and English gunners that the opposing armies were out of range.[93] An obvious move by Somerset would have been to mount a cavalry attack on the Scottish right flank. He had considerable superiority in numbers of horsemen and the previous day's skirmishing would have considerably boosted his men's confidence. None of our sources indicate whether this option was considered.

Instead, the Scots were to be subjected to an attack on their left flank in the form of gun fire from at least one of the English ships, *The Galley Subtle*. Not all early accounts knew about this or thought it significant enough to mention. The Battle of Pinkie Roll (see Figure 5.7) depicts the large English galley close to the shore to the east of Pinkie House, firing a large gun mounted in its bow. An ink line traces its shot passing between the house and Musselburgh and slamming into an unidentified unit of Scottish foot. The Copperplate engraving also shows the galley in action (Figure 7.8). Patten tells us the galley shot and killed the Master of Graham along with 25 near him, and the 4,000 archers brought by Argyll were so scared that they could never be made to come forward. So the Scottish army hastily moved, turning south-eastwards to Falside Brae (Figure 7.10).[94] Hume says the English galley was joined close to the shore by two pinnaces and their shot greatly annoyed the Scottish rear. The only casualty he was aware of was the Laird of Lochinvar.[95] Although from Galloway, as a Gordon he might be expected to have served in Huntly's command.

Estimates of the range of guns of the period, even when based on contemporary manuals and treatises, vary greatly. It is the view of Caldwell that few pieces of artillery in use in 1547 are likely to have had an effective range of more than about 2,000 yards (1828.8 m), but others, for example Arnold, have suggested ranges up to 4,000 paces (perhaps roughly equivalent to the same figure in yards).[96] A great deal obviously depends on what is meant by 'effective'. Assuming the English fleet was very close in, perhaps as near as 1300 m to the high ground occupied by the Scots when they moved out of their camp, making allowance for the reclamation of land to the north of Musselburgh Racecourse, the English shipboard guns might just about have mounted an effective bombardment of the Scots. However, it seems likely that with the exception of the galley and the two pinnaces that came close into the shore, the guns on many of the English ships were probably operating towards the limit of their range.

It would seem that the Scots moved because they were being shot at from the English ships; but was it just one or two 'lucky' shots that struck the Scottish rear-guard, or was it a sustained bombardment? If one or more English ships could fire effectively on the Scots, presumably the larger pieces of Scottish artillery could return

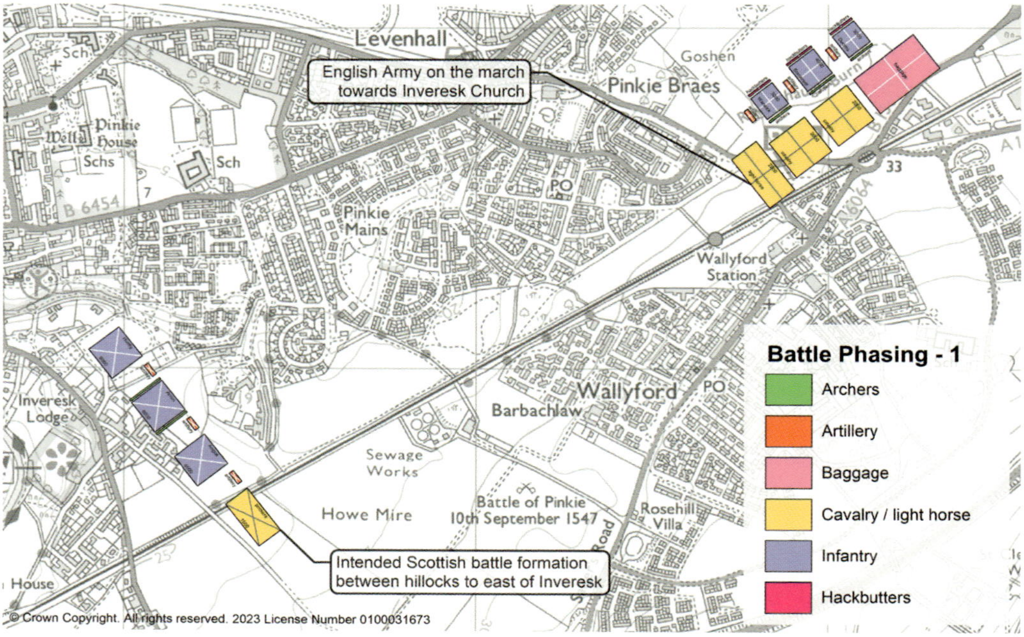

Figure 7.9: Battle Phasing, 10 September – 1: The Scots form a line of battle overlooking Pinkie Cleugh while the English march from their camp towards Inveresk Church (Geddes Consulting Ltd)

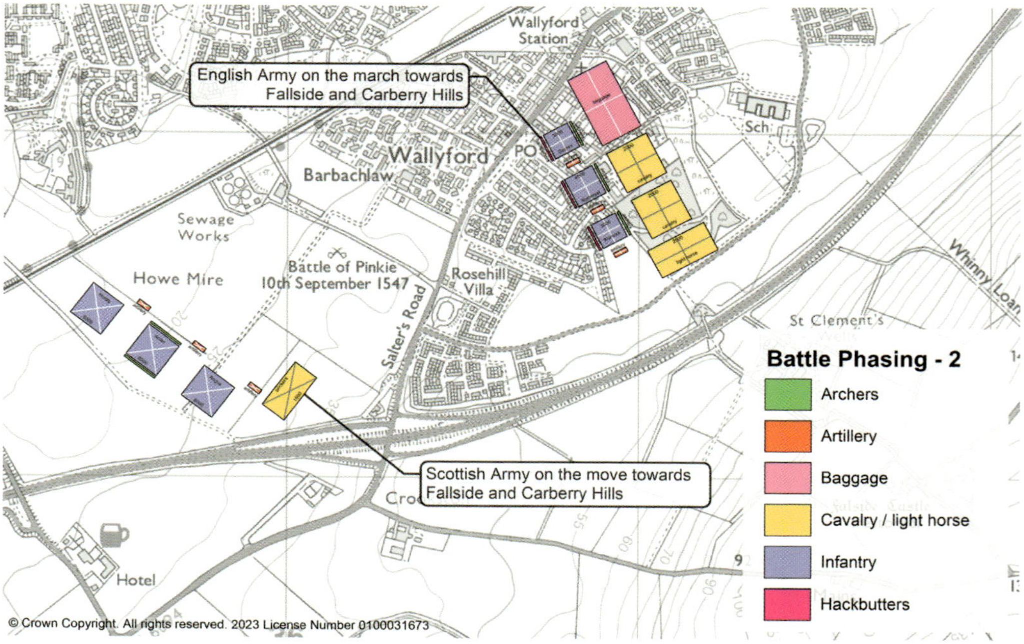

Figure 7.10: Battle Phasing, 10 September – 2: Both armies head inland towards Falside Hill, their routes gradually converging (Geddes Consulting Ltd)

that fire and put the ships at risk. We are not informed that that was the case. It is worth reminding ourselves here of what the pro-Angus, Hume of Godscroft had to say about how this naval bombardment was used as an excuse by Huntly and Arran for not coming to aid Angus at the height of the battle. The rear-guard had been unsettled by the gunfire and, as a result, their men, chiefly the Highlanders, refused to advance.[97] This sounds like special pleading. There is no mention of casualties amongst the Highlanders and they should, surely, have been happy to move well inland away from the ships.

Nevertheless, the naval bombardment must be considered a factor in the decision by the Scots to move from Pinkiehill. The only obvious direction to go was southwards. Doing so meant traversing Inveresk fields, relatively flat and unencumbered with trees, buildings or other obstacles. No doubt it was now deserted countryside, some of it fallow, some with crops still unharvested. This move potentially abandoned the Scottish camp to the enemy and might have meant that Somerset could press ahead to Edinburgh, but there were also considerable dangers for the English attempting to cross the Esk and push forwards with a Scottish army still nearby.

An alternative or additional reason for the move by the Scots was Arran's determination to draw Somerset into a pitched battle.[98] Since the English were not going to attack across Pinkie Cleugh perhaps they would be prepared to tackle the Scottish army if it made a stand in Inveresk Fields. With his battles properly deployed on open, level ground and supported by artillery is it possible that Arran could have fancied his chances of a win? He would have known about the dip and marshy ground at Colton Dean and perhaps it was even then the intention that it would flank his vanguard, compensating for his lack of cavalry. There are no obvious clues from early sources that this was Arran's thinking at this point in the day. Instead, all we have is the notion that the Scots wanted to occupy the high ground of Falside Hill with no analysis of how that might prevent Somerset from advancing to Edinburgh.

Arran probably correctly predicted that the English would try and match his move southwards, attempting, as they saw it, to beat him to the higher ground. He may also have seen how the English, in that case, would be at a disadvantage. Arran would have a head start and he may have foreseen how the English, in turning southwards, would end up with their horse behind their units of foot. Somerset also had to ensure that his baggage train was shielded from enemy action. It is possibly also the case that the terrain that the English had to cross was less convenient for large troop movements, broken up by mine workings and water courses. In contrast, the Scots were basically following the line of the Crookston Road from Pinkiehill.

Several early sources comment on the speed of the advance by the Scottish vanguard, leaving little doubt that Arran saw that he was engaged in a race. According to both Buchanan and Hume of Godscroft, Angus started off slowly, and had to be ordered by Arran to speed up.[99] The result was a trot, as if the men were on horseback.[100] The Scots also had their guns pulled by men rather than horses or oxen.[101] The thinking here appears to have been that well organised squads of men could move the guns faster and allow more manoeuvrability, enabling the guns to be fired quickly without having to unhitch animals and move them out the way.

When news of the Scottish advance southwards was brought to Somerset he lost no time in mobilising his own forces and progressing towards Falside Hill. As the two armies marched their courses converged to such an extent that the Scots thought it worthwhile to fire their guns, thus demonstrating the effectiveness of not having them lumbered with trains of beasts. This is only likely to have been a serious option if the Scots were as close as half a mile from the English footmen. The English may not have had an opportunity to unhitch and fire their guns at this time, their priority being to get them on to the high ground of Falside Hill.

At some point in the march southwards the Scottish army halted. Patten reports that Somerset thought that this was a sign that the Scots intended to avoid a pitched battle. Bishop Leslie's comment that the Scottish forces had become somewhat disordered due to the rapidity of their advance is a more likely explanation.[102] The main problems are likely to have been twofold. First spacing and cohesion within the battles, and second the distances between the main units. To what extent the Scottish commanders at this point were able to sort such problems is unclear, but they were soon all on the march again. The routes of the two armies continued to converge, the two vanguards ending up only about 500 m apart.[103]

The English high command perceived that the Scots were going to beat them to Falside Hill. Although there may not have been much difference in the overall distances that each army had to traverse, the Scots had had a head start and their route up the hillside, if that was their plan, was easier than the one facing the English. Somerset had put some effort into pushing his baggage train onwards to the comparative safety of the hilltop, no doubt also mindful that if his baggage were behind his footmen that would severely curtail his options in a battle. He also managed to get some of his artillery on the hill as well. Both baggage and guns were drawn by horses and could be whipped into action, the baggage perhaps taking a circuitous route to terrace the brae from the north and end up on the summit of the hill adjacent to Falside Castle. At least some of the guns may have been taken on a route more to the southwest, on the line of the present road from Clement's Wells to the castle, and not all of these had been positioned to fire on the Scottish battles by the time the two armies clashed.

There was a limit to how quickly Somerset could get his footmen to move while still maintaining their order. Clearly a desperate measure was called for, and that was releasing cavalry for an attack on the Scottish vanguard to prevent it from continuing its advance (Figure 7.11). A full-frontal assault of cavalry against men armed with pikes was neither a wise nor an easy option. Patten could not criticise anything that Somerset chose to do but he did play up the drama of the decision and sacrifice that the cavalry was prepared to make. Grey's request to Somerset that if things went badly for him he should look after his wife and children, is recorded, as well as the surprising admission that many of the men-at-arms had not armoured their horses before setting out from camp that morning, assuming that there would be no pitched battle.[104] Clearly Grey and his men had not envisaged that they might be required to ride against intact formations of enemy pikemen.

Somerset committed most (perhaps all) of his men-at-arms and demilances, with Lord Grey in overall command. Grey had to marshal his horsemen into one unit and lead them round from the left flank of the infantry, then still marching forwards, taking a wide sweep southward up Falside Brae and then down the slope in the direction of the advancing Scottish vanguard.

Angus should have had a reasonable amount of warning of this impending clash, both from Scottish scouts and visual observation. In any case, his battle was so positioned that it was protected from all-out assault by a slough, probably the place now known as Colton Dean. To his left Angus had four or five guns and, on his right, a contingent of horsemen, probably the full force of Scottish horse in the field that day. At this point the Scottish main battle and the rear-guard were some distance to the west of the vanguard and positioned side by side, in present day terms to the east of Crookston farm (see Figure 5.2).[105] The Scots were evidently in the process of turning from a marching formation to a line of battle facing eastwards, towards Falside Brae, already anticipating that an English attack was about to be unleashed from that quarter.

At this juncture it is appropriate to consider how decisions on the deployment of the forces involved in the fighting that day might have been made. On the one hand, Somerset was mounted and accompanied by a small support group and could ride out and take an overview of the disposition of his forces in relation to the enemy. Senior commanders like Warwick and Grey were able to confer directly with him, face to face, when necessary. Arran, on the other hand, although he had a horse within reach to whisk him away when his army collapsed, seems to have intended to command the main battle on foot from its ranks. There were riders and heralds that could pass on instructions from Arran to other units, but there is no evidence of face-to-face meetings between Arran and his divisional commanders after they set out that morning, nor any evidence for information flowing from the units back to Arran. It is surely the case that Arran would have received reports about what was happening elsewhere, and have sent revised orders, but it seems likely that he was at a considerable disadvantage in maintaining control of his army.

As the Scottish army marched towards Falside Hill, it is probable that Angus was best placed to understand what was happening and what changes might be necessary to the overall plan and its timing. Perhaps Arran should have been content to devolve overall command to such a man of experience and reputation in military matters. However, comments by Scottish writers (notably Buchanan and Hume of Godscroft)

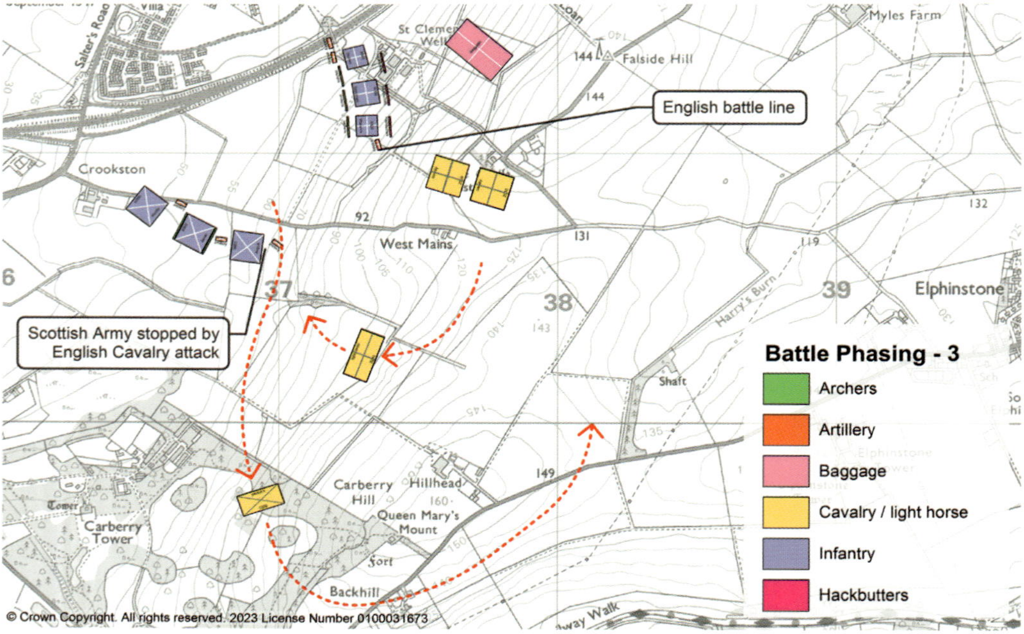

Figure 7.11: Battle Phasing, 10 September – 3: A cavalry attack is launched by the English on the Scottish vanguard while the English army is drawn up in line of battle. The Scots horse manoeuvres away, aiming to launch an attack along Falside Hill (Geddes Consulting Ltd)

stating that Arran sent instructions to Angus to speed up his march,[106] suggest that Arran was reluctant to allow Angus too much control.

The Scottish army, as already mentioned, was seen to pause on its march through the fallow Inveresk fields and that may have provided a last opportunity for the main commanders to confer. A decision that could well have been made was to launch a cavalry attack. Certainly, the whole force of Scottish horse moved from its position adjacent to the vanguard, sweeping southwards to the summit of Carberry Hill before turning to attack the English artillery and baggage train being gathered on Falside Hill. A combination of timing and routes meant that the Scottish light horse avoided making contact with the incoming English heavy cavalry, which from a Scottish point of view may have been a successful outcome.

The main thing for the Scottish commanders to agree on at this point must surely have been to turn their battles from marching order into a battleline. There is no reason to doubt that they were aware of the lie of the land ahead of them, especially the presence of Colton Dean. While obviously an inconvenient obstacle it would not necessarily have been viewed as too big a challenge by commanders who had already that day marched their men across the River Esk. Nevertheless, it would be understandable if the plan was to keep the army to the north of it. It probably seemed when the decision was made as if there was ample space to do this at a reasonable distance from the enemy forces.

It is probable that this manoeuvre was already underway when it became evident that an attack by the English heavy horse was about to be unleashed. The first table in Patten's book (see Figure 5.1) may show that as the English army was still on the march the Scottish rear-guard was already moving up to take its place on the left flank of the main battle. The Scottish vanguard is shown slightly separate, facing the English attack across the slough.

As matters turned out, only the Scottish vanguard was the target of this cavalry attack. It was probably no accident that Angus made his stand so that Colton Dean was between his battle and the approaching enemy horse. He had the presence of mind and skill to position his forces to provide maximum protection for his own men and serious inconvenience for the English. He would have had to wheel his battle around clockwise so that its front was facing the slough. He did not take up position right on its lip but left space, about 100 m, for the now disorganised English to cross rigs, their momentum lost, into the points of his pikes. Possibly his detachment of artillery could not be used to any great effect without endangering the gunners, but Patten does record that one Englishman, Sir Thomas Darcy, received a glancing blow from a piece of shot from a Scottish field piece which dented his armour, broke his sword hilt and damaged a finger.[107]

By trumpet blast the front ranks of the Scottish vanguard were ordered to lower their pikes as the English horse emerged from Colton Dean towards them.[108] The front rank placed the butts of their pikes on the ground and steadied them with their feet. They thus thrust forwards and upwards at an ideal angle to impale the bellies of the unprotected English horses, as Angus had instructed. The second, third, fourth and fifth Scottish ranks would have shouldered their pikes, creating a dense array of spear points that proved impenetrable.

We are lacking clarity on how the English attacked. Grey had been instructed to stop the Scottish advance and this order translated into an attack on the front of the enemy vanguard. It was probably in several waves as men were felled, beaten back, and regrouped to try again. English staves (lances) were pitted against Scottish pikes, the former being shorter in length. English casualties were possibly as high as 200. Lord Grey had a significant injury from a pike thrust into his mouth.[109] Edward Shelley, lieutenant of the men-at-arms from Boulogne, lost his life.[110] Scottish casualties were negligible.

The Scots fought courageously and with some confidence, shouting at, and taunting their opponents with insults, calling them loons, tykes and heretics. At one stage the left of the Scottish front was beaten back and compressed but it remained intact. Some Scots were detached to tackle the wounded and unhorsed Englishmen, and very nearly, by Patten's admission, captured the royal standard, coming away with part of its shaft.[111] After about an hour, the English retreated back the way they had come. Grey and his cavalry had achieved the goal they had been set of stopping the Scottish advance, and would have been able to see that the rest of Somerset's commanders had now drawn the units of foot soldiers into a line of battle, with the left flank of the English vanguard resting on a turf-banked enclosure at the foot of Falside Hill. This was probably at St Clement's Wells. The main battle and rear-guard stretched out in line on to the gently sloping Fore-Brae. The English line faced westwards, stretching northwards towards Wallyford. It was well positioned to engage in battle with the Scots forming their battleline further southwest on the same Fore-Brae.

Grey's manoeuvre had bought the English much needed time to deploy their forces, but now his retreat came close to bringing the whole army to disaster. His efforts to create an orderly withdrawal were not a complete success, with a number of his horsemen rushing back to the English lines in disorder. Many may have aimed to pass through the gap between their vanguard and main battle but some broke through the ranks of the vanguard. It was with difficulty that Warwick held it together and restored calm in the ranks and amongst the horsemen.[112]

There would have been many in the English ranks at this point who would have feared that this was a significant turning point, the Scots triumphant over the main strength of their army and ready now to do what they did best, advance their formations of pikemen and tackle the English foot. For most of the day the English had been reacting to moves by the Scots, trying to catch up with them or stop their progress. There must have been jubilation in the ranks of the Scottish vanguard at their success, but all was not well elsewhere. The Scottish horse, which had been ordered to tackle the artillery being planted on Falside Hill, as well as perhaps attacking the English baggage train, had failed in its objectives. The English gunners had managed to set up a battery of guns to fire on the incoming Scots, and the Scottish horse seem to have been unable to deal with a well-armed squad of carters. They rode off to Cousland and took no further part in the fighting that day.

All the time that the Scottish vanguard was being attacked by the English heavy horse the main battle and rear-guard remained inactive. They were probably both still in marching order, facing east to south-eastwards up the hill, with the rear-guard having begun to pull forwards alongside the main battle (Figure 7.12). There would have been an understandable reluctance to turnabout from marching to battle order while their vanguard was under attack. Now that the English cavalry had been seen off, the obvious next step was for the main battle and rear-guard to join the vanguard in line abreast, facing the English army.

The English were too distant to use their footmen to stop the Scots completing this manoeuvre and were understandably reluctant to commit their cavalry again. Their options at this point were limited to long distance fire from their artillery and bringing their hand gunners and archers into play. The large guns, both on the hill and with the main army, may have had some effect, though the fire was not all one way. Pitscottie claims that the Scots dismounted a large English gun by their fire.[113] It was, however, the English hackbutters who presented themselves as the biggest, immediate threat to the Scottish vanguard. There were 600 of them, a good number

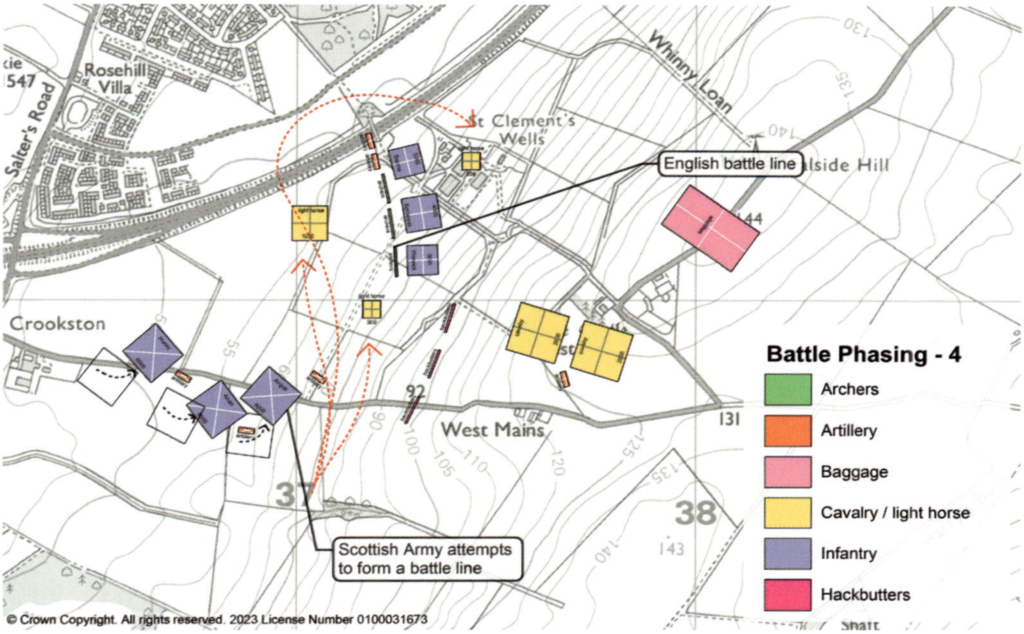

Figure 7.12: Battle Phasing, 10 September – 4: The English cavalry make a disorderly retreat after failing to break the Scottish vanguard. The Scots attempt to form a battle line but are under increasing fire from English artillery and hackbutters (Geddes Consulting Ltd)

of whom were now brought forward to line the slough. They were joined by the 200 mounted hackbutters captained by Pedro Gamboa.[114] The Scots had neither hand gunners of their own to return their fire nor horsemen to ride them down. They did, however, have a sizeable professional body of archers from the West Highlands and Islands, brigaded in two units either side of their main battle, and it is a legitimate question to wonder why they were not brought into play at this time.

Hume of Godscroft, perhaps reflecting a justification provided by Angus himself, says it was the gunfire from the mounted hackbutters that caused him to turn his battle 'softly' in such a way that Arran perceived that he was in the process of fleeing.[115] It is not certain how exactly Angus turned, in precisely which direction, but what is clear is that it was unexpected and unauthorised by Arran. Angus' decision at this juncture may reveal underlying challenges in the command structure of the Scottish forces and the cohesion of their army. On the one hand, Angus may not have had much respect for Arran and his actions at Pinkie suggest he needed to be reined in from making decisions without adequate orders or consultation. On the other hand, John Knox suggests that Arran and Huntly had decided that Angus' force, which probably had a large Protestant element, should be left to fight it out alone with the English army.[116] The antiquary and herald, Sir James Balfour of Denmiln (1600–57) wrote that the English won Pinkie by the multitude of their men and the treachery of the Earl of Huntly. No explanation is offered for this remark but it smacks of a sectarian outlook by this staunch Presbyterian.[117] This idea that underlying tensions between Catholic and Protestant factions in the Scottish army were influencing attitudes and events cannot be ignored. While it is clearly improbable that Arran and Huntly should have decided to abandon Angus, the latter might well have entertained doubts about the extent to which he could rely upon other elements in the army to support him. Angus is alleged to have complained to Mary of Guise that the defeat was down to the fact that he had been abandoned by Arran and Huntly.[118]

Angus' manoeuvre precipitated uncertainty if not panic in the Scottish army. He must have expected to take his place on the right wing of a new battle line facing towards, but not parallel to the English army, across level, open land at a distance of about quarter of a mile (about 400 m). This would involve Arran and Huntly swinging their battles around in an anti-clockwise direction, though not as far as Angus. If any reliance can be placed on Patten's first table (see Figure 5.1), the main battle and rear-guard were too close together at this point, limiting their opportunity to manoeuvre effectively. Much more serious was the consequence of the greater turn being made by the vanguard, which brought it crashing into the archers on the flank of the main battle. This gave the Scottish army the appearance of being one very large mass of footmen, a development specifically noted by the author of Harleian MS 540 and clear from the Battle of Pinkie Roll (see Figure 5.8).

We know of no precedents for such a move, nor can we suggest any line of reasoning that would have led the Scottish high command to think that it had any merit. At best, it produced a formation that was too large and unwieldy and which could more readily be outflanked by the enemy. Our explanation for this development is that it was the consequence of poor judgement by the Scottish leaders in the very basic military skill of marching and positioning their units. They had moved closer together in the process of the march from Pinkiehill and subsequent manoeuvres than was wise, and now Angus' unexpected shift was causing a disastrous bunching together.

Most pressure was on the main battle and the archers, now being pressed between the vanguard and rear-guard. Somerset could no doubt see and understand the predicament that his foes had inflicted upon themselves from his vantage point on Falside Hill, and any feelings of despair he may have harboured at his heavy cavalry being mauled would have been swept away by a new tide of optimism. More to the point, he was able to again take the initiative, bring his forces and guns to bear upon the Scots and precipitate their flight.

The sequence and duration of the final events in the confrontation between the two armies is not certain, but it is probable that the Scots had locked themselves together to such an extent that they could not immediately march in battle order towards the English line. The English hand gunners could therefore continue to fire unmolested on the Scots, especially their vanguard, and other forces of English gunners and archers were soon being ordered forward. Clearly the Scottish archers, whose function at this time should have been to pick off their English opposite numbers as well as their hackbutters, were so hemmed in that they could not fire their arrows. The English artillery was probably also having more and more effect on what was essentially a sitting target.

There may only have been minutes between the retreat of the English heavy cavalry from its attack on the Scottish vanguard and when it became evident that the Scottish main battle was beginning to break. A charitable explanation is that Arran and many of his men had little choice but to try and extricate themselves by turning or reversing backwards out of the squeeze they found themselves in. Similarly, this may be the explanation for why Argyll's men were also said to be amongst the first to break rank, as described by Leonard Digges, the English compounded the Scots' misery by taunting them with news that their general had already fled – whether strictly true or not.[119] Such 'fake news' could clearly have had a devastating effect on morale, and in this case can be recognised as a major cause of the Scottish collapse. Pitscottie describes how the Scottish vanguard with the remnants of the main battle then attempted to manoeuvre themselves alongside their rear-guard, but in the poor visibility some chose to identify them as an enemy force.[120]

At this point many generals in Somerset's situation would have advanced their battles of footmen to attack the Scots directly. Yet in reality there appears to have been a delay. We have seen above how Arran promoted the view that the English footmen were young and inexperienced. Perhaps Arran had a point and Somerset was cautious about committing his footmen, especially having just witnessed the near break up of his vanguard by the defeated English horsemen. According to the Pinkie Roll the English footmen did eventually advance and take part in the chase of the fleeing Scots (see Figure 5.11). However, it seems that the advance by the English foot took place quite late on and did not contribute in a major way to the turning point in the Scottish fortunes or the outcome of the battle.

The final blow for the Scots may have come in the form of another one or two cavalry attacks. English and diplomatic sources paint a confusing picture of what happened in the closing stages of the battle. Some of that uncertainty may result from political manipulation to give credit for events either to Somerset or Warwick. Only Hooper's informant claimed that such an attack was led by Grey of Wilton, but this is unlikely given the severity of the wound he had received earlier in the day.[121] The Battle of Pinkie Roll depicts a cavalry attack on the Scottish rear-guard which might have been led by Warwick. Another charge of the re-grouped men-at-arms may have been led by Somerset on the Scottish vanguard.

Confusion, the apparent retreat or flight of some units, shot from artillery, archers and hackbutters, renewed attacks by cavalry and, possibly, the sight of advancing English battles of footmen meant individual Scots had plenty of reasons to doubt whether continuing in the ranks was a sound strategy for preserving their life. Blind panic no doubt spurred many to flee, dropping not just their weapons but also shedding items of clothing and armour to enable them to run faster. Ahead of them was the River Esk or else a turn southwards towards Dalkeith. Beyond the river, Edinburgh was only a few miles away, and an obvious place to seek safety for those who could make it. Some men, notably including the Earl of Arran, had access to horses positioned nearby on the battlefield, and perhaps others were able to get to the horses that had been left in camp. Other Scots resorted to lying down and pretending to be dead or submerging themselves in the river.[122] Some units of men managed to retain some cohesion in marching away and thus discouraged attack from scattered English horsemen looking for easy wins. A notable example of this appears to have been Argyll's men, many of whom were professional warriors.[123] The pursuit of the fleeing Scots seems to have been led by the English cavalry. To what extent the English foot participated is not known. Possibly the English ships also targeted Scots who had made for the bridge over the Esk or an escape along the shore.[124]

The Scottish losses were clearly brutal. Some information on individual deaths can be gleaned from early Scottish sources. They included three lords – Cathcart, Elphinstone and Fleming. There were also several lairds, heirs and younger sons. Whole families and kin groups were cut down together, including at least seven Gordon lairds, eight Kennedy lairds, nine Ramsays, a whole generation of Ogilvies and seven sons of Thomas Urquhart of Cromarty. One of the Scottish trumpeters, Julian Drummond, was also killed.[125]

Patten describes the horrible wounds inflicted by the horsemen upon the fleeing Scots, in particular about the head and upper body.[126] Dead bodies were strewn over the land almost to the gates of Edinburgh and from the shore inland for four miles in the direction of Dalkeith. Further casualties resulted from men drowning in the river. There are vastly varying figures provided by contemporary sources regarding the number of Scottish dead (see Tables 5.1 and 5.2). One of the more conservative estimates is Huntly's claim that 6,000 Scots were killed. This amounted to a bit more than a quarter of the total Scottish fighting force. Some prisoners were also taken, though, relatively speaking not in as great numbers. Patten reported that above 1,500 prisoners were noted in the marshal's book.[127] According to Holinshed, they were held after the battle in a church in Leith, identified by Bishop Leslie as St Anthony's, actually an Augustinian hospital.[128] The wounded appear to have been released after a day. The only prisoner held for any length of time was the Earl of Huntly, who as the most prominent Scot captured was taken back to London as a hostage. The English lost only a few hundred men. Officially, it was given out that they were restricted to 200, although rumours at the Tudor court, fed by private letters from those in the army, indicated that 500 to 600 was more likely.[129] The highest estimate of the English deaths seems to be 800 men.

Protector Somerset appears to have brought the fighting to an end about five o'clock, having trumpeters call the retreat for his horsemen from the far side of the Scottish camp. The killing of the Scots was mostly done by mounted troops, none of which appear to have been held back. One incident late in the day that Patten reported with apparent glee was the burning of Falside Castle (see Figure 6.7) over the heads of its garrison who had had the temerity to fire their guns on the English earlier in the afternoon.[130]

By the evening of Saturday 10 September 1547, the English had won the Battle of Pinkie. The Earl of Arran and his army had fled from the fields of Inveresk, leaving behind their artillery, and dropping 'their weapons and armour'.[131] In the aftermath of the battle the English collected 'above' 30,000 items of Scottish kit, in particular jacks and swords, which they took south by ship.[132] Towards the end of Saturday, the English forces regrouped, many of them gathering in the remains of the Scottish camp, which Patten describes as being located at Edminston Edge. Here, the English soldiers 'made an universal noise and shout' in honour of their 'gladness and victory'.[133] Supposedly, the shouting was so loud it could be heard in Edinburgh. That night Somerset's army camped at Edgebuckling Brae, near Pinkie Cleugh, which Patten reckoned was about 'a mile beyond' the camp they had left that morning.[134] Shortly after the English had pitched their tents at Edgebuckling Brae, there was 'a great shower of rain that lasted well nigh an hour'. Some of the English army regarded this downpour as a 'token' of 'God's assent and applause' for their victory.[135]

In hindsight, the English victory at Pinkie can seem inevitable. Yet, the contemporary evidence clearly indicates that this outcome was far from assured. The Scottish army was larger and defending its own territory. Whilst the English did have certain advantages, such as their fleet and heavy cavalry, there was not a great technological gulf between the two sides. As a result, there were several moments at Pinkie that were very finely balanced. During the critical Friday and Saturday both Somerset and Arran had, on occasions, reason for optimism and cause for alarm. Somerset appears to have had a better grasp than Arran of what he could ask different units to do, and how to move men effectively around the battlefield. He was a flawed politician, but a relatively skilled general. He also had in his army a number of men who had already worked closely together in conflict situations in both the British Isles and France. Significantly, when things went wrong, it was these experienced cavalry men, hackbutters, and gunners that Somerset relied on. Ultimately, these men delivered, and, as night fell on Saturday 10 September 1547, Somerset was undoubtedly in control of the terrain around Pinkie Cleugh. However, what else the English would control was still unclear.

Notes

1 Patten, f. 39r.
2 Patten, f. 43v.
3 *CSP Scot* 1, 19.
4 Interestingly, Wharton appears to have been firmly convinced of the strategic significance of Castlemilk, whilst Somerset appears to have been less sure. See *CSP Dom Add*, 329.
5 *CSP Scot* 1, 11; *CSP Spain* 9, 181.
6 *Navy of Edward VI*, 26–27.
7 Patten, f. 36r–v.
8 *CSP Scot* 1, 19; Patten, ff. 36r–37r.
9 Patten, ff. 37r–38r.
10 Patten, f. 38r–v.
11 Patten, f. 39r.

12 R. Virgoe and A. Hawkyard, 'Brende (Brande), John (by 1515–1559), of London and Beccles, Suff.', biography from *The History of Parliament*.
13 Somerset, 'Proclamation'.
14 Merriman, *The Rough Wooings*, fig. 11.3.
15 *TA* 9, 110, 111.
16 Somerset, 'Proclamation'.
17 NRS, Register of Acts and Decreets, 1st series, especially CS7/3/1 and CS7/3/2. See, for instance, CS7/3/1 ff. 239v, 246r; CS7/3/2 ff. 276, 288v–289r.
18 Patten, f. 39r.
19 Patten, f. 39r.
20 Patten, ff. 43v–44r.
21 BL, Harleian MS 540.
22 Patten, f. 44.
23 Graham, 'Archaeology on a Great Post Road', 318–47, provides useful information on the Pease and on the early route from Berwick to Edinburgh. He, however (p. 324 n.1), misquotes Patten to say that the English crossed 'twenty skore' from the sea. Patten was indicating that it was 20 score paces or yards wide. There is no reason to doubt that the crossing was actually made by the shore of Pease Bay.
24 Patten, f. 45r.
25 Patten, f. 45r.
26 Patten, f. 46r.
27 Patten, ff. 48r, 52r.
28 Patten, ff. 47v–48r.
29 Patten, f. 48v.
30 Patten, ff. 48r–51v.
31 Patten, f. 51v.
32 Patten, f. 52r–v.
33 Patten, f. 52v.
34 Patten, f. 52v.
35 Patten, ff. 53r, 56r–58v.
36 In 1535 Haddington had the heaviest tax burden after the four major burghs of Edinburgh, Dundee, Aberdeen and Perth. J. D. Marwick (ed.), *Records of the Convention of the Royal Burghs of Scotland*, 5 vols (Edinburgh, 1866–1885) 1, 514–15.
37 Patten, f. 60v.
38 Patten, f. 61r–v.
39 For further discussion of the decision to muster at Fala see Chapter 4 of this work.
40 *TA* 9, 120.
41 *CSP Spain* 9, 181.
42 *CSP Scot* 1, no. 40, (p. 18).
43 *HP* 2, 363.
44 Clues for this, noted in Chapter 6, are the drawing up of a document at Gilberton on 7 September (*RMS* 1546–1580, no. 160), and the holding of a convention at Monktonhall on 8 September (RPS, A1547/9/1–3).
45 See Chapter 6 for more discussion of the question of the number of Scottish camps and their location.
46 Patten, f. 69r.
47 For further insights into the role that conventions played in early sixteenth-century Scotland see A. Blakeway, *Parliament and Convention in the Personal Rule of James V of Scotland, 1528–1542* (Cham, 2022).
48 RPS, A1547/9/1–3.
49 Pitscottie 2, 93–96; Buchanan, *History*, vol. 2, 366.

50 Maxwell, *Historical Memoirs*, 21.
51 Letter from the Lord Wharton and the Earl of Lennox, 6 November. TNA, SP 50/1, f. 97r.
52 Dalrymple 2, 297–98.
53 Patten, f. 62r.
54 Patten, f. 62r.
55 Patten, f. 62v.
56 Patten, f. 63r. H. R. Woudhuysen, 'Ferrers, George (c. 1510–1579)', *ODNB*.
57 Patten, f. 63r.
58 Patten, f. 63v.
59 Patten, ff. 63v–64r.
60 Patten, f. 64r.
61 Patten, f. 67r.
62 Grey, *A Commentary*, 10.
63 Grey, *A Commentary*, 10.
64 Grey, *A Commentary*, 11.
65 Patten, f. 67r–v.
66 Patten, f. 67r.
67 Grey, *A Commentary*, 11–12.
68 Grey, *A Commentary*, 12–13.
69 M. C. Fissel, *English Warfare, 1511–1642* (London, 2001), 32, wrote that English tactics, outflanking both ends of the Scottish cavalry, were decisive in this action on 9 September, but that interpretation does not seem to be solidly based on early accounts.
70 Patten, f. 69r.
71 *Diurnal*, 44–45.
72 Patten, f.69r.
73 Hume, *Douglas History*, 271.
74 Patten, f. 72r.
75 Patten, ff. 70v–73r.
76 Pitscottie 2, 96.
77 Buchanan, *History* 2, 364–67.
78 *MLSC*, 79–80.
79 *Selve*, 218–19 (no. 242).
80 Knox, *History*, vol. 1, 99.
81 Patten, ff. 114v–115r.
82 Skidmore, *Edward VI*, 78.
83 Knox, *History* 1, 98.
84 Patten, ff. 74r–75r.
85 Buchanan, *History* 2, 367; Pitscottie 2, 95.
86 Beaugué, *L'Histoire de la Guerre D'Escosse*, ff. 15v, 18r, 50v–55r; Holinshed, *The Laste Volume*, 1638; A. Teulet, *Relations Politiques De La France Et De L'Espagne Avec L'Écosse Au XVIe Siècle. Tome Premier. Correspondances Françaises 1515–1560* (Paris, 1862), 185–86; Pitcairn, *Ancient Criminal Trials*, 345.
87 Pitscottie 2, 99.
88 Dalrymple 2, 297–98.
89 Pitscottie 2, 95; Patten, ff. 79v–80r.
90 Patten, f. 80r.
91 Patten, ff. 88v–89r.
92 Patten, f. 88v. *The Battle of Pinkie Roll* is discussed and interpreted in chapter 5.
93 *Original Letters*, vol. 1, 43–44 (letter XXIV).
94 Patten, f. 80r.
95 Hume, *Douglas History*, 273.

96 See, for instance, the table of gun sizes in Caldwell, 'How Well Prepared Was James IV', 75; Arnold, *The Renaissance at War*, 40–41.
97 Hume, *Douglas History*, 273. In this context the Highlanders were presumably from the north and east of Scotland, lands under the sway of Huntly.
98 The authors are grateful to Jon Cooper for making this case to them.
99 Buchanan, *History* 2, 367; Hume, *Douglas History*, 272.
100 Patten, f. 82v.
101 Patten, f. 81r.
102 Patten, ff. 83v–84r; Dalrymple 2, 299.
103 Two 'flightshot' apart: Patten, f. 82v.
104 Patten, ff. 89r–90v.
105 Patten, f. 88v.
106 Buchanan, *History* 2, 367; Hume, *Douglas History*, 272.
107 Patten, f. 94r.
108 The reference to trumpet signals comes from Pitscottie 2, 97, and there are other useful, original pieces of information from Scottish sources like the *Diurnal*, 45. Most of the detailed information is provided by Patten, ff. 88v–95r.
109 Patten, f. 93v.
110 Patten, f. 112r.
111 Patten, f. 94v.
112 Patten, f. 96r.
113 Pitscottie 2, 99.
114 Patten, f. 99r.
115 Hume, *Douglas History*, 272–73. Eltis, *The Military Revolution*, 114, claims that Gamboa and his men executed a caracole, meaning they attacked in waves, firing their guns from horseback before turning away. This was a tactic being employed elsewhere in Europe at this time by mounted troops armed with pistols. It is more likely that these hackbutters dismounted to fire their guns.
116 Knox, *History* 1, 100.
117 Sir J. Balfour, *The Historical Works* (Edinburgh, 1824), vol. 1, 288.
118 Hume, *Douglas History*, 273.
119 Digges and Digges, *Stratioticos*, 158.
120 Pitscottie 2, 100.
121 *Original Letters* 1, letter XXIV.
122 Patten, ff. 101r–105r.
123 This assumes that they were the force identified by George Buchanan as *Scoti prisci* (Buchanan, *History* 2, 368).
124 Herries, *Memoirs*, 20.
125 See Caldwell, 'The Battle of Pinkie', 86, and especially n.90.
126 Patten, ff. 104r–v.
127 Patten, ff. 108r–v.
128 https://canmore.org.uk/site/51984 (accessed 14 December 2020); I. B. Cowan and D. E. Easson, *Medieval Religious Houses Scotland* (London, 1976), 184–85.
129 *CSP Spain* 9, 150, 152; *Selve*, 222.
130 Patten, ff. 116r–v.
131 Patten, f. 117.
132 Patten, f. 117.
133 Patten, f. 111r.
134 Patten, ff. 117v–118r.
135 Patten, f. 118r.

8

Pinkie: first and last

After Pinkie: the English policy

During the sixteenth century both English and Scottish commentators tended to agree that at Pinkie the Duke of Somerset won a 'great victory'.[1] Yet more recent writers have often felt that Somerset did surprisingly little with the military advantage he gained. The day after the battle the English buried their dead and 'did very diligently get together all the Scottish ordnance'.[2] They then marched along the edge of the Firth of Forth towards Leith, arriving 'about three of the clock in the afternoon'.[3] Somerset was among the first English soldiers to enter Leith, which was found 'desolate of resistance or anybody else'.[4] The port became the base for Somerset's forces over the next few days, as the English sought to project their military influence in the countryside around Edinburgh and the Forth. However, on Sunday 18 September, after burning much of Leith, Protector Somerset and most of the army 'rode to England again'.[5] On their way south some of the English troops went along the route where the 'chief of the chase' had taken place just over a week earlier, and found themselves marching past unburied Scottish corpses 'the colour of their skins changed greenish about the place they had been smitten'.[6] After 10 days of military activity in the Borders, Somerset 'passed over the Tweed' into England on Michaelmas Day (29 September) and 'took his way straight toward Newcastle and thence homeward'.[7] Meanwhile, a group of his officers rode to Berwick to await diplomatic representation from Scotland, which never arrived (Figure 8.1).

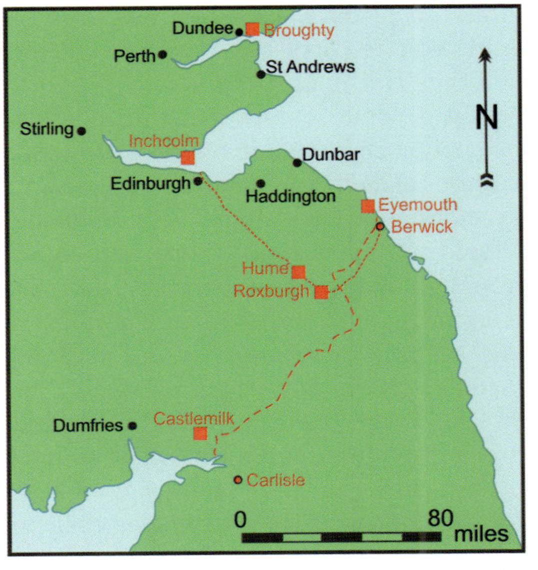

Figure 8.1: Map showing the route home taken by the English army at the end of September and the garrisons left at Broughty, Inchcolm, Eyemouth, Hume, Roxburgh and Castlemilk

Protector Somerset's hasty return has been criticised by a number of historians, who have argued that he threw away a moment of opportunity. In the 1960s, W. K. Jordan remarked on Somerset's 'inexplicably' sudden departure 'only a week after his great victory had been won', and criticised the 'compulsive haste involved in [his] precipitate return'.[8] More recently, Chris Skidmore asserted that Somerset chose 'to return to London rather than pursue his advantage up through Scotland' – a decision attributed to Somerset's alarm about his brother Sir Thomas Seymour's machinations at court.[9] Yet it is debatable whether Somerset's actions after Pinkie were as misguided as these comments suggest. Indeed, despite his seeming success on the fields of Inveresk, the options facing Somerset in the middle of September 1547 were still unenviable, and his decision to withdraw a significant proportion of his forces may have been the least worst option.

Before he left London in August, Somerset had intended that his personal involvement in the Scottish campaign should be a matter of weeks rather than months. Quite apart from the political problem of a new head of government absenting himself from the country for a long time, there were sensible practical reasons to plan a short campaign. In order to invade Scotland, the English had removed soldiers from their fortifications in France and redirected naval forces from the south coast. Such a state of affairs was made possible by the recent peace with France. However, it was unclear whether the more cordial Anglo-French dynamic would last. The newly crowned Henry II of France was adopting a more aggressive approach, reflected in the attack on St Andrews Castle in July 1547, which the French reputedly boasted about being able to carry out 'without contravening the treaties in force between them and the English' as it was held by 'Scottish rebels'.[10] Immediately before leaving for Scotland, Somerset informed the Imperial ambassador, Francis van der Delft, that 'he had not much hope of maintaining the peace' with France, although he was 'sincerely desirous of doing so'.[11] Somerset claimed to foreign diplomats that, despite his Scottish expedition, he had 'abundantly supplied' and manned all his fortifications 'on the French side' as well as 'the ports of England'.[12] In reality Somerset had withdrawn from Boulogne and southern England a significant number of his more experienced men for his 'enterprise' in northern Britain. With war in Europe looking ever more likely, a large-scale diversion of forces away from the Anglo-French border became increasingly risky.

Even more pressing than the shifting situation in international politics were problems regarding the time of year and supply. The 1547 attack on Scotland took place near the end of the campaigning season. Bad weather had already been an issue for the English as they assembled their forces prior to Pinkie. On 25 August it was reported in London that the weather had not been 'favourable' to the English ships moving troops and supplies north, and that 'three hundred of the best soldiers. . . taken out of Boulogne to send to Scotland' had been drowned.[13] Even in a good year, the challenges associated with moving large numbers of men and provisions across Scotland during late autumn and winter were almost insurmountable. The impending winter weather was an issue that regularly concerned English leaders in the weeks after Pinkie. Indeed, as Somerset's forces recrossed the Tweed into England on 29 September they encountered difficulties 'by reason of rain that lately fell' making 'the stream so swift' that 'one or two' men drowned and 'many carriages' were 'in great danger'.[14] The situation was not likely to improve as the autumn progressed. On 18 October Lord Grey of Wilton explained to Somerset the reasons for removing cavalry forces from Roxburgh to Warkworth Castle, noting among other points that 'when the water shall arise there [at Roxburgh] as this winter it will. . . no carriage may pass over as your grace well knoweth'.[15] In the same letter Grey complained how even 'in the little time' that he had 'lain upon this frontier' there had been 'such a scarcity' of food for horses and men that if he kept his cavalry forces at Roxburgh all winter the men-at-arms and demilances would be 'unfit for service' by 'the spring of the year'.[16] By 27 October, Grey felt that conditions had significantly worsened, and he informed Somerset that any plans for large scale military activity must be given up, as such 'great abundance of rain' had 'fallen and daily doth fall' that the waters had risen and the ground was 'so rotten' that 'neither carriage nor men on horseback be able to pass'.[17] The weather in the autumn of 1547, which was wetter than for 'many years', meant that Somerset would have struggled to campaign effectively in Scotland much beyond Michaelmas, traditionally regarded as the start of autumn and the day on which his forces crossed back into England.[18]

It is clear that the practicalities of transport and supply were a factor in Somerset's decision-making during the latter part of 1547. In mid-October the unreliable Scottish nobleman Sir George Douglas sent the English a scheme for a further invasion of Scotland. Somerset rejected these plans on the grounds that they would lead to 'butchery', and stressed that the English were 'not so ignorant' as to venture 'far into the heart' of Scotland with just a few days of 'victual'.[19] The Pinkie campaign was made possible by the provisions brought north by land and sea. But these supplies were not limitless. Indeed, on 24 September Lord Clinton reported that the English fleet's activities at Broughty Ferry had been cut short by 'lack of victual'.[20] The expense of maintaining an army in this way was also considerable. Somerset will have been aware that the costs of his intervention in Scotland were rapidly mounting. According to the account submitted by Sir Ralph Sadler in December 1547 the expenses of 'the king's majesty's army against Scotland' added up to more than £44,912 for the period between 1 August and 20 November.[21] This figure excludes the costs of victuals, and the expenses of the naval forces taken north. Nevertheless, it is still almost double the original budget for the army's invasion.[22]

The challenges facing Somerset's forces were not removed by their victory at Pinkie. Indeed, in some respects the battle worsened their problems. Despite having much smaller losses than the Scots, the English did not come away unscathed. In particular, a large number of horses were killed or injured. This equine tragedy had a noticeable impact on the English army's operational effectiveness. On 23 October Lord Grey reported that he had at his disposal 840 'able men and horses', 100 'unable men' and 588 'evil horses'.[23] Part of the horse crisis related to the difficulty of obtaining suitable fodder in the Borders. However, the shortage was also directly connected to the fighting at Pinkie. In November Grey wrote to Somerset specifically complaining of the 'great loss of horses in the late battle'.[24] The English cavalry paid a considerable price at Pinkie, and their decreased effectiveness removed a key advantage that Somerset held over the Scots.

Given all these challenges, Somerset's decision not to push further into Scotland appears fairly rational. Indeed, it could be argued that it is to his credit that he managed to return such a large proportion of his forces to England. William Patten's gratitude to Somerset for 'so small a loss' of his men, was not completely misplaced.[25] Yet what did those men achieve during the 25 days they were in Scotland? Had they secured anything of value by the end of September 1547?

From the vantage point of 'four months' after Pinkie, the effusive Patten certainly thought that Somerset had done something remarkable.[26] He claimed that through the 'valiant policy of my lord Protector's grace' the English had:

> overturned many of our enemies' rebellious holds, and then overcome the double of our number and strength in open field. . . slain so great a multitude of them. . . taken of their chiefest prisoners, won. . . a great sort of their strongest forts, builded many new, taken and destroyed their whole navy, and brought the townships in the hither part of their bounds. . . in an honest obedience unto the King's Majesty.[27]

Clearly, this account is partial. Yet it contains several valid points. As 1547 drew to a close, there were reasons why Somerset might have felt that the Pinkie campaign had delivered real results. First and foremost, the English had destroyed a significant proportion of Scotland's potential fighting forces. In the days before Pinkie, the Earl of Arran had assembled one of the largest Scottish armies ever seen. Had the Scots won at Pinkie, Arran may well have chosen to use his forces against English targets. Certainly, nobles on the northern border of England had spent the summer of 1547 being deeply concerned about the prospect of a Scottish attack.[28] Indeed, by capturing Langholm in July, Arran had already demonstrated his willingness to conduct offensive operations. Somerset's victory on 10 September largely eradicated this threat.

Somerset's actions in the days after Pinkie also neutralised much of Scotland's naval forces, which had often harassed English shipping. At the beginning of April 1547 Edward VI's council had complained how the *Mary Willoughby* and other Scottish war ships were on every tide despoiling English merchant vessels.[29] That same month, the Imperial ambassador in London, Francis van der Delft, reported that the Scots had 'captured some English merchant ships' and as a result Somerset's government were reinforcing their 'fleet at sea'.[30] Apparently, the Scots were 'no less vigilant' and 'thought of nothing but war against the English'; information van der Delft had obtained from 'one who is very intimate with one of the Scottish ambassadors'.[31] However, on 15 September 1547 Lord Clinton and the English fleet in the Forth successfully captured the *Mary Willoughby*, as well as a 'large vessel' called the *Bosse* and the *Anthony* of Newcastle (which the Scots had previously taken from the English), all of which had been put 'for safeguard' in the harbour by Blackness Castle.[32] The English also burned a number of Scottish ships in the same incident. By 22 September it was being claimed in London that the English had 'captured all the largest of the Scottish ships to the number of thirteen'.[33] The action at Blackness appears to have largely disabled the Scottish navy.[34] A couple of days later, on 17 September, the English burned six 'great ships' which had been left in the harbour at Leith; although because of 'age and decay' these vessels 'were not so apt for use', the military advantage gained by this decision is questionable.[35] Nevertheless, the overall actions of the English in the days after Pinkie seem to have struck a major blow to Scottish naval power, which had been built up at considerable expense during the reigns of James IV and James V.[36]

However, the damage to Scotland's naval and land forces was not the only advantage the English had gained by the end of September 1547. After his return to London, Protector Somerset had a lengthy meeting with Francis van der Delft, in which he told the diplomat that with God's help the English had won 'not a battle alone, but a country'.[37] Somerset went on to emphasise that his forces had 'occupied and held. . . three strong places. . .all well provided with munitions, and he hoped at another time to push further forward'.[38] Whilst the claim that the English garrisons were 'well provided' was a little optimistic, Somerset's statement that the English had 'three strong places' was arguably conservative, and did not reflect the full scale of the fortifications that the English were building on Scottish soil. It is not completely clear which three fortifications Somerset meant, but he may have been referring to Broughty Ferry (manned by 200 hackbutters and 'a sufficient number of pioneers'), Hume Castle (occupied by 60 hackbutters, 60 horsemen and 100 pioneers) and Roxburgh (garrisoned by 300 soldiers and 200 pioneers, as well as for a brief period housing Lord Grey's cavalry forces).[39]

The establishing of English garrisons in southern Scotland was an integral part of Somerset's plan for the 1547 expedition, which sought to create a pale, or defended sphere of influence, held down by a series of artillery forts and other strongpoints – a strategy the Tudor government had also pursued in France and Ireland.[40] Throughout the Pinkie campaign Somerset paid attention to places where he could build defences, even visiting the site of a possible fort at Eyemouth before the main English army had crossed the border.[41] Following Pinkie, the English further implemented Somerset's garrison scheme. On the Tuesday after the battle, Somerset inspected the island of Inchcolm in the Firth of Forth (Figure 8.2).[42] A few days later, on Saturday 17 September, the experienced soldier Sir John Luttrell was despatched to hold the island with 100 hackbutters, 50 pioneers and 70 'mariners'.[43] Naval forces also played a major role in the English occupation of the castle at Broughty Ferry (see Figure 2.6), then more commonly known as Broughty Crag, at the mouth of the River Tay. On 20 September Lord Clinton and his fleet arrived at Broughty Ferry. The English sent the *Galley Subtle* before the castle and 'shot off three pieces'.[44] The garrison immediately surrendered – the handover having previously been agreed by the Scottish Lord Gray and the castle's

Figure 8.2: Inchcolm Abbey, on an island in the Firth of Forth. Somerset identified that this was a good place to plant a garrison to control or annoy Scottish shipping (David Caldwell)

captain Henry Durham.[45] The main English fleet remained at Broughty Ferry for four days, during which time they nearly 'finished' a trench to provide extra defence from the land, and began 'rampiring the walls and making a platform of earth within the castle'.[46] On 24 September Lord Clinton and much of the fleet departed, leaving Sir Andrew Dudley (who had helped lead the naval operations to assist St Andrews Castle in the spring of 1547) in charge of the newly installed English garrison.

The English army acquired further sites for garrisons as they journeyed south through the Borders. On Thursday 22 September the relatives of Lord Hume, who had been wounded at Pinkie, surrendered Hume Castle to Somerset (see Figure 4.7). The English seem to have regarded Hume Castle as a useful strongpoint, with Patten noting how 'the castle standeth upon a rocky crag. . . on every side well nigh fenced by marsh'.[47] A day later the English occupied Roxburgh (see Figure 2.2), where almost immediately Somerset and the military engineer Sir Richard Lee set about inspecting how to make the site of the former medieval castle as 'defensible, as shortness of time and season of the year' permitted.[48] Somerset was clearly anxious to complete the defences at Roxburgh quickly, even apparently digging with a spade himself – an example that led other 'lords, knights, and gentlemen' to take up 'spade, shovel or mattock' to advance the earthworks.[49] Around this date work was also progressing on the coastal promontory at Eyemouth in Berwickshire, which Somerset had identified as a potential location for a fort right at the beginning of the Pinkie campaign (Figure 8.3). On 15 October 1547, Lord Grey of Wilton reported that at Eyemouth there was 'already raised a bulwark and two curtains', whilst at Roxburgh the fortifications were also 'well forward for so short a time'.[50] The diversionary military intervention on the west side of the country, led by Lord Wharton and the Earl of Lennox, had also secured Castlemilk for the English, where a garrison was similarly installed (see Figure 7.1).[51]

English military activity during September 1547 had therefore given them control of coastal strongpoints at Broughty Ferry, Inchcolm and Eyemouth, and garrisons further inland in the Scottish Borders at Hume, Roxburgh and Castlemilk. The English also briefly contemplated fortifying Leith – Scotland's largest port and the burgh of Edinburgh's link to international trade. On 12 September Somerset and Richard Lee

Figure 8.3: Aerial view of the fort at Eyemouth commenced by the English in September 1547. They erected a rampart across the neck of a promontory with a large, centrally placed, pointed bastion. An outer line of defence with two bastions was commenced ten years later by the French (photo: Colin Martin)

'rode about the town, and to the plots and hillocks on either side' to consider if Leith 'might be made tenable and defensible'.[52] Somerset ultimately decided against this project, for reasons which are unclear, but may have been connected to the sheer size of Leith. Indeed, during the religious conflict of 1560 the French had about 3,000 men defending Leith – a significantly larger force than Somerset left at any of the fortifications he acquired during 1547.[53] There is also some evidence that Somerset was concerned that at low tide the harbour at Leith was 'dry', an explanation the English gave to van der Delft when justifying why they had not kept Scotland's leading port.[54] Had Somerset held Leith he could have established an economic stranglehold on Edinburgh, and exerted control over much of central Scotland. Yet given the difficulties the English had in supplying the forts they did establish, Leith would almost certainly have been a garrison too far.

The English did manage to place garrisons at a number of critical locations. In particular, the island of Inchcolm enabled the English to threaten shipping in the Forth, and so impact water-borne trade to Edinburgh and Stirling. Meanwhile the castle of Broughty Ferry controlled the mouth of the Tay, and so impacted on Dundee and Perth. The strategic potential of these sites was clearly apparent to the English. For example, Patten asserted that together 'St Colm's Inch and Broughty Crag' kept the Scots from the 'whole intercourse of merchants'.[55] Francis van der Delft reported that with 'these strongholds' the English 'consider themselves the masters of the principal part of Scotland and the whole of its navigation'.[56]

By the beginning of October 1547, the English had made worthwhile gains, and were preparing to keep them. From his service in France, Somerset was aware of how garrisons in up-to-date artillery fortifications could hold down enemy countryside. This was a lesson he now sought to implement in Scotland. Excavations at Eyemouth, and plans and written evidence regarding other sites, show that the defences Somerset's forces built in the autumn of 1547 were heavily influenced by recent Continental developments in military architecture, specifically the adoption of what later scholars have termed *trace italienne* fortifications.[57] Such fortifications were characterised by massive earthworks with large pointed bastions, creating a difficult target for enemy artillery and providing effective protection for the guns positioned to defend them. If supplied and manned effectively these structures were extremely difficult to assault. Of course, in the long run the question of supply would turn out to be the Achilles' heel of Somerset's garrison strategy.

Yet in the autumn of 1547 a combination of the victory at Pinkie and the newly planted garrisons seemed to be transforming the situation in southern Scotland. The garrisons were not simply instruments of oppression but were also intended to create protective zones for Scots who were sympathetic to England and the Protestant cause – part of Somerset's 'amicable' approach to invasion. Unlike what happened in the English pales in Ireland and around Boulogne, where many of the men who served at Pinkie implemented policies akin to ethnic cleansing, the garrisons established in Scotland were meant to ally with sympathetic locals.[58] Indeed, in contrast to other Tudor colonial projects, Somerset's occupation of Scotland does not seem to have been predicated on displacing the native inhabitants with English civilian settlements. Instead, the plan was based on winning over to the English cause dissatisfied Scots.

It was a policy that initially seemed to be working. Whilst Somerset was overseeing the building work at Roxburgh, more than 37 'lairds and gentlemen' from the area came in and took an oath of loyalty – supposedly won over by the English Protector's 'wisdom and policy without any fighting or bloodshed'.[59] In early November, Somerset informed van der Delft that Scots 'in the neighbourhood' of the English forts 'were coming in every day in numbers to give their adhesion'.[60] Somerset further claimed that 'other chiefs with their followers in more distant parts of the country were offering their services' but he did not wish to receive them until he 'was in a position to aid and support them'.[61] Reports from English commanders serving in Scotland suggest that Somerset's assessment of the situation was not purely wishful thinking. A blend of factors, including religion, politics, fear, bribery and opportunism encouraged significant numbers of Scots to make 'assurance' (defined by Patten as 'a friendship' and 'a trust') with the English following Pinkie.[62] On 15 October

Grey of Wilton informed Somerset that many of the 'lords and gentlemen' near the garrisons at Roxburgh, Hume and Eyemouth had initially been 'loathe to receive' the English soldiers, but once the Scottish lairds were provided with 'victuals' they were 'well content' to welcome the occupying forces.[63] On 1 November, shortly after the burgh officials of Dundee had pledged their support for the English at Broughty Ferry, Andrew Dudley reported that 'the most part of the town favours the word of God and loveth not the [Catholic] priests'.[64] Dudley furthermore claimed that the 'substantial men' of Dundee 'would be glad their town were English so that it might be fortified to be strengthened against the Governor [Arran]'.[65] The number of assured Scots was considerable, particularly in areas close to the border. In the west Lord Wharton applied significant pressure to Scottish communities to get them to side with the English. On 5 October 1547 Wharton informed Somerset that 'sundry lairds', 'gentlemen' and 'others' of Annandale and Nithsdale had recently come to support the English, and that he now had in total 2,400 Scots serving as soldiers, as well as 'oaths and hostages' from additional local gentry.[66] Wharton also maintained that he laboured 'for the order of justice' in the region 'to the contentment of the reasonable sort'.[67]

The genuineness of the 'contentment' of the assured Scots is a matter for debate. Nevertheless, it is clear that in the autumn of 1547 numerous Scots were willing to contemplate collaboration with the English. Why then, did Somerset's occupation of southern Scotland go so wrong? The eventual Anglo-Scottish peace treaty agreed at Norham Castle in 1551 delivered the English no gains from all the blood and toil of the late 1540s. The causes of Somerset's ultimate failure in Scotland were complex and beyond the scope of this book. However, it is unlikely that the chief cause was Somerset's rapid return to London after Pinkie. Of far greater importance were issues with provisioning the garrisons Somerset left behind. Questions of supply routinely reduced the effectiveness of the English strongholds in Scotland, and significantly hampered the building of fortifications. On 15 October 1547 Lord Grey bemoaned that labourers at Eyemouth 'for lack of victuals and payment do daily... convey themselves away'.[68] A few weeks later, on 2 November, Sir John Luttrell complained that since sending a ship from Inchcolm to Newcastle 'for timber, plank and coal and such other necessaries' he had not 'heard from her' leaving him 'with no help'.[69] The English supply failures also undermined the morale of their garrisons. On 1 November Sir Andrew Dudley wrote from Broughty Ferry criticising the quality of the provisions he had been sent, asserting that 'such rotten biscuit and sour beer was never had' and claiming that on account of the poor victuals he was 'in as much danger' from his own 'soldiers and mariners' as from the Scots.[70] The shortages of food and essential supplies also negatively affected the English garrisons' relationship with surrounding Scottish communities, from whom they sought to obtain necessities, sometimes through purchase, at other times by force. For instance, when the English on Inchcolm had a lack of coal and wood they sailed to Fife to steal boats to burn – an activity which unsurprisingly resulted in a 'skirmish'.[71] The commanders of the garrisons in Scotland clearly felt they were handicapped by a lack of resources. On

3 January 1548 Andrew Dudley informed Somerset that 'we lack but men and money here, the which having we might do wonders'.[72] This failure in support was partly attributable to the varied burdens on Somerset's regime, but it was also a result of the logistical challenges of getting supplies from northern England up into Scotland during the autumn and winter. In November 1547 three ships were sent north to victual Broughty Ferry: two of the vessels sank in stormy weather and the third had to take refuge on the coast of Northumberland.[73] In December, Thomas Wyndham, an experienced naval captain and occasional privateer, reported that although it was Protector Somerset's 'pleasure' that Broughty Ferry and Inchcolm be 'victualled and well-furnished' for at least four months, this was not possible as the fort at Broughty Ferry did not have sufficient storage whilst the 'dangerous' winter weather impeded provisioning efforts at Inchcolm.[74]

The military ambitions of Protector Somerset in 1547 were at the limits of what the Tudor state had the capacity to fulfil. During the Pinkie campaign Somerset managed to secure victory in battle, bring the majority of his men (though perhaps not most of the horses) back to England, and avoided a major crisis in supply. However, as the winter weather worsened, and with a proportion of the autumn campaign's forces redeployed or disbanded, properly supplying the English garrisons in Scotland proved beyond the power of Somerset's regime. The logistical limitations of the Tudor navy and army both restricted Somerset's options in the aftermath of Pinkie, and undermined the garrison strategy he settled upon.

The invasion of 1547 was a gamble right from the start. At Pinkie the bet paid off; in the long run it was ruinous. By the end of 1549 Somerset had expended vast sums of money and destroyed the lives and livelihoods of thousands of Scots and English, to very little benefit. This dismal result was a key factor in his arrest and removal from power that October. Among the charges levelled at him when arrested was the fault of 'entering into rash wars'.[75] It was in many respects a valid criticism. Yet it is questionable whether the outcome of Somerset's Scottish policy would have been as disastrous for the English, and the Protector personally, had Arran, and the wider circle around Mary Queen of Scots, not navigated the aftermath of Pinkie with remarkable resilience and diplomatic dexterity.

After Pinkie: the Scottish response

Following the Battle of Pinkie, both the Earl of Arran and Scotland faced a grim situation. In late September 1547 a messenger representing the Earl of Angus to the English described the Scottish defeat as 'such a scourge as the world might take example at them forever'.[76] The Fife laird William Bruce of Earlshall was similarly gloomy, informing Mary of Guise just after the arrival of the English at Broughty Ferry, that he feared he was 'destroyed forever and the [rest] of the country in peril'.[77] Unsurprisingly, Arran was heavily blamed for the disaster at Pinkie, and was deeply unpopular in the weeks afterwards. Thousands of families were grieving, and many deeply resented the man who had hazarded so many Scottish lives. When Arran briefly ventured out into the burgh of Edinburgh local women 'were like to have stoned him to death', forcing him to seek refuge in St Giles' Kirk, which he eventually 'left at the back gate'.[78] The anger of the 'wives' of Edinburgh is perhaps understandable – around 360 of them had been made widows by the events at Pinkie.[79]

Many other Scots were captured at Pinkie. Patten claimed that over 1,500 were recorded as prisoner by the English.[80] Meanwhile, reports circulating in diplomatic circles in October 1547 claimed that more than 2,000 Scots had been captured.[81] Among them were several government officials, most notably the Earl of Huntly, who was described by Francis van der Delft as being 'a person of great estimation among his people'.[82] Huntly had been appointed chancellor in the summer of 1546, shortly after the assassination of Cardinal David Beaton, who had previously held this key role.[83] The capture of such a key official arguably created its own crisis for the Scottish government.[84]

Scotland's misfortunes were not confined to the men killed or captured near Musselburgh. Despite Somerset's hope of limiting devastation, his forces had severely disrupted Scottish agriculture and supply chains. In November 1547 the lairds of Ormiston and Longniddry (who were both Protestants and supporters of the English) complained that when Somerset's 'army' was 'last in these parts' they were 'heavily hurt' by the loss of 'corns and other necessary things'.[85] That same month John Luttrell, then commanding the English garrison at Inchcolm, noted the 'extremities' of 'pestilence and famine' affecting communities around the Forth.[86]

Afflicted by illness and food shortages, politically and religiously divided, and grappling with the consequences of a major military defeat, the people of Scotland faced profound challenges in the autumn of 1547. Yet, despite these problems, the Scottish government responded to the crisis relatively effectively. They took a poor hand and played it well. Part of the credit for this lies with Arran. However, the role played by the queen mother, Mary of Guise, was also pivotal (Figure 8.4). Indeed, in the aftermath of Pinkie she significantly expanded her influence in Scottish politics, paving the way for her to replace Arran as regent in 1554.[87]

Figure 8.4: Mary of Guise, c. 1537, by Corneille de Lyon (National Galleries of Scotland. Presented by E. P. Jones 1950)

Among the chief tasks facing Arran and Guise in the weeks after Pinkie was keeping Mary Queen of Scots safe and out of English hands – something they did successfully. Although the Scottish monarch was just a small child (at the time of Pinkie she was approaching her fifth birthday) her person was of great political significance. Indeed, when Hume Castle surrendered to Somerset in September 1547 one of the demands the English made was that the Humes should work 'for the delivery of the young Queen of Scotland into my lord Protector's hands'.[88] The itinerary of Mary Queen of Scots, and her mother Mary of Guise, in the days around Pinkie is not completely clear, but both managed to avoid the English. Shortly before the battle, Guise appears to have been in Edinburgh, where on 2 September it was reported that she had been sending out proclamations and helping Arran to assemble the Scottish forces.[89] John Knox, who of course disliked both queens, claimed that Guise fled from Edinburgh to Stirling upon hearing news of Pinkie, although it is possible that she actually relocated there slightly earlier.[90] According to Bishop Leslie's history, it was at Stirling that the decision was taken to move Mary Queen of Scots to Inchmahome Priory on

Figure 8.5: The Priory of Inchmahome, on an island in the Lake of Menteith. The young Queen Mary was sent here for safety after the defeat at Pinkie (© Crown Copyright: HES)

the Lake of Menteith, a religious site about 15 miles further away from the area of conflict and conveniently located on the edge of the Highlands (Figure 8.5).[91] In early October, Somerset's trusted advisor Sir William Paget informed van der Delft that the Scottish queen had 'retired from Stirling to a more remote place on an island in a river or large lake very difficult of access'.[92] It is unclear when, or whether, Mary of Guise stayed with her daughter at Inchmahome, although on 16 September the dowager queen seems to have been at Stirling with the Scottish Privy Council.[93] Arran remained in contact with his child monarch and her mother throughout the difficult days following Pinkie. He despatched a series of messengers to Inchmahome, including sending letters with 'a boy direct to the Queen's grace' on 12 September – a mere 48 hours after the battle.[94]

Keeping the young queen physically away from the threat of capture was only part of the challenge. The negotiating table posed almost as great a risk to the Scottish monarch. It was after all through the discussions of diplomats that royal marriages were usually arranged and new alliances agreed. Having just broken the Scottish army at Pinkie, the English may have expected that Arran and his colleagues would rush to negotiate. Indeed, international observers, including the French, seem to have assumed that after their defeat the Scots would make significant concessions

Figure 8.6: Stirling Castle, the approach from the town of Stirling, photographed sometime about 1883–1902. The castle was out of reach of English hostile intentions and with its recently built palace made a fitting home for the Queen Mother, Mary of Guise (© Courtesy of HES: Miss Murray's Album)

to the English, perhaps even handing over their queen. In early October the Imperial ambassador in Paris reported that Henry II was seeking a suspension to the Anglo-Scottish hostilities and that the French king would try 'to get the Scots to consent to any reasonable and tolerable conditions'.[95]

However, Arran and Guise defied expectations. The Scots do not appear to have engaged diplomatically until a few days after the battle, when the Scottish Protestant Alexander Crichton, laird of Brunstane, set about facilitating discussions.[96] On 16 September the English Norroy herald, an experienced negotiator named Gilbert Dethick, was despatched to Stirling (Figure 8.6). There he met with Mary of Guise and the Scottish Privy Council.[97] Arran does not appear to have been present at the meeting, instead being preoccupied with reorganising the defences at several Scottish strongholds, including Edinburgh Castle, where he had taken refuge after the battle.[98] A copy of Somerset's instructions to Dethick for his meeting with the Scottish leaders survives.[99] The line taken by the English was far from conciliatory, emphasising the 'provocation' offered by the Scots, and in particular 'the Governor of Scotland'.[100] The English demanded that the Scots commit to the 'already promised' marriage between Britain's two child monarchs, and hand over Mary to the English to be brought up at the Tudor court – Somerset pledging that she would be treated in as 'honourable' a fashion 'as any Queen of England', hardly a reassuring statement in the light of the experiences of some of Henry VIII's consorts.[101]

The outcome of the discussions at Stirling are unclear, but they do not appear to have led to any firm understanding, and there was another meeting on 28 September at Roxburgh. Apparently 'a Scottish herald accompanied with certain Frenchmen' came to speak with Somerset, assuring him that commissioners would soon 'come to commune' with the English at Berwick-upon-Tweed.[102] The French presence possibly indicates the influence of Mary of Guise, although it may also reflect the fact that as France was technically at peace with England they could be perceived as more neutral intermediaries. Interestingly, the list of expenses 'disbursed' by Arran's 'precepts and special commands' in September 1547 include a charge for 'hiring a horse' for 'a Frenchman sent to the English camp' – which implies that Arran assented to the French involvement in negotiations.[103] We do not know if the Scots ever meant to keep the appointment at Berwick. The Earl of Glencairn claimed that the Earl of Cassilis, George Douglas and the Sheriff of Ayr were all to act as commissioners for the Scots, but the day before they were due to depart for England 'a gentleman of France' using 'fair words' successfully 'altered' the purpose of 'the queen and governor'.[104] Whether or not this is precisely what happened, it is clear that despite the Earl of Warwick, Lord Grey of Wilton and Sir Ralph Sadler travelling to Berwick 'to abide the coming' of the commissioners, the Scottish diplomats never turned up.[105]

The English appear to have genuinely expected that the Scots would continue negotiating even without the presence of a foreign army. On 30 September 1547 the bishop of Durham, Cuthbert Tunstall, was hurriedly drafting and sending to Somerset commissions for Warwick and his colleagues to represent the English government in the proposed negotiations at Berwick. The bishop had also looked out copies of previous peace treaties, including the 1543 agreement regarding the marriage of Edward Tudor and Mary Queen of Scots – efforts that ultimately proved irrelevant.[106] Somerset arguably handled the diplomatic interaction with the Scots rather naively, failing to lock them into any firm agreement before he departed to England. Significantly, Francis van der Delft had assumed that Somerset would not 'leave the enemy's country in the full flood of success without some sort of treaty, understood or projected with the Scots'.[107] Somerset himself soon acknowledged that he had perhaps miscalculated. In early November, he remarked to van der Delft on the 'underlying intrigue of the war in Scotland; which he confessed that he had not previously understood so well as he did at present'.[108] The English protector continued to state that 'he saw no appearance now of any arrangement being made with the Scots, the Regent, who had previously solicited. . . to treat for peace having now changed his mind as soon as the English army had marched out of the country'.[109]

The decision to play for time by seemingly being open to discussion, without actually making any commitments, was probably the wisest course the Scottish government could have pursued in the circumstances. As the Scots were adopting this delaying tactic, Arran was attempting to regroup what remained of his country's military forces and gathering funds to continue the war. At Pinkie, the Scots suffered a 'great loss of men, ordnance, munitions, harness, and weapons', leaving Arran with fewer options than he had at the start of September.[110] Nevertheless, Arran rapidly set about trying to rebuild the Scottish forces and deploying his limited resources effectively. On 17 September, the day after Mary of Guise met with the Norroy herald, Arran was despatching culverins and artillery experts to Dunbar Castle 'for the resisting of the Englishmen'.[111] Arran was himself at Edinburgh Castle for much of the time after Pinkie and was clearly concerned that this vital fortification was defended. Immediately 'after the field' Arran made payments to soldiers at Edinburgh to 'conduce' them 'to remain at the castle'.[112] He also gave orders for 'others' to be 'solicited' to 'come to the castle for the keeping of the same'.[113] Arran seems to have been anxious to retain skilled gunners and restore his artillery capabilities. For example, £6 was paid to Andrew Stratoun and James Fethy 'gunners, who after the field came to the castle of Edinburgh and remained there by the space of a month'.[114] There are also records of coal being sent to Edinburgh 'to help melt metal to the artillery'.[115]

By November 1547 the Earl of Arran had assembled sufficient forces to contemplate action against the English garrison at Broughty Ferry. An intelligence report sent to the English on 17 November by the spy Ninian Cockburn reported that to this end the Scottish government had just supplied 300 soldiers and two 'cannons and bastard culverins' which were sent to Arbroath in readiness. Meanwhile, Arran was raising forces in Fife and Angus.[116] Unfortunately for Arran, although the attack on Broughty Ferry put the English under pressure, it was unsuccessful. The English reported that the force that attacked them was in the region of 3,000 'horsemen and footmen' and that the Scottish 'ordnance' was 'two cannon, a culverin, two sakers, a bastard and diverse other small pieces'.[117] Given the catastrophe of Pinkie only two months before, it is to the credit of the Scots that they were able to assemble this moderately sized force – what is more they did this during a period of bad weather at the beginning of winter. The fact that the Scots were once again undertaking offensive operations on land was a significant milestone. The Scots had also restarted small-scale naval activity. For instance, in late October they were sending ships from Leith to duel with the English forces based on Inchcolm.[118] These localised actions added considerably to the difficulties of the already under-resourced English garrisons.

To fund such operations, and to have any hope of continuing resistance to the English, the Scottish government had to raise substantial sums of money. Arran seems to have made this a priority almost as soon as the battle was over. As early as 15 September Arran sent messages to the burghs of Perth, Dundee and St Andrews 'to crave the rest of their tax'.[119] Pressure was also placed on the Catholic clergy to assist financially with the 'recovering' of Broughty Ferry, Inchcolm, Hume Castle and Roxburgh.[120] In response to the national crisis the Scottish churchmen agreed to 'advance' Arran £5,000 and also to pay half the cost of sending 100 hackbutters and 100 'spearmen' to attack Broughty Ferry.[121] The local 'barons and landed men' in eastern Perthshire, and in the sheriffdoms of Forfar and Kincardine meanwhile pledged to fund a hundred horsemen. It was also reported that the Scottish Privy Council sought to take the 'chalices' and 'jewels of the Church' to raise funds for 'the wars'.[122] However, these measures were ultimately stop-gaps. The resources of the Stewart kingdom did not compare with the resources of the Tudor state, even overstretched as it was. To continue to resist, the Scots required external assistance – they needed France to intervene actively on their behalf.

The French would ultimately commit substantial money and men to assist the Scots. In June 1548 a French fleet of 27 warships and 86 transport vessels arrived in Scotland, bringing with them more than 5,440 footmen and additional cavalry forces.[123] Their involvement transformed the situation in Scotland, and was a major factor in the eventual defeat of the English. However, the journey to acquiring this help was complex, with critical negotiations taking place in the weeks and months after Pinkie. Despite his decision to send military aid to St Andrews Castle, the new king of France, Henry II, was initially wary about triggering a full-scale war with England.[124] When news of the Scottish loss at Pinkie reached France, the royal court was shocked. The Duke of Montmorency, then Constable of France, wrote to Mary of Guise assuring her that the French king and 'all of the court. . . would not have felt greater sorrow if the defeat had been suffered here'.[125] Yet, despite the words of condolence, the French government was uncertain how to act. In October 1547 Jean de St Mauris, the Imperial ambassador to France, reported that Henry II was anxious for the Scots to reach an understanding with the English, as he currently 'could not succour the Scots' and 'did not wish, moreover, to engage himself in this labyrinth'.[126] Yet despite this discouraging situation, the Scottish government did a commendable job of maintaining awareness of their issues and ultimately persuading Henry II into action.

The Scottish ambassador, David Paniter, had been at the French court for some time in the autumn of 1547. However, in the aftermath of Pinkie, Mary of Guise and the Earl of Arran repeatedly sent additional diplomatic representatives to Henry II. Immediately after the battle Sir Walter Ogilvy and the French ambassador to Scotland, Henry Cleutin, often known as d'Oisel, brought news of the disaster.[127] Further Scottish representation arrived in Paris in the weeks that followed. On 25 October St Mauris noted that four days earlier 'a Scottish gentleman came to this Court sent by the Queen Dowager of Scotland and the Governor'.[128] The Scottish representative emphasised the 'disastrously large' losses at Pinkie, and sought French aid, without which the Scots' claimed they would have to 'make what terms they may with the King of England'.[129] In November, the Scots once again despatched d'Oisel to intercede on their behalf, this time accompanied by the elderly laird, John Hamilton of Milnburn, for whom the Scottish government provided a new doublet and a black cloak with a velvet lining when he departed 'to France in my lord governor's affairs'.[130] The Scottish government also tried to persuade the Emperor Charles V, who at that stage was at peace with France and allied to England, of the justice of their cause. To this end they stressed

Figure 8.7: Dumbarton Castle, from John Slezer's Theatrum Scotiae, *1693. Dumbarton was an important royal castle guarding the upper reaches of the Clyde estuary. The young queen was sent here for safety in 1548 prior to her being taken off by a French fleet to France (The Trustees of the National Library of Scotland)*

the religious dimension of the conflict, with David Paniter explaining to St Mauris how marriage to Edward VI would place their queen 'in the hands of one, who. . . would for the whole of his life be alienated from the Catholic faith, and might well draw Scotland into the same heresy as himself' – a situation that Paniter asserted the Scots would 'hate' as they were 'so firmly Christian'.[131]

The Scottish lobbying bore fruit. By November 1547 it was being reported that Henry II of France would either provide money, or 'in the spring' send military aid.[132] It was also noted at this time that the Papacy had decided 'to contribute funds to the Scots'.[133] Significant sums of money from the Pope (enough to pay 10,000 Scots for a year) and 50 French military advisors arrived in Scotland on Christmas Day 1547, with more aid coming in the following months.[134] Of course, there was a price for this assistance. In January 1548 Arran agreed that the young queen could be taken to France to be betrothed to Henry II's eldest son Francis, and the decision was approved by the wider Scottish government at a convention at Stirling in February (Figure 8.7).[135] In hindsight it was a decision a number of Scots regretted. Looking back, Robert Lindsay of Pitscottie felt great harm followed, with the betrothal causing 'crueller wars between us and England' and leading the French to 'desire us and our realm [of Scotland] to be a province or pertinent unto them as their own subjects'.[136] However, in the short term the French alliance provided the money, men, and military expertise the Scottish government so desperately needed to defeat Somerset's forces, and undo at least part of the damage done at Pinkie. The hope some Scots expressed in the autumn of 1547, that the French would 'come at the spring', largely came to pass.[137]

Together the Earl of Arran and Mary of Guise managed to pull Scotland back from the brink in the autumn of 1547. Nevertheless, the disaster near Musselburgh had consequences for Arran's career and was arguably a factor in his eventual loss of the governorship of Scotland. There was, in the aftermath of Pinkie, little faith in Arran as a military leader. In November 1547 the spy Ninian Cockburn reported to the English that the Scots would have more confidence if Arran did not lead them into battle in person, and that if he 'be on his horse back' the soldiers would 'flee'.[138] Meanwhile on 31 December 1547 Lord Methven wrote to Mary of Guise detailing Arran's failings as a commander, which he regarded as 'discouraging' to the Scots, and suggesting that command be given to one of the newly arrived French advisors 'who had intelligence of order of men on the fields'.[139] Yet, in the end, the outcome for Arran was still rather more satisfactory than for Somerset. Following his loss of power, Somerset was eventually tried for treason and executed on 22 January 1552.[140] In contrast, Arran was awarded the French dukedom of Châtelherault, remained a major player in Scottish politics and died of natural causes in his own home on 22 January 1575 – exactly 23 years after the demise of his English opponent.[141]

Pinkie and military change in early modern Britain

Pinkie clearly influenced the politics of both Scotland and England, sometimes in unexpected ways. To what extent, though, can it help us understand the development of warfare in early modern Britain? Pinkie has been popularly depicted as 'the first modern battle in the British Isles' – an assertion that is in the introduction to the battle's Wikipedia page and hence is probably one of the first judgments about Pinkie that many will read.[142] In a more official context, the Inventory of Historic Battlefields designation for Pinkie claims that the battle demonstrates 'some of the major military innovations' of the sixteenth century.[143] But how useful are ideas of 'modernity' and 'new' styles of warfare in relation to Pinkie? Should we see the battle as representing a break with earlier military traditions and heralding a new age in British warfare, or is this a problematic way to perceive what happened in 1547?

For much of the twentieth century, historians exerted considerable efforts tracing the origins of modernity in European warfare, and in particular debating the concept of the 'military revolution' – a tradition that colours how Pinkie has been portrayed. The idea of a military revolution is particularly associated with Michael Roberts, whose inaugural lecture on the topic in 1955 at Queen's University in Belfast is frequently regarded as sparking its own 'historiographical revolution'.[144] Roberts argued that there was in the late sixteenth and early seventeenth centuries a period of radical development in the art of war, which 'stands like a great divide separating mediaeval society from the modern world'.[145] Central to this age of change was an increasing reliance on firepower and the deployment of larger, more professional armies with greater administrative support. Yet Roberts' theory owed a considerable debt to a wider historiographical interest in big military 'turning points' and the pathway to 'modernity'.[146] This trend can be seen in the earlier writings of Charles Oman about Pinkie.

Oman believed that Somerset's army at Pinkie was 'unlike any that had marched for the invasion of Scotland'. Indeed, according to Oman, Pinkie saw the 'tactics of the Renaissance' employed 'for the first time' in Britain.[147] The depiction of Pinkie as a departure from what went before, secured by the, albeit rather belated, military modernisation of the English has proved remarkably enduring. At the start of the twenty-first century Marcus Merriman depicted Somerset's army as 'perhaps the finest military machine hitherto put together in English history'.[148] Meanwhile, as recently as 2016, Dan O'Sullivan described Pinkie as 'the victory of a Renaissance army over a medieval one'.[149]

A more nuanced take on Pinkie, modernity, and the military revolution was provided by Gervase Phillips in the late 1990s.[150] In his work on the Anglo-Scots wars of the early sixteenth century, Phillips sought to challenge common assumptions about the isolated and backwards nature of military activity in the British Isles, stressing the parallels between trends in Continental Europe, and practices in Scotland and England. He also questioned the idea that the 1540s formed a break with what went before, and that the Pinkie campaign was indicative of a sea-change in military tactics and organisation. According to Phillips, 'the successful combined arms force that Somerset took to Scotland in 1547 was not the product of a military revolution', instead it reflected 'a steady accretion of novel military techniques, combined with the gradual adaptation of existing practices'.[151] The evolutionary model that Phillips proposed is probably a more helpful way to understand the forces at Pinkie than a simple binary of 'Renaissance' versus 'Medieval'. Analysis of the English and indeed the Scottish forces that assembled near Musselburgh in 1547 reveals a mix of tradition, adaptation and innovation. Yet even with a more 'evolutionary' model we should be wary of seeing Pinkie as part of a journey towards military 'progress'. The armies that met outside Musselburgh were impressive, but it is debatable to what extent they laid the foundations for things to come.

So, what can we learn from Pinkie about the nature of military change in early modern Britain, starting with the English? Much of the twentieth- and twenty-first-century discussion of Pinkie has stressed the novel way in which Somerset exploited cavalry and artillery. Notably, Charles Oman perceived Pinkie as a battle in which 'the main part was played by cavalry and artillery'.[152] According to Oman this was a departure from previous English practice, with Somerset having 'noted the deficiency of cavalry' in Henry VIII's campaigns.[153] Oman emphasised the presence of 'cosmopolitan foreign men-at-arms' in the English cavalry and the innovatory nature of the mounted hackbutters, which he described as 'a troop of the new sort'.[154] This was part of his effort to present the English forces at Pinkie as reflecting recent trends in mainland Europe. According to Oman, 'the recrudescence' at Pinkie 'of cavalry as the mainstay of battle' echoed 'already well developed' tactics on 'the Continent'.[155] In particular, Oman likened the 'general engagement' of cavalry and artillery at Pinkie to the Battle of Marignano, fought near Milan in 1519, where the French broke Swiss pikemen 'by keeping the enemy fixed to the ground by constant... cavalry charges, till cannon were brought up'.[156] Oman regarded the integration of cavalry and artillery at Pinkie as unlike anything that had previously taken place 'on British soil'.[157] Echoes of this interpretation can be found in the modern Battlefield Inventory for Pinkie, which asserts that this was 'the first' British battle in which 'gunpowder weapons proved decisive' and that it was 'also the first time that artillery, infantry, cavalry and naval support had combined in an action recognisable in modern terms'.[158] The Inventory further states how at Pinkie 'the standard English medieval tactics of archery and dismounted men-at-arms were replaced by heavy cavalry charging the enemy... with arquebuses firing into the sides of schiltrons' – tactics which the inventory's authors regarded as a significant departure for battles 'fought on British soil'.[159]

The English cavalry and artillery undoubtedly played significant roles at Pinkie. However, the revolutionary nature of these forces and how they were used has perhaps been overstated. The English had a variety of horsemen at the battle, including men-at-arms, the slightly less heavily armed demilances, light horsemen and mounted hackbutters. Oman of course perceived the mounted hackbutters as a symbol of modernity – they were professional mercenaries who carried firearms.

Yet the mounted hackbutters at Pinkie probably used horses to move quickly and then dismounted to fight, in the manner of later dragoons. It is significant that this unit appears to have fought at Pinkie alongside the foot hackbutters led by Sir Peter Mewtas.[160] The mounted hackbutters at Pinkie are an interesting insight both into how Somerset was using firearms and the Tudor government's recruitment of mercenaries. However, they were not what turned the tide of battle.

It was the contribution of men-at-arms and demilances which proved crucial. The main charge against the Scottish battle on Saturday 10 September appears to have consisted of the 'men at arms of Boulogne' and Lord Grey's 'own band of lances only'.[161] These units had been 'carried over' from northern France, where they had been involved in relatively brutal fighting and scorched earth policies in 1544, 1545 and 1546.[162] This experience was almost certainly key to their effectiveness.

Traditionally, historians often assumed that the English largely eschewed cavalry during the Late Middle Ages.[163] According to Oman 'the English upper military classes. . . ceased for the most part to fight on horseback in the fifteenth century'.[164] Yet, there is increasing evidence for the use of light and heavy cavalry during the Wars of the Roses, with horsemen playing significant roles at Towton in 1461, Tewkesbury in 1471 and Bosworth in 1485.[165] Some of these engagements saw cavalry and artillery on the same battlefield. For example, at Bosworth Richard III had a 'substantial' artillery presence, and personally led a heavy cavalry charge.[166] Research by Anthony Goodman into English armies during the Wars of the Roses suggests that 'infantry, cavalry and artillery were used in conjunction in the field, probably in increasingly sophisticated combinations'.[167] The English also deployed horsemen and 'certain pieces of small ordnance' at the Battle of the Spurs near Guinegate (now Enguinegatte) in 1513, where combined English and Imperial forces defeated the French – an engagement in which Protector Somerset's own father fought.[168] The integration of cavalry and artillery at Pinkie did not form a complete departure from previous English tactics, but arguably echoed practices of the civil wars of the fifteenth century and techniques trialled during the French campaigns of the early sixteenth century.

The idea that the English forces at Pinkie reflected a mixing of old and new approaches can also be seen in the infantry. An issue that preoccupied the military theorists of early modern England, and indeed many more recent writers, was the extent to which longbows should be replaced by guns.[169] For hundreds of years the former had proved effective in the hands of well-trained archers. In contrast the technically more complex firearms, and in particular hackbuts, achieved less good results in many circumstances and were subject to the vagaries of weather. Indeed, when the old soldier Humphrey Barwick remembered in the 1590s the hackbuts he came across during his early soldiering in the time of Edward VI he reckoned they were 'mean stuff' and did not compare to the quality of later firearms.[170] At Pinkie archers and hackbutters were present. Both were employed effectively, but in circumstances in which they could be used offensively without themselves being exposed to counterattack. Men armed with the old and new missile weapons were brigaded separately from the main battles of footmen, with a sleeve of archers to the right and hackbutters to the left; a formation that is clearly shown on early illustrations of the battle.

Yet such a set-up was not unique to Pinkie. Indeed, a similar formation seems to have been used by the English in their earlier battle against the Scots at Ancrum Moor in 1545, when the Earls of Arran and Angus successfully defeated the forces of Sir Ralph Eure, the warden of the English Middle March, and Sir Brian Layton, the governor of Norham Castle.[171] The sixteenth-century Fife chronicler, Robert Lindsay of Pitscottie, claims that at Ancrum the English army was 5,000 men strong, brigaded in two battles. The first consisted of 1,000 spears (perhaps pikemen), with 500 hackbutters on the right wing and 500 archers on the left. The second battle also had 1,000 spears, but it had wings of 1,000 hackbutters and 1,000 bowmen.[172] Although Pitscottie's figures for the number of combatants should perhaps be treated with a degree of caution, the set-up he describes for Ancrum does reflect contemporary English practice. A slightly more complex variation on the same theme was employed in the campaigning around Boulogne in the mid-1540s. According to Giovacchino da Coniano, an Italian sergeant-major who served with the Tudor army in France, the English used rectangular units of pikemen with a core of halberdiers (perhaps a reference to billmen), and with soldiers armed with guns in between. On the wings were archers and hackbutters combined. Giovacchino was told by his English colleagues that the pikemen placed in front would stoop low so that the hackbutters placed behind could fire over their heads.[173] This approach could help at least some of the hackbutters shelter amongst those with long-shafted weapons and the latter could benefit more directly from the firepower of the missile weapons.

In the 1540s the English were exploring how best to use archers and hackbutters on the same battlefield. Pinkie was part of this period of experimentation, but it was hardly a departure from what was being done elsewhere. What is more, the arrival of the hackbut was not the immediate death knell of the longbow. Indeed, the English state continued to see a value in archers into the late sixteenth century, with Elizabeth I in 1591 ordering that 'bowls, dicing and carding' be discouraged, and that her subjects instead practice archery 'an exercise not only of good recreation, but otherwise of good use and defence to the realm'.[174]

Pinkie's depiction as a joint land and sea operation has also been regarded as indicative of modernity.[175] Ships certainly were integral to Somerset's campaign in 1547. The English fleet helped supply the army, and also conducted raids along the Scottish coastline. These were long-established roles for English naval forces – William the Conqueror, Edward I and Henry IV had all used shipping to support their military interventions in Scotland. However, it is debatable how large a role the English fleet played in the fighting on 9 and 10 September. With the exception of the *Galley Subtle* (see Figures 3.10 and 7.8), there is little evidence for the English ships coming close to shore. This is unsurprising given the hazards associated with bringing sailing ships into shallow water on a coast with extensive sand banks. Many of the ships Somerset had at his disposal were newly built, but the way in which they were deployed was quite traditional and had little bearing on how the battle unfolded. The use of ships at Pinkie did not amount to 'a major innovation'.[176]

The role of the *Galley Subtle* at Pinkie was slightly different from the sailing ships and did influence events on land. As a galley, this vessel was less dependent on wind direction, was able to manoeuvre in shallow waters, and could be beached if necessary. Nations such as France and Spain used galleys as close-support gun boats, very much the purpose that the *Galley Subtle* had at Pinkie.[177] The English experimentation with galleys was of relatively recent date, with Henry VIII developing an interest in them around 1540, when he sought shipwrights from Italy to assist with their construction.[178] Yet the English involvement with this form of watercraft proved limited and short-lived. For most of the late 1540s and early 1550s the English navy had at most two galleys; although they did have other rowing vessels at their disposal.[179] By 1559 English interest in galleys had declined and Elizabeth I was advised to sell or dispose of the *Galley Subtle*, which by then was in poor repair.[180] The Elizabethan navy occasionally had galleys in its possession, but they saw little service. The *Galley Subtle*'s presence at Pinkie is a reminder of the Tudor government's awareness of Continental military trends, but it hardly constituted a revolutionary shift in English naval equipment or tactics.

The *Galley Subtle* met a sad end in part because of a lack of maintenance in the 1550s. A similar trend could be seen across the English forces. Protector Somerset had an effective fighting force at Pinkie, which blended tradition and innovation. Yet the strength of the English at Pinkie did not derive from any great technological or tactical leap forward: it was the result of recent exposure to conflict. These were battle-hardened men with a range of weapons that had largely been proven to work. The Tudor state spent most of the 1540s at war – in the process the English forces acquired relevant expertise and invested in military equipment. However, these gains were not retained, let alone built upon, following Somerset's downfall. A combination of the financial and political crises of the mid-Tudor years, and Elizabeth I's parsimonious approach to defence, meant that the experience and equipment acquired in the 1540s was squandered and dispersed. When the English found themselves involved in a major international conflict in the 1580s, they had to build anew.

The sense that Pinkie was an interesting moment rather than a foundation for Britain's military development is even more apparent when we consider the Scottish forces. There is little reason to view the Scottish army at Pinkie as a startling break with what went before. As at Flodden more than 30 years earlier large formations of pikemen remained central to the Scottish approach. Yet it is also unfair to characterise the Scots as 'medieval' in outlook, completely cut-off from wider European military trends.

The Scottish army at Pinkie had relatively similar military kit to other European armies of the period. In particular, the Earl of Arran had at his disposal significant artillery. This was hardly a departure from previous Scottish practice. Strong Scottish artillery trains had been brought down into the Borders in 1496, 1497, 1513 and 1523.[181] Indeed, in 1523 the Scottish governor, the Duke of Albany, had experimented with armoured carts or waggons mounted with guns, although these were not put to the test in actual conflict.[182] One feature of the Scottish artillery at Pinkie was relatively experimental – they tried having the guns drawn by men rather than animals. Presumably the rationale was to enable the guns to be fired, moved and fired again without wasting time and effort in hitching and unhitching trains of horses. In the manoeuvres on Inveresk Fields on 10 September, it does appear that this tactic had some success, allowing the Scottish gunners to fire on the English army without the latter being able to respond. Perhaps if the Scots had won the day this development would have been copied. As it was, the experiment was not reproduced.

The lack of firearms among the Scots is worthy of comment. The two previous Scottish monarchs, James IV and James V, were both interested in guns. When Governor Albany attacked England in 1523 his force of 8,000 men included 1,000 culveriners, hackbutters and crossbowmen.[183] By the time of James V's death in 1542 Scotland's royal armouries included several hundred handguns, and further firearms were supplied by the French in 1543 and 1545.[184] Parliamentary legislation in the 1530s had also required Scots with land worth 100 merks to have two culverins, whilst holders of land worth above £40 had to have at least one.[185] Arran himself had demonstrated a willingness to employ bands of hackbutters, using such units to garrison fortifications and in 1544 paying 62 men with hackbuts to act as his bodyguard when he attended parliament.[186] By 1547 there should therefore have been significant quantities of firearms available in Scotland, and a number of men proficient in using them. Why were these weapons not at Pinkie? It is possible that their absence reflects a deliberate decision on the part of the Scottish commanders to rely on Argyll's archers rather than on firearms. The Scottish archers at Pinkie have not received a good press from later historians. Charles Oman regarded them as being discouraged by 'the first salvos' from the English fleet and never really coming 'into action'.[187] This should not be taken as indicative of the wider effectiveness of archers from the Highlands and Islands during the 1540s. For example, the French soldier Jean de Beaugué was impressed by the Highland archers' enthusiasm and bravery during the siege of Haddington in 1548.[188]

Another element in the Scottish forces at Pinkie that is sometimes portrayed as disappointing is the light horse. Clearly the Scottish horse came off worse in the fighting on Friday 9 September when facing heavier English units. They did, though, undertake a worthwhile role shadowing the English forces in their march from Linton Bridge to their camp at Prestonpans. The French clearly valued them, and from late 1548 to early 1550 paid for a force of about 800 light horse to remain active, under their colonel, Gilbert Kennedy, Earl of Cassilis. As a noted Protestant and sometime supporter of the English, Cassilis might seem a surprising choice, but his ability and effectiveness was demonstrated by a victory over a force of 600 English horse.[189] In 1547 Protector Somerset seems to have had a relatively high opinion of the Scottish light cavalry, telling Lord Grey about 'the goodness of their horsemen' and initially giving orders forbidding the English from skirmishing with them.[190] The Scottish light horse struggled at Pinkie, but in the main seem to have been useful troops. Indeed, the French would subsequently use Scottish light horse in northern France in the late 1550s.[191] It would be possible to regard the light horsemen at Pinkie as part of a wider early modern European interest in light cavalry.[192] Certainly, these troops clearly had a use on sixteenth-century campaigns. However, Scotland had a tradition of light horse, particularly in the Borders, stretching far back into the Middle Ages. As so often, neither 'modernity' nor 'medievalism' seem particularly helpful lenses through which to understand this aspect of the Scottish forces.

The army that Arran brought to Pinkie was in many ways an impressive achievement. The Scots lost not because they were a 'medieval' army coming up against 'modern' land and sea forces, but primarily because Arran proved, on the day, a worse general than Somerset. Yet Pinkie is a turning point in Scottish military history. It was the last time that the Scottish government sought to fight a pitched battle against a foreign power without considerable external assistance. The real significance of Pinkie is not what happened on the battlefield, but that it marked the end of Scotland's ambition to be an independent military power.

During the 1550s the Scots depended heavily on the French for defence – a strategy that proved a double-edged sword. As religious divisions worsened towards the end of the decade, the French forces were seen in some circles as working 'to oppress' Scotland and putting the country 'in thraldom to strangers'.[193] By the end of 1559 many Scots had resolved 'to banish the French'.[194] To accomplish this aim, Scottish Reformers turned to Elizabeth I of England. In the spring of 1560 the English queen reluctantly agreed to provide military aid to Scotland's Protestant rebels, and both sides pledged to resist 'all strangers that should invade the Isle of Britain'.[195] Encouraging Elizabeth in this unusual military intervention was her advisor William Cecil, a veteran of Pinkie, who shared Somerset's vision of a Protestant Britain, but had rather more political acumen.[196] The expeditionary force Elizabeth despatched north was led by Lord Grey of Wilton, who by then was in his fifties and in poor health. Grey handled matters in 1560 rather less competently than Somerset had 13 years earlier. Indeed, it is not impossible that Grey had a degree of brain injury from Pinkie which affected his decision-making.[197] However, the deaths of Mary of Guise and Henry II of France in the summer of 1560 ultimately helped the Scottish Protestants to victory.

In the years that followed, Scotland's Protestant governments increasingly relied on England to deal with internal and external threats.[198] In 1573 the Scottish Privy Council wrote in fulsome terms to thank Elizabeth I for her military aid in 1560 and 1570, and her more recent supply 'of men, ordnance and munition'.[199] They went on to welcome English forces to Edinburgh, noting gratefully the 'care, travails and charges' Elizabeth's government had 'sustained for the safety and preservation of Scotland'.[200] A lot had changed in both the British kingdoms since the time of Pinkie.

For a variety of reasons, in the latter part of the sixteenth century successive Scottish administrations allowed their country's existing military capability to wither away. Instead of engaging with an international arms race, the Scots used their allies to fight their battles for them. As a country that increasingly did not rely on its own military capability to preserve its independence and project its influence, Scotland was something of an anomaly in early modern Europe.[201] Yet it was an approach that largely worked for Scotland. When James VI of Scotland went south in 1603 to peacefully occupy the palaces from which Somerset planned the Pinkie campaign, the late sixteenth-century Scottish strategy of leaving military might to other nations seemed to have turned out rather well.

While many traditional analyses see a definitive 'break' in warfare 'between the Middle Ages and modern times', this binary is not particularly helpful for Pinkie.[202] Both sides at Pinkie were engaging with technological developments such as field artillery. Both also had aspects of their armies that would have seemed familiar to earlier generations. Military practice in sixteenth-century Britain was not cut off from the rest of Europe, but nor was it necessarily following the 'broad and straight' road to 'modern' war, with its 'mass armies, strict discipline [and] control of the state'.[203] Pinkie forms a reminder of the large and varied forces that the mid-sixteenth-century kingdoms of Scotland and England were able to assemble. Yet in neither nation did their military capabilities in the 1540s prove the basis for a 'permanent transformation'.[204] Governments north and south of the border noticeably failed to build upon where they had reached by 1547. Quite apart from any ethical reservations over so-called 'improvements' in warfare, in purely practical terms Pinkie is very hard to situate on a road-map of military 'progress' – perhaps indicating that we should be looking for alternative ways to understand the military situation in early modern Britain.

Pinkie: future directions

Pinkie is an exceptionally well-recorded battle. There are contemporary descriptions of the fighting, relevant administrative records and early illustrations. As well as these broadly historical materials, there has been topographical study of the battlefield and archaeological investigation. This book has sought to integrate these diverse sources of information to create an unprecedentedly detailed analysis of the events of 9 and 10 September 1547 and what they meant for the peoples of Scotland and England. There is, though, still room for more research.

The results of archaeological investigation regarding Pinkie have, thus far, been relatively disappointing. There is not a single artefact that can be firmly identified as having been lost in September 1547. Probably the most promising items are the horse badges with images of a crown and roses (one of which is certainly Tudor) recovered during metal detecting at Crookston, south of the A1. There are also a few cannon balls and pieces of lead shot that might be connected to the battle, but an improved technological and scientific understanding would be necessary even to tie them down to the sixteenth century, never mind a particular day. Yet this does not mean that archaeology should not play an important role in future studies of Pinkie.

One of the most secure ways of identifying where the main clash between the two armies took place would be to find the graves of the fallen English soldiers. William Patten describes how the morning after the battle the English returned to the 'place of onset' where their comrades 'lay slain' and buried there all those who could be identified as their own.[205] Battlefield burials at sites such as Visby in Sweden (where a series of fourteenth-century mass graves have been uncovered) and Towton in Yorkshire (where a significant fifteenth-century mass burial was found in the 1990s) have proved transformative for understanding those conflicts.[206] The English burials from Pinkie might well provide considerable information on the soldiers who took part in the battle and the injuries they suffered, as well as indicating where the fighting took place.

The treatment of the Scottish dead after the battle was less systematic. Of course, far more Scots died at Pinkie and the nature of the rout means their bodies were distributed over a larger area. Patten claims that by Sunday 18 September a few of the Scottish fallen had been interred in Inveresk Churchyard, although the majority still lay in the open air.[207] Supposedly, beside several of the unburied corpses there were sticks with rags or other markers, which Patten assumed were put there by friends and relatives who were planning to 'convey away' the bodies for burial – a practice which would have dispersed the dead even further.[208] There may have been some centrally organised efforts to inter the Scots who fell at Pinkie, as the Earl of Arran's expenses for September 1547 include a payment of 22 shillings for 'carts to help earth the dead folks by the space of two days'.[209] Discovery of any of these Scottish burials would be of considerable interest, although it is likely that a proportion of the Scots were buried some distance from where they were killed.

Yet burials are not the only way to identify battlefields. Recently, Glenn Foard and Anne Curry suggested a revised location for the Battle of Bosworth in Leicestershire, even though no burial pits were found. Foard and Curry combined documentary research with archaeological survey data, in particular artefact distribution, to argue that the main fighting at Bosworth took place in countryside near Fen Hole, a couple of miles away from where the battlefield was traditionally assumed to be located. Metal detecting produced 'a silver-gilt badge in the shape of a boar' (a heraldic device used by King Richard III), as well as a large quantity of round shot.[210] The distribution of these items and a significant corpus of artefacts of medieval and probable medieval date were used to situate the fighting and tease out new perspectives on the battle, including the significant role played by artillery. There are, though, notable challenges associated with attempting to apply this methodology to Pinkie. Indeed, efforts by Foard and Curry to undertake a similar study for Pinkie were unsatisfactory and led them to conclude that the extant data was too poor for effective analysis.[211]

At Pinkie a significant amount of effort has already been expended in attempting to recover relevant artefacts from within the Battlefield Inventory area. Thousands of metal artefacts have been found, but few could plausibly date from the sixteenth century. Indeed, the vast majority are from the eighteenth century or later. Thus far there has been strikingly little archaeological evidence of the use of artillery, or any other weapons or military kit. It would be unlikely for pikes, swords or pieces of armour to be found in significant quantities – as noted above the English army deliberately collected Scottish weapons and armour after the battle.[212] There is also anecdotal evidence of more informal scavenging. For instance, the corpse of an English cavalry man known as 'Little Preston' was found shortly after the battle 'with both his hands cut off by the wrists' where scavengers had supposedly sought to remove 'from each arm a bracelet of gold'.[213] Yet pieces of lead shot and arrowheads that were buried in the ground after being fired might have been overlooked by scavengers, along with small fittings like buckles and badges.

Currently, no arrowheads have been recovered from the Pinkie Battlefield Inventory area. There are several possible explanations for this absence. Relatively small iron projectile points can disintegrate quite rapidly in the soil. Mechanised farming activity could have caused further destruction. The settings used by local metal detectorists (which are often set to exclude small ferrous signals) may also lead to items such as arrowheads being overlooked. In this context, it is worthwhile noting that no arrowheads were recovered at Bosworth, even though it is known that archers played a significant part in the fighting.[214] However, arrowheads have been recovered from some British battlefields, such as Towton.[215] Later changes to the landscape mean that it is not feasible to do a scientific programme of sampling of the whole area around Pinkie. However, if future archaeological research reveals a significant number of arrowheads of a sixteenth-century type, that would be an important indicator for where the climax of the battle took place.

There has been some lead and round shot recovered from the Pinkie area. Round shot (as fired from artillery pieces) has been found in relatively small quantities. Whilst some, particularly the composite pieces, could be broadly contemporary with the Battle of Pinkie, it has not been found in sufficient quantities to further our understanding of the battle. Similarly, whilst lead shot (as fired from firearms) has been recovered, it is also largely non-diagnostic and typical of recovery throughout Lowland Scotland.[216] At present we cannot reliably date lead shot or determine its provenance on the basis of technology or chemical composition. Lead shot was the main projectile fired from firearms from the late fifteenth to the mid-nineteenth century. Guns were commonly used throughout that period for sporting and hunting activities and this is a likely explanation for the lead shot found around Pinkie (and across most of Scotland). We should also consider the possibility that some of the round shot and lead shot may be connected with activity by the soldiers at the local barracks dating to the Napoleonic era. The limited number of pieces of round shot and the lead shot recovered from the

Battlefield Inventory area do not amount to significant evidence for a battle on a particular day in 1547.

The artefact evidence for Pinkie is therefore at present problematic. There is a tendency for modern battlefield archaeologists to concentrate on the recovery of arrowheads, bullets, and artillery shot – a practice shaped by the success of American battlefield investigations. Yet most of the notable American studies relate to post-1800 battles fought in landscapes which have since remained relatively undisturbed. For example, the Battle of Little Bighorn in Montana (which has produced extraordinarily rich archaeological finds) took place on open land which subsequently remained undeveloped. In contrast, the area around Musselburgh was already an intensively used landscape in the sixteenth century, with both farming and mining activity. Agricultural and industrial activity continued into modern times, with associated disruption to archaeological remains. Major transport infrastructure such as the building of the railway and the A1 have also led to the movement of large quantities of soil. The methodologies appropriate to undisturbed nineteenth-century American battlefields are perhaps not best suited to Pinkie (or indeed several other British battlefields). Unless many additional sixteenth-century objects are uncovered, statistical analysis of artefact distribution is probably not the most productive approach for Pinkie. Instead, there are other directions in which archaeological research might be taken forward.

There is scope for further archaeological research regarding the landscape and environment around Pinkie in 1547. A better understanding of the sixteenth-century landscape might help locate more securely the site of the fighting and cast additional light on the factors influencing the movements of the forces. Of considerable importance for understanding and placing the fighting on Saturday 10 September is the position of the slough which impeded the English cavalry attack on the Scottish vanguard, and then later provided protection for the English hackbutters. It seems likely that this was Colton Dean – an identification which largely fits with Patten's descriptions and diagrams. Colton Dean has been less developed than many parts of the local landscape, and archaeological survey and excavation in this area would be highly desirable. Indeed, some nearby finds of artefacts from Crookston hint at the passage of forces through this area. More detailed study of the historic landscape of Colton Dean, and how past environments compare to what we see today, should be a priority.

A future archaeological research strategy for Pinkie might hope both to examine the key sites in the hinterland of Musselburgh and to explore other locations connected with the campaign of 1547, an approach that might yield valuable comparative data. Obvious locations to consider include the Scottish muster place on Fala Moor and the sites of the English camps at Reston and Linton Bridge. More study of the forts constructed by the English in 1547 could also be undertaken. In this context, it should be noted that excavations at the demolished fort at Eyemouth provided invaluable information on the nature of English military engineering in the 1540s and the conditions in which the garrison were housed.[217]

In recent decades many conflict archaeologists have emphasised the importance of considering how warfare affected wider communities. More detailed archaeological study of sixteenth-century disruption to economic activity and settlement in the Musselburgh area, and along the routes of the campaigns of the 1540s, could be of great interest. It is likely that for local residents the consequences of Pinkie went well beyond the autumn of 1547. Yet, this broader story of how the war affected sixteenth-century Scottish society is poorly understood.

Of course, written records are also essential for understanding the impact of the events of 1547 and the development of the landscape around Pinkie. It is to be hoped that future researchers will continue to integrate archaeological and historical evidence. The wealth of surviving written material for Pinkie means that there is considerable room for new readings and more detailed analysis. This book has far from exhausted the potential of the extant primary sources. There is also the possibility of additional documents being identified. Both the National Records of Scotland and the National Library of Scotland have numerous manuscripts concerning property holding in the Musselburgh area, which may provide helpful insights into the historic landscape around Pinkie.[218] Further relevant materials almost certainly exist in local and family archives in Scotland and England. Closer analysis of local records might provide new insights into the preparations for fighting in 1547, and the impact of conflict on communities north and south of the border.

It is important that scholars gather these scattered grains of evidence associated with Pinkie. Traditionally, much of the discussion of Pinkie has focused on the actions and decisions of the Duke of Somerset and the Earl of Arran. Yet Pinkie was not only fought by the generals. Thousands of ordinary Scottish and English people had their lives changed, or indeed abruptly ended, by the events near Musselburgh. In November 1547 the Earl of Arran gave alms 'to a poor man who had his arm struck from him at the field of Pinkie'.[219] We do not know the name of this injured man, but he, and thousands like him, helped shape the outcome of the battle. The voices of the poorer people involved in the upheaval of Pinkie are less easy to hear, but traces of their experiences can be found, often in passing comments in unexpected places. The task of interpreting their tales is just beginning.

Notes

1 Interestingly the phrase 'great victory' is a term that was sometimes used by Scottish commentators regarding Somerset's success at Pinkie. See, for instance, Pitscottie 2, 102.
2 Patten, f. 121v.
3 Patten, f. 122r.
4 Patten, f. 122v.
5 Pitscottie 2, 102; Patten, f. 128v.
6 Patten, f. 129r.
7 Patten, f. 146r.
8 Jordan, *Edward VI*, 262.

9 Skidmore, *Edward VI*, 78.
10 *CSP Spain* 9, 139; Bonner, 'The recovery of St. Andrews Castle', 578–98.
11 *CSP Spain* 9, 140.
12 *CSP Spain* 9, 143.
13 *CSP Spain* 9, 143–44.
14 Patten, ff. 145v–146r.
15 TNA, SP 50/2, f. 22r. *CSP Scot* 1, 27.
16 TNA, SP 50/2, f. 22r. *CSP Scot* 1, 27.
17 TNA, SP 50/2, f. 67r. *CSP Scot* 1, 32.
18 TNA, SP 50/2, f. 67r. *CSP Scot* 1, 32.
19 SP 50/2, f. 57r. *CSP Scot* 1, 31–32.
20 SP 50/1, f. 119v. *CSP Scot* 1, 21.
21 Clifford, *State Papers and Letters of Sir Ralph Sadler*, vol. 1, 364.
22 Jordan, *Edward VI*, 262; Merriman, *Rough Wooings*, 248.
23 TNA, SP 50/ 2, f. 44r. *CSP Scot* 1, 30.
24 TNA, SP 50/2, f. 104r. *CSP Scot* 1, 40.
25 Patten, f. 152r.
26 Patten, f. 148r.
27 Patten, f. 7r.
28 *CSP Dom Add*, 324–32.
29 *CSP For*, 10.
30 *CSP Spain* 9, 72.
31 *CSP Spain* 9, 72.
32 Patten, f. 125r–v.
33 *CSP Spain* 9, 162.
34 *CSP Spain* 9, 169.
35 Patten, f. 127v.
36 Murdoch, *The Terror of the Seas?*, 60–61.
37 *CSP Spain* 9, 196.
38 *CSP Spain* 9, 196.
39 Patten, f. 145r-v.
40 Murphy, *Tudor Occupation of Boulogne*, 230–55.
41 Patten, f. 39r.
42 Patten, f. 123r–v.
43 Patten, f. 126v.
44 SP 50/1, f. 119r. *CSP Scot* 1, 21.
45 *Navy of Edward VI*, 31.
46 SP 50/1, f. 119r. *CSP Scot* 1, 21.
47 Patten, f. 135r.
48 Patten, ff. 135v–137r.
49 Patten, f. 139r–v.
50 TNA, SP 50/2, f. 17r. *CSP Scot* 1, 26.
51 *CSP Scot* 1, 19.
52 Patten, ff. 122v-123r.
53 T. Pollard, 'The Archaeology of the Siege of Leith', *Journal of Conflict Archaeology* 4 (February 2008), 161.
54 *CSP Spain* 9, 168.
55 Patten, ff. 151v-152r.
56 *CSP Spain* 9, 168.

57 For more information on Eyemouth Fort and a discussion on early *trace italienne* fortifications in Britain see Caldwell and Ewart, 'Excavations at Eyemouth, Berwickshire', 61–119.
58 For discussion of the English efforts to clear the local population of the Boulonnais see Murphy, *Tudor Occupation of Boulogne*, 77–86.
59 Patten, ff. 137r–139r.
60 *CSP Spain* 9, 197.
61 *CSP Spain* 9, 197.
62 Patten, f. 137v. For discussion of the complexities surrounding the assured Scots see M. H. Merriman, 'The Assured Scots: Scottish collaborators with England during the Rough Wooing, 1543–50', *SHR* 47 (1968), 10–35.
63 TNA, SP 50/2, f. 17v. *CSP Scot* 1, 26. For further discussion of the English providing Scots with foodstuffs and its implications see A. Blakeway, 'The Sixteenth-Century Price Rise: New Evidence from Scotland, 1500–85, *Economic History Review* (2015) 68, 167–90.
64 TNA, SP 50/2, f. 78r. *CSP Scot* 1, 35.
65 TNA, SP 50/2, f. 78r. *CSP Scot* 1, 35.
66 TNA, SP 15/1, f. 66r. *CSP Dom Add*, 331.
67 TNA, SP 15/1, f. 66r. *CSP Dom Add*, 331.
68 TNA, SP 50/2, f. 17r. *CSP Scot* 1, 26.
69 *Navy of Edward VI*, 34.
70 TNA, SP 50/2, f. 78v. *CSP Scot* 1, 41.
71 *Navy of Edward VI*, 36.
72 TNA, SP 50/3, f. 2r. *CSP Scot* 1, 56.
73 *CSP Scot* 1, 43.
74 *Navy of Edward VI*, 52.
75 Jordan (ed.), *Chronicle of Edward VI*, 18.
76 TNA, SP 15/1, f. 64v. *CSP Dom Add*, 330.
77 *MLSC*, 204.
78 *CSP Scot* 1, 34.
79 Maxwell, *Historical Memoirs*, 21.
80 Patten, f. 108r–v.
81 *CSP Spain* 9, 173.
82 *CSP Spain* 9, 181–182.
83 White, 'Gordon, George, fourth earl of Huntly (1513–1562)', *ODNB*.
84 We are grateful to Amy Blakeway for highlighting the deeply problematic wider implications of Huntly's capture.
85 TNA, SP 50/2, f. 92r. *CSP Scot* 1, 38.
86 *Navy of Edward VI*, 37.
87 Mary of Guise's path to power has commonly been attributed to her visit to France in 1550 – described by Pamela Ritchie as 'the watershed' in Guise's career. However, it is striking what a prominent role Guise was playing in Scottish politics directly after Pinkie, relative even to that played by her a few months earlier. P. E. Ritchie, *Mary of Guise in Scotland, 1548–1560: a political career* (East Linton, 2002), 61.
88 TNA, SP 50/1, f. 117r. *CSP Scot* 1, 20.
89 *CSP Scot* 1, 18.
90 Knox, *History*, vol. 1, 101.
91 Dalrymple 2, 301.
92 The published translation of the letter notes that this was the 'Queen Dowager', but this seems to be editorial conjecture. *CSP Spain* 9, 188.
93 Patten, f. 125v.
94 *TA* 9, 122.

95 *CSP Spain* 9, 175.
96 Patten, f. 125v.
97 Patten, f. 125v.
98 CSP Scot 1, 34. *TA* 9, 115.
99 TNA, SP 50/1, ff. 111r–114v. *CSP Scot* 1, 22.
100 TNA, SP 50/1, ff. 111r–v. *CSP Scot* 1, 22.
101 TNA, SP 50/1, ff. 113r. *CSP Scot* 1, 22.
102 Patten, ff. 140v–141r.
103 *TA* 9, 114.
104 TNA, SP 50/2, f. 46r.
105 Patten, f. 146.
106 *CSP Scot* 1, 22–23.
107 *CSP Spain* 9, 178.
108 *CSP Spain* 9, 196.
109 *CSP Spain* 9, 196.
110 TNA, SP 15/1, f. 64v. *CSP Dom Add*, 330.
111 *TA* 9, 114.
112 *TA* 9, 115.
113 *TA* 9, 115.
114 *TA* 9, 125.
115 *TA* 9, 127.
116 TNA, SP 50/2, ff. 110r–111v. *CSP Scot* 1, 41.
117 It is possible that the original letter stated that the Scots had 3,000 or 4,000 men. There is apparently some damage to the original letter right beside the figure of 3,000. *Navy of Edward VI*, 41.
118 *Navy of Edward VI*, 34–37.
119 *TA* 9, 121.
120 *RPC* 1, 79–80.
121 *RPC* 1, 80–81.
122 TNA, SP 50/2, ff. 110r. *CSP Scot* 1, 41.
123 Merriman, *Rough Wooings*, 308. French support for Scotland, especially their reaction to Pinkie, is fully dealt with by Bonner, 'The French Reactions to the Rough Wooings'.
124 *CSP Spain* 9, 130.
125 *Balcarres Papers* (SHS, 1923–25), vol. 1, 172. Translation from Merriman, *Rough Wooings*, 293.
126 *CSP Spain* 9, 175.
127 Merriman, *Rough Wooings*, 293.
128 *CSP Spain* 9, 189.
129 *CSP Spain* 9, 189.
130 *TA* 9, 127; *CSP Scot* 1, 35.
131 *CSP Spain* 9, 215.
132 *CSP Spain* 9, 217.
133 *CSP Spain* 9, 217.
134 *CSP Scot* 1, 55.
135 Ritchie, *Mary of Guise*, 24.
136 Pitscottie 2, 106.
137 TNA, SP 50/2, f.77r. *CSP Scot* 1, 34.
138 TNA, SP 50/2, f. 117r. *CSP Scot* 1, 42.
139 *MLSC*, 210.
140 Scard, *Tudor King in All But Name*, 392.

141 Merriman, 'Hamilton, James, second earl of Arran, and duke of Châtelherault in the French nobility', *ODNB*.
142 Wikipedia, 'Battle of Pinkie': https://en.wikipedia.org/wiki/Battle_of_Pinkie (accessed 22 December 2022).
143 HES, Inventory of Historic Battlefields, Designation for Battle of Pinkie: https://portal.historicenvironment.scot/designation/BTL15 (accessed 24 April 2020).
144 M. Roberts, 'The Military Revolution, 1560–1660: Inaugural Lecture Delivered Before the Queen's University, Belfast' in C. Rogers (ed.), *The Military Revolution Debate: Readings on the Military Transformation of Early Modern Europe* (Boulder, 1995), 13–33. In the same volume see also C. Rogers, 'The Military Revolution in History and Historiography', 3.
145 Roberts, 'The Military Revolution', 13.
146 Roberts, 'The Military Revolution', 13, 29.
147 Oman, 'The Battle of Pinkie', 6.
148 Merriman, *Rough Wooings*, 236.
149 It should perhaps be acknowledged that this assertion was made in a book that was not primarily about Pinkie, or indeed military history. Nevertheless, the remark gives an indication of the views that still circulate in the historical community. D. O'Sullivan, *The Reluctant Ambassador: The Life and Times of Sir Thomas Chaloner* (Stroud, 2016). The claim about Pinkie is made by O'Sullivan as part of a brief overview of Pinkie at the beginning of chapter 5.
150 Phillips, *The Anglo-Scots Wars*.
151 Phillips, *The Anglo-Scots Wars*, 257.
152 Oman, 'The Battle of Pinkie', 6.
153 Oman, *History of the Art of War*, 359.
154 Oman, *History of the Art of War*, 359.
155 Oman, *History of the Art of War*, 367.
156 Oman, 'The Battle of Pinkie', 6.
157 Oman, 'The Battle of Pinkie', 6.
158 HES, Inventory of Historic Battlefields, Designation for Battle of Pinkie.
159 HES, Inventory of Historic Battlefields, Designation for Battle of Pinkie.
160 Patten, f. 99r.
161 Grey, *A Commentary*, 14.
162 Grey, *A Commentary*, 10.
163 Michael Prestwich has argued that it was the English defeat at Bannockburn that led them to reject heavy cavalry. M. Prestwich, *Armies and Warfare in the Middle Ages: The English Experience* (New Haven, 1996), 328–329.
164 Oman, *History of the Art of War*, 289.
165 A. Goodman, *The Wars of the Roses: Military Activity and English Society, 1452–97* (Abingdon, 1981), 178–179.
166 G. Foard, 'Bosworth Battlefield: A Reassessment', Report for Battlefield Trust. Available at: https://www.battlefieldstrust.com/media/269.pdf (accessed 22 December 2022).
167 Goodman, *Wars of the Roses*, 181.
168 E. Hall, *Hall's chronicle: Containing the history of England, during the reign of Henry the Fourth, and the succeeding monarchs, to the end of the reign of Henry the Eighth, in which are particularly described the manners and customs of those periods* (London, 1809), 530. R. L. Davids, 'Seymour, Sir John (1473/4–1536) of Wolf Hall, Wilts.', *History of Parliament*, available at: http://www.historyofparliamentonline.org/volume/1509-1558/member/seymour-sir-john-147374-1536 (accessed 22 December 2022).
169 G. Phillips, 'Longbow and Hackbutt: Weapons Technology and Technology Transfer in Early Modern England', *Technology and Culture*, 40/3 (July 1999), 576–93.
170 Barwick, *Breefe Discourse*, f. 5r.

171 HES, Battlefield Inventory Designation for Ancrum Moor: http://data.historic-scotland.gov.uk/data/docs/battlefields/ancrummoor_full.pdf (accessed 22 December 2022).
172 Pitscottie 2, 36, 38.
173 J. R. Hale, *Renaissance War Studies* (London, 1983), 266–67.
174 *APC* 21, 174.
175 See for instance, HES, Inventory of Historic Battlefields, Designation for Battle of Pinkie.
176 HES, Inventory of Historic Battlefields, Designation for Battle of Pinkie. Patten, f. 99r.
177 C. Martin and G. Parker, *The Spanish Armada* (London, 1992), 51.
178 Bennell, 'The Oared Vessels', 34.
179 E. Adair, 'English Galleys in the Sixteenth Century', *English Historical Review* 25 (October 1920), 503.
180 Adair, 'English Galleys', 504.
181 Caldwell, Guns in Scotland, 1, 147–63, 169–76.
182 These primitive tanks are described in contemporary spy reports. See *L&P* 3/2, nos 3365, 3368, 3403, 3446, 3451. It is fair to point out that the use of waggons, specifically designed or modified for use on the battlefield, goes back in Europe to the 1420s and 1430s when they were deployed by the Hussites. See A. Querengässer, *Before the Military Revolution. European Warfare and the Rise of the Early Modern State 1300–1490* (Oxford, 2021), 71–76.
183 Caldwell, 'Royal Patronage of Arms and Armour Making', 78–82.
184 HP 2, 103; *TA* 7, 498; *TA* 8, 31, 46–47, 93–94, 118–19, 120, 381. It is not clear how consistently and rigorously the terminology for these early firearms was applied. All the weapons in question were single shot long guns firing lead bullets. Some may have been so heavy that they required a rest for support when being fired. Many would have been fired with a simple mechanism using a lighted match (matchlocks); others would have had technologically more advanced 'snap' mechanisms in which ignition was provided by striking sparks from a flint.
185 *RPS* 1535/29; NRS, PA 2/8, II, f.19r-v (accessed 4 October 2022).
186 *TA* 5, 203; *TA* 7, 150; *TA* 9, 100, 114, 138, 307.
187 Oman, 'The Battle of Pinkie', 13.
188 Beaugué, *L'Histoire de la Guerre D'Escosse*, f. 22v. We also have here the arrival of the quintessential tartan clad Highland soldier. See Caldwell, 'The Origins of Plaid Wearing', 437–54.
189 Fourquevaux *Miss*, 15–16, 26: Merriman, *Rough Wooings*, 333; Marcus Merriman, 'Kennedy, Gilbert, third earl of Cassillis (c.1517–1558)', *ODNB*.
190 Grey, *A Commentary*, 10–11.
191 Phillips, 'In the Shadow of Flodden', 167.
192 For discussion of the wider question of light horsemen in the sixteenth century see G. Phillips, '"Of Nimble Service": Technology, Equestrianism and the Cavalry Arm of Early Modern Western European Armies' in P. E. J. Hammer (ed.), *Warfare in Early Modern Europe 1450-1660* (London, 2007), 59–79.
193 Anonymous, 'History of the Estate of Scotland from July 1558 to April 1560', in D. Laing (ed.), *The Miscellany of the Wodrow Society* (Edinburgh, 1844), 68.
194 Maxwell, *Historical Memoirs*, 44.
195 Maxwell, *Historical Memoirs*, 47.
196 For more detailed discussion of the relationship between Somerset and Cecil's visions of Britain see R. Mason, 'Scotland, Elizabethan England, and the Idea of Britain', *Transactions of the Royal Historical Society* 14 (2004), 279–293.
197 Grey appears to have been personally courageous. However, in the years after Pinkie he made a series of military miscalculations. He could also be reckless, highly emotional and on occasions cruel or lacking in empathy – behaviours that can be associated with traumatic brain injuries. Certainly, the head injuries that he is described as suffering at Pinkie could plausibly have caused brain damage. There are, of course, considerable issues connected to diagnosing the

health problems of historical figures, but the possibility of some form of trauma to the brain does deserve consideration when analysing Grey's career after 1547. For an outline of Grey's later career see Lock, 'Grey, William, thirteenth baron Grey of Wilton (1508/9–1562)', *ODNB*.

198 Scottish military capability in the later sixteenth and early seventeenth century is effectively surveyed by J. Goodare, *State and Society in Early Modern Scotland* (Oxford, 1999), 133–71; and M. Glozier, 'The Wars of Mary and James VI and I, 1560–1625', in E. M. Spiers, J. A. Crang and M. J. Strickland (eds), *A Military History of Scotland* (Edinburgh, 2014), 235–47.

199 *RPC* 2, 214.

200 *RPC* 2, 213–214.

201 Compare Goodare, *State and Society*, 157, 308–09.

202 Oman, *History of the Art of War*, 30.

203 Roberts, 'The Military Revolution', 29.

204 Roberts, 'The Military Revolution', 29.

205 Patten, f. 121v.

206 B. Thordeman, P. Norlund and B. E. Ingelmark, *Armour from the Battle of Wisby, 1361*, 2 vols (Stockholm, 1939); T. Sutherland, 'The Bloody Battle of Towton, England', in M. Carver and J. Klápště (eds), *The Archaeology of Medieval Europe Vol. 2, Twelfth to Sixteenth Centuries* (Aarhus, 2011), 272–76.

207 Patten, f. 129r.

208 Patten, f. 129v.

209 *TA* 9, 121.

210 G. Foard and A. Curry, *Bosworth 1485. A Battlefield Rediscovered* (Oxford, 2013), 124, 156.

211 Foard and Curry, *Bosworth 1485*, 179.

212 Patten, f. 117v.

213 Patten, f. 112r.

214 Foard and Curry, *Bosworth 1485*, 132.

215 Foard and Morris, *The Archaeology of English Battlefields*, fig. 2.10.

216 This observation is based on our understanding of the reporting of finds for Treasure Trove and anecdotal information provided by museum curators, including one of the authors.

217 Caldwell and Ewart, 'Excavations at Eyemouth, Berwickshire'.

218 Collections of interest in the National Records of Scotland include, but are not limited to: B52, Records of Musselburgh Burgh; GD122, Papers of the Gilmour family of Craigmillar and Liberton, Midlothian; GD237, Records of Messrs Tods Murray and Jamieson WS, lawyers; RH6, Register House Charters; RH9, Miscellaneous Papers. Collections of interest in the National Library of Scotland include, but are not limited to: Ch.11830–11841; MS.14757, Papers Concerning Pinkie Household and Estate.

219 *TA* 9, 133.

Bibliography

Manuscripts

Bibliothèque Nationale, Paris, C. V. Colbert 35: 'De expeditione in Scotiam commentarius'

British Library, Harleian MS 540, fols 70–71: 'Two Warlike Voiages into Scotland the first a° 1547. A°. 1°. E.6. The second a°. 1560. A° 2°. Eliz.'

Hatfield House, Cecil Papers

National Records of Scotland, Register of Acts and Decreets, 1st series, especially CS7/3/1 and CS7/3/2

The National Archives (Kew), State Papers Scotland, Series 1, Henry VIII, Letters and Papers, especially SP 49/8

The National Archives (Kew), State Papers Domestic, Edward VI, Letters and Papers, especially SP 10/1, 10/2, 10/3, 15/1, 50/1, 50/2, 50/3

Primary sources (printed and online)

Aberdeen Council Register, Extracts from (Spalding Club, 1844–48) <AQ: not referenced in the text. Add citation or remove from bibliography>

Accounts of the Treasurer of Scotland, 13 vols, eds T. Dickson, J. Balfour Paul, C. T. McInnes and A. L. Murray (Edinburgh, 1877–1970)

Acts of the Lords of Council in Public Affairs 1501-1554, ed. R. K. Hannay (Edinburgh, 1932)

Acts of the Privy Council of England, new series, 32 vols, ed. J. R. Dasent (London, 1890–1907)

Anonymous, *The Statutes Which the Justices of Peace, Mayors, Sheriffs, Bailiffs, Constables and Other Officers Were of Late Commanded by the King's Majesty to put in Execution* (London, 1538)

Anonymous, *Statutes and Ordinances for the War* (London, 1544)

Anonymous, 'History of the Estate of Scotland from July 1558 to April 1560', in D. Laing (ed.), *The Miscellany of the Wodrow Society,* vol. 1 (Edinburgh, 1844), 49–85

Balcarres Papers, Foreign Correspondence with Mary de Lorraine, Queen of Scotland, from the Originals in the Balcarres Papers, ed. M. Wood (Scottish History Society, 1923–25)

Barwick, H., *A breefe discourse, concerning the force and effect of all manuall weapons of fire and the disability of the long bowe or archery, in respect of others of greater force now in use* (London, 1592)

Beague, M., *The History of the Compagnes 1548 and 1549,* trans. Dr [Patrick] Abercromby (Edinburgh, 1707)

Beaugué, I. de, *L'Histoire de la Guerre D'Escosse* (Paris, 1556)

Berteville, Le Sieur de, *Recit De L'Expedition En Ecosse L'An MDXLVII Et De La Battayle de Muscleburgh Par Le Sieur Berteville Au Roy Edouard VI* (Edinburgh, 1825)

Brosse, J. de la, *Two Missions of Jacques de la Brosse*, ed. G. Dickenson (Edinburgh, 1942)

Buchanan, G., *The History of Scotland*, trans. J. Aikman (Glasgow and Edinburgh, 1827–29)

Buchananus, G., *Rerum Scoticarum Historia* (Aberdeen, 1762)

Calendar of Letters, Despatches and State Papers relating to the Negotiations between England and Spain, 11 vols, eds G. A. Bergenroth, P. de Gayangos, M. A. S. Hume and R. Tyler (London, 1862–1916)

Calendar of State Papers Domestic of the Reigns of Edward VI, Mary, Elizabeth 1547–1580, ed. R. Lemon (London, 1856)

Calendar of State Papers, Foreign Series, of the Reign of Edward VI, 1547–1553, ed. W. B. Turnbull (London, 1861)

Calendar of State Papers Domestic of the Reign of Mary I 1553–1558, ed. C. S. Knighton (London, 1998)

Calendar of the State Papers relating to Scotland and Mary, Queen of Scots, 1547–1603, 13 vols in 14, eds J. Bain, W. K. Boyd, A. I. Dunlop and H. W. Meikle (Edinburgh, 1898–)
Calendar of Writs preserved at Yester House, 1166–1625, eds C. C. H. Harvey and J. MacLeod (Edinburgh, 1930)
Churchyard, T., *The Firste parte of Churchyardes Chippes* (London, 1575)
Clifford, A. (ed.), *The State Papers and Letters of Sir Ralph Sadler, Vol. 1* (Edinburgh, 1809)
Digges, L. and T. Digges, *Arithmeticall militare treatise named Stratioticos* (London, 1579, reprinted by Da Capo, Amsterdam and New York 1968)
Diurnal of Remarkable Occurrents in Scotland A.D. M.D.XIII – A.D. M.D.LXXV (Edinburgh, 1833)
English and Scottish Popular Ballads, 5 vols, ed. F. J. Child (Boston, 1882–98)
Exchequer Rolls of Scotland, 23 vols, eds G. Burnett, A. J. G. MacKay, G. P. Mcneill and J. Stuart (Edinburgh, 1878–1908)
Fourquevaux, R. de Rouer, baron de, *Instructions sur le faict de la Guerre* (Paris, 1548)
Fraser, Sir W., *The Scotts of Buccleuch*, 2 vols (Edinburgh, 1878)
Froissart, J., *Oeuvres De Froissart*, 25 vols in 27, ed. K. de Lettenhove (Brussels, 1867–77)
Grafton, R., *Chronicle or History of England to which is added his table of the Bailiffs, Sheriffs and Mayors of the City of London from the year 1189 to 1558 inclusive*, 2 vols (London, 1809)
Grey, A., *A Commentary of the services and charge of William Lord Grey of Wilton, by his son Arthur Grey* (Camden Society, 1847)
Hall, E., *Hall's chronicle: Containing the history of England, during the reign of Henry the Fourth, and the succeeding monarchs, to the end of the reign of Henry the Eighth, in which are particularly described the manners and customs of those periods* (London, 1809)
Hamilton Papers: Letters and Papers Illustrating the Political Relations of England and Scotland in the XVIth Century, 2 vols, ed. J. Bain (Edinburgh, 1890)
Harrison, J., see Henrisoun, J.
Henrisoun, J., *An Exhortation to the Scotts to Conforme Themselves to the Honourable Expedient and Godly Union Betwene the Two Ralmes of Englande and Scotland* (London, 1547) [published under the name 'James Harrison']
Holinshed, R., *The Firste Volume of the Chronicles of England, Scotlande, and Irelande* (London, 1577)
Holinshed, R., *The Laste Volume of the Chronicles of England, Scotlande, and Irelande, with their descriptions* (London, 1577)
Hume, Master David, of Godscroft, *The History of the Houses of Douglas and Angus* (London, 1648)
Inquisitionum Ad Capellam Domini Regis Retornatarum quae in Publicis Archivis Scotiae adhuc servantur, abbreviato, ed. Thomas Thompson, 3 vols (London, 1811)
Jordan, W. K. (ed.), *The Chronicle and Political Papers of King Edward VI* (London, 1966)
Kirk, J. (ed.), *The Books of the Assumption of the Thirds of Benefices* (Oxford, 1995)
Knighton, C. S. and D. M. Loades (eds), *The Anthony Roll of Henry VIII's Navy: Pepys Library 2991 and British Library Additional MS 22047 with Related Documents* (Ashgate, 2000)
Knighton, C. S. and D. Loades (eds), *The Navy of Edward VI and Mary I* (London, 2011)
Knox, J., *History of the Reformation in Scotland*, ed. W. C. Dickinson, 2 vols (Edinburgh, 1949)
Late Expedicion in Scotlande Made By the Kynges Hyhnys Armye, Under the Conduit of the Ryght Honorable the Erle of Hertforde, The Yere of Oure Lorde God 1544 (edition by W. Dalyell, *Fragments of Scotish* [sic] *History*) (Edinburgh, 1798)
Leslaeus, J., *De Origine, Moribus, Et Rebus Gestis Scotorum* (Rome, 1578)
Lesley, J., *The History of Scotland, from the death of King James I in the year MCCCCXXXVI to the year MDLXI* (Edinburgh, 1830)
Leslie, J., *The Historie of Scotland, written first in Latin by the most reverend and worthy Jhone Leslie, Bishop of Rosse, and translated in Scottish by Father James Dalrymple 1596*, 2 vols (Edinburgh, 1888–95)
Letters and Papers Foreign and Domestic of the Reign of Henry VIII, eds J. S. Brewer, J. Gairdner and R. H. Brodie, 21 vols in 35 (London, 1862–1910)
Liber Cartarum Sancte Crucis (Edinburgh, 1840)

Lindesay, R., of Pitscottie, *The Historie and Cronicles of Scotland*, 3 vols (Edinburgh, 1899–1911)
Major, J., *A History of Greater Britain as well England as Scotland compiled from the ancient authorities*, trans. A. Constable (Edinburgh, 1892)
Mary of Lorraine, *Scottish Correspondence*, ed. A. I. Cameron (Edinburgh, Scottish History Society, 3rd series, vol. 10, 1927)
Marwick, J. D. (ed.), *Records of the Convention of the Royal Burghs of Scotland*, 5 vols (Edinburgh, 1866–85)
Maxwell, J. (Lord Herries), *Historical Memoirs of the reign of Mary Queen of Scots and a portion of the reign of King James the Sixth* (Edinburgh, 1836)
Mission de Beccarie de Pavie, Baron de Fourquevaux, en Ecosse, 1549. Documents originaux du fonds Fourquevaux, ed. G. Dickinson (Oxford, 1948)
Original Letters relating to the English Reformation, vol. 1, ed. Rev. Hastings Robinson (Cambridge, 1846)
Papiers d'état, pièces et documents inedits ou peu connus relatifs à l'histoire de l'Écosse au XVIeme siècle, ed. A. Teulet, 3 vols (Edinburgh, 1852)
Patten, W., *The Expedicion into Scotlande of the most worthy fortunate Prince Edward, Duke of Soomerset* (London, 1548)
Perlin, M. E., *Description Des Royaulmes D'Angleterre et D'Ecosse* (Paris, 1558)
Pitcairn, R., *Ancient Criminal Trials in Scotland*, 3 vols (Edinburgh, 1833)
Pollard, A. F. *Tudor Tracts 1532–1588* (Westminster, 1903)
Records of the Parliaments of Scotland to 1707, eds K. M. Brown, G. H. MacIntosh, A. J. Mann, P. E. Ritchie and R. J. Tanner (St Andrews, 2007-2010): https://www.rps.ac.uk/(accessed 17 April 2023)
Register of the Privy Council of Scotland, eds J. Hill Burton, P. Hume Brown, D. Masson and H. Paton (Edinburgh, 1877–)
Registrum de Dunfermelyn (Edinburgh, 1842)
Registrum S. Marie de Neubotle (Edinburgh, 1849)
Registrum Secreti Sigilli Regum Scotorum, The Register of the Privy Seal of Scotland, eds M. Livingstone, D. H. Fleming, J. Beveridge and G. Donaldson, 8 vols (Edinburgh, 1908–82)
Selve, O. de, *Correspondance Politique de Odet de Selve, Ambassadeur de France en Angleterre, 1546–1549*, ed. G. Lefèvre-Pontalis (Paris, 1888)
Silver, G., *Paradoxes of Defence* (London, 1599)
Somerset, E., Duke of, 'Proclamation' (London, 1547). Available from Early English Books Online, https://www.proquest.com/books/edward-duke-somerset-erle-hertford/docview/2264205643/se-2 (accessed 16 January 2023)
Somerset, Duke of, *An Epistle or Exhortacion, to Unitie and Peace, sent from the Lorde Protector, and Others the Kynges moste Honorable Counsaill of England: to the Nobilitie, Gentlemen, and Commons, and al Others the Inhabitauntes of the Realme of Scotlande* (London, 1548)
Starkey, D. and P. Ward (eds), *The Inventory of King Henry VIII* (London, 1998)
Styward, T., *The Pathwaie to Martiall Discipline* (London, 1582)
Teulet, A., *Relations Politiques De La France Et De L'Espagne Avec L'Écosse Au XVIe Siècle. Tome Premier. Correspondances Françaises 1515–1560* (Paris, 1862)
Thomas of Erceldoune, *Romance and Prophecies*, ed. J. A. H. Murray (London, 1875)
Waldegrave, R., *The Whole Prophesies of Scotland, England, Ireland, France and Denmark* (Edinburgh, 1603)

Maps and plans

Adair, J., East Lothian, 1682 [manuscript]. NLS: Adv.MS. 70.2.11: https://maps.nls.uk/counties/rec/65 (accessed 6 May 2019)
Battle of Pinkie Roll [manuscript], Bodleian Library, Oxford: MS. Eng. Misc. C 13 (R)
Englishe Victore Agaynste The Schottes By Muskelbroghe 1547 [copper plate engraving], BL: CC.5.a.409
Eyemouth, plan of Fort Point [manuscript], BL: Cotton Augustus 1.i.60: https://imagesonline.bl.uk/asset/19762 (accessed 8 April 2023)

Great Reform Act Plan of Musselburgh (London, House of Commons, 1832). NLS: https://maps.nls.uk/view/74491914 (accessed 29 June 2020)

Hay, J., *New Plan of Musselburgh and its environs* (Edinburgh, 1824). NLS: https://maps.nls.uk/towns/rec/7504 (accessed 3 July 2020)

Johnston, T., Plan of the fields of Pinkie and Inveresk, 1778 [manuscript], NRS: RHP 24995

Kirkwood, R. and Son, *A Map of the Environs of Edinburgh* (Edinburgh, 1817). NLS: https://maps.nls.uk/counties/rec/611 (accessed 7 May 2022)

Knox, J., *Map of the Shire of Edinburgh* (Edinburgh, 1816). NLS: https://maps.nls.uk/view/74400232 (accessed 7 May 2022)

Laurie, J., *A Plan of Edinburgh and Places Adjacent* (Edinburgh, 1766). NLS: https://maps.nls.uk/view/74400229 (accessed 12 December 2021)

Lee, R., Bird's eye view of Edinburgh, 1544 [manuscript], BL: Cotton MS Augustus I ii 56

Phinn, T., *Plan of the Fields of Inveresk as distinguished by the valuators and division of the same among the several heritors* (1756). NLS: https://maps.nls.uk/estates/rec/8023 (accessed 23 June 2020)

Roy, W., The Great Map: the Military Survey of Scotland, 1747–55 [manuscript], BL: Maps K.Top.48.25-1, a-f: NLS: https://maps.nls.uk/roy/(accessed 11 December 2021)

Siege of Leith, 1560 [manuscript: *The Plat of Lythe w'th'aproche of the Trenches Thereunto*], West Sussex Record Office (Chichester): PHA 4640

Secondary sources (printed and online)

Abbott, D. M., 'Buchanan, George (1506 – 1582), poet, historian, and administrator, *Oxford Dictionary of National Biography* (25 May 2006), https://doi.org/10.1093/ref:odnb/3837 (accessed 18 February 2019)

Adair, E., 'English Galleys in the Sixteenth Century', *English Historical Review* 25 (October 1920), 497–512

Anderson, C. and C. Fleet, *Scotland: Defending the Nation: Mapping the Military Landscape* (Edinburgh, 2018)

Arnold, T., *The Renaissance at War* (London, 2001)

Audley, T., 'A Treatise on the Art of War', *Journal of the Society for Army Historical Research* 6/24 (April–June 1927), 65–78

Baillie, R., *Letters & Journals* (Edinburgh, 1841)

Balfour, Sir J., *The Historical Works* (Edinburgh, 1824)

Balfour Paul, J. (ed.), *The Scots Peerage*, 9 vols (Edinburgh, 1904–14)

Barber, P., 'Putting Musselburgh on the map: Two recently-discovered cartographic documents from the "Rough Wooing"', in P. van Gestel-vanhet Schip and P. van der Krogt (eds), *Mapæ antiquæ: liber amicorum Günter Schilder* (Houten, Netherlands, 2007), 327–38

Bedford, C. H., 'Notice of the Fawsydes of the ilk', *Proceedings of the Society of Antiquaries of Scotland* 24 (1889), 370–78

Beer, B. L., 'Seymour, Edward, duke of Somerset [known as Protector Somerset] (c.1500–1552), soldier and royal servant', *Oxford Dictionary of National Biography* (23 September 2004), https://doi.org/10.1093/ref:odnb/25159 (accessed 28 November 2022)

Bennell, J. 'The Oared Vessels', in C. S. Knighton and D. M. Loades (eds), *The Anthony Roll of Henry VIII's Navy: Pepys Library 2991 and British Library Additional MS 22047 with Related Documents* (Ashgate, 2000), 34

Blakeway, A., *Regency in Sixteenth-Century Scotland* (Woodbridge, 2015)

Blakeway, A., 'A New Source for Holinshed's 1577 Hystorie of Scotland', *Notes & Queries*, vol. 62/1 (2015), 53–56

Blakeway, A., 'The Sixteenth-Century Price Rise: New Evidence from Scotland, 1500–85', *Economic History Review* 68 (2015), 167–90

Blakeway, A., 'Spies and Intelligence in Scotland, *c.* 1530 – 1550', in S. M. Butler and K. J. Kesselring (eds), *Crossing Borders: Boundaries and Margins in Medieval and Early Modern Britain* (Leiden, 2018), 83–104

Blakeway, A., *Parliament and Convention in the Personal Rule of James V of Scotland, 1528–1542* (Cham, 2022)

Bonner, E., 'The recovery of St. Andrews Castle in 1547: French Naval Policy and Diplomacy in the British Isles', *English Historical Review*, 111(1996), 578–98
Bonner, E., 'The French Reactions to the Rough Wooings of Mary Queen of Scots', *Journal of the Sydney Society for Scottish History* 6 (1998), 78–161
Brigden, S., 'Bryan, Sir Francis [called the Vicar of Hell] (d. 1550)', *Oxford Dictionary of National Biography* (3 January 2008), https://doi.org/10.1093/ref:odnb/3788 (accessed 29 December 2022)
Briquet, C.-M., *Les filigranes; dictionnaire historique des marques du papier dès leur apparition vers 1282 jusqu'en 1600* (Leipzig, 1923)
Brown, W., *Select Views of the Royal Palaces of Scotland* (Edinburgh, 1830)
Bush, M. L., *The Government Policy of Protector Somerset* (London, 1975)
Caldwell, D. H., 'Royal Patronage of Arms and Armour Making in Fifteenth- and Sixteenth-Century Scotland', in D. H. Caldwell (ed.), *Scottish Weapons & Fortifications 1100–1800* (Edinburgh, 1981), 73–93
Caldwell, D. H., 'The Battle of Pinkie', in N. Macdougall (ed.), *Scotland and War AD 79–1918* (Edinburgh, 1991), 61–94
Caldwell, D. H., 'Tantallon Castle, East Lothian: a catalogue of the finds', *Proceedings of the Society of Antiquaries of Scotland* 121(1992), 335–57
Caldwell, D. H., *Scotland's Wars and Warriors, Winning Against the Odds* (Edinburgh, 1998)
Caldwell, D. H., 'Having the right kit: West Highlanders fighting in Ireland', in S. Duffy (ed.), *The World of the Galloglass* (Dublin, 2007), 144–68
Caldwell, D. H., 'The Defence of the Scottish Border', *Journal of the Sydney Society for Scottish History*, 12 (2010), 59–82.
Caldwell, D. H., 'How Well Prepared Was James IV to Fight by Land and Sea in 1513?', *Journal of the Sydney Society for Scottish History* 14 (2013), 33–75
Caldwell, D. H., 'The Sea Power of the Western Isles of Scotland in the Late Medieval Period', in J. H. Barrett and S. J. Gibbon (eds), *Maritime Societies of the Viking and Medieval World* (Society for Medieval Archaeology monograph 37, 2015), 350–68
Caldwell, D. H., 'Scottish Ways to War 1513 – The Mobilisation for the Flodden Campaign', in *Flodden Legends & Legacy. The findings of the Flodden 500 Project* (The Flodden 1513 Ecomuseum, 2016), 81–86
Caldwell, D. H., 'Bannockburn: the Road to Victory', in M. Penman (ed.), *Bannockburn 1314–2014: Battle and Legacy* (Donington, 2016), 15–35
Caldwell, D. H., *Islay. The Land of the Lordship* (Edinburgh, 2017)
Caldwell, D. H., 'The Origins of Plaid Wearing', *Scottish Historical Review* C3 (2021), 437–54.
Caldwell, D. H. and G. Ewart, 'Excavations at Eyemouth, Berwickshire, in a mid 16th-century *trace italienne* Fort', *Post-Medieval Archaeology* 31 (1997), 61–119
Cameron, J., *James V* (East Linton, 1998)
Campbell, A., of Airds, *A History of Clan Campbell Volume 2 From Flodden to the Restoration* (Edinburgh, 2002)
Catalogue of the Harleian Manuscripts, vol. 1 (London, 1808)
Cathcart, A., *Kinship and Clientage. Highland Clanship 1451–1609* (Leiden, 2006)
Connor, R. D., and A. D. C. Simpson, *Weights and Measures in Scotland* (Edinburgh, 2004)
Cook, M., *'Howe Mire: excavations across the cropmark complex at Inveresk, Musselburgh, East Lothian', Proceedings of the Society of Antiquaries of Scotland 134 (2005), 131–60*
Coombs, B., 'John Stuart, Duke of Albany and his contribution to military science in Scotland and Italy, 1514–36', *Proceedings of the Society of Antiquaries of Scotland* 148 (2019), 231–66
Cowan, I. B., *The Parishes of Medieval Scotland* (Edinburgh, 1967)
Cowan, I. B. and D. E. Easson, *Medieval Religious Houses Scotland* (London, 1976)
Dalyell, W., *Fragments of Scotish* [sic] *History* (Edinburgh, 1798)
Davids, R. L., 'Seymour, Sir John (1473/4–1536) of Wolf Hall, Wilts.', *History of Parliament*: http://www.historyofparliamentonline.org/volume/1509-1558/member/seymour-sir-john-147374-1536 (accessed 22 December 2022)
Davies, C. S. L., 'Provisions for Armies, 1509–50; a Study in the Effectiveness of Early Tudor Government', *Economic History Review*, new series 17/2 (1964), 234–48

Davies, J., 'Painful Pastime Versus Present Pleasure: Tudor Archery and the Law', *Journal of the Society for Army Historical Research* 85, no. 343 (autumn 2007), 224–36
Dawson, J. E. A., 'Campbell, Archibald, fourth earl of Argyll', *Oxford Dictionary of National Biography* (23 September 2004), https://doi.org/10.1093/ref:odnb/4469 (accessed 18 January 2023)
Defoe, D., *A Tour Thro' The Whole Island of Great Britain* (1724–1727), http://www.visionofbritain.org.uk/travellers/Defoe/(accessed 9 December 2022)
Dennison, E. P., *Historic Musselburgh: the archaeological implications of development* (Edinburgh, 1996)
Dennison, E. P., S. Eydmann, A. Lyell, M. Lynch and S. Stronach, *Painting the Town. Scottish Urban History in Art* (Edinburgh, 2013)
Duffin, A., 'Clinton, Edward Fiennes de, first earl of Lincoln (1512–1585)', *Oxford Dictionary of National Biography* (3 January 2008), https://doi.org/10.1093/ref:odnb/5679 (accessed 17 January 2023)
Duffy, A. R., *European Armour in the Tower of London* (London, 1968)
Duffy, E., *The Stripping of the Altars: Traditional Religion in England, 1400–1580* (New Haven, 1997)
Ellis, S. G., 'Dacre, William, third Baron Dacre of Gilsland and seventh Baron Greystoke (1500–1563)', *Oxford Dictionary of National Biography* (3 January 2008), https://doi.org/10.1093/ref:odnb/46514 (accessed 26 December 2022)
Eltis, D., *The Military Revolution in Sixteenth-century Europe* (London, 1995)
Esper, T., 'The Replacement of the Longbow by Firearms in the English Army', *Technology and Culture* 6/3 (summer 1965), 382–93
Ferguson, M. G., 'Grafton, Richard (1506/7–1573)', *Oxford Dictionary of National Biography* (17 September 2015), https://doi.org/10.1093/ref:odnb/11186 (accessed 31 October 2022)
Fergusson, Sir J., *The White Hind* (London, 1963)
Finlay, J., 'Otterburn, Sir Adam (*d.* 1548)', *Oxford Dictionary of National Biography* (23 September 2004), https://doi.org/10.1093/ref:odnb/20938 (accessed 15 June 2019)
Fissel, M. C., *English Warfare, 1511-1642* (London, 2001)
Fleet, C. and D. MacCannell, *Edinburgh, Mapping the City* (Edinburgh, 2014)
Foard, G. and A. Curry, *Bosworth 1485. A Battlefield Rediscovered* (Oxford, 2013)
Foard, G. and R. Morris, *The Archaeology of English Battlefields* (York, 2012)
Fox, A., *The Press & The People, Cheap Print & Society in Scotland 1500–1785* (Oxford, 2020)
Friedman, A. B., 'A New Version of "Musselburgh Field"', *Journal of American Folklore* 66, no. 259 (January–March 1953), 74–77
Gabra-Sanders, T., 'Part of a 16th century quilted jack of plate found at Craigievar Castle, Aberdeenshire', *Journal of the Arms & Armour Society* 14 (1993), 147–52
Glozier, M., 'The Wars of Mary and James VI and I, 1560–1625', in E. M. Spiers, J. A. Crang and M. J. Strickland (eds) *A Military History of Scotland* (Edinburgh, 2014)
Goodare, J., *State and Society in Early Modern Scotland* (Oxford, 1999)
Goodman, A., *The Wars of the Roses: Military Activity and English Society, 1452–97* (Abingdon, 1981)
Gorman, M. A. F., 'Jean Ribault's Colonies in Florida', *Florida Historical Quarterly*, vol. 44, no. 1/2 (July–October 1965), 51–66
Graham, A., 'Archaeology on a Great Post Road', *Proceedings of the Society of Antiquaries of Scotland* 96 (1965), 318–47
Graham, A., 'Archaeological Notes on Some Harbours in Eastern Scotland', *Proceedings of the Society of Antiquaries of Scotland* 101 (1971), 200–85
Grant, A., *Independence and Nationhood Scotland 1306-1469* (London, 1984)
Greene, D. G., 'The Court of the Marshalsea in Late Tudor and Stuart England', *American Journal of Legal History* 20/4 (October 1976), 267–81
Gregory, D., *History of the Western Highlands and Islands of Scotland* (Edinburgh, 1836)
Hale, J. R., *Renaissance War Studies* (London, 1983)
Hardy, R., *Longbow: A Social and Military History* (Sparkford, 1992)
Henshall, A., 'A Long Cist Cemetery at Parkburn Sand Pit, Lasswade, Midlothian', *Proceedings of the Society of Antiquaries of Scotland* 89 (1958), 252–83

Hewitt, G. R., 'Maxwell, John, fourh Lord Herries of Terregles (c. 1512-1583)', *Oxford Dictionary of National Biography* (23 September 2004), https://doi.org/10.1093/ref:odnb/18403 (accessed 15 April 2023)
Hildred, A. (ed.), *Weapons of Warre. The Armaments of the Mary Rose*, 2 parts (Portsmouth, 2011)
Hodnett, E., *Image & Text. Studies in the illustration of English literature* (Aldershot, 1986)
Hume, D., *De Familia Humia Wedderburnensi Liber* (Edinburgh, 1839)
Johnston, G. H., *The Heraldry of the Johnstons* (Edinburgh and London, 1905)
Johnston, S., 'Digges, Leonard (c. 1515 – c. 1559), mathematician', *Oxford Dictionary of National Biography* (23 September 2004), https://doi.org/10.1093/ref:odnb/7637 (accessed 18 February 2019)
Johnstone, C. L., *History of the Johnstones 1191–1909* (Edinburgh, 1909)
Jones, P. M., 'Gemini [Geminus, Lambrit], Thomas (*fl.* 1540–1562)', *Oxford Dictionary of National Biography* (3 January 2008), https://doi.org/10.1093/ref:odnb/10513 (accessed 23 December 2018)
Jordan, W. K., *Edward VI: The Young King: The Protectorship of the Duke of Somerset* (Cambridge, MA, 1968)
Kaufmann, M., 'Sir Pedro Negro: what colour was his skin?', *Notes & Queries*, 253/2 (June 2008), 142–46.
Kewes, P., I. W. Archer and F. Heal (eds), *The Oxford Handbook of Holinshed's Chronicles* (Oxford, 2013)
Kimber, M., *Archaeological monitoring in the streets of Musselburgh* (Edinburgh, 2009), https://doi.org/10.5284/1017938 (accessed 18 June 2020)
Loach, J., *Edward VI* (New Haven and London, 1999)
Loades, D., 'Woodhouse, Sir William (b. in or before 1517, d. 1564), naval commander and administrator', *Oxford Dictionary of National Biography* (3 January 2008), https://doi.org/10.1093/ref:odnb/47407 (accessed 15 April 2023)
Loades, D. M., *Tudor Government: Structures of Authority in the Sixteenth Century* (Oxford, 1997)
Lock, J., 'Grey, William, thirteenth Baron Grey of Wilton (1508/9–1562)', *Oxford Dictionary of National Biography* (3 January 2008), https://doi.org/10.1093/ref:odnb/11568 (accessed 27 April 2019)
MacGibbon, D. and T. Ross, *The Castellated and Domestic Architecture of Scotland*, 5 vols (Edinburgh, 1887–92)
MacIvor, I., 'Artillery and Major Places of Strength in the Lothians and the East Border, 1513–1542', in D. H. Caldwell (ed.), *Scottish Weapons & Fortifications 1100–1800* (Edinburgh, 1981), 94–152
Marshall, R. K., 'Lesley [Leslie], John (1527 – 1596), bishop of Ross, historian, and conspirator', *Oxford Dictionary of National Biography* (24 May 2007), https://doi.org/10.1093/ref:odnb/16492 (accessed 18 February 2019)
Martin, C. and G. Parker, *The Spanish Armada* (London, 1992)
Mason, R., 'Scotland, Elizabethan England, and the Idea of Britain', *Transactions of the Royal Historical Society* 14 (2004), 279–93
Mason, R. A., 'Writing Scotland's History', *Scottish Historical Review* 76 (1997), 55, 65
McCulloch, D., *Tudor Church Militant. Edward VI and the Protestant Reformation* (London, 2001)
McGinley, J. K., 'Lyndsay (Lindsay), Sir David (c. 1486 – 1555), writer and herald', *Oxford Dictionary of National Biography* (25 May 2006), https://doi.org/10.1093/ref:odnb/116691 (accessed 18 February 2019)
McGinnis, P. M. and A. H. Williamson, 'Hume, David, of Godscroft (1558 – 1629 x 31), political theorist and poet', *Oxford Dictionary of National Biography* (24 May 2012), https://doi.org/10.1093/ref:odnb/9780 (accessed 8 March 2019)
McKean, C., 'Craignethan: the castle of the Bastard of Arran', *Proceedings of the Society of Antiquaries of Scotland* 125 (1995), 1069–90
Meikle, M. M., 'Hume [Home], George, fourth Lord Hume (d. 1549), nobleman', *Oxford Dictionary of National Biography* (23 September 2004), https://doi.org/10.1093/ref:odnb/13641 (accessed 5 February 2023)
Merriman, M. H., 'The Assured Scots: Scottish collaborators with England during the Rough Wooing, 1543–50', *Scottish Historical Review* 47 (1968), 10–35
Merriman, M., *The Rough Wooings: Mary Queen of Scots 1542–1551* (East Linton, 2000)
Merriman, M., 'Douglas, Archibald, sixth earl of Angus (c. 1489-1557), magnate and lord chancellor of Scotland', *Oxford Dictionary of National Biography* (5 January 2006), https://doi.org/10.1093/ref:odnb/7866 (accessed 15 April 2023)

Merriman, M., 'Hamilton, James, second earl of Arran, and duke of Châtelherault in the French nobility (c. 1519–1575)', *Oxford Dictionary of National Biography* (23 September 2004), https://doi.org/10.1093/ref:odnb/12081 (accessed 16 January 2023)
Merriman, M., 'Hepburn, Patrick, third earl of Bothwell (c. 1512 – 156)', *Oxford Dictionary of National Biography* (23 September 2004), https://doi.org/10.1093/ref:odnb/13007 (accessed 3 January 2020)
Merriman, M., 'Kennedy, Gilbert, third earl of Cassillis (c.1517–1558)', *Oxford Dictionary of National Biography* (23 September 2004), https://doi.org/10.1093/ref:odnb/15368 (accessed 22 October 2022)
Millar, G. J., 'Henry VIII's Colonels', *Journal of the Society for Army Historical Research* 57/231 (Autumn 1979), 129–36
Murdoch, S., *The Terror of the Seas? Scottish Maritime Warfare, 1513-1713* (Leiden, 2010)
Murphy, N., *The Tudor Occupation of Boulogne* (Cambridge, 2019)
Murphy, N., 'The Duke of Albany's Invasion of England in 1523 and Military Mobilisation in Sixteenth-century Scotland', *Scottish Historical Review* 99/1, no. 249 (April 2020), 1–25
Norman, A. V. B., *Arms and Armour in the Royal Scottish Museum* (Edinburgh, 1972)
New Statistical Account, The Statistical Account of Scotland by the Ministers of the Respective Parishes (Edinburgh, 1834–45). Available online at https://stataccscot.edina.ac.uk (accessed 27 April 2022)
Ogier, D. M., 'Mewtas [Mewtis], Sir Peter, d. 1562', *Oxford Dictionary of National Biography* (24 October 2019), https://doi.org/10.1093/ref:odnb/68013 (accessed 15 April 2023)
O'Kill, B., 'The Printed Works of William Patten (c. 1510 – c. 1600), *Transactions of the Cambridge Bibliographical Society*, vol. 7/1 (1977), 28–45
Old Statistical Account, The Statistical Account of Scotland, ed. Sir J. Sinclair (Edinburgh, 1791–99). Available online at https://stataccscot.edina.ac.uk (accessed 27 April 2022)
O'Sullivan, D., *The Reluctant Ambassador: The Life and Times of Sir Thomas Chaloner* (Stroud, 2016)
Oman, C. W. C., 'The Battle of Pinkie, Sept. 10, 1547', *Archaeological Journal* 90 (1933), 1–25
Oman, C. W. C., *The Art of War in the Middle Ages* (Ithaca and London, 1968)
Oman, Sir C., *History of the Art of War in the Sixteenth Century* (London, 1937)
Oxford English Dictionary, 2nd edition, 20 vols (Oxford, 1989)
Paterson, J., *History of the Regality of Musselburgh* (Musselburgh, 1857)
Pettegree, A., 'Wolfe, Reyner [Reginald, Reynold] (d. in or before 1574)', *Oxford Dictionary of National Biography* (22 September 2011), https://doi.org/10.1093/ref:odnb/29835 (accessed 23 December 2018)
Phillips, G., 'In the Shadow of Flodden: Tactics, Technology and Scottish Military Effectiveness, 1513–1550', *Scottish Historical Review* 77 (1998), 162–82
Phillips, G., *The Anglo-Scots Wars 1513-1550* (London, 1999)
Phillips, G., 'Longbow and Hackbutt: Weapons Technology and Technology Transfer in Early Modern England', *Technology and Culture*, 40/3 (July 1999), 576–93
Phillips, G., '"Of Nimble Service": Technology, Equestrianism and the Cavalry Arm of Early Modern Western European Armies', in P. E. J. Hammer (ed.), *Warfare in Early Modern Europe 1450-1660* (London, 2007), 59–79
Phillips, G., 'Scotland in the Age of the Military Revolution', in E. M. Spiers, J. A. Crang and M. J. Strickland (eds), *A Military History of Scotland* (Edinburgh, 2014), 182–208
Pollard, T., 'The Archaeology of the Siege of Leith', *Journal of Conflict Archaeology* 4 (February 2008), 159–88
Potter, D., *Renaissance France at War. Armies, Culture and Society c.1480-1560* (Woodbridge, 2008)
Potter, D., *Henry VIII and Francis I: The Final Conflict, 1540-47* (Leiden, 2011)
Prestwich, M., *Armies and Warfare in the Middle Ages: The English Experience* (New Haven, 1996)
Pryde, G. S., *The Burghs of Scotland, a Critical List* (Oxford, 1965)
Querengässer, A., *Before the Military Revolution. European Warfare and the Rise of the Early Modern State 1300–1490* (Oxford, 2021)
Rae, T. I., *The Administration of the Scottish Frontier 1513-1603* (Edinburgh, 1966)
Ritchie, P. E., *Mary of Guise in Scotland, 1548–1560: a political career* (East Linton, 2002)

Roberts, M., 'The Military Revolution, 1560–1660: Inaugural Lecture Delivered Before the Queen's University, Belfast' in C. Rogers (ed.), *The Military Revolution Debate: Readings on the Military Transformation of Early Modern Europe* (Boulder, 1995), 13–33

Robertson, G., *General View of the Agriculture of the County of Midlothian* (Edinburgh, 1793)

Rogers, C. (ed.), *The Military Revolution Debate: Readings on the Military Transformation of Early Modern Europe* (Boulder, 1995)

Rogers, C., 'The Military Revolution in History and Historiography', in C. Rogers (ed.), *The Military Revolution Debate: Readings on the Military Transformation of Early Modern Europe* (Boulder, 1995), 1-12.

Ryrie, A., *The Origins of the Scottish Reformation* (Manchester, 2006)

Scard, M., *Tudor King in All but Name: The Life of Edward Seymour* (Cheltenham, 2020)

Scott, W. W., 'Lindsay, Robert, of Pitscottie (c. 1532 – c. 1586), historian', *Oxford Dictionary of National Biography* (23 September 2004), https://doi.org/10.1093/ref:odnb/16715 (accessed 18 February 2019)

Sherlock, P., 'William Patten (*d.* in or after 1598)', *Oxford Dictionary of National Biography* (23 September 2004), https://doi.org/10.1093/ref:odnb/21573 (accessed 5 January 2019)

Simpson, B., 'Land to the South-West of Barbachlaw', *Discovery and Excavation in Scotland* 8 (2007), 73

Skidmore, C., *Edward VI: The Lost King of England* (London, 2007)

Slezer, J., *Theatrum Scotiae* (1693)

Steer, K. A. and J. W. M. Bannerman, *Late Medieval Monumental Sculpture in the West Highlands* (Edinburgh, 1977)

Stirling, R. McD., *Inveresk Parish Lore from Pagan Times* (Musselburgh, 1894)

Strickland, M. and R. Hardy, *The Great Warbow* (Stroud, 2005)

Summerson, H., 'Sources: 1577', in P. Kewes, I. W. Archer and F. Heal (eds), *Oxford Handbook of Holinshed* (Oxford, 2013), 61–76

Sutherland, T., 'The Bloody Battle of Towton, England', in M. Carver and J. Klápště (eds), *The Archaeology of Medieval Europe Vol. 2, Twelfth to Sixteenth Centuries* (Aarhus, 2011), 272–76

Thordeman, B., P. Norlund and B. E. Ingelmark, *Armour from the Battle of Wisby, 1361*, 2 vols (Stockholm, 1939)

Tucker, T., *Report by Thomas Tucker Upon the Settlement of the Revenues of Excise and Customs in Scotland, A.D. MDCLVI* (Edinburgh, 1824)

Virgoe, R. and A. Hawkyard, 'Brende (Brande), John (by 1515–1559), of London and Beccles, Suff.', biography from *The History of Parliament*: https://www.historyofparliamentonline.org/volume/1509-1558/member/brende-%28brande%29-john-1515-59 (accessed 16 January 2023)

Whetham, D., 'The English Longbow: A Revolution in Technology', in L. J. Andrew Villalon and D. J. Kagay (eds), *The Hundred Years War: Pt. 2. Different Vistas* (Leiden, 2008), 211–32

White, A., 'Gordon, George, fourth earl of Huntly (1513–1562)', *Oxford Dictionary of National Biography* (23 September 2004), https://doi.org/10.1093/ref:odnb/11034 (accessed 18 January 2023)

Wormald, J., *Court, Kirk, and Community Scotland 1470–1625* (London, 1981)

Wormald, J., *Lords and Men in Scotland. Bonds of Manrent 1442–1603* (Edinburgh, 1985)

Woudhuysen, H. R., 'Ferrers, George (c. 1510–1579), courtier and poet', *Oxford Dictionary of National Biography* (23 September 2004), https://doi.org/10.1093/ref:odnb/9360 (accessed 21 January 2023)

Unpublished archive reports

AOC Archaeology Group (https://www.aocarchaeology.com) and CFA Archaeology Ltd (https://www.cfa-archaeology.co.uk) are commercial archaeology companies. The majority of reports listed below have been produced following archaeological research and fieldwork undertaken by the companies. These reports are archived with the East Lothian Historic Environment Record (https://www.eastlothian.gov.uk/uk/info/210596/archaeology/12108/historic_environment_record).

Anderson, S., *Wallyford Settlement Expansion Project, Wallyford, East Lothian: Metal Detector Survey 2007* (CFA Report No. 1403, 2007)
Anderson, S., *Wallyford Settlement Expansion Project, Wallyford, East Lothian: Metal Detector Survey, Area 4* (CFA Report No. 1548, 2008)
Anderson, S. and T. Neighbour, *Goshen Farm, Wallyford, East Lothian: Archaeological Metal Detecting Survey, Artefact Assessment Report* (CFA Report No. 2087, 2012)
Caldwell, D. H., Guns in Scotland. The manufacture and use of guns and their influence on warfare from the fourteenth century to c.1625 (University of Edinburgh PhD, 1982)
Caldwell, D. H., *The Battle of Pinkie 1547 – The Location* (Report for Sirius Sport & Leisure Ltd, Dirleton, 2015, available from AOC Archaeology Group)
Caldwell, D. H., *Pinkie Battlefield: an assessment of threats* (Report for Sirius Sport & Leisure Ltd, Dirleton, 2016)
Caldwell, D. H., *Preliminary metal detection finds from fields around Crookston* (Unpublished Report, 2016, available from AOC Archaeology Group)
Carruthers, G., *Pinkie Mains Farm, Archaeological Evaluation* (CFA Report no. 2032, 2012)
Carruthers, G., *Galt Terrace, Musselburgh, East Lothian: Archaeological Metal Detector Survey and Evaluation* (CFA Report No. 3644, 2018)
Carruthers, G. and S. Anderson, *Pinkie Mains, East Lothian, Archaeological Metal Detecting Survey* (CFA Report no. 2024, 2012)
CFA Archaeology Ltd, *2008 Report on Pinkie Battlefield*, prepared by *History Tomorrow* (Centre for Environmental History and Policy, University of Stirling, 2008)
Davies, C. S. L., Supply Services of English armed forces, 1509–50 (Oxford University Thesis, 1963)
Dixon, N., The Placenames of Midlothian (Edinburgh University PhD Thesis, 1947)
Ellis, C., *Stadium Site, Wallyford: Archaeological Works* (AOC Data Structure Report, 2002)
Ellis, C., *Barbachlaw Farm, Wallyford, East Lothian* (AOC Data Structure Report, 2002)
Engl, R., *Victory Lane Car Park* (AOC Report, 2014)
Engl, R., *Wallyford Expansion (Areas 1 & 4), East Lothian: Archaeological Works Data Structure Report* (AOC Report, 2014)
Engl, R., *Wallyford Expansion Area 4* (AOC Report, 2015)
Engl, R., *Land at Dolphingstone Farm, Prestonpans, East Lothian: Archaeological Works* (AOC Report, 2016)
Engl, R., *Crookston Metal Detecting: Data Structure Report* (AOC Report, 2016)
Engl, R. and D. McLaren, *Victory Lane Car Park* (AOC Report, 2014)
Engl, R. and S. Wilson, *Crookston Metal Detecting: Data Structure Report* (AOC Report, 2017)
English Heritage, Battlefield Report: Solway Moss 1542, https://historicengland.org.uk/content/docs/listing/battlefield/solway-moss/(accessed 3 August 2022)
Foard, G., 'Bosworth Battlefield: A Reassessment', Report for Battlefields Trust. Available at: https://www.battlefieldstrust.com/media/269.pdf (accessed 22 December 2022)
Foard, G., *Lead munitions and other metal finds from the CFA Investigation at Wallyford in 2005 & 2007 of part of Pinkie battlefield* (Report for AOC, 2008)
Foard, G., *Report on CFA 2008 Lead munitions and other metal finds from the CFA Investigation at Wallyford* (Report for CFA, 2008)
Foard, G., *A report on the metal finds from investigation of Pinkie battlefield by AOC Archaeology* (Report for CFA, 2008)
Foard, G., *Pinkie Battlefield Report on survey undertaken in 2005–6 by B Simpson for East Lothian Council* (Report for East Lothian Council, 2008)
Franklin, J., *Inveresk Lodge: Metal Detecting Survey, Trial Trenching and Test Pitting* (2013)
Hills, C. and S. Anderson, *Goshen Farm, Wallyford, East Lothian: Archaeological Metal Detecting Survey* (CFA Report No. 2070, 2012)
Historic Environment Scotland, Battlefield Inventory Designation for Ancrum Moor, https://data.historic-Scotland.gov.uk/data/docs/battlefields/ancrummoor_full.pdf (accessed 22 December 2022)
Historic Environment Scotland, Haddon Rig Battlefield Research Report, https://historicenvironment.scot/archives-and-research/publication/(accessed 3 August 2022)

Historic Environment Scotland, Inventory of Historic Battlefields, Designation for Battle of Pinkie, https://portal.historicenvironment.scot/designation/BTL15 (accessed 24 April 2020)
Historic Environment Scotland, *The Inventory of Historic Battlefields, Battle of Pinkie* (March 2011, updated December 2012), https://portal.historicenvironment.scot/document/600000940 (accessed 12 December 2021)
Hodgkins, A., 'Reconstructing Rebellion: Digital Terrain Analysis of the Battle of Dussendale (1549)' *Internet Archaeology* 38 (2015), available online at: https://doi.org/10.11141/ia.38.3 (accessed 28 December 2022)
Hodgkins, A. J., Rebellion and Warfare in the Tudor State. Military Organisation, Weaponry and Field Tactics in Mid-Sixteenth Century England (Leeds University PhD Thesis, 2013)
Lichfields UK, *The Inventory of Historic Battlefields, Battlefield Planning Best Practice* (March 2022, prepared for Historic Environment Scotland) https://www.historicenvironment.scot/archives-and-research/publications/publication/(accessed 15 November 2022)
Mackay, F. L., Reading Pitscottie's Cronicles: a case study on the history of literacy in Scotland, 1576–1814 (Glasgow University PhD Thesis, 2016)
McLaren, D., *Crookston Farm, Wallyford, East Lothian Report on metal detected finds assemblage* (AOC Report, 2017)
McNutt, R. K., Finding Forgotten Fields: A Theoretical and Methodological Framework for Historic Landscape Reconstruction and Predictive Modelling of Battlefield Locations in Scotland, 1296–1650 (Glasgow University PhD Thesis, 2014)
Merriman, M. H., The Struggle for the Marriage of Mary Queen of Scots: English and French Intervention in Scotland, 1543–1550 (London University PhD Thesis, 1975)
Mitchell, S., *Wallyford Settlement Expansion Project, Wallyford, East Lothian: Archaeological Evaluation, Area 1* (CFA Report No. 1469, 2008)
Mitchell, S., *Wallyford Settlement Expansion Project, Wallyford, East Lothian: Archaeological Evaluation, Area 4* (CFA Report No. 1539, 2008)
Mitchell, S., *Wallyford Settlement Expansion Project, Wallyford, East Lothian. Archaeological Evaluation of SAM No. 5658, Area 1* (CFA Report No. 1635, 2009)
Neighbour, T., *Galt Terrace, Musselburgh, East Lothian. Impact Assessment Review* (CFA Report No. 3657, 2018)
O'Connell, C., *Wallyford Settlement Expansion Project, Wallyford, East Lothian. Archaeological Evaluation* (CFA Report No 1076, 2005)
O'Connell, C. and B. Glendinning, *Wallyford, East Lothian: Metal detector Survey and Fieldwalking.* (CFA Report No 1145, 2006)
O'Connell, C., *Wallyford Settlement Expansion Project, Wallyford, East Lothian. Archaeological Evaluation* (CFA Report No 1076, 2005)
Oleksy, V., and R. Engl, *Archaeological Investigations at Gula Flats* (AOC Report, 2008)
Oleksy, V., B. Salter, and R. Miller, *Battle of Pinkie 1547: Heritage Assessment* (AOC and Geddes Consulting, Report, 2015)
Oleksy, V., and S. Wilson, *Gula Flats Metal Detecting Survey* (AOC Data Structure Report, 2016)
Oleksy, V., and S. Wilson, *Victory Lane, Wallyford, East Lothian* (AOC Data Structure Report, 2016)
Ross, A., *Goshen Farm, Musselburgh, East Lothian: Pinkie Battlefield (Historical Research)* (CFA Report No. 2200, 2011)
Savory, G. and B. Glendinning, *Goshen Farm, Musselburgh, East Lothian: Archaeological Evaluations* (CFA Report No. 3497, 2016)
Starley, D. and G. Rimer, *Lead Shot from Pinkie Battlefield* (Royal Armouries Report No. AM 2089, 2008)
Wallace, M. and C. O'Connell, *Whitecraig, East Lothian: Metal Detecting, Trial Trenching and Excavation* (CFA Report, 2019)
Watt, S., *Craighall, Musselburgh, East Lothian* (AOC Data Structure Report, 2019)
White, R., *Wallyford Settlement Expansion Project, Wallyford, East Lothian: Archaeological Evaluation, Areas 2 and 3* (CFA Report No. 1479, 2008)
Wood, A., *Land East of Wallyford (Dolphingstone), East Lothian* (AOC Data Structure Report, 2018)

Websites

AOC Archaeology Group, https://www.aocarchaeology.com/(accessed 17 April 2023)
A Vision of Britain Through Time, http://visionofbritain.org.uk/(accessed 14 April 2023)
Canmore, National Record of the Historic Environment (Historic Environment Scotland), https://canmore.org.uk/(accessed 17 April 2023)
CFA Archaeology Ltd, https://www.cfa-archaeology.co.uk (accessed 17 April 2023)
Dictionaries of the Scots Language Online, https://dsl.ac.uk/(accessed 17 April 2023)
East Lothian Council Historic Environment Record, https://www.eastlothian.gov.uk/info/210596/archaeology/12108/historic_environment-record(accessed 24 April 2020)
English Heritage, Battlefield Report: Solway Moss 1542, https://historicengland.org.uk/content/docs/listing/battlefields/solway-moss/(accessed 8 April 2023)
Historic Environment Scotland Portal, https://portal.historicenvironment.scot/(accessed 17 April 2023)
Musselburgh Museum, https://musselburghmuseum.org.uk/(accessed 16 February 2023)
National Library of Scotland – Map Images, https://maps.nls.uk/(accessed 17 April 2023)
Oxford Dictionary of National Biography, http://www.oxforddnb.com/(accessed 17 April 2023)
Records of the Parliaments of Scotland to 1707, eds K. M. Brown, G. H. MacIntosh, A. J. Mann, P. E. Ritchie and R. J. Tanner (St Andrews, 2007-2010): https://www.rps.ac.uk/(accessed 17 April 2023)
ScotlandsPlaces, https://scotlandsplaces.gov.uk/(accessed 17 April 2023)
Scottish Remote Sensing Portal, https://remotesensingdata.gov.scot/(accessed 17 April 2023)
Statistical Accounts of Scotland, https://stataccscot.edina.ac.uk/(accessed 17 April 2023)
The Battlefields Trust, http://www.battlefieldstrust.com/(accessed 24 April 2020)
The History of Parliament: http://www.historyofparliamentonline.org/(accessed 17 April 2023)
Wikipedia, 'Battle of Pinkie': https://en.wikipedia.org/wiki/Battle_of_Pinkie (accessed 22 December 2022)

Index

Numbers in *italics* denote pages with illustrations

aketons 85
Ancrum, battle of 72, 90, 242
Angus *see* Douglas, Archibald
Annan Steeple 64, *68*
Anthony Roll 50, *51*, *52*
Ardmore 27
Argyll *see* Campbell, Archibald
Arran *see* Hamilton, James
artillery
  range of 161–62, 205
  types 48, 97, 156
Assured Scots 72, 228–30
Audley, Thomas 46, 52
axes *81*, 85

bagpipes 86
bale-fires 60, *62*, 63, 68
Balfour, Sir James 213–14
Bannockburn, battle of 6, 13, 35
Barbachlaw 151, 173, 181
barracks (19th century) 173
Barr, Laird of 34
Barwick, Humfrey 47, 241
battards (pieces of artillery) 48, 236
bases (pieces of artillery) 48
Battle of Pinkie Roll *see* Pinkie, Battle of, Roll
Battlefields Trust 12
Beaton, Archibald 196
Beaton, Cardinal David 22
Beaugué, Jean de 85–86, 89
Beccarie, Raymond de, Baron de Fourquevaux 77, 155
berses (pieces of artillery) 48
Berteville, Sir John 107–8
Berwick *31*, 53, 189, 221
bills *45*
Blackness Castle *66*, 225
Border Lairds 84–85, 161
Bosworth, Battle of 247–48
bows 17, *81*, 85, 167
breech-loading guns 48
Brende, John 41, 49
Brosse, Jacques de la 58–59, 81
Broughty Castle *26*, 225–27, 230
Bryan, Sir Francis 41, 43–44
Buchanan, George *130*, 131
bucklers 80, *81*, 85
Bulmer, Sir Ralph 200
burials 174, 247

Campbell, Archibald, Earl of Argyll 73
Campbell, Captain Andrew 66
cannon 48, 236
Canochson *see* MacDonald, James
Car, Dandy (Andrew Kerr) 85
Carberry, encounter at 160
Carberry Castle 148
Carberry Hill 160, 200
case shot 177
Castlemilk 188, *189*, 226
casualties 1, 4, 14, *99*, *128*, 216, 224
Cathcart, Lord 216
catholics in the Scottish Army 202
Cecil, William 5, 137, 245
Charles V, Emperor 4
Churchyard, Thomas 46
cleugh, meaning of 7
Clinton *see* Fiennes, Edward
Cockburn, James 28, 33
Cockburn, John 34
Colton Dean 164, *166*, 167, 249
composite shot 176–77
Convention at Monktonhall 97, 155, 196
Copperplate engraving *see* Musselburgh, English victory

Cousland (Castle) 84, *147*, 161, 200
Crookston 178–80
Crouch, Robert 200
Culloden, battle of 6
culverins 48, 235, 236
Cunningham, William, Earl of Glencairn
 27, 33, 34, 77

Dalkeith Castle, siege of 70
Darcy, Sir Thomas 41, 211
Defoe, Daniel 5
demi-culverins (pieces of artillery) 48
demilances *43*, 199, 209
Digges, Leonard 80–81, *109*, 155
Diurnal of Remarkable Occurrents 125–26
Dethick, Gilbert, Norroy Herald 21, 234
Douglas, Archibald, Earl of Angus 71, *72*,
 207–11, 213–14
Douglas, Sir George 67, 145, 223
Dudley, Andrew 23, 28, 33, 226
Dudley, John, Earl of Warwick *24*, 39, 50, 84,
 188, 193, 212, 215
Dumbarton Castle *237*
 siege of 70
Dunbar Castle *64*, 192
Dundee 28, 34
Dunfermline Abbey *143*
Dunfermline, Abbot of *see* Durie, George
Dunglass Castle 67, 191
Durie, George, Abbot of Dunfermline
 68, 196

Edgebuckling Brae 151, 217
Edenhall Hospital *see* Pinkieburn House
Edinburgh *71*
 Castle *63*
Edward VI 1, *4*, 108–9
Elmes, William 23
Elphinstone (Castle) 147–48, 161
Elphinstone, Lord 216
English Army 39, *40*, 41, *42*, 43–49, 242–43
 archers 46–47
 artillery 48
 camp (8–9 September) 159–60, *199*
 camp (10 September) 169
 cavalry 42, *43*, 44, 223–24
 footmen, English 44–45
 hackbutters 44, 47, 81–82, 213
 invasion by *3*, *63*, 188, *189*, 190–94
 logistics 52–55
 pioneers 49, 89
 return home *221*, 222–23
 transport 53–54
English Government records 97–98
English Navy 50–52, 197–98, *199*, 224–25
Englefontaine camp 159
Esk, River, course of 141
Eyemouth Fort 190, 226, *227*, 228, 249

Fala Moor *62*, 68, 194, 249
falcons (pieces of artillery) 48, 88
Falside, Land of 145
 Castle 8, 147, *148*, 216
Fane, Sir Ralph 41, 42, 163
Fergusson, Sir James 11
Ferrers, George 197
Fiennes, Edward, Lord Clinton *25*, 41, 50,
 193–94
fire crosses 60
Fleming, Lord 216
Fleming, Sir Francis 41
flight shot 167
Flodden, battle of *82*, 89
Fourquevaux *see* Beccarie
fowlers (pieces of artillery) 48
French aid to Scotland 58–59, 236–38

Galley Subtle 19, 50, *51*, 194, *199*, 205, 225,
 242–43
Gamboa, Sir Pedro de 41, 44, 213
Gainford, Nicholas 200
Glasgow Castle, siege of 70
Glencairn *see* Cunningham, William
Gordon, George, Earl of Huntly 28, 58, 72–73,
 99, 231
Goshen 181
Governor of Scotland *see* Hamilton, James
Gower, Thomas 200
Grafton, Richard 123
Graham, Robert, Master of 161
Gray, (Scottish) Lord 26, 225
Grey, Arthur, of Wilton 109–10
Grey, Lord William of Wilton 5, 39, *41*, 44,
 209–11, 223, 245

Gula Flats *170*, 173, 181
Guthrie, Alexander 87

hackbuts (hand guns) *47*
hackbuts of crok (pieces of artillery) 156
hackbutters 44, 47, 81–82, 213
  Scottish 64, 68, 81–82, 244
Haddington, siege of 85–86
Haddon Rig, battle of 72, 89
hail-shot 48
Hailes Castle 67, 193, *194*
halberds 81
Hamilton, James, Earl of Arran 1, *3*, 69
  close advisers 126, 196
  military experience 70–71
  policy of 17, 34, 69–70, 230–32, 235–38
  strategy 195–96, 202–3
Hamilton, John, Archbishop of St Andrews 196
Hamilton, Robert, of the Briggs 64, 73
Harleian MS 540 122–23
Henrisoun, James 17–18, 27
Henry II of France 4–5, 24, 234
Hepburn, Patrick, Earl of Bothwell 66, 67, 77
Herries, Lord *see* Maxwell, John
Hertford, Earl of *see* Seymour, Edward
Holinshed, Raphael *123*, *124*
Hooper, John 5, 102
Howe Mire 9, 11, 12, 152, *153*, 154, 173–74
Hume, David of Godscroft 111–12
Hume, George, Lord Hume 67, 73, 84, 199, 200
Hume, Master of 84, 200
Hume Castle 64, *65*, 225–26

Inchcolm 45, 225, *226*, 227, 230
Inchgarvie Blockhouse 19
Inchmahome Priory *232*, 233
Innerwick Castle 67, 191, *192*
Inventory of Historic Battlefields 12
Inveresk, Land of 143
  St Michael's Church 148, 157, *158*

jacks 46, 79, *80*, 84, 85
  Arran's 80

Kennedy, Gilbert, Earl of Cassilis 244
Knox, John *125*

lances 84
'lane' 149–50, 200
Langholm Castle, siege of 28, *29*, 30–31, 62, 70
lead shot 176
Lee, Sir Richard 41, *71*, 112, 226
Leith 64, *65*, 221, 226
Lennox *see* Stewart, Matthew
Leslie, John, Bishop of Ross *127*, 128–30
Levenhall 174
Lewisvale Park 169, 204
light horsemen, English 43, 199, 203
light horsemen, Scottish *43*, 193, 199–200, 210, 212
Lilliard's Edge, Battle of *see* Ancrum
Lindisfarne 53, 189
Lindsay, Robert, of Pitscottie 126–27
Lindsay, Sir David, of the Mount 126–27
Linton Bridge *193*, 249
Little Bighorn, Battle of 249
Lochleven Castle 27
Lochore Castle 27
Longniddry 193
Loraine, Thomas 111
Lord's Mount, Berwick 31
Loretto 160
Luttrell, Sir John 227

MacCulloch 87
MacDonald, James 74, 85
Mangerton, Laird of 85
Mary of Guise *231*, 232, 236–38
Mary of Hungary 4, 32
Mary Queen of Scots 1, *4*, 232–33
  marriage prospects 17, 18, 32, 201, 234–35
Mary Rose 46, 48, 167, 177
Maxwell, John, Lord Herries 131, 196
Maxwell, Richard 85
men-at-arms 43, 199–200, 209
Methven *see* Stewart, Henry
Mewtas, Sir Peter 41, 44, 47
Military revolution, the 12, 239–40, 242
mining 151–52, 197
Monktonhall 68
Montgomery, Jacques, Seigneur de Lorges 58, 71, 74
mounted hackbutters 41, 44, 199, 213

moyens 48
Musselburgh (town) 1, 146
  lands 145
  old bridge *149*
  tolbooth *146*, 154
Musselburgh Field, Ballad of 121–22
Musselburgh, English victory, copperplate engraving *2*, 116, 121
Musselburgh, Lordship of 143
muster of Scottish army *62*, 63, 68

Newcastle 188
non-combatants 88–89
Norroy Herald see Dethick, Gilbert

Oman, Charles *7*, *8*, 9–10, 75, 240–41, 244
Ormiston, Laird of see Cockburn, John
Otterburn, Adam 16, 18, 19–20, 23, 33, 60

Paget, William 24, 98–99
Paniarhough, Battle of *see* Ancrum
Paniter, David 28
Patten, William 4, 33, 46, 49, 50, 96, 102–4, *105*, *106*, 107, 110–11, 197
Pauncy 51, *52*
Peace attempts 130, 201–2
Pease, the 34, *49*, 67
Perth 27
Phillips, Gervase 10, 240
pikes 45–46, 82–83
Pinkie Battle, alternative names 137, 140
Pinkie, battle of
  cavalry engagement on 9 September *113*, 160–61, 199–200
  legacy of, for the Scots 245–46
  phase 1: 160–63, 203–5, *206*
  phase 2: 163, 205, *206*, 207–9
  phase 3: 163–68, 209, *2010*, 211–12
  phase 4: 212, *213*, 214–15
  rout *106*, *118*, *119*, 168–69, 215–16
Pinkie, battle of, described by
  Ballad of Musselburgh Field 121–22
  Berteville, Sir John 107–8
  Buchanan, George *130*, 131
  Caldwell, David *9*, *10*, 11–12
  Digges, Leonard 109
  Diurnal of Remarkable Occurrents 125–26
  Edward VI *4*, 108–9
  Fergusson, Sir James 11
  Gordon, George, Earl of Huntly, 99
  Grafton, Richard 123
  Grey, Arthur, of Wilton 109–10
  Harleian MS 540 122–23
  Holinshed, Raphael *123*, *124*
  Hooper, John 102
  Hume, David of Godscroft 111–12
  Knox, John *125*
  Leslie, John, Bishop of Ross *127*, 128–30
  Lindsay, Robert, of Pitscottie 126–27
  Maxwell, John, Lord Herries 131, 196
  Oman, Charles *7*, *8*, 9–10, 75, 240–41, 244
  Patten, William 4, 102–4, *105*, *106*, 107, 110–11
  Phillips, Gervase 10, 240
  Ribault, Jean 99–100
  Selve, Odet de 98–100
  Van der Delft, Francis 100–1
Pinkie, Battle of, Roll 8, 112, *113*, 114, *115*, 116, *117*, *118*, *119*, 120
Pinkie, engagement between English and Franco-Scots Army, 1548 203
Pinkie, Land of 144–45, 171
Pinkie battle memorials *6*, *7*, *169*
Pinkie Battlefield *8*, *9*, *10*, *11*, *138*, *139*, *142*, 169–70, *171*, 172–73, *198*
  finds *170*, 173, *174*, *175*, 176–78, *179*, 180, 246–49
  LiDAR analysis *165*
Pinkie Brae 173
Pinkie Cleugh *139*, 140
Pinkie Cleugh Battlefield Group 12
Pinkie House 146–47
Pinkieburn House (Edenhall Hospital) *139*, 173–74
Pinkiehill 162
Pitscottie *see* Lindsay, Robert, of Pitscottie 126–27
plaids 85

plate armour 46, 79, 80
Huntly's 80
port pieces (pieces of artillery) 48
Prestonpans 146
prickers 42. See also light horse
prickshot 158, 167
prisoners *99*, 129, 231
Protector of England *see* Seymour, Edward

Ravenscraig Castle 27
Ramsay, John 112
Reston 103, 249
Ribault, Jean 99–100
Rigg, Master Hugh 196
round shot *176*
Roxburgh Castle/Fort 19, *20*, 48, 223, 225–26

Sadler, Sir Ralph 39, 97, 188, 223
St Andrews *22*
St Andrews, Archbishop of *see* Hamilton, John
St Andrews Castle, siege of 22–25
St Clement's Wells 168
St Michael's Church *see* Inveresk
sakers (pieces of artillery) 48, 236
Saltpreston *see* Prestonpans
Scottish army 58, 59, 74, *75*, 76–77, *78*, 79, 243–45, 235–36
archers 75–76, 85, 205, 214–16, 244
artillery 48, 76, *87*, *88*, 97, 156, 235–36, 244
camp 154–5, *156*, 157–59
footmen 76–77, 83–85
light horse 75, *83*, 89, 193, 197, 244–45
mobilisation 60, *61*, *62*, 63–69
religious factions 74, 126, 131, 213–14
Scottish Government records 96–97
Scottish navy 66, 224–25
Scottish religious tensions 214
Selve, Odet de 32, 98–100
Seymour, Edward, Duke of Somerset 1, *3*
as Earl of Hertford 18–19, 45
military commander 39
policy of 1, 6, 20–22, 33, 222–25, 228–30, 234–35
proclamation to the Scots 33, 190
rise to power 17
Seymour, Thomas 42
Shelley, Edward 41, 44, 211
Sliman, Master Thomas 155
slough, the 10, 12, 164, 166–67, 249
Solway Moss, battle of 90
Somerset *see* Seymour, Edward
Spanish morion *45*
spies 60
steel bonnets 79
Stewart, Henry, Lord Methven 73–74
Stewart, Matthew, Earl of Lennox 34, 77, 188
Stewart, William 87
Stirling Bridge, Battle of 157
Stirling Castle *233*, 234
Strozzi, Leone 24
supplies of English army 190
swords 80, *81*

Tantallon Castle 66, *67*, 192
Thomas of Ercildoune 137
Thornton Castle 67, 191, *192*
Towton, battle of 247–48
trace italienne fortifications 228
Tucker, Thomas 141
'turf banked enclosure' 168
'two hillocks' 162–63, 173
Two Warlike Voyages into Scotland see Harleian MS 540

van der Delft, Francis 1, 25, 28, 32, 39, 100–1, 225
Visby, Batle of 247

Wallyford, Land of 145, 173
wappenshaws 16, 59–60
Warwick *see* Dudley, John
West March, invasion of 188–89
Wharton, Lord 34, 188
Wilford, Sir James *41*
Woodhouse, Sir William 50

York 53